W9-APF-564

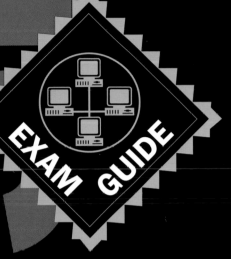

EXAM GUIDE

Microsoft® Networking Essentials Chapter Notes

SECOND EDITION

Quick review of the most important
concepts and terms from the *Exam Guide*

MCSE

Que®

Dan York

Chapter 2

Introduction to Networks
Network Terminology

Client: A computer that uses resources available on the network.

Server: A computer that provides resources (files, printers, and so on) on the network that other computers can use.

Peer: A computer that shares its own resources while also using resources available on other computers on the network.

Media: The physical mechanism for connecting computers in a network. An example would be copper or fiber-optic cable.

Network Interface Card (NIC): The card that connects a computer to the network media and translates the internal digital data into electrical or optical signals on the network.

Local area network (LAN): Several computers connected in a relatively confined area such as an office building or campus.

Resource: Any component that you would like to use on the network. This can be anything from a file on a remote machine, to a printer located down the hall.

Wide area network (WAN): A larger network that connects multiple LANs over some geographic distance.

Topology: The physical layout or design of a network. Three major variations:

- *Bus*—Computers are connected by the media in a line.
- *Star*—Computers are connected to a central point, usually a hub.
- *Ring*—Computers are connected into a logical ring, with the last computer being connected back to the first.

Network Architecture: The method by which data is actually transmitted across the network media. Examples include Ethernet and Token Ring.

Network Protocol: The communication mechanism used by two computers to communicate across the network. Think of it as similar to a human language. Both participants in a conversation must speak the same language to be understood. Examples include TCP/IP, IPX/SPX, and NetBEUI.

Types of Networks

Peer-to-Peer

Computers can act as both servers sharing resources and as clients using resources.

Advantages

- Easy to set up.
- Inexpensive.
- Additional computers or software packages are not required beyond the operating system.
- Local control of resources is maintained by individual users.
- Specific staff is not required to maintain the network.
- Individual computers are not dependent on the functioning of a central computer.

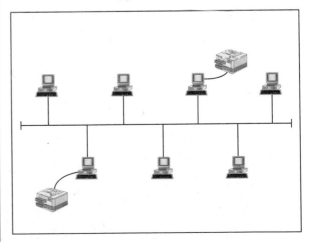

Peer-to-Peer

Disadvantages

- Network security is weak and limited to only password protection.

- Users might have to remember multiple passwords to access shared resources.

- It is difficult and time-consuming to back up data stored on many different computers.

- A decreased performance of computers exists due to the increased load of network sharing.

- There is a lack of a central organizational scheme. Users have to seek out data on different computers.

Server-Based

Server-based networks provide centralized control of network resources and rely on server computers to provide security and network administration.

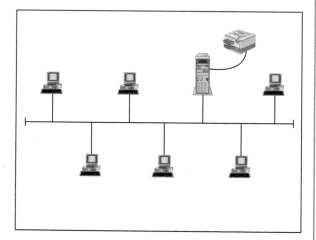

Server-Based

Advantages

- Security is centrally controlled.

- Simplified administration for large numbers of user accounts.

- Faster access to files/resources because of optimized equipment.

- Protecting data through backups can be easier because of central location of data files.

- Because they only have to remember one password, it is easier for users to access network resources.

Disadvantages

- The hardware and software are both more expensive.

- Additional staff and staff training are usually required.

- If a server fails, the entire network can be unusable.

Types of Servers

File Servers

Servers that provide users with a central repository of documents and other files. Data can be easily backed up and protected.

Print Servers

Printers connected to a print server can be accessed by all network users. Print servers provide a central point of control over printing. Print servers have *print queues* and are said to *spool* each individual print job to an actual printer for printing.

Communication/Mail Servers

Servers dedicated to providing email, messaging, or groupware functions. Such servers often run an application such as Microsoft Exchange Server or Lotus Notes.

Application Servers

A term generically applied to servers that provide access for users to applications. An application server might run a database or email program. In some contexts, it might also be used to refer to a file server where all users store the network versions of applications such as Microsoft Office.

Network Media

The physical connection between computers on a network.

Copper

Copper cable has been in use for well over 100 years and is used in most network cables. It provides strong transmission of the electrical signal, is extremely flexible, and has transmission properties that are well understood.

Copper network media comes more commonly in the form of coaxial cable or twisted-pair cable.

Fiber-Optic

Fiber-optic cable uses light through typically a glass core to achieve extremely high data transmission speeds. Using the cable as the network media is both extremely fast and secure, but it is also much more expensive and difficult to work with compared to copper cable.

Wireless

Wireless media connect computers without the use of a physical cable. Typical mechanisms include infrared, radio, and microwave (satellite) transmission.

Chapter 3

The OSI Reference Model

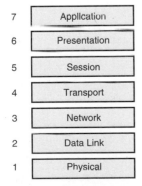

The OSI Reference Model consists of seven layers.

Application Layer

At the application layer, user applications interact with the network.

Presentation Layer

Think of the *presentation layer* as preparing the data to be presented to either the network (if outbound) or the applications (if inbound).

Session Layer

Remember the *session layer* as opening, using, and closing a session between two computers. In Microsoft networks, the NetBIOS protocol operates at this layer.

Transport Layer

Remember the *transport layer* as ensuring error-free and properly sequenced transportation for the data. Protocols such as TCP and SPX operate at this layer.

Network Layer

Remember that the *network layer* routes messages to the appropriate address by the best available path. Protocols such as IP and IPX operate at this layer. Devices such as routers operate at this layer.

Data Link Layer

Remember the *data link layer* as the layer packaging data into frames and providing an error-free link between two computers. Ethernet and Token Ring act at this layer. Devices such as *bridges* operate at this layer.

Physical Layer

Remember the *physical layer* as the actual physical connection between computers. Devices such as *hubs* and *repeaters* operate at this layer.

IEEE Enhancements to the OSI Model

The IEEE 802 Project further divided the data link layer into two sublayers:

- Logical Link Control
- Media Access Control

It also developed a series of specifications, of which the important ones for the exam are shown in the following table.

Number	Category
802.2	Logical Link Control
802.3	Carrier-Sense Multiple Access with Collision Detection LAN (CSMA/CD, or Ethernet)
802.4	Token-Bus LAN
802.5	Token-Ring LAN
802.12	Demand Priority Access LAN, 100 BaseVG-AnyLAN

Chapter 4

Network Topology
What Is a Topology?

The term *topology* describes the physical layout of computers, cables, routers, and other equipment on the network. Note that there is a subtle difference between the *physical* and *logical* topology of a network. For instance, in a Token Ring network, the signal might travel logically from computer to computer in a ring, even though it might be physically connected in a star.

Bus Topology

In a bus topology, each computer is connected directly to the primary network cable in a single line.

Advantages of the Bus Topology

- The cable and hardware used are very inexpensive.
- Installation can be both easy and rapid.

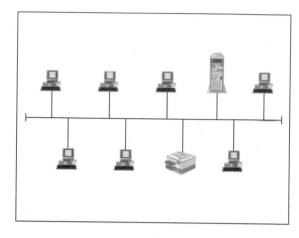

Bus Topology

- The topology is simple to understand. (The cable runs from one computer to the next; can it be any simpler?)
- A bus network can be easily extended.

Disadvantages of the Bus Topology

- It can be painfully difficult to troubleshoot. Because a break in the network *anywhere* can bring down the entire network, each and every connection might have to be checked to find the problem.
- Increased network traffic can significantly decrease the network performance.
- The overall physical length of the network is limited.

Star Topology

In a star topology, all computers are connected using a central hub. A separate cable runs from each computer back to the hub.

Advantages of the Star Topology

- Failure of a single computer will not stop communication between other computers.
- Because the connections are between the hub and individual computers, troubleshooting can be relatively easy.
- It is easy to add computers to the network and reconfigure connections.

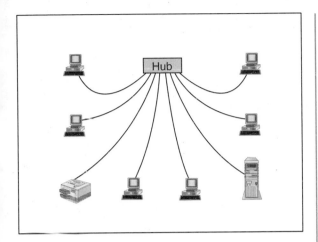

Star Topology

Disadvantages of the Star Topology

- Cabling can be expensive due to the need for a separate cable between the hub and each computer.
- Failure of the hub will terminate all network communication.
- Distance can be limited due to the need for separate cables.

Ring Topology

In a ring topology, all computers are connected in a loop. Most rings use a *token* to control which computer has access to the network media.

A *token* is a small data packet that is continually passed around the ring between computers. Each computer can only transmit a message when it has the token.

Advantages of the Ring Topology

- The mechanism for fair access (token passing) can provide equal opportunities for all computers to communicate.
- Installation can be simple.
- Because the signal is regenerated at each computer, signals do not degrade as much as in other topologies.

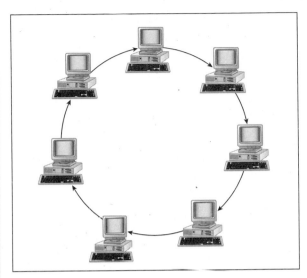

Ring Topology

Disadvantages of the Ring Topology

- As with a bus, the failure of any one connection can bring the network down. (Note that some ring networks, such as those using FDDI, might incorporate a second ring to minimize network failures.)
- Reconfiguration can be difficult because the network might need to be brought down while the new connection is added.
- Distance can be limited due to the physical media limitations.

Hybrid Networks

A *star bus* network involves connecting several hubs on a separate bus network.

A *mesh* network is one in which each computer is connected to every other computer resulting in multiple redundant connections.

Choosing the Appropriate Topology

The topology you use will depend on several factors, including cost, distance, installation timeframe, and physical environment. Factors to consider include the following:

- If you are installing a small network in a room or office and are looking for an inexpensive mechanism to do so, a *bus* or *star* topology will probably provide the best solution.
- If you know you will be adding and reconfiguring your network, a *star* topology is by far the easiest to reconfigure.
- If you have a large number of users in a relatively confined area, a *star bus* topology might provide you with all the expansion that you need.
- If you are looking for a mechanism that will provide equal access to the network media even under conditions of high network traffic, choose a *ring* topology.
- If you want an extremely fault-tolerant network, choose a *mesh* topology.

Chapter 5

The Physical Connection

Baseband: The data signal uses the entire bandwidth of the cable. The signal is either on or off. Most LANs today use baseband.

Broadband: Multiple frequencies are used allowing more than one signal to be sent down the wire at the same time; used most commonly in cable modem technology.

Cable Terminology

Attenuation

Attenuation: Degeneration of a signal over distance on a network cable; measured in decibels. Copper attenuates rapidly = used for short distances. Fiber-optic suffers little attenuation = used over large distances.

Bandwidth: Number of bits that can be sent across the cable at any given time; measured *in Megabits per second (Mbps)*(1Mbps = 1 million bits transmitted per second).

Ethernet = 10Mbps–100Mbps. Token Ring = 4Mbps or 16Mbps. Fiber-optic networks = 2–200Gbps.

Gigabits per second (Gbps): Billions of bits per second.

Impedance: Resistance of a wire to the transmission of an electric signal; measured in ohms. Higher impedance = greater energy needed to transmit.

Interference

Interference: (Also known as *Electromagnetic Interference* or *EMI*). When radiating energy (*noise*) interferes with the signals of other wires and devices.

Crosstalk: When two wires are placed next to each other inside a cable and noise from each line ruins the signal in the other line.

Corporate security issue.

- Energy radiating from a cable interferes with other devices.
- Can be intercepted by eavesdroppers.

Fiber-optic medium is not susceptible to EMI; best choice for high security.

Cables

Plenum: False ceiling where cables (electrical, phone, and network) needed for office work are run; also used to circulate air throughout the building.

In the case of fire, the type of cable in this airspace is crucial. Most cables are covered with inexpensive *polyvinyl chloride (PVC)*, which gives off extremely noxious and deadly gases. Fire codes require *plenum cabling* in false ceilings.

Plenum cables: Resistant to fire; produce fewer fumes.

Shielding: Foil or woven steel mesh wrapped around the cable to minimize interference; increases cost and decreases the flexibility; harder to install.

Twisted-pair cable: Two copper wires wrapped around each other. Each cable usually consists of two pairs (telephone wire) or four pairs (network cables). Two types: unshielded twisted-pair (UTP) and shielded twisted-pair (STP).

Unshielded twisted-pair (UTP): Most common type of cable used for PC networking; used in a star topology; connected from the computer to a hub. UTP typically uses an RJ-11 connector (telephone) or an RJ-45 connector (network). Rated in five categories:

Cat	Speed	Notes
1	None	Used in older telephone systems
2	4Mbps	
3	10Mbps	The minimum required for data networks
4	16Mbps	
5	100Mbps	Most new installations go directly for Cat 5

Category 3 is the minimum for Ethernet networks. Category 5 is the only type that will work for 100Mbps Fast Ethernet.

Shielded twisted-pair (STP): Pairs of wires like UTP, but their covering is a foil or mesh shielding around the individual pairs, the entire cable, or both; uses specialized connectors.

Coaxial cable: Central copper core down which the data signal is transmitted, followed by a layer of insulation, a layer of mesh shielding, and an outer plastic or vinyl jacket. There are two main types: thinnet and thicknet.

Thinnet cables: 1/4-inch in diameter and usually have a *British Naval Connector (BNC)* on each end; very flexible; part of the RG-58 family of cables.

Coaxial Cables	
Cable	**Description**
RG-58 /U	50 ohm, solid copper core
RG-58 A/U	50 ohm, stranded wire core
RG-58 C/U	Military specification of RG-58 A/U
RG-59	75 ohm, broadband transmission such as cable TV
RG-62	93 ohm, used primarily in ArcNet

Only RG-58 A/U and RG-58 C/U are usable in Ethernet networks.

Thinnet cables are connected together using a T-connector and have a *terminator* on each end to absorb the signal.

Thicknet coaxial: 1/2-inch thick and inflexible; installed as a single length of cable going throughout the office area. Computers are connected to the thicknet cable by *piercing tap* (or *vampire tap*) that pierces through the jacket and insulation and makes contact with the central core.

Fiber-optic cables: Glass (or plastic) core down which a light signal is transmitted. The core is surrounded by *cladding* layer that keeps the light focused and traveling. Resistant to interference and highly secure. More expensive and less flexible than copper cables. Of all cables, fiber-optic can cover the longest distances and transmit data at the highest speeds.

Cable media

The following table summarizes the characteristics of the cables discussed in this book.

UTP

Maximum cable length	100 meters (328 feet) ·
Transmission speed	Usually 10Mbps, can be 4–100Mbps
Installation/maintenance	Easy to install and maintain. Very flexible. Components readily available.
Interference	Highly susceptible to interference.
Cost	Least expensive of all media.

STP

Maximum cable length	100 meters (328 feet) (identical to UTP).
Transmission speed	Usually 16Mbps, can be up to 155Mbps.
Installation/maintenance	Moderately easy, although cables can require special connectors. The cable is also generally quite rigid.
Interference	Resistant to interference.
Cost	More expensive than UTP or Thinnet, but less than Thicknet or Fiber-optic.

Thinnet Coaxial Cable

Maximum cable length	185 meters (607 feet).
Transmission speed	10Mbps.
Installation/maintenance	Easy to install. Very flexible.
Interference	Resistant to interference.
Cost	Inexpensive.

Thicknet Coaxial Cable

Maximum cable length	500 meters (1,640 feet).
Transmission speed	10Mbps.
Installation/maintenance	Rigid structure makes it difficult to install in tight spaces.
Interference	Resistant to interference.
Cost	More expensive than all other media except fiber-optic cable.

Fiber-optic Cable

Maximum cable length	2 kilometers (6,562 feet).
Transmission speed	Usually 100Mbps, although speeds have been demonstrated up to 2Gbps.
Installation/maintenance	Difficult.
Interference	Not subject at all to electromagnetic interference.
Cost	Most expensive of all cable media.

Comparison of Different Network Media

Medium	Maximum Cable Length	Transmission Speed	Installation	Inter-ference	Cost
UTP	100 meters (328 feet)	10–100Mbps	Easy	High	Least expensive
STP	100 meters (328 feet)	16–155Mbps	Moderately easy	Low	Moderate
Thinnet	185 meters (607 feet)	10Mbps	Easy	Low	Inexpensive
Thicknet	500 meters (1,640 feet)	10Mbps	Difficult	Low	High
Fiber-optic	2 kilometers (6,562 feet)	100Mbps–2Gbps	Difficult	None	Most expensive

Chapter 6

Wireless Connections

Three primary types: radio, microwave, and infrared.

Radio

Radio utilizes a transmitter and antenna/receiver. Several possible media types:

Low-power, single frequency: Low-power radio setups where both transmitter and receiver are tuned to same frequency. Only works in a very limited area and can be blocked by walls and other obstructions. Susceptible to eavesdropping.

Low-power, Single-frequency	
Maximum distance	10s of meters.
Transmission speed	Can be 1–10Mbps.
Installation/maintenance	Relatively easy to install.
Interference	Highly susceptible to interference.
Cost	Moderate.
Security .	Highly susceptible to eavesdropping, although due to low power, the signal is generally limited to the immediate building.

High-power, single frequency: Can transmit over a larger area but again is easy to eavesdrop on.

High-power, Single-frequency	
Maximum distance	A function of power and frequency of transmitters. Can be line-of-sight or over the horizon.
Transmission speed	Can be 1–10Mbps.
Installation/maintenance	Difficult. Requires licensing.
Interference	Highly susceptible to interference.
Cost	Moderate to very expensive.
Security	Highly susceptible to eavesdropping, especially as the signal is broadcast over a large area.

Spread-spectrum radio: Transmits on multiple frequencies according to a predetermined plan known to both the transmitter and receiver. One variation is called *frequency hopping*.

Spread-spectrum radio	
Maximum distance	Depends on power and frequency. Often limited, but can be over several miles.
Transmission speed	Direct-sequence 902MHz systems offer 2–6Mbps. GHz systems offer higher rates. Frequency-hopping typically lower (under 1Mbps).
Installation/maintenance	Depends on design. Can range from simple to complex.
Interference	Resistant to interference.
Cost	Relatively inexpensive.
Security	Highly resistant to eavesdropping.

Microwave

Microwave communication uses high frequency signals to transmit at high data rates over long distances. Major disadvantage is that there must be a *line of sight* between both the transmitter and receiver.

Terrestrial microwave: Uses towers or other antennas to transmit from one point on the ground to the other. Moderate to high cost. Interference might not be a problem over short distances, but longer distances might be susceptible.

Satellite microwave: Uses ground stations to bounce a signal off a satellite and back down to another ground station. Very expensive and often difficult to set up. Vulnerable to interference and also easy to eavesdrop on. Can have *propagation delays* due to the extreme distance that must be covered.

Infrared

Infrared communication uses technology similar to TV remote controls and usually works with either a *light-emitting diode (LED)* or a laser. Two forms:

Point-to-point infrared: Requires a line of sight between the transmitter and receiver. Highly resistant to interference and eavesdropping. Can cover long distances at high speeds with laser technology.

Broadcast infrared: Involves sending out the signal in such a way that multiple stations can receive it, often by bouncing it off some type of reflective material or having a repeater available to resend the signal out. Although very convenient because it does not require line of sight, it operates at slower speeds and can only operate within a confined area.

Applications for Wireless Media

Wireless media can be used to extend your LAN to other locations. One such use is as a *wireless bridge* to link two LANs in a location where cable is not an option (for instance over a highway or river).

Another option is for mobile computing to allow stations on your LAN to move around within a certain area.

Chapter 7

Data Transmission

Network Interface Cards

Operate at the OSI data link and physical layers and connect your computer to the network.

Utilize the bus inside the computer. Four major types:

- *ISA*—Original PC bus—16 bits.
- *EISA*—Compatible with ISA, but 32 bits.
- *Micro Channel Architecture*—IBM proprietary, 32 bits.
- *PCI*—New de facto PC standard—32 bits.

The *MAC address* or *hardware address* is a unique address burned into the card at the time of manufacture.

Configuration Settings

Most NICs configured today by software, but older ones might use jumpers or DIP switches. Three main settings to configure:

- Interrupt request
- Base I/O port
- Base memory address

IRQs signal the CPU that a device needs service. Must be unique inside of computer. Standard IRQs are in the following table.

IRQ	Typical Usage
0	System timer
1	Keyboard
2	Secondary IRQ controller or video adapter
3	Unassigned (unless used for COM2, COM4, or bus mouse)
4	Serial ports COM1 and COM3
5	Unassigned (unless used for LPT2 or sound card)
6	Floppy disk controller
7	Parallel port LPT1
8	Real-time clock
9	Unassigned, redirected IRQ2, sound card, or third IRQ controller
10	Unassigned or primary SCSI controller
11	Unassigned or secondary SCSI controller
12	PS/2 Mouse
13	Math coprocessor (if installed)
14	Primary hard-drive controller
15	Unassigned or secondary hard-drive controller

Base I/O port is essentially the address of a device on the computer's internal bus. Consists of hexadecimal addresses in format "0x300" or "300h". Common values for a NIC are 0x300, 0x310, or 0x280.

Base memory address is the buffer area within the computer's RAM that the NIC can access.

Performance Enhancements

Possible NIC performance enhancements include:

- RAM buffering
- Direct memory access (DMA)
- Bus mastering
- Onboard microprocessor
- Shared memory

Drivers

A driver is a small piece of software that is installed into your operating system to allow it to use a specific device.

NIC drivers are installed through the Network Control Panel in Microsoft operating systems.

Getting Data on the Network

NIC also controls when the computer can transmit data onto the network. A *collision* occurs when two computers transmit simultaneously, and data is lost. Part of network access is avoiding these collisions. Four primary methods:

Contention

Network devices compete with each other to transmit. Two main methods:

Carrier-Sense Multiple Access with Collision Detection (CSMA/CD)—If the network media is free, a computer can transmit. If two computers transmit simultaneously, a collision is detected, and both computers back off and transmit again. The most common implementation of CSMA/CD is Ethernet.

Carrier-Sense Multiple Access with Collision Avoidance (CSMA/CA)—If the network media is free, a computer first transmits a small packet indicating that it will be transmitting more data. Most common implementation is early Apple LocalTalk.

Think of contention as driving to an intersection with no stoplight. If all is clear, you can go. If many people are coming, you might have to wait.

Advantages of Contention

- Fast in low-traffic environments
- Inexpensive

Disadvantages of Contention

- Slow in high-traffic environments
- No guarantee of access to the network media
- No way of prioritizing packets

Token Passing

In token passing, computers are connected in a ring. A small data frame called a *token* circulates. Only when a computer has the token can it transmit. There are no collisions, and every computer is guaranteed access to the network media. The most common implementation is IBM's Token Ring.

Think of token passing as driving to an intersection where a stoplight gives equal access to all approaching the intersection.

Advantages of Token Passing

- Fast in high network-traffic environments
- Guaranteed access to media for all network stations
- Allows time-critical transmission

Disadvantages of Token Passing

- Slower than contention in low-traffic environments
- More expensive than most contention-based networks

Demand priority

With demand priority, computers are connected to intelligent hubs that sense a *demand* for service when a computer wants to transmit. That packet is then sent to its destination port. Hubs can also prioritize the traffic. The only implementation is HP's 100VG-AnyLAN.

Advantages of Demand Priority

- Fast access
- Can set priority of data packet

Disadvantages of Demand Priority

- Hubs and NICs are expensive

Polling

Polling occurs when a central controller (such as a mainframe) repeatedly checks each network device to see if it has anything to transmit. One example is IBM's SNA.

Advantages of Polling

- Guaranteed access

Disadvantages of Polling

- Inefficient use of the network

Chapter 8

Network Architecture

Ethernet

Most popular network architecture in use today. Breaks data into *frames*, uses baseband signaling, and uses CSMA/CD for access control. IEEE specification is 802.3. Operates at either 10Mbps or 100Mbps.

Most versions of Ethernet are subject to the *5-4-3 rule*, which indicates that between any two devices on the network, there can be no more than five network segments connected by four repeaters with no more than three of those segments being populated. A *populated* segment is one that has more than just the start and end connections and is only possible with coaxial cable.

In Ethernet networks, there are four possible *frame types* that can be used:

- *Ethernet 802.3.* Used primarily in Novell NetWare 2.x and 3.x networks.
- *Ethernet 802.2.* Used in Novell NetWare 4.x networks by default.
- *Ethernet SNAP.* Used in some AppleTalk networks.
- *Ethernet II.* Used in TCP/IP networks.

For communication to occur between two computers on an Ethernet network, they both must use the *identical* frame type.

10BASE5

Original Ethernet design uses thicknet coaxial cable. Stations are connected to the cable by way of a *transceiver* that has a *piercing tap* (also called a *vampire tap*). A *drop cable* extends from the transceiver to the *Attachment Unit Interface (AUI)* port on a NIC.

Information Category	10BASE5 Specifics
Advantage	Long distances
Disadvantages	High cost, difficult to install
Topology	Bus
Cable type	50-ohm thicknet
Connector type	Vampire tap transceiver, AUI/DIX connector
Media access method	CSMA/CD
Maximum segment length	500 meters (1,640 feet)
Maximum length between any two points	2,500 meters (8,200 feet)
Minimum length between nodes	2.5 meters (8 feet)
Maximum # of connected segments	5, with only 3 populated
Maximum # of nodes per segment	100
Maximum # of nodes for network	1,024
Transmission speed	10Mbps
IEEE specification	802.3

10BASE2

10BASE2 Ethernet uses thinnet cable of type RG-58A/U or RG-58C/U. The cable has an impedance of 50 ohms. Cable segments are connected by a *T-connector* or a *barrel connector*. The T-connector attaches to the NIC. Cheaper and more flexible than thicknet, 10BASE2 was the most popular Ethernet until rise of 10BASE-T. Like 10BASE5, it is subject to the 5-4-3 rule.

Information Category	10BASE2 Specifics
Advantages	Simple to install, relatively inexpensive
Disadvantage	Bus topology is difficult to troubleshoot
Topology	Bus
Cable type	50-ohm thinnet—RG-58A/U and RG-58C/U

Information Category	10BASE2 Specifics
Connector type	BNC
Media access method	CSMA/CD
Maximum segment length	185 meters (607 feet)
Maximum distance between two points	925 meters (3,035 feet)
Minimum length between nodes	0.5 meters (20 inches)
Maximum # of connected segments	5, with only 3 populated
Maximum # of nodes per segment	30
Maximum # of nodes for network	1,024
Transmission speed	10Mbps
IEEE specification	802.3

10BASE-T

Most popular form of Ethernet today. Uses unshielded twisted-pair (UTP) with a minimum of Category 3 in a star topology. UTP cables have an RJ-45 connector on end. Subject to 5-4-3 rule, but because UTP will never have a "populated" segment (with more than the two endpoints), only the 5-4 part of the rule applies in a pure 10BASE-T network.

Note that to connect two hubs in any twisted-pair Ethernet network (10BASE-T or 100BASE-T), you need to use some means to swap the signal between the transmit and receive pairs inside the UTP cable. The usual methods are either to use a *crossover cable* or to use a special port on one of the hubs.

Information Category	10BASE-T Specifics
Advantages	Very inexpensive, simple to connect, easy to troubleshoot
Disadvantage	Limited distance
Topology	Star
Cable type	Unshielded twisted-pair (Categories 3–5)
Connector type	RJ-45
Media access method	CSMA/CD
Maximum segment length	100 meters (328 feet)
Maximum distance between any two points	500 meters
Minimum length between nodes	0.5 meters (1.5 feet)

…continues

Information Category	10BASE-T Specifics
Maximum # of connected segments	1,024
Maximum # of nodes per segment	1
Maximum # of nodes for network	1,024
Transmission speed	10Mbps
IEEE specification	802.3

10BASE-F

Ethernet over fiber-optic cable. Several variations, but the important fact to remember is 10BASE-F will go to 2 kilometers.

Information Category	10BASE-F Specifics
Advantage	Long distances
Disadvantages	Very expensive, difficult to install
Topology	Star
Cable type	Fiber-optic
Connector type	Specialized
Media access method	CSMA/CD
Maximum segment length	2,000 meters (6,561 feet)
Maximum overall network length	N/A
Minimum length between nodes	N/A
Maximum # of connected segments	1,024
Maximum # of nodes per segment	1
Maximum # of nodes for network	1,024
Transmission speed	10Mbps
IEEE specification	802.3

100BASE-T

Also called *Fast Ethernet* or *100BASE-X*. Three variations:

- *100BASE-T4*. Four-pair Category 3, 4, or 5 UTP.
- *100BASE-TX*. Two-pair Category 5 UTP.
- *100BASE-FX*. Two-strand fiber-optic cable.

Information Category	100BASE-T Specifics
Advantages	Fast, simple to connect, easy to troubleshoot
Disadvantages	Limited distance, expensive hardware
Topology	Star
Cable type	Category 5 UTP—100BASE-TX; Category 3, 4, 5 UTP – 100BASE-T4; Fiber-optic cable—100BASE-FX
Connector type	RJ-45
Media access method	CSMA/CD
Maximum segment length	100 meters (328 feet)—100BASE-TX, 100BASE-T4; 2,000 meters (6,561 feet)—100BASE-FX
Maximum overall network length	N/A
Minimum length between nodes	2.5 meters (8 feet)
Maximum # of connected segments	1,024
Maximum # of nodes per segment	1
Maximum # of nodes for network	1,024
Transmission speed	100Mbps
IEEE specification	802.3

100VG-AnyLAN

Uses *demand-priority* instead of CMSA/CD. Developed by HP and not in widespread use. Uses special hubs that can prioritize traffic.

Information Category	100VG-AnyLAN Specifics
Advantages	Fast, simple to connect, easy to troubleshoot, can be used with either Ethernet or Token-Ring packets
Disadvantages	Limited distance (UTP), expensive hardware
Topology	Star
Cable type	Unshielded twisted-pair (Categories 3–5), shielded-twisted-pair, fiber-optic
Connector type	RJ-45
Media access method	Demand priority

...*continues*

Information Category	100VG-AnyLAN Specifics
Maximum segment length	100 meters (328 feet) if using Category 3 UTP or STP; 150 meters (492 feet) if using Category 5 UTP; 2,000 meters (6,562 feet) if using fiber-optic
Maximum overall network length	N/A
Minimum length between nodes	2.5 meters (8 feet)
Maximum # of connected segments	1,024
Maximum # of nodes per segment	1
Maximum # of nodes for network	1,024
Transmission speed	100Mbps
IEEE specification	802.12

Token Ring

Developed by IBM, implements token passing. Usually configured physically like a star, but the hub (called a *Multistation Access Unit [MAU])* is wired internally like a ring.

Token ring uses a *larger frame size* of 4–17KB compared to Ethernet's 1,500-byte frame.

Beaconing is a process whereby a computer detects that the ring might be broken and sends out a signal forcing all computers on the ring to check their connection and reconfigure the ring if necessary.

Information Category	Token-Ring Specifics
Advantages	Fast and reliable
Disadvantages	More expensive than comparable Ethernet solutions and can be difficult to troubleshoot
Topology	Ring
Cable type	IBM cable types, typically Types 1 (STP) and 3 (UTP)
Connector type	RJ-45 or IBM Type A
Media access method	Token passing
Maximum cable length	45 meters (150 feet) with UTP, 101 meters (330 feet) with STP
Maximum overall network length	N/A
Minimum length between nodes	2.5 meters (8 feet)
Maximum # of connected segments	33 hubs

Information Category	Token-Ring Specifics
Maximum # of nodes per segment	Depends on hub
Maximum # of nodes for network	72 nodes with UTP; 260 nodes with STP
Transmission speed	4 or 16Mbps
IEEE specification	802.5

ARCNet

Older architecture developed in late 1970s. No longer used much due to 2.5Mbps transmission rate. Uses token passing, although structured more like a bus as in Ethernet. Uses RG-62 A/U 93-ohm cable.

Information Category	ARCnet Specifics
Advantages	Inexpensive, easy to install, reliable
Disadvantages	Slow, does not interconnect well with other systems
Topology	Star and bus
Cable type	RG-62 A/U coaxial (93 ohm), UTP, fiber-optic
Connector type	BNC, RJ-45, others
Media access method	Token-passing
Maximum segment length	600 meters (2,000 feet)—RG-62 A/U; 121 meters (400 feet)—UTP; 3,485 meters (11,500 feet)—fiber-optic; 30 meters (100 feet)—from a passive hub
Maximum overall network length	6,060 meters (20,000 feet)
Minimum length between nodes	Varies
Maximum # of connected segments	Varies
Maximum # of nodes per segment	Varies
Maximum # of nodes for network	255
Transmission speed	2.5Mbps
IEEE specification	No IEEE specification, but ANSI 878.1

AppleTalk

Simple, easy-to-use networking built in to Macintosh computers. At first, *AppleTalk* referred to protocols and hardware. In 1989, AppleTalk became protocols, and **LocalTalk** became the hardware.

LocalTalk used CSMA/CA and operated at 230.4 Kbps. Very easy to install cabling system.

AppleTalk now supports *EtherTalk* (Ethernet) and *TokenTalk* (Token Ring) and is subject to the advantages and disadvantages of those architectures.

Information Category	LocalTalk Specifics
Advantages	Simple, easy to install
Disadvantages	Slow, limited size
Topology	Bus
Cable type	STP
Connector type	Specialized
Media access method	CSMA/CA
Maximum segment length	300 meters (1,000 feet)
Maximum overall network length	300 meters (1,000 feet)
Minimum length between nodes	N/A
Maximum # of connected segments	8
Maximum # of nodes per segment	32
Maximum # of nodes for network	254
Transmission speed	230.4Kbps
IEEE specification	None

FDDI

Fiber Distributed Data Interface (FDDI), pronounced as "fiddy" uses fiber-optic cable and token-passing. FDDI has two different configurations: Class A and Class B. A Class A FDDI network uses two counter-rotating rings. A Class B FDDI network uses only one ring to transmit data. On a Class A FDDI network, a break in one ring can cause the signal to go back in the opposite direction on the inner ring for fault tolerance. A hub in FDDI is called a *concentrator*. It can operate at 100Mbps over a large distance (as much as 100km).

Information Category	FDDI Specifics
Advantages	Very fast, long distances, highly secure, resistant to EMI
Disadvantages	Very expensive, difficult to install
Topology	Ring
Cable type	Fiber-optic
Connector type	Specialized
Media access method	Token-passing

Information Category	FDDI Specifics
Maximum segment length	N/A
Maximum overall network length	100km (60 miles)
Minimum length between nodes	N/A
Maximum # of connected segments	N/A
Maximum # of nodes per segment	N/A
Maximum # of nodes for network	500
Transmission speed	100Mbps
IEEE specification	No IEEE specification, but ANSI X3T9.5

Chapter 9

Network Protocols

Computer communication protocols are usually grouped in a *protocol stack* or *protocol suite* and installed onto a computer before it can connect to a network.

Connection-Oriented Versus Connectionless

Connection-oriented protocols provide a reliable point-to-point connection that guarantees that data will be sent correctly (TCP or SPX).

Connectionless protocols merely send the data to the recipient with no guarantee of delivery (UDP and IPX).

Routable versus Nonroutable

Routable protocols can work with routers and are suitable for networks, from small office networks to large enterprisewide networks (TCP/IP and IPX/SPX).

Nonroutable protocols do not pass through routers and are designed primarily for small networks (NetBEUI and DLC).

TCP/IP

Consists of several protocols:

Internet Protocol (IP): Provides data transportation

Transmission Control Protocol (TCP): Provides reliable connection-oriented data transportation on top of IP.

To communicate within TCP/IP networks, all computers are assigned a unique 32-bit *IP address* consisting of a portion identifying the network and a portion identifying the individual computers, referred to as *hosts*.

Subnet mask: Used to determine which part of the IP address refers to the network and which part refers to an individual computer.

IP addresses are either assigned manually or provided dynamically using the *Dynamic Host Configuration Protocol (DHCP)*. DHCP eases network administration and allows computers to be easily moved around within an organization.

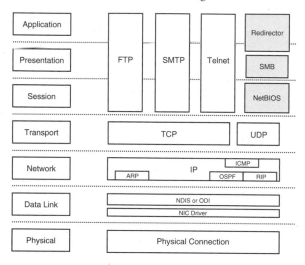

The TCP/IP compared to OSI

IPX/SPX

Used primarily within Novell NetWare networks. Like TCP/IP, the suite consists of a number of protocols:

Internetwork Packet Exchange (IPX): Like IP, provides basic data transmission across a network

Sequenced Packet Exchange (SPX): Like TCP, provides reliable connection-oriented communication. In Windows NT, *NWLINK* is Microsoft's implementation of IPX/SPX.

One concern with IPX/SPX is to make sure that the correct Ethernet frame type is being used.

Microsoft Networking

Microsoft and IBM jointly developed the *Network Basic Input Output System (NetBIOS)* and *NetBIOS Extended User Interface (NetBEUI)* to support communication over small- to medium-sized networks.

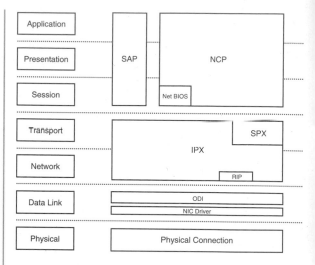

IPX/SPX protocol compared to OSI

Developed to work together, NetBIOS and NetBEUI have been separated.

NetBIOS

- Can work with a variety of protocols.
- Provides a session-layer application programming interface that PC applications can use to access network resources.
- Can now be used on top of TCP/IP and IPX/SPX networks.

NetBEUI

A small, fast, nonroutable protocol designed to carry NetBIOS and found primarily in small PC networks. Server Message Block (SMB) is the Microsoft file-sharing protocol.

Other Protocols

- DLC (a nonroutable protocol used for printing)
- NFS (Network File System—UNIX/Linux file sharing)
- AppleTalk (Apple networking protocol suite)

NDIS and ODI

Network Driver Interface Specification (NDIS) and *Open Driver Interface (ODI)* are specifications that allow multiple protocols to be bound to the same network interface card.

NetBIOS Naming

NetBIOS uses unique computer names that are 16 characters long but of which you can only assign the first 15. Names are resolved into network addresses by either broadcast or by the *Windows Internet Name System (WINS)*.

Chapter 10

Network Operating Systems

A network operating system provides functions such as file and printer sharing, user account administration, and network security.

Examples: Novell NetWare and Windows NT Server.

For a network operating system to work, there must be software installed on both the client and the server.

Client

Redirector: Program that intercepts resource requests from applications, determines whether those requests are local or on the network, and forwards the request appropriately.

Redirectors work primarily at the presentation layer, but also at the application OSI layer.

Universal naming convention (UNC): Pathname that is a method of referencing shared network resources. The format of a UNC name is `\\servername\pathname`.

Server

Operating system maintains a user account database and allows users to log on to the network.

File Sharing

sharing: The process of making a directory/folder available for network use.

Microsoft networks use the *Server Message Block (SMB)* protocol for file sharing. UNIX/Linux servers use the *Network File System (NFS)* protocol.

Network Printing

When the user submits a print job, it is spooled into a print queue, where a spooler monitors the status of printers and permits the print job to be printed when a printer is available.

Printers can be managed remotely, and network administrators are usually able to cancel or reprioritize queued print jobs.

Chapter 11

Network Applications
Types of Applications

Standalone: Applications designed to be used on a single computer.

Network versions: Applications that can be run from a network server and offer the administrator more control over upgrading and administering the programs. Network versions cost less than standalone, but they generate a lot of network traffic and are unavailable in the event of a network failure.

Network-only: Applications that rely on a network for operation such as an email or shared database system.

Network-Only Applications

Three modes of operation:

Centralized applications: All processing takes place on a central (mainframe) computer, and all the client computers merely have terminal windows open in which the application is run. Such applications generate a great deal of network traffic and do not efficiently use the power of desktop systems today.

Shared-file-system applications: All the processing takes place on the client systems, and the network file server is used only to store the central data repository. Examples include many PC email programs and database applications. Although often simple to set up, they generate a lot of network traffic and can have security problems.

Client/server applications: Some of the processing takes place on the client and some on the server end. Examples include many of the recent database applications, email systems such as Microsoft Exchange Server or Lotus Notes, and the World Wide Web.

Electronic Mail

Mail user agent: The email client.

Mail transfer agent (MTA): The program delivering messages in the background.

Do not confuse email protocols with network protocols. Email protocols include *Simple Mail Transport Protocol (SMTP), POP3, IMAP4, MIME,* and *X.400.* Related directory protocols include *LDAP* and *X.500.*

MAPI, Microsoft's *Messaging API,* is used to allow desktop applications to communicate with an underlying email system.

Shared Databases

Do not confuse database protocols with network protocols. The two main database standards of interest are *Structured Query Language (SQL)* and Microsoft's *Open Database Connectivity (ODBC).*

Chapter 12

Remote Access
Modems

Translate between the digital signal from the computer and the analog signal (sound) of the telephone lines.

Two primary types of modems: asynchronous and synchronous.

Asynchronous

Commonly used in personal computers and provide connections over regular telephone lines.

Use start and stop bits to identify where individual bytes of data begin and end. With error correction and compression, operate around 56Kbps.

Synchronous

Do not use start and stop bits, but instead, rely on exact coordination of timing between the sending and receiving computers.

Less overheard than asynchronous modems, synchronous modems can attain higher speeds, but are limited to dedicated leased lines.

Types of Connections

- *Dial-up connections:* Use modems typically up to 56Kbps.
- *ISDN:* Provides a connection up to 128Kbps but is more expensive.
- *Dedicated leased lines:* Can provide the same bandwidth as dial-up connections (or higher) but are much more expensive.

Remote Access Service

Remote Access Service (RAS) is provided for remote connections.

Operates on Windows NT and provides up to 256 inbound connections on NT Server and 1 connection on NT Workstation.

The client software comes in the form of a RAS client (Windows NT 3.51 and Windows for Workgroups) and a Dial-Up Networking (DUN) client (Windows 95/98 and Windows NT 4.0).

Communication Protocol

Serial Line Internet Protocol (SLIP): An older protocol that only supports TCP/IP connections to remote networks and provides no error checking, compression, or encryption for password authentication.

PPP: Is the successor to SLIP and is widely used because it supports the transmission of packets using multiple network protocols. PPP also provides sophisticated error checking and compression (faster and more reliable than SLIP). Almost all dial-up connections today use PPP.

Although RAS/DUN clients support outbound connections using either SLIP or PPP, the RAS server incorporated into Windows NT supports only inbound PPP connections.

Providing remote network access does introduce security threats. Microsoft RAS provides several options to reduce this threat, including the following:

- Windows NT user account security.
- User callback capability.
- Encryption between the RAS/DUN client and the RAS server.

Chapter 13

Creating Larger Networks

Repeaters

Repeaters function at the physical layer of the OSI Reference Model to take incoming signals from one network segment, boost the signal strength, and retransmit the signal onto another network segment. Repeaters deal only with electrical and optical signals and have no knowledge of the data or any addresses. They cannot be used to connect network segments with dissimilar architectures, such as Token-Ring and Ethernet.

They operate at a fast speed and enable you to connect network segments using different physical media (for instance, UTP and coaxial cable).

For disadvantages, they simply pass along the electrical signal and do nothing to eliminate network congestion or noise.

Hubs are "multiport repeaters".

Bridges

Bridges operate at the data link layer of the OSI Reference Model and are used primarily to segment a network to reduce network traffic. Bridges listen to network traffic and build a table based on *MAC (hardware) addresses* of what network devices are on which bridge ports.

It is important to understand that a bridge checks the destination address against the addresses it knows to be on the same network as the source. If the destination is not on the same network, the bridge forwards the packet. Note that the bridge does not have to know that the destination address is, in fact, on the other segment. It only knows that the destination is *not* on the same segment as the source.

Bridges offer many advantages, including the following:

- Bridges can act as repeaters and extend a network to greater distances.
- Bridges can restrict the flow of traffic between network segments and ease network congestion.
- They can connect network segments using different physical media.
- Bridges called *translation bridges* can connect networks with different architectures.

However, bridges do have some disadvantages, including the following:

- Because bridges examine hardware addresses, they are slower than repeaters.
- Broadcast packets, intended for all computers on a network, are forwarded by bridges to all network segments.
- Bridges are more expensive and complex than repeaters.

Bridges forward all broadcast packets. Additionally, when a bridge encounters an unknown destination address, its default action is to forward the packet to all other network segments.

Routers

Routers operate at the Network Layer of the OSI Reference Model and connect networks using network protocols, determine the best path for a data packet to travel, and send the packet to the appropriate destination. Because routers work with network protocols, they can send packets over different network architectures (such as Ethernet and Token Ring).

Routers consult an internal *routing table* to determine where the packet should be sent. For the exam, remember the following: Upon receiving a broadcast packet or a packet with an unknown destination address, *bridges forward* the packet, whereas *routers discard* the packet.

Routers only work with *routable protocols* such as TCP/IP and IPX/SPX. Packets using *nonroutable protocols* such as NetBEUI and DLC will not be forwarded through the router.

Routers can use *static* routing, where the routing table is manually constructed, or *dynamic* routing, where the router builds the table itself.

Note that routers use *routing protocols* such as RIP and OSPF to determine the best path for a packet to travel.

Routers offer many advantages, including the following:

- Routers can interconnect networks using different network architectures and media access methods, such as Ethernet and Token-Ring.
- When there are multiple paths across a network, a router can choose the best path and make the most efficient use of network resources.
- Routers can reduce network congestion because, unlike bridges, they do not retransmit broadcast messages or corrupted data packets.

However, routers do have some disadvantages, such as the following:

- Routers are more expensive and complex than bridges or repeaters.
- Routers work only with routable network protocols.
- When using dynamic routing, continuous updates of router information generate additional network traffic.
- Routers are slower than bridges because they need to perform more processing on the data packet.

Windows NT 4.0 Server and Windows 2000 can act as either a static or dynamic router.

Brouters

Brouters are devices that function at both the network and data link layers of the OSI Reference

Model and combine elements of both bridges and routers. They route packets that use routable protocols and bridge packets that use nonroutable protocols.

Gateways

Gateways function at the application and other upper layers of the OSI Reference Model to connect systems that use completely different protocols or data formats.

Advantages of gateways include the following:

- Gateways can connect completely different systems.
- They specialize in one task and can do that task well.

Disadvantages of gateways include the following:

- Gateways are often more expensive than other devices.
- Gateways are frequently more difficult to install and configure.
- Because of the processing involved with data translation, gateways can be quite slow.

Chapter 14

Wide Area Networks (WANs)

WAN Basics

Wide area network (WAN): Links multiple LANs across a large geographic distance. Consists of the following:

- Connections leased from service providers
- Dial-up telephone connections
- Dedicated telephone lines
- Connections over packet-switched networks.

Dedicated connections: Establish an exclusive, permanent, full-time open connection between two points.

Switched networks: Enable multiple users to share the same connection line.

Packet-switching networks: Break data into small packets that are sent across the network with each packet potentially following a different route and with the data being reassembled into the proper sequence at the destination.

Virtual circuits: Establish a path for data to travel across a packet-switched network. Most common type is a *permanent virtual circuit (PVC)*.

Many dedicated connections use a **Channel Service Unit/Data Service Unit (CSU/DSU)** to connect your network to the line.

Types of Connections

Dedicated Digital Service (DDS): Leased lines are inexpensive connections provided at up to 56Kbps.

The T-carrier system: Uses multiplexors to combine several voice or data channels for transmission on a single line. Most common form is a *T1* line, which consists of 24 64Kbps channels for a maximum transmission speed of 1.544Mbps. A *T3* line goes up to 45Mbps. *Fractional* service is also available.

Integrated Services Digital Network (ISDN): Enables users to combine voice and data over a digital line. Basic Rate ISDN provides two 64Kbps B-channels and one 16Kbps D-channel (for control) for a total data bandwidth of 128Kbps. Primary Rate ISDN provides 23 64Kbps B-channels and one 64Kbps D-channel, using the full bandwidth of a T1 line.

X.25: Is a CCITT/ITU series of protocols that defines how packet-switching can occur across an internetwork. Used primarily in Public Data Networks (PDNs) to which organizations can connect, X.25 provides reliable and virtually error-free communication up to 64Kbps.

Frame relay: Provides packet-switching like X.25, but assumes that it will be running on top of a more reliable medium and leaves error checking to devices at the end connections. Maximum speed of frame-relay is up to 1.544Mbps.

Asynchronous Transfer Mode (ATM): Uses an advanced form of packet-switching referred to as cell-switching, where all data is packaged into 53-byte cells for transmission. ATM can have speeds up to 622Mbps and beyond.

Switched Multi-megabit Data Service (SMDS): Is a service offered by some local telephone companies using ATM technology to provide connections from 1.544 to 45Mbps. Like both frame relay and ATM, SMDS does not provide any error checking.

Synchronous Optical Network (SONET): Is a physical layer standard that defines transmission speeds and other characteristics of fiber-optic cables. Both ATM and SMDS can use SONET as the underlying physical transportation medium. The measurement units within SONET are intervals of 51.8Mbps.

Chapter 15

The Internet
Internet Overview

Internet: A large network of networks all based on the TCP/IP protocol.

Intranet: An internal network based on Internet services and technologies.

Internet services include the following:

World Wide Web: A network of servers that communicate with Web *browsers* using the *Hypertext Transfer Protocol (HTTP).* Web pages are created in the *Hypertext Markup Language (HTML).*

Email: Enables transmission of electronic messages between people. The *Simple Mail Transport Protocol (SMTP)* is used for sending and receiving messages, and the *Post Office Protocol (POP3)* is used for retrieving messages by computers that are not always online.

File Transfer Protocol (FTP): Enables you to upload and download files to and from FTP servers.

Newsgroups: Allow for the discussion of a wide range of topics. Also referred to as *Usenet* because of its origins.

Telnet: Enables you to log in to a remote host (usually a UNIX or Linux system) and execute commands on that system.

Chat: Enables you to communicate in real time with others around the globe, commonly text-only, although video and audio have recently started to develop.

The Domain Name System (DNS)

All communication on the Internet occurs between computers using IP addresses. However, to aid in remembering addresses, the *Domain Name System (DNS)* was created. DNS enables you to associate a *domain name* with an IP address and use meaningful names for communication purposes. Note that a DNS domain name is different from a Windows NT domain name.

Getting Connected

To connect to the Internet, you need to arrange for a connection with an *Internet service provider (ISP).* Many different types of ISPs exist, and the choice for your organization can be a difficult one. When you have chosen an ISP, you need to obtain a range of valid IP addresses and a domain name.

Security

Firewall: A series of hardware and/or software solutions that combine to protect your network from external intruders.

Proxy server: One of the tools used in a firewall. It retrieves Web pages on behalf of the browsers on your internal network and therefore only exposes one computer (the proxy server) to the Internet and possible intruders.

Chapter 16

Network Administration
Domain Versus Workgroup

Workgroup

Workgroup: A logical collection of computers in a peer-to-peer network.

Each computer maintains its own list of users and security settings.

When users want to connect to a shared resource, they must know the password or have a local user account on that system.

Domain

Domain: Uses a server-based model where user account administration is handled from a central location.

All users are added to the central database, and permissions are assigned based on that central list. When a user has logged on to the network, she can access all resources for which she has been given permission without reentering her password.

One Windows NT Server is the *Primary Domain Controller (PDC)* that has the master account database. The PDC might be supported by one or more *Backup Domain Controllers (BDCs)*, which

help share the load of authenticating users and serve as a backup should the PDC fail.

Workgroups are suitable for small networks (under 10 users), but above that the domain model is easier to administer.

Accounts

User accounts: Are created for each user who will be on the network. Accounts are given passwords and can be given settings such as expiration dates.

Special administrative accounts: Are present in most network operating systems. In Windows NT, the account is Administrator. In NetWare, the account is Supervisor. In UNIX/Linux, it is root. This account has permission to add other users and perform administrative tasks.

Group accounts: Can be created to simplify assigning permissions to large blocks of users.

User and Group accounts are created on Windows NT using the *User Manager* tool.

Security

Part of security is establishing an *account policy*, which determines how often users must change their password, how long the password must be, and so on.

Share-Level Security

A password is assigned to each shared resource (folder or printer) and must be provided to gain access to that resource. It is used in a *workgroup* setting where each computer maintains its own list of account. *Windows 95/98* and *Windows for Workgroups* can use share-level security when not part of a Windows NT domain.

User-Level Security

Involves assigning permissions for resources to individual user or group accounts, typically from a central database such as a Windows NT domain. User-level security is easier to administer and provides higher security than share-level security, but it usually involves more initial setup work. Users typically need to know only their one logon password to access resources.

Auditing

Auditing is tracking user account activities and network events. Audit logs can be used to find out who has been accessing what resources or exercising certain privileges.

In NT, auditing is established by choosing Audit from the Policies menu of the User Manager and then completing the dialog box. Log entries are visible in the NT Event Viewer.

Chapter 17

Network Problem Prevention

Overview

In *documenting your network*, you should develop documents that outline the hardware and software components and configuration of your network. Including information such as key contact phone numbers, vendor relationships, and any successful problem resolutions will greatly increase the value of your documentation when you are trying to diagnose problems.

Monitoring network performance involves searching for network *bottlenecks*, including network devices that are too slow or are stretched beyond their capabilities due to the level of network traffic.

Performance Monitor is a tool in Windows NT to help with monitoring many aspects of system performance.

The *Simple Network Management Protocol (SNMP)* is a protocol that enables you to collect data from SNMP-enabled devices and display it in

a management station.

An *Uninterruptible Power Supply (UPS)* protects devices from power failures and surges. Your servers and network devices should be plugged in to UPS systems.

Backup Procedures

Backups are crucial to protecting your system. There are several types:

A *Full Backup* backs up all selected files, regardless of whether they have changed since the last backup, and marks them as being backed up.

A *Copy* backs up selected files without marking them as backed up.

An *Incremental* backs up and marks selected files only if they have changed since the last backup.

A *Daily Copy* backs up all files modified on a given day, without marking the files as backed up.

A *Differential* backs up selected files only if they have changed since the last backup, but does not mark files as backed up.

Fault-Tolerant Disk Storage

To protect disk data, one mechanism is to use a RAID (Redundant Array of Inexpensive Disks) system. RAID systems are labeled as RAID 0 through RAID 5. Windows NT Server supports RAID 0, RAID 1, and RAID 5.

RAID Level 0 uses disk striping to enhance disk performance by spreading data across multiple drives. RAID Level 0 does not provide any degree of fault tolerance.

RAID Level 1 uses *disk mirroring* to write the identical data to two separate disk drives. In the event of the failure of one drive, users can continue using the second drive.

Disk duplexing is a variation on disk mirroring where each disk drive uses a separate disk drive controller card.

RAID Level 5, known as *disk striping with parity*, writes data and parity information across three or more disks. If any disk fails, data can be reconstructed from the data and parity information stored on all other disks.

Beyond RAID, Windows NT also supports **sector-sparing**. Sector-sparing is a fault-tolerant mechanism where data is moved from a bad sector to a good sector and the bad sector is removed from use. Windows NT supports sector sparing on SCSI disk drives.

Disaster Recovery

Lastly, as a network administrator, you should develop a comprehensive disaster recovery plan to address what happens when you experience a catastrophic failure such as a fire, extended power outage, flood, or other natural disaster.

Chapter 18

Troubleshooting Overview

Network troubleshooting involves the process of collecting information about what is wrong, isolating the problem, and correcting the situation. Microsoft outlines a five-step approach to network troubleshooting:

1. Set the problem's priority.
2. Collect information to identify the symptoms.
3. Develop a list of possible causes.
4. Test to isolate the cause.
5. Study the results of the test to identify a solution.

By using a structured approach such as this, you can methodically identify and solve network problems.

Troubleshooting Tools

A **digital volt-meter (DVM)** can be used to test for the existence of a break or a short in a cable. A DVM operates at the physical layer of the OSI Reference Model.

A **time-domain reflectometer (TDR)** uses a sonar-like pulse to determine where a break or short has occurred within a cable. A TDR operates at the physical layer of the OSI Reference Model.

A **cable tester** will examine a cable to see whether it meets the performance standards for its type. Can also include DVM and TDR functionality. Will also test for impedance and other variables. Advanced testers might have some data link layer data-collection capabilities.

A **protocol analyzer** is a hardware and/or software tool that can monitor network traffic, find faulty network components, and analyze the overall network performance. A protocol analyzer operates at many layers of the OSI model, although primarily the physical through network layers.

A **network monitor** is a software program that can monitor the network performance and gather statistics. Operates from data link layer up through top of OSI model.

There are also **operating system tools** that are available that can assist you in identifying system configuration problems. In Microsoft networks, such tools include the Control Panel and the Windows NT Diagnostics tool.

Troubleshooting Resources

In your search for solutions, many resources are at your disposal. Microsoft TechNet is a CD-ROM–based resource to which you can subscribe that provides a monthly set of CDs with a searchable database of technical support problems and product information. Microsoft also maintains a Knowledge Base on the Web, which provides another searchable database. Most vendors are now making information available through the Web, as are numerous networking periodicals.

Common Problems

Finally, the most common problems plaguing network users usually involve (the problem is followed by the common troubleshooting tools used to solve these problems):

- Cable problems (DVM, TDR, cable tester)
- Faulty network interface cards (operating system tools, protocol analyzer)
- NIC configuration issues (IRQ and Base I/O port) (operating system tools)
- Network driver problems (operating system tools)
- Incorrect network protocol settings (operating system tools, protocol analyzer)
- Network protocol mismatch (operating system tools, protocol analyzer)
- Connectivity device failure (protocol analyzer)
- Network traffic congestion (protocol analyzer, network monitor)
- Broadcast storms (protocol analyzer, network monitor)
- Network applications (protocol analyzer, network monitor)
- Power fluctuations (DVM)

MCSE
Networking
Essentials
Exam Guide

Second Edition

Dan York

Contents
at a Glance

A Division of Macmillan Publishing USA
201 W. 103rd Street
Indianapolis, Indiana 46290

MCSE Networking Essentials Exam Guide

Copyright © 2000 by Que

International Standard Book Number: 0-7897-2265-8

Library of Congress Catalog Card Number: 99-65934

Printed in the United States of America

First Printing: November 1999

01   00   99   4   3   2   1

Trademarks

All terms mentioned in this book that are known to be trademarks or service marks have been appropriately capitalized. Que cannot attest to the accuracy of this information. Use of a term in this book should not be regarded as affecting the validity of any trademark or service mark.

Microsoft is a registered trademark of Microsoft Corporation in the United States and other countries. Que is an independent entity from Microsoft Corporation, and not affiliated with Microsoft Corporation in any manner. This book may be used in assisting students to prepare for a Microsoft Certified Professional Exam. Neither Microsoft Corporation, its designated review company, nor Que warrants that use of the book will ensure passing the relevant Exam.

Warning and Disclaimer

Every effort has been made to make this book as complete and as accurate as possible, but no warranty or fitness is implied. The information provided is on an "as is" basis. The authors and the publisher shall have neither liability nor responsibility to any person or entity with respect to any loss or damages arising from the information contained in this book or from the use of the CD or programs accompanying it.

Use of the Microsoft Approved Study Guide Logo on this product signifies that it has been independently reviewed and approved in complying with the following standards:

- acceptable coverage of all content related to Microsoft exam number 70-058, entitled Networking Essentials.
- sufficient performance-based exercises that relate closely to all required content; and
- technically accurate content, based on sampling of text.

Credits

Publisher
Paul Boger

Associate Publisher
Jim Minatel

Executive Editor
Angie Wethington

Series Editor
Jill Hayden

Development Editor
Jill Hayden
Angelique Brittingham

Acquisitions Editor
Tracy Williams

Managing Editor
Lisa Wilson

Project Editor
Natalie Harris

Copy Editor
Kelly Talbot

Indexer
Rebecca Salerno

Proofreader
Benjamin Berg
Bob Laroche

Technical Editor
Edward Herzog

Team Coordinator
Vicki Harding

Software Development Specialist
Michael Hunter

Interior Design
Anne Jones

Cover Design
Karen Ruggles

Layout Technicians
Stacey DeRome
Ayanna Lacey
Heather Hiatt Miller

Composed in ***AGaramond*** and ***Futura*** by Que Corporation.

To Lori—my wife, partner, editor, and friend.

About the Author

Dan York, MCSE, MCT, served as both a regional technical instructor and the manager of technical operations for the Bedford, NH office of Productivity Point International. Having spent over 20 years working with personal computers, Dan brings a powerful breadth of knowledge to the classroom. Schooled in adult learning techniques, he has spent the past 10 years training in the corporate world seeking to demystify computer technology and make it available and understandable to novice users.

After attaining his bachelor's degree at the University of New Hampshire, Dan continued to pursue graduate courses in Education. He interrupted his study to start up the training division of CIC/Copley Systems, initially focusing on desktop publishing and UNIX. Prior to joining PPI in early 1996, Dan had grown this division into one of the top FrameMaker, UNIX, and Internet training centers in New England. With PPI, he became a Microsoft Certified Trainer and utilized his strong UNIX, Internet, and PC background to enhance his Windows NT, Microsoft Exchange, and Internet courses.

An accomplished speaker and presenter, Dan has presented workshops at national conferences such as *Computer Training and Support 1995, Training Director's Forum 1996,* and the Information Technology Training Association's *Strategies for Success '96* and *'99.* Dan currently resides in southern New Hampshire with his wife Lori and a greyhound named Atticus. He is now employed by Linuxcare, Inc. and is active in the development of a certification program for the Linux operating system through the Linux Professional Institute. He can be contacted electronically at dyork@lodestar2.com. You can also visit his Web page at http://www.lodestar2.com/netess2/.

Acknowledgements for the Second Edition

There are many people to thank for this updated book:

First, my wife Lori for all the support, encouragement, and assistance she has provided—and for all the lost evenings and weekends she has endured! Sorry, hon, this one still isn't a murder mystery!

All the many readers of the first edition who wrote in to me with comments, suggestions, thoughtful insights, and feedback. It was great to communicate with so many people pursuing certification. This second edition is a much better book because of their comments.

Nancy Maragioglio, formerly of Que, for all her help during the time between the first and second editions.

Angie Wethington, Tracy Williams, Jill Hayden, Angelique Brittingham, and the technical editors (especially Ed Herzog) at Macmillan for making this book possible.

Peter Squier at PPI for asking me to do this new edition.

Neal Allen at Fluke Corporation who *greatly* increased my knowledge and understanding of Ethernet.

All the great staff at PPI who remain dedicated to making PPI a world-class training organization.

All my students over the years who have constantly asked tough questions and demanded comprehensive answers.

And finally, thanks to Linus Torvalds and all the people in the Linux community who have made computing fun for me again!

Acknowledgements for the First Edition

No book of this size could be published without the help of many individuals. I would like to thank:

Caroline Kiefer, Rebecca Mounts, Don Essig, and the technical editors at Que, who made this book possible.

Pam Bernard at Productivity Point International who provided me the opportunity to write this book.

Kurt Hudson from PPI of Texas for his excellent technical editing.

All the staff of Productivity Point International of Northern New England, with special thanks to: Peter Poulin, the franchise owner, for all his support and for inadvertently beginning this whole process by simply forwarding an email message requesting authors with only the comment "F.Y.I."; Stephen Wallace, Terry McCarthy, and Scott O'Halloran for either answering questions I had or asking me questions that clarified my own knowledge; and Steve Urban for reading many of the chapters and for trying out the sample questions and lab exercises.

Mark Sangillo for his technical hardware assistance.

Dan Ryan, who first nurtured my interest in computers, and all those students and peers who have challenged my mind and continued my growth.

My parents, David and Sue York, for constantly fostering intellectual curiosity.

Our cat, Gremlin, for sitting in the middle of whatever I was working on, getting cat hair all over my keyboard and putting paw prints on top of drawings.

Most importantly, my wife Lori, who spent many nights and weekends reading every word of this book, providing endless amounts of constructive feedback, drawing some of the graphics, and learning far more about computer networking than she ever wanted to know. This text is a far better book because of her participation. Thank you, Lori.

Table of Contents

Tell Us What You Think!

As the reader of this book, *you* are our most important critic and commentator. We value your opinion and want to know what we're doing right, what we could do better, what areas you'd like to see us publish in, and any other words of wisdom you're willing to pass our way.

As a publisher for Que, I welcome your comments. You can fax, email, or write me directly to let me know what you did or didn't like about this book—as well as what we can do to make our books stronger.

Please note that I cannot help you with technical problems related to the topic of this book, and that due to the high volume of mail I receive, I might not be able to reply to every message.

When you write, please be sure to include this book's title and author as well as your name and phone or fax number. I will carefully review your comments and share them with the author and editors who worked on the book.

Fax: 317.581.4666

E-mail: certification@macmillanusa.com

Mail: Publisher
               Que
               201 West 103rd Street
               Indianapolis, IN 46290 USA

Introduction

This book was written by Microsoft Certified Professionals for Microsoft Certified Professionals and MCP Candidates. It is designed, in combination with your real-world experience, to prepare you to pass the Networking Essentials Exam (70-058) in addition to giving you a background in general networking.

At the time of this book, the Microsoft certification exams cost $100 each. Each exam consists of a range of questions with time limits for completion ranging from 25 minutes to two hours. If you are currently on the path to becoming a Microsoft Certified Systems Engineer (MCSE), you will be required to take as many as six exams, covering Microsoft operating systems, application programs, networking, and software development. The certification exams involve preparation, study, and the ability to apply the information learned through real-world experience. Are the benefits of certification worth the time, cost, and test anxiety? Microsoft has cosponsored research that provides some answers regarding the benefits of Microsoft certification.

Benefits for Your Organization

At companies participating in a previous Dataquest survey, a majority of corporate managers stated that certification is an *important factor* to the overall success of their companies because of the following:

■ *Certification increases customer satisfaction.* Customers look for indications that their suppliers understand the industry and have the ability to respond to their technical problems. Having Microsoft Certified Professionals on staff reassures customers by conveying to them that your employees have used and mastered Microsoft products.

■ *Certification maximizes training investment.* The certification process specifically identifies skills that an employee is lacking or areas where additional training is needed. By so doing, it validates training and eliminates the costs and loss of productivity associated with unnecessary training. In addition, certification records enable a company to verify an employee's technical knowledge and track retention of skills over time.

In October 1995, International Data Corporation (IDC) released a study regarding employee certification. IDC categorized survey respondents into two categories: advocates and nonbelievers. The advocates were those companies that require certification when hiring information-technology employees, whereas the nonbelievers did not require certification. The IDC study found that the benefits to companies supporting employee certification included the following:

■ *Reduced downtime.* Nonbelievers experienced an average of 5.3 hours of unscheduled downtime, with a per-incident cost per server of $1,102. Advocates, on the other hand, reported an average of 3.5 hours of unscheduled downtime with a per-incident cost per server of $669. On a monthly basis, it cost nonbelievers $866 more per server than it did advocates.

■ *Higher productivity.* On the average, advocate companies support roughly the same number of PCs as do nonbeliever companies. However, at advocate companies, the PCs are distributed across almost twice as many sites and across more distributed environments with roughly the same number of employees (144 employees for advocate companies, and 146 employees for nonbelievers).

■ *An ROI payback of less than nine months.* The IDC research found that a certified employee costs about $9,500 more per year than an uncertified employee (based on an average cost of $3,728 to certify added to a pay difference of 11.7 percent). IDC then weighed this against a monthly support cost difference for advocates of $285 less per month and the monthly server downtime costs of $866 less per month. The result? A total annual saving of $13,812 for the advocates and a return-on-investment in less than nine months.

Personal Benefits for You

Microsoft also cites a number of benefits that the Microsoft Certified Professional will accrue:

■ Industry recognition of expertise, enhanced by Microsoft's promotion of the Certified Professional community to the industry and potential clients.

- Access to technical information directly from Microsoft through a secured area on the MCP Web site.
- A complimentary one-year subscription to *Microsoft Certified Professional Magazine.*
- Microsoft Certified Professional logos and other materials to publicize your MCP status to colleagues and clients.
- Invitations to Microsoft conferences, technical training sessions, and special events.

Additional benefits, depending upon the certification, include the following:

- Microsoft TechNet or Microsoft Developer Network membership or discounts.
- Eligibility to join the Network Professional Association, a worldwide independent association of computer professionals.

Some intangible benefits of certification are as follows:

- Enhanced marketability with current or potential employers and customers, along with an increase in earnings potential.
- Methodology for objectively assessing current skills, individual strengths, and specific areas where training is required.

How to Use This Networking Essentials Exam Guide to Prepare for the Exam

One of the challenges that has always faced the would-be Microsoft Certified Professional is to decide how to best prepare for an examination. In doing so, there are always conflicting goals, such as how to prepare for the exam as quickly as possible and still actually learn how to do the work that passing the exam qualifies you to do.

Our goal for this book is to make your preparation and studying easier by filtering through the seemingly endless amounts of technical material on computer networking. The chapters and lab exercises are designed to present only the information that you actually need to *know* when installing and supporting computer networks as a Microsoft Certified Professional. Additional relevant information has been relegated to the appendixes.

How to Study with This Book

The chapters in this book are intended to be read in sequential order. Each chapter builds on the material learned in previous chapters. At the beginning of each chapter, you will find a list of skills and topics that are prerequisites for a comprehensive understanding of the material to be discussed in the chapter.

The lab exercises are arranged by topic rather than by chapter. This enables you to explore the areas and concepts of computer networks that are unfamiliar to you or those in which you would like additional reinforcement. It is strongly recommended that you do not skip the lab exercises in this book. Some of the knowledge and skills necessary to pass the Networking Essentials Exam can only be acquired by working with computer networks. The lab exercises are designed to help you acquire those skills.

How This Book Is Organized

The book is broken up into 18 chapters, each focusing on a particular topic that is an important piece of the overall picture:

- Chapter 1, "Microsoft Certified Professional Program," provides an overview of the Microsoft Certified Professional program, what certifications are available to you, and how Networking Essentials and this book fit in.

- Chapter 2, "Introduction to Networks," is an overview of computer networks. You will learn the basic terminology, the different types of networks, and the components that comprise a network. This chapter will also introduce the computer networking concepts that will be covered throughout the rest of the book.

- Chapter 3, "The OSI Reference Model," introduces a theoretical model of how a network should work. This model provides the framework for discussion for the remainder of the book. The concept of layered networking will be introduced, and each layer of the OSI Reference Model will be discussed in detail. Real-world networks will also be compared with the theoretical model.

- Chapter 4, "Network Topology," provides you with information critical to designing a network. Bus, star, and ring networks will be discussed, and you will learn which are appropriate for different situations.

- Chapter 5, "The Physical Connection," begins at the physical layer of the OSI Model and introduces the actual physical components necessary to create a computer network. Different media will be evaluated, and their advantages and disadvantages will be weighed.

- Chapter 6, "Wireless Connections," discusses wireless alternatives to the cable connections described in Chapter 5.

- Chapter 7, "Data Transmission," looks at the functions at the data link layer of the OSI Model—specifically, how the data is actually packaged for transmission onto the physical network media. You will learn about installing network interface cards and some common problems you will encounter. This chapter will also review the different methods that networks use to determine which computer can transmit data onto the network.

- Chapter 8, "Network Architecture," integrates the information discussed in the first seven chapters. Five different network architectures will be introduced and defined according to their topology, physical media, and data access method for a network. You will learn the advantages and disadvantages of the five network architectures and when each is appropriate.

- Chapter 9, "Network Protocols," introduces the different protocols that comprise the upper layers of the OSI Model. Special attention will be given to TCP/IP, IPX/SPX, and NetBEUI because these three protocols are the most prevalent in Microsoft environments.

- Chapter 10, "Network Operating Systems," discusses the role of operating systems within a networked environment. The benefits of different operating systems will be reviewed with a special focus on Windows NT Server.

- Chapter 11, "Network Applications," focuses on the types of applications found in a typical network environment. Also considered will be the factors involved with implementing network applications in a real-world environment.

- Chapter 12, "Remote Access," provides an understanding of the issues around allowing users to access your network remotely. Both the technologies involved and the security issues raised will be discussed.

- Chapter 13, "Creating Larger Networks," introduces different methods of expanding your network as your organization grows larger. Devices such as bridges, routers, and gateways will be described and compared.

- Chapter 14, "Wide Area Networks (WANs)," explains the options available as you seek to link multiple networks across large geographic areas. You will descend into the world of telecommunication acronyms and learn what they actually mean.

- Chapter 15, " The Internet," describes how the Internet functions and what services are available when you connect your network to the Internet.

- Chapter 16, "Network Administration," discusses issues and techniques relating to the actual administration of a network. You will learn how to create users and address security concerns in different Microsoft environments.

- Chapter 17, "Network Problem Prevention," focuses on methods you can use to prevent or minimize problems on your network. This chapter will explain available technologies, what their benefits are, and how they are implemented.

- Chapter 18, "Troubleshooting," introduces the resources and technology available to assist you in troubleshooting a network.

The Networking Essentials exam objectives are covered in the material contained in the text of the chapters and the lab exercises. The companion Chapter Notes booklet provides memory boosters to help you study in conjunction with the book. Finally, the appendixes in this book provide you with additional resources and information that can be helpful to you as you prepare and take the Networking Essentials Microsoft Certified Professional exam and as you work as a Microsoft Certified Professional:

- Appendix A, "Glossary," provides you with definitions of terms that you need to be familiar with as a network professional.
- Appendix B, "Certification Checklist," provides an overview of the certification process in the form of a to-do list, with milestones you can check off on your journey to certification.
- Appendix C, "How Do I Get There from Here?," provides step-by-step guidelines for successfully navigating the process between initial interest and final certification.
- Appendix D, "Testing Tips," gives you tips and pointers for maximizing your performance when you take the certification exam.
- Appendix E, "Contacting Microsoft," lists contact information for certification exam resources at Microsoft and at Sylvan Prometric testing centers.
- Appendix F, "Suggested Reading," presents a list of additional reading resources that can help you prepare for the certification exam and increase your knowledge of networking in general.
- Appendix G, "Internet Resources," is a list of places to visit on the Internet where related computer network information may be found.
- Appendix H, "Using the CD-ROM," gives you the basics of how to install and use the CD-ROM included with this book. The CD-ROM includes the TestPro adaptive test engine, which scores your test electronically with several options for results available.
- Appendix I, "Lab Exercises," provides some hands-on opportunities to explore computer networking.
- Appendix J, "Objectives Index," contains a list of the objectives for the Networking Essentials Exam, as well as where the corresponding information can be found in this book.

Special Features of This Book

The following features are used in this book.

Chapter Prerequisites

Chapter prerequisites help you determine what you need to know before you read a chapter. You meet the prerequisites either by reading other chapters in this book, or through your prior work experiences.

Key Concept

A Key Concept points out those concepts that are vital to your success as a network professional. You will be tested on these concepts on the Networking Essentials Exam. Pay close attention to these, and make sure you understand all of the Key Concepts.

 Key Concept

For communication to occur between two computers on an Ethernet network, they both must use the identical frame type.

In addition to these special features, there are several conventions used in this book to make it easier to read and understand. These conventions include shortcut key combinations, menu commands, and typeface enhancements.

Underlined Hot Keys, or Mnemonics

Hot keys do not appear in this book. In general when studying for MCP exams, you should be aware that most environments are mouse-centric and you will be expected to know how to navigate them using the mouse—clicking, right-clicking, and using drag and drop.

Shortcut Key Combinations

In this book, shortcut key combinations are joined with plus signs (+). For example, Ctrl+V means hold down the Ctrl key while you press the V key.

Menu Commands

In the text, instructions for choosing menu commands follow the form:

Choose File, New.

This example means open the File menu and select New, which in this case opens a new file.

Typeface Enhancements

This book also has the following typeface enhancements to indicate special text, as indicated in the following table.

Typeface	Description
Italic	Along with adding emphasis to text, italic is used to indicate terms and variables in commands or addresses.
Boldface	Bold is used to indicate text you type.
`Computer type`	This command is used for on-screen messages and commands (such as `DOS` copy or `UNIX` commands), and Internet addresses and other locators in the online world.
`My Filename.doc`	Filenames and folders are set in a mixture of upper- and lowercase characters, just as they appear in Windows 95 or Windows NT.

Final Thoughts

As you begin your preparation for the Networking Essentials exam, do realize that many candidates have found this exam to be one of the toughest exams you will take on your way toward MCSE. The importance of gaining hands-on experience cannot be emphasized enough. The labs in Appendix I have been provided to help you and should definitely be explored. Studying the glossary in Appendix A will also be a great help as some of the struggle with the exam is simply remembering all the terminology.

Finally, do note that this book discusses settings within Windows NT 3.51 and Windows for Workgroups, even though those two operating systems have been almost entirely displaced by Windows NT 4.0 and Windows 95/98. Likewise, the book spends a great deal of time discussing coaxial networks using thinnet and thicknet even though such networks are extremely hard to find today given the popularity of twisted-pair.

The reason for covering these older topics is because the Network Essentials *exam* still covers the material, and therefore, you do need to know it to pass the exam.

Now, on to the preparation for the exam!

CHAPTER PREREQUISITE

This chapter has no prerequisites. You need only a desire to become a Microsoft Certified Professional.

Microsoft Certified Professional Program

WHILE YOU READ

1. An MCP is any individual who has passed a current exam in any Microsoft Professional track, with one exception. What is the exception?

2. True or False: The MCSE is a widely respected certification because it focuses on one aspect of computing.

3. Which certification instructionally and technically qualifies you to deliver Microsoft Official Curriculum through Microsoft-authorized education sites?

4. To maintain certification, a Microsoft Certified Trainer is required to pass the exam for a new product within how many months of the exam's release?

5. An MCP+I is an MCP who has specialized in _____ technologies.

As the demand for Microsoft products continues to remain strong, the demand for trained personnel grows, and the number of certifications follows suit. By September 1999, the team of Microsoft Certified Professionals had grown close to 400,000 members.

This chapter covers the Microsoft Certified Professional Program. Terms and concepts covered include the following:

- Microsoft Certified Professional
- Microsoft Certified Systems Engineer (MCSE)
- Microsoft Certified Systems Engineer + Internet
- Microsoft Certified Solutions Developer (MCSD)
- Microsoft Certified Professional + Internet
- Microsoft Certified Trainer (MCT)

Exploring Available Certifications

When Microsoft first began certifying people to install and support its products, there was only one certification available: the *Microsoft Certified Professional (MCP)*. As time went on, demand by employers and prospective customers of consulting firms for more specialized certifications grew.

There are now eight available certifications in the MCP program, as described in the following sections. Note that because Microsoft is constantly growing the MCP program, you should visit http://www.microsoft.com/train_cert/ to make sure that you have the most up-to-date information

Microsoft Certified Systems Engineer (MCSE)

Microsoft Certified Systems Engineers are qualified to plan, implement, maintain, and support information systems based on Microsoft Windows NT and the BackOffice family of client/server software. The MCSE is a widely respected certification because it does not focus on a single aspect of computing, such as networking. Instead, MCSEs demonstrate skills and abilities on the full range of software, from client operating systems to server operating systems to client/server applications. The full requirements of the MCSE Certification are listed later in this chapter.

Microsoft Certified Systems Engineer + Internet (MCSE+Internet)

Building on the success of the MCSE program, Microsoft launched the *Microsoft Certified Systems Engineer + Internet* to certify candidates who are qualified to deploy and manage Internet- or intranet-based solutions that involve Web servers, proxy servers, browsers, and messaging solutions. The MCSE+Internet program consists of seven core exams and two electives.

Microsoft Certified Database Administrator (MCDBA)

The *Microsoft Certified Database Administrator* credential recognizes MCPs who are able to implement sophisticated Microsoft SQL Server databases.

Microsoft Certified Solution Developers (MCSD)

Microsoft Certified Solution Developers are qualified to design and develop custom business solutions with Microsoft development tools, platforms, and technologies, such as Microsoft BackOffice and Microsoft Office.

Microsoft Certified Professional (MCP)

To recognize the skills of candidates working with specific products, Microsoft created the *Microsoft Certified Professional* program. With the exception of the *Networking Essentials exam (70-058)*, passing *any* other Microsoft certification exam will qualify you as an MCP. The MCP credential is intended to serve as a building block for those pursuing additional certifications.

MCP+Site Building

The *Microsoft Certified Professional + Site Building* certifies people who are planning to design and build Web sites using Microsoft products and technologies.

Microsoft Certified Professional (MCP+Internet)

The *Microsoft Certified Professional + Internet* recognizes individuals who specialize in implementing Internet solutions using Microsoft Internet technologies. Note that this credential is easy to attain on your way toward MCSE because it requires two of the electives (IIS and TCP/IP) that are *also* required for MCSE.

Microsoft Certified Trainers (MCT)

Microsoft Certified Trainers are instructionally and technically qualified to deliver Microsoft Official Curriculum through Microsoft-authorized education sites. Not only do MCTs have to pass the exams required for each subject they want to instruct, but they must also take, and participate in as a student, each course they are going to instruct. Additionally, they must demonstrate appropriate levels of instructional ability and must attend a Microsoft-approved "Train-the-Trainer" course.

Understanding the Exam Development Process

The exams are computer-administered tests that measure your ability to implement and administer Microsoft products or systems; to troubleshoot problems with installation, operation, or customization; and to provide technical support to users. The exams do more than test your ability to define terminology and/or recite facts. Product *knowledge* is an important foundation for superior job performance, but definitions and feature lists are just the beginning. In the real world, you need hands-on skills and the ability to apply your knowledge—to understand confusing situations, to solve thorny problems, and to optimize solutions to minimize downtime and maximize current and future productivity.

To develop exams that test for the right competence factors, Microsoft follows an eight-phase exam development process:

1. In the first phase, experts analyze the tasks and skill requirements for the job being tested. This job analysis phase identifies the knowledge, skills, and abilities relating specifically to the performance area to be certified.

2. The next phase develops objectives by building on the framework provided by the job analysis. That means translating the job function tasks into specific and measurable units of knowledge, skills, and abilities. The resulting list of objectives (the *objective domain*, in educational theory-speak) is the basis for developing certification exams and training materials.

3. Selected contributors rate the objectives developed in the previous phase. The reviewers are technology professionals who are currently performing the applicable job function. After prioritization and weighting based on the contributors' input, the objectives become the blueprint for the exam items.

4. During the fourth phase, exam items are reviewed and revised to ensure that they are technically accurate, clear, unambiguous, plausible, free of cultural bias, and not misleading or tricky. Items also are evaluated to confirm that they test for high-level, useful knowledge rather than for obscure or trivial facts.

5. During alpha review, technical and job function experts review each item for technical accuracy, reach consensus on all technical issues, and edit the reviewed items for clarity of expression.

6. The next step is the beta exam. Beta exam participants take the test to gauge its effectiveness. Microsoft performs a statistical analysis based on the responses of the beta participants, including information about difficulty and relevance, to verify the validity of the exam items and to determine which will be used in the final certification exam. When the statistical analysis is complete, the items are distributed into multiple parallel forms, or versions, of the final certification exam.

7. As the beta exam results are returned, a group of job function experts determine the cut, or minimum passing score, for the exam. (The cut score differs from exam to exam because it is based on an item-by-item determination of the percentage of candidates who answered the item correctly.)

8. The final phase, *Exam Live!,* is administered by Sylvan Prometric, an independent testing company. The exams are always available worldwide at Sylvan Prometric testing centers.

If you participate in a beta exam, you might take it at a cost that is lower than the cost of the final certification exam, but it should not be taken lightly. Beta exams actually contain the entire pool of possible questions, of which about 30 percent are dropped after the beta. The remaining questions are divided into the different forms of the final exam. If you decide to take a beta exam, you should review and study as seriously as you would for a final certification exam. Passing a beta exam counts as passing the final exam; you receive full credit for passing a beta exam.

Also, because you will be taking all the questions that will be used for the exam, expect a beta to take two to three times longer than the final exam. For example, the final version of the Windows 95 exam has a time limit of one hour. The beta version has a time limit of more than three hours and has more than three times as many questions as the final versions of the exams!

If you're interested in participating in any of the exam development phases (including the beta exam), contact the Microsoft Certification Development Team by sending a fax to (206) 936-1311. Include the following information about yourself: name, complete address, company, job title, phone number, fax number, email or Internet address, and product areas of interest or expertise. You can also visit Microsoft's Web site at http://www.microsoft.com/train_cert/.

Microsoft Certified Systems Engineer Core Exams

To achieve the MCSE certification, a candidate must pass four required (*core*) exams plus two elective exams. There are two possible paths, or *tracks*, that lead to an MCSE certification: the Windows NT 4.0 track and the Windows NT 3.51 track. (You can be certain that Microsoft will also have a Windows 2000 track available when Windows 2000 exams start being created.) For your information, the Networking Essentials exam (for which this book is written) can be waived for those candidates who also are Novell Certified NetWare Engineers (CNE) or Certified Banyan Engineers (CBE).

Note that Microsoft has retired a number of exams over the past few years, and for the sake of clarity, those retired exams are not listed here. If you have previously taken older

Microsoft exams (such as those involving Windows 3.1), visit Microsoft's Web site at `http://www.microsoft.com/train_cert/` to see if your previous exams still count toward certification and what steps you will need to take to make sure you maintain your certification.

The following pages list only the existing exams that will prepare you for certification.

Microsoft Windows NT 4.0 Track to an MCSE

The Microsoft Windows NT 4.0 track to an MCSE includes four core exams. The first two required exams focus specifically on Windows NT 4.0:

- *Exam 70-067: Implementing and Supporting Microsoft Windows NT 4.0.* This exam covers installing and supporting Windows NT 4.0 in a single-domain environment.
- *Exam 70-068: Implementing and Supporting Microsoft Windows NT 4.0 in the Enterprise.* This exam covers installing and supporting Windows NT 4.0 in an enterprise computing environment with mission-critical applications and tasks.

The third required core exam can be fulfilled by one of the following exams:

- *Exam 70-073: Implementing and Supporting Microsoft Windows NT Workstation 4.0.* This exam tests a candidate's ability to implement and support Microsoft Windows NT Workstation 4.0.
- *Exam 70-064: Implementing and Supporting Microsoft Windows 95.* This exam tests a candidate's ability to implement and support Microsoft Windows 95 in a variety of environments.
- *Exam 70-098: Implementing and Supporting Microsoft Windows 98.* This exam tests a candidate's ability to implement and support Microsoft Windows 98 in a variety of environments.

The fourth core exam can be fulfilled by only one exam at the current time:

- *Exam 70-058: Networking Essentials.* This exam tests the candidate's networking skills required for implementing, administrating, and troubleshooting systems that incorporate Windows 95 and BackOffice.

Windows NT 3.51 Track to the MCSE Certification

Many of the original Microsoft Certified Systems Engineers followed the Windows NT 3.51 track. This continues to be a valid track for MCSE certification, although Microsoft has indicated that these exams will be retired when the Windows 2000 exams become available.

There are four core exams. The first required exams focus specifically on Windows NT 3.51:

- *Exam 70-042: Implementing and Supporting Microsoft Windows NT Workstation 3.51.* This exam covers installing and supporting Windows NT Workstation 3.51.
- *Exam 70-043: Implementing and Supporting Microsoft Windows NT Server 3.51.* This exam covers installing and supporting Windows NT Server 3.51 in a variety of environments.

The third required core exam can be fulfilled by one of the following exams:

- *Exam 70-064: Implementing and Supporting Microsoft Windows 95.* This exam tests a candidate's ability to implement and support Microsoft Windows 95 in a variety of environments.
- *Exam 70-078: Implementing and Supporting Microsoft Windows 98.* This exam tests a candidate's ability to implement and support Microsoft Windows 98 in a variety of environments.

The fourth core exam can be fulfilled by only one exam at the current time:

- *Exam 70-058: Networking Essentials.* This exam tests the candidate's networking skills required for implementing, administrating, and troubleshooting systems that incorporate Windows 95 and BackOffice.

Electives for the Microsoft Certified Systems Engineers

In addition to the core exam requirements, to complete an MCSE certification you must pass two elective exams. The list in Table 1.1 was current as of September 1999. (Visit Microsoft's Web site at http://www.microsoft.com/mcp/ for the current list.)

Table 1.1 Microsoft Certified System Engineer Electives	
Exam Title	*Exam Number*
Implementing and Supporting Microsoft SNA Server 3.0	70-013
Implementing and Supporting Microsoft SNA Server 4.0	70-085
Implementing and Supporting Microsoft Systems Management Server 1.2	70-018
Implementing and Supporting Microsoft SystemsManagement Server 2.0	70-086

...continues

Table 1.1 continued	
Exam Title	*Exam Number*
Designing and Implementing Data Warehouses with Microsoft SQL Server 7.0	70-019
System Administration of Microsoft SQL Server 6.5	70-026
Implementing a Database Design on Microsoft SQL Server 6.5	70-027
Administering Microsoft SQL Server 7.0	70-028
Designing and Implementing Databases with Microsoft SQL Server 7.0	70-029
Internetworking Microsoft TCP/IP on Microsoft Windows NT 3.5 (scheduled for retirement)	70-053
Internetworking Microsoft TCP/IP on Microsoft Windows NT 4.0	70-059
Implementing and Supporting Web Sites Using Microsoft Site Server 3.0	70-056
Implementing and Supporting Microsoft Exchange Server 5.0	70-076
Implementing and Supporting Microsoft Exchange Server 5.5	70-081
Implementing and Supporting Microsoft Internet Information Server 3.0 (scheduled to be retired)	70-077
Implementing and Supporting Microsoft Internet Information Server 4.0	70-087
Implementing and Supporting Microsoft Proxy Server 1.0	70-078
Implementing and Supporting Microsoft Proxy Server 2.0	70-088
Implementing and Supporting Microsoft Internet Explorer 4.0 by Using the Internet Explorer Administration Kit	70-079
Implementing and Supporting Microsoft Internet Explorer 5.0 by Using the Internet Explorer Administration Kit	70-080
Deploying, Implementing, and Supporting Microsoft Office 2000	70-090

In cases where there are exams for multiple versions of a product, be aware that only one of the exams can usually count toward certification. For instance, with Exchange Server only one of exams 70-076 (Exchange Server 5) and 70-081 (Exchange Server 5.5) will count toward certification. Likewise, candidates choosing SQL Server electives can only count one of the database implementation exams (70-026 or 70-028) and one of the database administration exams (70-027 or 70-029) towards their certification. In other words, your two electives can't both be database implementation exams.

Continuing Certification Requirements

When you attain an MCP certification, such as the MCSE certification, your work isn't over. Microsoft requires you to maintain your certification by updating your exam credits as new products are released and old products are retired.

An MCT is required to pass the exam for a new product within three months of the exam's release. For example, the Windows 95 exam (70-63) was released on October 9, 1995. All MCTs were required to pass Exam 70-63 by January 9, 1996, or lose certification to teach the Windows 95 course.

Holders of the other MCP certifications (MCSD, MCSE) are required to replace an exam that is giving them qualifying credit within six months of the retirement of that exam. For example, the Windows for Workgroups 3.10 exam was one of the original electives for the MCSE certification. When it was withdrawn, MCSEs had six months to replace it with another elective exam, such as the TCP/IP exam.

Summary

Microsoft has now created a comprehensive certification program testing candidate's skills when utilizing Microsoft products and technologies. Beginning with the *Microsoft Certified Professional* credential, the program goes on to provide the *MCP+Internet* certification and then, finally, the *Microsoft Certified System Engineer (MCSE)* and *Microsoft Certified System Engineer + Internet* certifications.

This book prepares students for one of the certification exams in the MCSE program. To become an MCSE for Windows NT 4.0 and 3.51, candidates must take four core exams (of which this is one) and then two elective exams. When you complete all six exams, you will retain your MCSE status until Microsoft retires one of the exams you took, at which point you will usually have a year to take a replacement exam.

┌─ QUESTIONS AND ANSWERS ────────────────────┐
│   None for this chapter.   │
└───┘

PRACTICE TEST

None for this chapter.

CHAPTER PREREQUISITE

Before beginning this chapter, you should have some basic familiarity with computers, their components, and the Microsoft family of Windows products.

Introduction to Networks

WHILE YOU READ

1. What is the difference between a client and a server?

2. A computer that acts as both a client *and* a server can be referred to as a _____.

3. What is the topology of a network?

4. Identify three different network topologies.

5. Name the two major types of networks.

6. True of False. Security is a major advantage of peer-to-peer networks.

7. What are the advantages of server-based networks?

8. What types of servers do you see on a typical network?

9. Identify the major categories of media used in networks.

Why Should You Use Networks?

How do computer networks simplify work? How can your business benefit from computer networking? Why should you get involved with computer networking? Consider any of the following cases:

- You work in a small office where individual computers are not connected to a printer. Every time you want to print, you have to save the information to a floppy disk and physically bring it to a computer connected to a printer. In the course of a day, you might make this trip several times, disrupting both your work flow and that of your colleagues.

- In the consulting firm where you are employed, multiple people need to work on the same set of documents. You spend a significant amount of time copying files to disks and then transferring the information onto everyone else's computers so they can use the files. As time goes on, you find it more difficult to keep track of who has the most recent version of each document. As a result, people wind up working with different versions, creating more headaches as you try to work together.

- Your company has several offices spread out over a wide geographic area. Because of the need for inter-office communication, each office spends a large amount of time, energy, and money creating information on computers and then either faxing information between offices or preparing packages for delivery via courier or overnight express.

- Employees in your sales organization are constantly using your fax machine and spend a significant portion of their day waiting around for the fax machine to be available. It has become a bottleneck for getting out your sales quotes and other information. You have a fax modem on one of your computers, but only one person can use it.

In all these cases, computer networks could solve real business problems and increase the efficiency and productivity of the organizations involved. This book is about solving these and many other similar problems that plague the computerized world. Whether the answer is sharing printers and fax modems, centralizing file storage, or allowing easy communication throughout an organization, computer networking is the tool for implementing these solutions.

From the local network in an office to the global Internet, computers surround us and play a crucial role in the daily operations of organizations of all sizes. This book helps you understand how these networks function and how you can use them to assist your organization.

Network Terminology

Before you go further, you need to take a detour, and I'll discuss the language used to describe networks. Computer networks have created a seemingly endless list of new terms, and half the battle of learning networking is just getting past all the terminology.

Clients, Servers, and Peers

To begin with, each computer on a network functions as a *client* or a *server*. A *server* computer shares resources on the network. A *client* computer uses those resources. In every interaction between computers on a network, one of the computers will function as the client and the other as the server. A typical network setup can be seen in Figure 2.1.

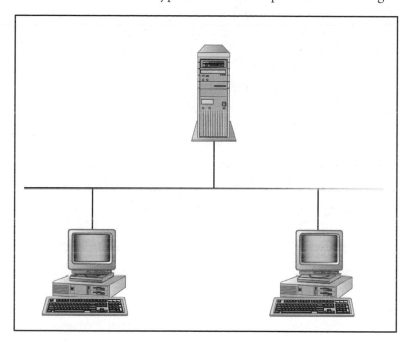

Figure 2.1
Within a computer network, server computers share resources, whereas client computers use those shared resources.

Although some types of networks limit computers to functioning only as a client or a server, other types of networks allow computers to act as both a client *and* a server, using network resources while sharing their own resources with others. Computers operating in this fashion are referred to as *peers.* Operating systems such as Windows 2000, Windows 95/98, Windows NT, and Windows for Workgroups support this type of *peer-to-peer* network.

Network Media, LANs, and WANs

Computers are connected using *network media.* In most networks, this is simply copper cable running between the systems. However, it can also be fiber-optic (glass) cable or a wireless technology such as microwave or infrared. Whatever the physical connection method, it is referred to as the *medium.* A computer is connected to that medium through the use of a *Network Interface Card (NIC),* also referred to as a *network adapter.*

When several computers are connected in a relatively confined area, such as an office building or campus, the network is referred to as a *Local Area Network,* or *LAN* for short. As shown in Figure 2.2, a LAN can include many different computers as well as resources such as printers. The characteristics of a LAN include the following:

- They exist in a limited geographical area.
- They transfer data at high speeds.
- Resources and connectivity are managed by the organization running the LAN.

A *resource* is any component that you would like to use on the network. This can be anything from a file on a remote machine to a printer located down the hall.

As these LANs grow larger and two or more networks are connected, often over larger geographic distances, they are then referred to as a *Wide Area Network,* or *WAN.*

Figure 2.3 depicts a WAN linking five different regional networks.

Topology

If you were to draw a diagram of how your computers are physically connected, your picture would represent the *topology* of the network. There are three major types of network topologies. Although these terms are described in detail in later chapters, the terms are briefly introduced now to help create a clearer picture of networking.

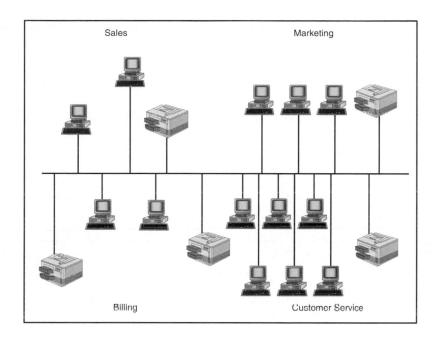

Figure 2.2
A Local Area Network connects computers within a small area.

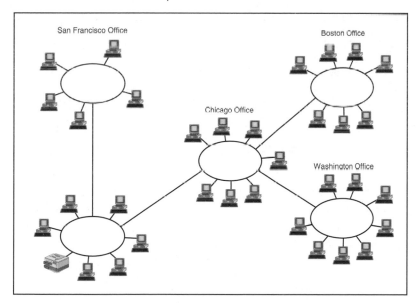

Figure 2.3
A Wide Area Network links separate LANs, usually over a large geographic distance.

In a *bus* network, as depicted in Figure 2.4, all the computers are connected in a line. Messages are passed between computers along a single *backbone* connecting them. At each end of this backbone is a *terminator* to stop the network signal.

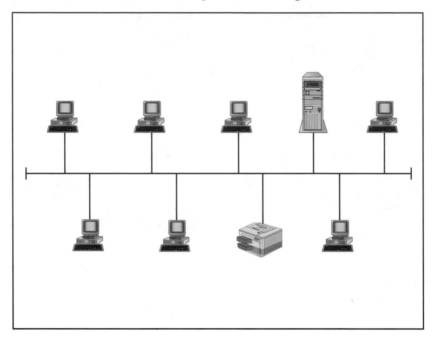

Figure 2.4
A bus network connects all computers in a line.

As shown in Figure 2.5, a *star* network uses a central hub to connect all the computers. The hub acts as a central collection and distribution place for all network traffic.

Finally, a *ring* topology connects all the computers in a single loop. As shown in Figure 2.6, information is passed along in a continual circle.

Now, just to confuse the issue, you will also hear discussion of the term *network architecture*. Typically, the term refers to the actual method in which *packets* of information are transmitted on the network media. For example, when people speak of an *ethernet* or *token-ring* network, they are describing the architecture of the network. People will sometimes use the term *network architecture* to refer to the overall structure of the network, including the topology.

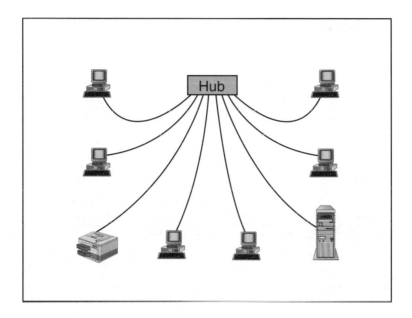

Figure 2.5
In a star topology, a hub connects all the computers.

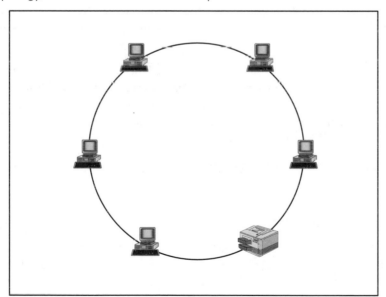

Figure 2.6
A ring topology connects all computers in a circle.

Network Protocols

When connected, the computers have to know how to communicate. In terms of human communication, if I called you on the telephone and I spoke only German and you spoke only French, our chances of having a meaningful conversation would be essentially zero. Likewise, two computers have to use the same language in order to communicate. The language they use is referred to as the *network protocol*, and it is usually described in the cryptic form of TCP/IP, IPX, DLC, and so on.

Key Concept

The term *network protocol* refers to the "language" two computers use to communicate, whereas the term *network architecture* refers to the underlying mechanism that transports the data from one computer to another.

Network Software

On top of the protocol, computers use a *network operating system*, which controls who can gain access to network resources. The most common network operating systems are Windows NT and Novell NetWare.

Resting on top of the operating systems are the *network applications*, which communicate over the network. These applications, or programs, can range from email programs to the File Manager and the printing systems.

So, to combine all this into one paragraph full of network communication buzzwords: Your *network applications* run on top of a *network operating system*, which uses a *protocol* to communicate across the network *media* to other computers on the *Local Area Network*; this LAN is constructed in some type of *topology* and uses a *network architecture* to actually transmit *packets* of data between computers.

Got all that? Don't worry. By the end of this book, you'll actually understand that sentence!

Types of Networks

Computer networks can be divided into two major categories: *peer-to-peer* and *server-based*. Although server-based networks are the standard in most organizations today and will be the focus of much of this book, both types of networks need to be understood.

Peer-to-Peer Networks

In *peer-to-peer* networks such as that shown in Figure 2.7, each computer can act as both a server (sharing resources) and a client (using resources). There is no centralized control over resources such as files or printers. Individual users simply share resources whenever and with whomever they want. All computers are equal in the sense that no computer has a higher priority for network resources.

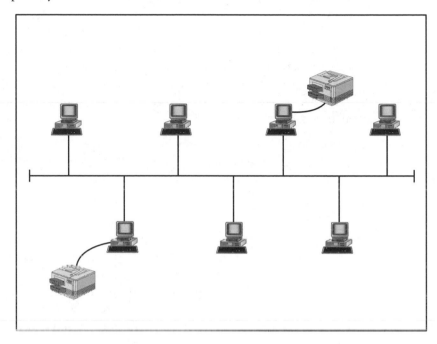

Figure 2.7
In a peer-to-peer network, each computer can share resources as well as use resources from other computers.

Access is controlled by the user sharing the resource. The user can grant full control to all network users, grant restricted access, or choose to require a password before another user can use the resource.

For this reason, security is a major issue in peer-to-peer networks. All computers are loosely grouped into *workgroups*. However, there are no networkwide security controls. If you know the password to gain access to a particular resource, you can do so. The downside of this is that because a separate password can be required for *each* shared resource, users can easily wind up drowning in a sea of different passwords that they need to remember.

Another major concern with peer-to-peer networks is that computers in these networks are generally not optimized for network performance. The computers are primarily intended for office applications, but they also have the capability to share resources. What this means is that when another user begins to use shared resources on your computer, you will notice a decrease in your system's performance. If you share your printer with the network, your system will slow down whenever anyone else prints to your printer.

Organization of information can also be an issue in a peer-to-peer network. If everyone can share information, how do you keep track of where things are? For example, in a small office, one user might share a folder containing newsletters. Another user might share a folder containing finances and press releases. Still another might share the latest sales quotes. If you are looking for a specific document, you might have to search through several different computers before you can find the information. Without a central storage area, finding information can be quite difficult.

This lack of a central storage area also makes if very difficult to protect data through a backup procedure. If data is stored on many separate computers, each computer will need to be backed up individually. There is no way to easily back up all data.

With all these concerns, why would someone choose to use a peer-to-peer network? Quite simply, these networks are the easiest and cheapest to implement. In most instances, nothing is needed beyond the basic operating system and the actual network connections. Users in a small office environment would only need to connect their computers and begin sharing information through the network. Peer-to-peer networks do not require extensive staff training, nor do they need staff support to keep the network operational. Because there is no central control, if one computer on the network goes down, all the other computers will continue to function. For many small businesses, this can be an easy way to begin accessing information in a more efficient manner.

Some examples of operating systems that can work in a peer-to-peer network include Microsoft Windows 2000, Windows NT Workstation, Windows NT Server (acting as a "member server"), Windows 95/98, Windows for Workgroups, and Apple's Macintosh operating system.

 Key Concept

In a peer-to-peer network, computers can act as both servers sharing resources and as clients using resources.

Advantages of Peer-to-Peer Networks

Peer-to-peer networks have many advantages, including the following:

- They are relatively easy to set up.
- They are inexpensive.
- Additional computers or software packages are not required beyond the operating system.
- Local control of resources is maintained by individual users.
- Specific staff is not required to maintain the network.
- Individual computers are not dependent on the functioning of a central computer.

Disadvantages of Peer-to-Peer Networks

Although peer-to-peer networks might be appropriate for small environments, some disadvantages that need to be mentioned include the following:

- Network security is weak and limited to only password protection.
- Users might have to remember multiple passwords to access shared resources.
- It is difficult and time-consuming to back up data stored on many different computers.
- A decreased performance of computers exists due to the increased load of network sharing.
- There is a lack of a central organizational scheme. Users have to seek out data on different computers.

Server-Based Networks

Server-based networks provide for centralized control of network resources, unlike the peer-to-peer networks discussed earlier. Server-based networks are also known as *client/server* networks because they divide computer roles between client computers and server computers. As shown in Figure 2.8, the client computers use the resources available on the network, whereas the server computers provide shared resources, security, and system administration for the network.

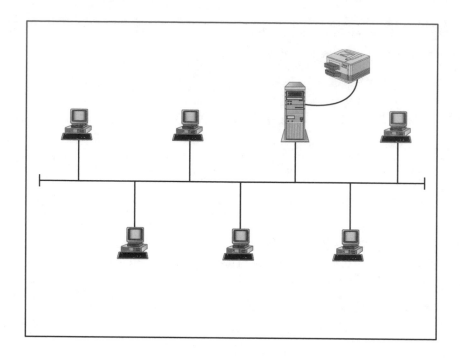

Figure 2.8
In a server-based network, server computers provide centralized control of network resources.

Note that the term *client/server* can be used in different contexts. Although it is used here to describe a network, it can also be used to describe applications running on the network such as database and electronic mail systems.

Computers used as servers are optimized for network use with faster processors, more system memory, larger disk drives, and extra devices such as tape drives and CD-ROM drives. They are usually designed to allow multiple users to simultaneously access shared resources. In most instances, servers are not used for general-purpose office functions, but rather for specific functions such as providing access to shared files. Often, a server will be located in a separate room in the building away from the office area.

In a server-based network, all user accounts and passwords are verified or authenticated by some central server. For example, within a Windows NT Server network, users can be part of a *domain*. Before users can gain access to resources on the network, their username and password must be authenticated by the domain controller, which is one of the servers on the network. Only system administrators can modify these access privileges and control who has access to what. Security in this type of network can be very tight.

For users, server-based networks are easier to use than peer-to-peer networks in the sense that users do not have multiple passwords. The files and programs are easier to find in most cases because they are located on specific servers, rather than being located on various computers spread throughout the network. This centralized organization is less time-consuming compared to peer-to-peer networks and makes it easier to back up data.

Another major advantage to server-based networks is the growth potential. With centralized user account management and network administration, server-based networks can grow from only a few users to literally thousands of users as the company grows in size.

The major drawback to server-based networks can be summed up in one word—cost. Both the server software and the hardware can be extremely expensive. Additionally, a full-time network administrator is usually required. This position often requires extensive training for the administrator to adequately perform her job.

One other concern is server failure. In a peer-to-peer network, if one computer fails, the others will still operate, although they will not be able to access whatever resources were shared from the failed computer. With a server-based network, not only is failure of a client computer an inconvenience to a specific user, but the failure of a server can bring down the entire network! Users can be denied access to resources or, conceivably, to the network itself.

 Key Concept

Server-based networks provide centralized control of network resources and rely on server computers to provide security and network administration.

Advantages of Server-Based Networks

The advantages of server-based networks include the following:

- Security is centrally controlled.
- Simplified administration for large numbers of user accounts.
- Faster access to files/resources because of optimized equipment.
- Protecting data through backups can be easier because of central location of data files.
- Because they only have to remember one password, it is easier for users to access network resources.

Disadvantages of Server-Based Networks

Although very effective, server-based networks do have their downside, including the following aspects:

- The hardware and software are both more expensive.
- Additional staff and staff training are usually required.
- If a server fails, the entire network can be unusable.

Combination Networks

Today, desktop operating systems such as Windows 2000, Windows 95/98, Windows for Workgroups, and Windows NT Workstation have blurred the line between true peer-to-peer networks and server-based networks. In fact, it is quite common to find a server-based network where many client workstations are actually functioning as peers.

A typical scenario might involve a Windows NT Server running on the network servers, providing central security and file storage. The network users, running Windows 2000, Windows 95/98, or Windows NT Workstation, would have access to all the server-based resources, but would also be able to share their files or printers.

Combination networks have most of the advantages of *both* types of networks. However, the disadvantages are really the same as those of server-based networks.

Types of Servers

Within a server-based network, the server computers themselves might fulfill different roles. Some servers will be dedicated to one function, whereas others might perform several different roles. For example, a network such as that in Figure 2.9 might have server computers dedicated to printing, messaging, and file storage.

File Servers

On almost every network, you'll find a server functioning as a central repository for files. Consider these the electronic equivalent of a room full of wall-to-wall file cabinets. Users will store their documents, graphics, and other files on this server. File servers are one of the main reasons for networking and are a key ingredient for any network plan. This central storage of data provides several benefits, including the following:

- *Central organization.* Instead of searching numerous computers as in a peer-to-peer network, users can go directly to the file server for the information.

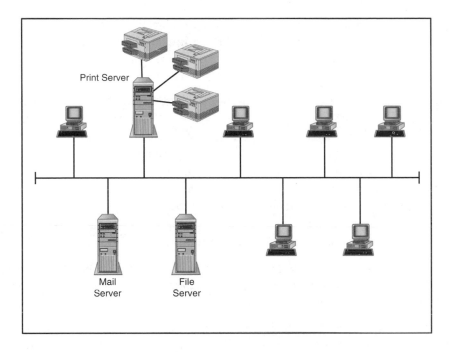

Figure 2.9
A server-based network can include server computers dedicated to a specific task.

- *Ease of data protection.* If all the files are in one location, they are easier to back up for protection against data loss. A typical file server will usually be attached to a backup device, possibly a tape drive or optical disk drive. Regular backups, usually performed daily, can ensure that data will not be lost due to equipment failure.
- *Speed.* Most file servers are fast computers running a network operating system such as Windows NT Server or Novell NetWare, which are specifically designed for server usage. These operating systems are optimized to provide fast access to files. Usually, these servers are also equipped with fast disk drives and other storage media.

Print Servers

Another main goal of networking is to share printers. In a small network, a printer might just be attached to a single computer and then simply be *shared* through peer-to-peer networking using an operating system such as Windows 2000, Windows 95/98, or Windows NT Workstation. Other users would simply print to that printer across the network.

Although this works fine in a small environment, a problem occurs as the printer use increases. The user of the computer linked to the printer will find his computer slowing down when the printer is in use. Ultimately, this will affect the productivity and efficiency of that individual's workstation.

At this point, a print server can be an appropriate solution. Print servers are often dedicated computers that function only to provide people with access to printers. On these servers, there are multiple *print queues.* When a user prints a document to a specific printer, it is *spooled* into the appropriate print queue, where it waits its turn to be printed. As far as the user is concerned, it is really no different from printing to a printer directly connected to the computer. She simply prints her document to the queue; the print server does the rest. This has the added benefit that the document is transferred to the print server at the high speed of the network, freeing up the user to go back to her work, while the print server handles the low-speed communication to the actual printer.

In addition to solving speed issues, print servers can also more efficiently utilize office space. Printers can be located in a central area or separate room instead of being restricted to an individual's desk.

Print servers have the benefit of enabling you to share expensive equipment among all users. For instance, a company can make available a laser printer, color inkjet printer, and color laser printer, all from the same print server. Additionally, because fax modems are usually handled in a similar manner to printers, central fax services can be established for the organization through a print server.

Communication/Message Servers

As networks are increasingly used for internal communication, it is now common to find servers on a network dedicated solely to the task of handling communications. Following are some examples:

- *Electronic mail.* These systems have become so large and complex that some systems can't exist without a dedicated server. Especially in cases where networks are connected to the Internet, it is not uncommon to find a mail server that exists primarily to cope with exchanging email with other sites on the Internet.

- *Workgroup or groupware.* Programs such as Lotus Notes or Microsoft Exchange Server also place heavy demands on hardware resources. Such programs go beyond simple email to also include discussion bulletin boards, workflow applications, and databases. In large settings, they simply cannot coexist on a system that is also being used for other services.

■ *Internet publishing and Internet services.* These are also playing a larger role in the makeup of network environments. The explosion of the World Wide Web and other Internet services has created a new role within the network. For instance, Microsoft has released a suite of Internet publishing products including the Internet Information Server (for the World Wide Web), Internet Chat Server, Personalization Server, Merchant Server, and Index Server. Although all these services might not run on separate computers, it is quite likely that at least one machine will be dedicated to their operation.

Application Servers

Referring to a computer as an "application server" can be a bit misleading because there are two different definitions in use today.

First, many people use the term to refer to a server that is running some large application, such as a database like Microsoft SQL Server or a communication package like Microsoft Exchange Server. These servers are often more specifically referred to as *database servers* or *mail servers*, but they sometimes might be referred to generically as *application servers.*

The second use of the term is for a server that contains all the applications that users run. For instance, in an office environment, the system administrators might install the network version of Microsoft Office into a folder on a server, rather than installing the programs onto each individual computer. In this situation, users have icons on their desktop that actually point to a drive (such as "F:") that is connected to the server. Although this setup has a couple of advantages in that it is easy to upgrade the version of the applications (because all the executable files are on a central server) and easy to back up, there is also the potential to generate a large amount of network traffic.

Key Concept

Regardless of whether the server holds a database, a mail routing product, or a software program, the important concept to remember is that an *application server* is one that provides users access to applications in some manner.

Network Media

The *media* of a network is simply the mechanism that physically carries a message from computer to computer. In terms of the physical world, think of the different media you use to communicate between people. If you wanted to get a message to someone, you might write a letter, or you might call the person on the telephone. Perhaps with some people, you might send a fax or electronic mail message. If you really wanted to get your message to someone hard to reach, you might broadcast it on television, run an ad in the newspaper, or have a banner towed behind an airplane! All these mechanisms are the *media* through which people communicate.

In the world of computer networks, there are three different types of media used: copper wire, glass fiber-optics, and wireless technologies. Figure 2.10 shows examples of media used in computer networks.

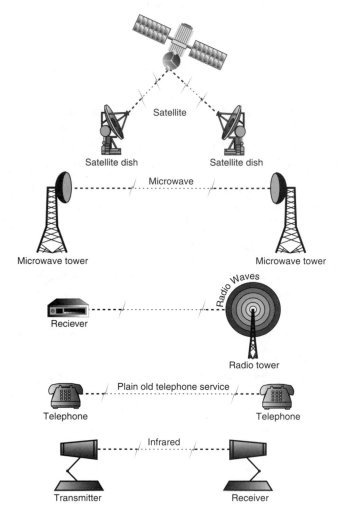

Figure 2.10
Network media can take many different forms.

Copper

Copper is the primary communication medium for computer networking. It is the primary component of internal circuit boards. Copper has been used for more than 100 years, and its characteristics and capabilities are well-known. The method in which electricity flows through copper has been extensively researched, and copper has been adapted for many different electrical needs. Most network cables use copper at their core.

Fiber Optics

As good as copper is, it simply can't match the raw speed of light. Fiber-optic cables are composed of glass strands that transmit beams of light. These beams of light can carry a signal over much greater distances than copper cables and are not subject to radio or other electromagnetic interference.

The major disadvantage of fiber-optic cables is the high cost associated with both the cables and the equipment necessary for data transmission. They are also more difficult to install and work with than copper cables.

Because of the high cost and difficult installation, fiber-optic cables are frequently used as *backbones* between other networks. Fiber-optic cables can also be found in situations where cables will be run through areas with high electromagnetic interference. Such interference will distort the electrical signal in a copper cable, but it will not damage the light signal in a fiber-optic cable.

Key Concept

Copper cable is the primary medium used to transmit electrical signals in computer networks due to its inexpensive cost, years of testing, and extreme flexibility. Fiber-optic cable utilizes signals of light to achieve much higher speeds than copper, but it is comparatively much more expensive to deploy than copper cable.

Wireless

Wireless network media actually includes several different technologies. The common theme is that an actual cable is not required. There are three types of wireless technologies in use today: infrared, microwave, and radio.

Infrared networks are common in a confined office space where the signals do not have to travel far. For instance, if you are a salesperson for a company and your schedule finds you frequently in and out of the office throughout the day, you might use a laptop equipped with an infrared adapter. When you arrive back in the office, you simply place your laptop on your desk and line up the adapter with an infrared port on the desk. As soon as you do this, you'll be connected with your network. When you leave, you just pick up your laptop and go. There is no need to mess with any cables or network cards.

The problem with infrared networks is that they are generally limited to *line of sight*, meaning that the network adapter on the computer has to be able to "see" its companion network port. Because of office furnishings and other equipment that can block this line of sight, infrared networks are not practical for many office environments.

Infrared networks are also quite slow and are limited in range. Typically, they might operate at less than 1/2 or 1/10 the speed of an equivalent copper-based network and cover distances no longer than 30 feet.

Microwave networks are used primarily to link networks over long distances or in areas where cables cannot be used. Although microwave communication requires a line of sight similar to infrared, it can cover great distances due to the frequencies used. Microwave networks might use a series of relay towers to carry a signal across the ground, or they might use satellites to transmit a signal to another part of the globe. The primary disadvantage of microwave networks is that they can be affected by weather conditions such as rain or fog.

Radio networks are becoming increasingly popular as new communication technologies are evolving. Because radio waves can penetrate walls, are resistant to weather conditions, and, courtesy of new satellite systems, can reach most parts of the globe, they will undoubtedly play a larger role in future networks. New paging and cellular technologies are also offering advanced options. The primary barriers at this time for expansion of radio usage are the cost of the networks and the scarcity of electromagnetic frequencies with which to operate. However, as both political and technological solutions evolve, look to this type of network to continue to grow.

Summary

Computer networks can solve real business problems and increase the overall productivity and efficiency of an organization.

In every interaction with another computer on a network, a computer functions either as a *client* when using resources from another computer or as a *server* when sharing resources to others.

The two major types of networks are *peer-to-peer* and *server-based*. In *peer-to-peer* networks, all computers are equal in the sense that there is no central control of resources. Each computer can function as both a client and a server. In *server-based* networks, access to resources is tightly controlled. Resources might also be centrally located and organized in an efficient manner.

Within a *server-based* network, there might be several different types of servers on the network. File servers provide a central storage location for files. Print servers enable easy sharing of printers and other similar devices. Communication servers are dedicated to providing efficient electronic mail or groupware services.

Ultimately, computer networks are about transmitting data over a physical *medium*. The *medium* used for a network might be copper, glass (fiber-optics), or wireless technologies such as radio and infrared.

QUESTIONS AND ANSWERS

1. What is the difference between a client and a server?

   A: A *server* computer shares resources out on a network. A *client* computer accesses those shared resources.

2. A computer that acts as both a client *and* a server can be referred to as a

   _____.

   A: Peer

3. What is the topology of a network?

   A: The physical layout of your network—a diagram of how all the computers are connected.

4. Identify three different network topologies.

   A: Bus, star, and ring

5. Name the two major types of networks.

   A: Server-based and peer-to-peer

6. True of False. Security is a major advantage of peer-to-peer networks.

   A: False

...continues

CH
2

...continued

> **7.** What are the advantages of server-based networks?
>
> A: Heightened security, simplified administration, potentially faster access to resources, and easier to back up data
>
> **8.** What types of servers do you see on a typical network?
>
> A: Answers might include file, print, mail, Web, database, application, and communication
>
> **9.** Identify the major categories of media used in networks?
>
> A: Copper, fiber-optic, and wireless

PRACTICE TEST

1. A network in which all computers are connected in a line is called what?

   a. Line
   b. Ring
   c. Bus
   d. Star

Answer a is incorrect because line is not a type of topology. Answer b is incorrect because a ring topology connects the last computer in line to the first, creating a ring. **Answer c is correct; a bus topology connects computers in a line.** Answer d is incorrect because a star topology connects each computer to a central device.

2. In your organization, security is not a great concern. You simply want to get a network operational as soon as possible. What type of network should you use?

   a. Server-based
   b. Peer-to-peer

Answer a is incorrect because it will typically take longer to get a server-based network operational. **Answer b is correct; peer-to-peer networks, although providing little or no security, can be rapidly put into operation.**

3. The _____ is the generic term for the material used to physically connect computers.

   a. Topology
   b. Media
   c. Architecture
   d. Packets

Answer a is incorrect because the topology is the physical design and layout of the network. **Answer b is correct.** Answer c is incorrect because the architecture is the mechanism for transmitting data across the media. Answer d is incorrect because it is a generic term for data transmitted across the media.

4. Your company currently employs 10 people, but as part of a new project, it will soon be adding 20 new employees and possibly even more in the months ahead. You've been asked to design and implement a new network for all users. You are concerned about security and also want to simplify network administration. What type of network should you choose?

   a. Server-based
   b. Peer-to-peer

Answer a is correct; server-based networks will provide both security and simplified network administration. Answer b is incorrect because peer-to-peer networks meet neither of these requirements.

5. The topology of a network refers to what?

   a. The method in which data is transmitted across a cable.
   b. The manner in which all computers are connected.
   c. The physical material used to connect computers.
   d. The "language" used by two computers to communicate.

Answer a is incorrect because it is the definition for *network architecture*. **Answer b is correct.** Answer c is incorrect and defines the network *media*. Answer d is incorrect because it defines the network *protocol*.

6. What are the advantages of using server-based networks? (Choose all that apply.)

   a. Increased security.
   b. Easier administration of large numbers of users.
   c. Specific staff people are not required to maintain the network.
   d. Faster access to files/resources because of optimized equipment.

Answer a is correct. Answer b is correct. Answer c is incorrect because server-based networks do typically require staff to ensure the continued operation of the network. **Answer d is correct.**

7. Ethernet is an example of what?

   a. Network protocol
   b. Network architecture
   c. Network topology
   d. Network application

Answer a is incorrect. **Answer b is correct.** Answer c is incorrect. Answer d is incorrect.

8. Computers that can use network resources while also making their own resources available to other computers are called what?

   a. Clients

   b. Servers

   c. Peers

   d. Media

Answer a is incorrect because clients *only* access resources. Answer b is incorrect because servers *only* share resources. **Answer c is correct; peers both access and share resources.** Answer d is incorrect because the media is the network cable.

9. The two major types of networks are which of the following?

   a. Peer-to-peer

   b. Client-based

   c. Peer-server

   d. Server-based

Answer a is correct. Answer b and c are incorrect because both are fictitious terms. **Answer d is correct.**

10. Which of the following are disadvantages of peer-to-peer networks? (Choose all that apply.)

   a. Weaker security

   b. Require additional staff to maintain

   c. Users might need multiple passwords to access resources

   d. Require expensive hardware and software

Answer a is correct; peer-to-peer networks have weak (or non-existent) security. Answer b is incorrect because peer-to-peer networks typically require little or no dedicated staff. **Answer c is correct; because peer-to-peer networks do not have centralized control over passwords, users must have a separate password for each machine from which they want to use resources.** Answer d is incorrect because peer-to-peer networks can typically use low-end hardware, and the networking is usually part of the operating system.

CHAPTER PREREQUISITE

Before reading this chapter, you should understand the networking terminology and concepts discussed in Chapter 2, "Introduction to Networks."

The OSI Reference Model

── WHILE YOU READ ──

1. Why should you care about the OSI Reference Model?

2. What are the seven layers of the OSI Reference Model?

3. True or false. The transport layer handles the actual transmission of data between two computers.

4. How did the IEEE enhance the OSI model? What are the names of the sublayers?

5. What is the role of the network layer?

6. What does the Media Access Control sublayer do?

7. What does the IEEE 802.3 specification define?

8. What does the IEEE 802.5 specification define?

The Need for a Conceptual Framework

Have you gone shopping for a computer recently or looked at advertisements for computers? If so, you'll know that it is extremely easy to become completely overwhelmed by the sheer number of options available. Different manufacturers make various models with a whole range of capabilities. Yet, as you are swept away in the sea of acronyms and computer jargon, some of it actually makes sense, and ultimately you are able to make some comparisons between computers.

Why? Well, if you think about it, most people have an idea of what the basic components of a personal computer are. For instance, your component list might resemble the following:

- Processor chip/CPU
- Memory/RAM
- Hard-disk drive
- Floppy disk drive
- CD-ROM drive
- Printer
- Monitor
- Keyboard
- Mouse
- Sound card
- Modem

Additionally, the processor has a type (Pentium Pro, Pentium, 486, and so on) and a clock speed (200MHz, 160MHz, and so on). The memory is measured in terms of megabytes, and the hard disk drive is measured in terms of megabytes or gigabytes.

You know all this because it is part of the reference model that you can use to think about computers. This model enables you to compare different computers and have some understanding of their differences. It enables you to use a common notation to describe computers.

Like the process of describing a computer, describing a network can be quite difficult. Networks are by their very nature quite complex, and some framework is needed within which to discuss their existence.

In the late 1970s, the *International Standards Organization (ISO)* began to develop a theoretical network model. In 1978, the organization released the first version of what was to become know as the *Open Systems Interconnection (OSI) Reference Model*. In 1984, a revision was published that has now become an international standard and the basis for most discussions of networking.

Layered Networking

The OSI Reference Model describes networked communication as a series of layers. To understand the concepts of layered communication, you should consider an example of how communication can happen in the physical world.

Say that Fred is an executive with a large corporation in one city who would like to send a document to Sally, an executive with the same corporation but in another city.

The process on Fred's end might occur as follows:

1. Fred writes or dictates his document and passes it to his assistant.
2. His assistant types up the document.
3. The assistant then puts the document into an interoffice mail envelope, addresses it, and leaves it out for pickup.
4. The internal mail clerk picks up the envelope and delivers it to the mail room.
5. The mail room staff reads the address and determines whether the envelope is for a local recipient or, if not, to which office the mail should be routed.
6. The staff determines how that mail should be delivered. Can it be sent with a courier service? Should an overnight express service be used?
7. The staff then places the envelope inside another envelope for the appropriate service.
8. They fill out whatever forms are necessary and determine how much it will cost and the appropriate payment options.
9. They arrange for a pickup of the package.

At this point, the package enters the network of the transportation provider. In most cases, it is probably brought to a central hub and is then sent to a regional facility, where it ultimately winds up in some van or truck being driven to Sally's location.

Now look at the process on Sally's end:

1. The package is delivered to the mail room at Sally's facility.
2. The mail room staff removes the outer envelope.
3. They determine who the mail is for and sort it into the appropriate pile for delivery.
4. A mail clerk takes the mail for Sally's area, goes to that area, and starts delivering envelopes.
5. Fred's envelope is delivered along with other mail to Sally's assistant.

CH

3

6. Her assistant opens the mail and screens the material.

7. In the end, Fred's document is delivered to Sally.

All these steps are necessary simply to deliver a document. Yet through this layered approach, documents *do* get delivered from office to office. Notice that there was a sequence followed on both ends of the communication path. Several layers were involved before the document even reached the transportation provider. Likewise, several layers were involved after the package reached the destination building.

The Seven Layers of the OSI Reference Model

For a computer network, the OSI Reference Model breaks down the communication into seven layers, as shown in Figure 3.1.

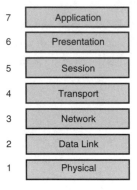

Figure 3.1
The OSI Reference Model consists of seven layers.

At the top of the model, in the *application layer,* are the actual programs operated by the computer users. A program of this type could be an email package, database program, or something as basic as the Windows File Manager or Explorer. On the bottom is the *physical layer,* comprised of the network media that makes the actual physical connection between computers. In between lie all the layers that make the actual communication occur.

Before discussing the individual layers, you should first understand a bit more about how the model actually works. Each computer on a network needs to have a *protocol stack* (sometimes referred to as a *protocol suite*), which provides the software necessary for the computer to communicate on the network. Common protocol stacks include the following:

- The ISO/OSI protocol stack
- TCP/IP (also known as the *Internet protocol suite*)
- Novell NetWare
- IBM's System Network Architecture (SNA)
- Microsoft's NetBEUI
- Apple's AppleTalk

These stacks are each comprised of several different *protocols* that perform the functions of the various layers of the OSI Reference Model. For more information about how different protocol stacks fit the OSI Reference Model, see the section "Real-World Application of the OSI Reference Model" later in this chapter.

When an application sends information from one computer to another, that data is passed down through the protocol stack on the sending computer, across the network, and then up through the protocol stack on the receiving computer. This relationship is shown in Figure 3.2.

CH
3

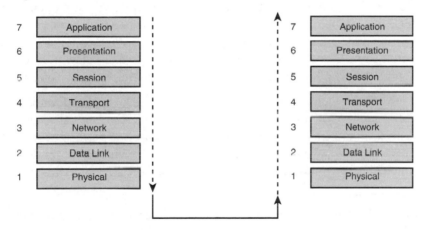

Figure 3.2
When two computers communicate, data passes down through the sender's protocol stack, across the network, and up through the receiver's protocol stack.

The actual process is a bit more complex. In truth, at each level of the process, header information is attached to the data as it is sent. On the receiving end, those headers are stripped off until the data is finally available to the receiving application. The actual transmission resembles Figure 3.3.

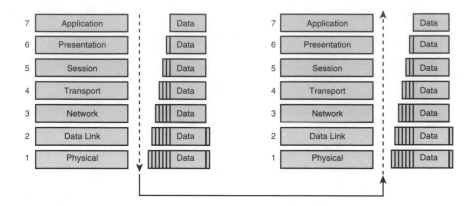

Figure 3.3

When data is sent between two protocol stacks, information is added and removed at the beginning and end of the data packet as it passes through a protocol stack.

Each layer can *only* communicate with the layer above and below it. A request from one computer for a file on another computer *must* pass down through all the layers on the sending computer and up through all the layers on the receiving computer. Each layer knows only how to transfer the information to the layer above or below it, but does not know (or need to know) how that information is passed on to the lower (or upper) layers.

The beauty of this approach is that a programmer can write an application that interacts with the application layer of a protocol stack, and the application should always work with the network, regardless of whatever lower-level protocols are used. For instance, the Windows File Manager or Explorer will enable you to access files on a remote file server, regardless of whether the network is using a TCP/IP, NetBEUI, or Novell NetWare protocol stack.

However, one of the details of this model is that each layer of the receiving protocol stack must know how to remove the header information added by each layer of the sending protocol stack. To go back to the earlier example, suppose that Fred had written his document entirely in French and sent it on to Sally. If Sally knows French, the communication can happen perfectly fine. However, if she does not, Fred's letter will be meaningless, and the communication will fail.

As another variation, suppose that Fred and Sally both spoke English, but change the scenario and say that Sally is with another company. All Fred has for an address is a U.S. Post Office box. Because almost all overnight express services (except, of course, the U.S. Postal Service) will *not* deliver to a P.O. Box, the package will not be delivered to that address if Fred's mail-room staff tries to send it through one of those services.

In both cases, the communication failed because somewhere along the way there were significant differences in the layers of communication.

Back in the realm of computer networking, this same problem can occur when two computers are set up to use two different types of networks. If one computer uses IPX/SPX and the other computer uses TCP/IP, no communication can occur.

You should understand, too, that only the protocol stacks on the two computers must be similar. One of the strengths of computer networking is that the actual computers can be quite different. A Windows PC can easily communicate with an Apple Macintosh, provided that they both use the same protocol stack (for instance, TCP/IP).

Note that it is possible in today's computer networks to actually run multiple protocol stacks on one computer. For instance, a computer might run TCP/IP to communicate with the Internet and UNIX workstations, but it might also run Novell NetWare to communicate with file servers. This will be discussed in more detail in Chapter 7, "Data Transmission."

CH
3

Key Concept

It goes without saying that for the exam you should know and understand the layers of the OSI Reference Model and IEEE 802 enhancements. You might find it helpful to come up with a phrase that includes all the letters of the OSI model. For instance: All Pilots Seek To Not Destroy Planes, Angry Patrons Seek To Not Deliver Payments, All People Should Try New Data Processors.

Application Layer

At the top of the OSI Reference Model, the application layer is primarily concerned with the interaction of the user with the computer. Services at this level support user applications such as electronic mail, database queries, and file transfer. Network protocol stacks provide programmers with functions that enable the programmers to interact with the network. This interaction is usually accomplished through an *Application Programming Interface (API)* incorporated into the protocol stack.

Returning to the earlier interoffice mail example, this OSI layer could be compared to Fred composing his document and again to Sally reading the document.

Within Microsoft networks, a service called a *redirector* operates at both this layer and the presentation layer. Essentially, the redirector represents network information to the applications that are calling network resources. For example, when you are in the Windows Explorer and want to see the directory listing of a folder on a server, the

Windows Explorer makes the same request that it would make to a local disk drive. That request, however, is redirected to the appropriate network server. The *redirector* intercepts that request and passes it along through the network. The redirector also handles network printing requests.

Key Concept

At the application layer, user applications interact with the network.

Presentation Layer

The presentation layer performs several functions with the data. Its main function is to take the data from the application layer and translate it into a format understandable to all computers. For instance, some computers encode the actual characters differently from others. Other computers order the actual bits and bytes differently. The presentation layer is responsible for translating the data to an intermediary format on outbound messages and translating the data from the intermediary format to the computer-specific format on inbound messages.

If any type of encryption is used in the communication, this is the layer at which the encryption occurs. Outbound messages are encrypted for transmission, and inbound messages are decrypted for presentation to the application layer.

Finally, the presentation layer might apply some type of data compression to reduce the size of the data as it goes across the network.

When the presentation layer is finished, the data is in its final form to be sent across the network. It might be sliced into smaller pieces by the lower levels, but there is no more manipulation of the actual data.

Going back to the interoffice mail example, the OSI presentation layer roughly compares to Fred's assistant typing the message and placing it in an envelope for transmission. The assistant is preparing it for transmission. Likewise, on the receiving end, Sally's assistant opens the envelope and prepares the document to be seen by Sally.

Key Concept

Think of the *presentation layer* as preparing the data to be presented to either the network (if outbound) or the applications (if inbound).

Session Layer

Have you ever sat at a railroad crossing and waited for a *very* long train to pass? If you haven't had that experience, I'm sure you can imagine that it isn't too much fun. You sit there wishing that there could be a pause so that you could get across the tracks and go on your way. The operators of the train, on the other hand, want to move as much cargo as they can with the fewest number of trains.

Within a computer network, you frequently do want to move large amounts of data, but you also want others to be able to use the network at the same time. To solve this, networks break data down into small *packets* for transmission. When you save a large document to a network file server, that document isn't just sent across the network in one large block. It is actually broken down into many small packets and sent individually.

Somehow, though, the receiving computer has to know when a transmission begins and ends. This role belongs to the session layer. When you want to save that document, your computer indicates to the file server that it wants to open a *session* with the server. If security permissions are okay, the connection begins. After that document has been successfully saved, the session layer indicates that the transfer has been successful and terminates the connection.

The session layer also performs an important function by placing and verifying *checkpoints* in the data stream as the data is being sent out. If there should be some temporary network failure, the sending computer will only need to retransmit the data sent after the last checkpoint.

Key Concept

Remember the *session layer* as opening, using, and closing a session between two computers.

Transport Layer

Go back to the layered networking example with Fred and Sally. The mail room staff might use a delivery service that requires that all packages not exceed five pounds. If someone wants to send 12 pounds worth of documents from one office to the other, the mail room staff is going to have to break that material up into three separate boxes. Two of those boxes will have five pounds of material and the last will contain two pounds. If the staff is cost-conscious, they will try to find any additional mail that is going to that office to fill up the last box so that it can be as close to five pounds as possible. Finally, they will number the boxes ("1 of 3", "2 of 3", and "3 of 3") and ship them out.

On the receiving end, the other mail room staff will sign for the delivery to acknowledge receipt. Next, they will open those boxes, reassemble the 12 pounds of documents, and also sort out any other mail that was sent along. If they notice that a box is missing, they will call the sending office to track down the problem.

This, in essence, is what happens at the *transport layer* of the protocol stack. Its mission is to break the data into segments and deliver the data without any errors and in the proper sequence. Protocols at this layer know the packet size required by the lower levels and break the data into the appropriate-sized packets. They also combine smaller pieces of data to reach the optimum packet size.

On the receiving end, the transport layer typically acknowledges the receipt of each packet and resequences the packets if they arrived out of order. If any packets are missing, it will request a retransmission of the missing packet.

Key Concept

Remember the *transport layer* as ensuring error-free and properly sequenced transportation for the data.

Network Layer

Returning to the interoffice mail example, when Fred's document reaches the mail room, the mail room staff determines how the package should get to Sally. The staff might evaluate different shipping options and choose the option best suited to deliver Fred's document. When the document is sent, it might travel through several different mail hubs and be carried by multiple transportation devices, such as trucks or airplanes. Fred doesn't care how the document gets to Sally as long as it gets there. His mail room staff and the transportation company are responsible for the delivery.

This routing of messages to addresses is the primary responsibility of the *network layer* in a computer network. The network layer is responsible for addressing a message and determining the best route based on network traffic, priority levels, and other conditions.

If one of those routes requires a different packet size from what was received from the transport layer, the network layer can refragment data before it is sent. On the receiving end, the network layer will reassemble the fragmented data.

In large networks, devices known as *routers* operate at the network layer to allow packets to be sent between different networks or network segments. For instance, if your organization is directly connected to the Internet, you will have a router allowing computers on your network to interact with other routers out on the Internet.

Ultimately, the network layer is responsible for converting a logical name into a physical address (such as the address of the Ethernet card) for delivery on a local network. Even if the network layer determines that the packet must be sent to a router for delivery to another network, it will still generate the physical address for the router so that the packet can be delivered to the router.

Key Concept

Remember that the *network layer* routes messages to the appropriate address by the best available path.

Data Link Layer

At the data link layer, all these packets sent down from the upper layers are placed into data *frames* for actual transmission by the physical layer. In addition to header information, this layer usually adds a trailing *Cyclical Redundancy Check (CRC)*, which the receiving computer can use to verify that the data was received intact, as shown in Figure 3.4.

Figure 3.4
At the data link layer, a CRC is added to the data frame.

The data link layer is responsible for ensuring that the frames are received error-free. After sending the frame, the layer waits for an acknowledgment from the recipient. If no acknowledgment is received, the frame is re-sent.

On the receiving end, the data link layer is responsible for uniquely identifying the computer on the network (usually through the address encoded into the network adapter card). When it detects an incoming packet to its address, it assembles all the bits from the physical layer into a frame, verifies the CRC to check the integrity of the packet, and then passes the packet up to the network layer. If the CRC check fails, this layer will request that the packet be retransmitted.

This layer is also responsible for controlling which computer can access the physical network connection at any given time. As you could imagine, if every computer on the network started transmitting data all at once, it would be hard to determine whose data belonged to whom. Several methods of controlling access will be discussed in Chapter 7.

In large networks, devices called *bridges* typically work at this layer to essentially combine different segments of a network into one large network.

Key Concept

Remember the *data link layer* as the layer packaging data into frames and providing an error-free link between two computers.

Physical Layer

Just as the communication between Fred and Sally ultimately uses trucks, trains, and planes, all computer networking communication comes down to 1s and 0s, which themselves are merely electrical impulses traveling across a wire. At the physical layer, the data is finally converted into bits to be sent across whatever physical media is being used to connect computers. In a protocol stack, this layer defines the actual medium used for connection, the physical topology of the network, how the signal is sent over the medium, as well as how that medium is connected to the computer (for example, how many pins are used on the physical connector). This layer defines the voltage used and any kind of encoding necessary to convert the bits into electrical signals.

In most networks, devices such as *hubs*, *repeaters*, and *transceivers* operate at this layer.

Key Concept

Remember the *physical layer* as the actual physical connection between computers.

IEEE 802 Enhancements to the OSI Model

At the same time as the International Standards Organization was developing the OSI Reference Model, the Institute of Electrical and Electronics Engineers (IEEE) was also engaged in the process of developing standards for the network interface card and the physical connection. This effort became known as *Project 802* (after the year and month when it started—February 1980).

The IEEE project resulted in the *802 specifications*, which define the way in which data is actually placed on the physical network media by network interface cards. The standards fall into 12 categories, as outlined in Table 3.1.

Table 3.1	IEEE 802 Specifications
Number	Category
802.1	Internetworking
802.2	Logical Link Control
802.3	Carrier-Sense Multiple Access with Collision Detection LAN (CSMA/CD, or Ethernet)
802.4	Token-Bus LAN
802.5	Token-Ring LAN
802.6	Metropolitan Area Network (MAN)
802.7	Broadband Technical Advisory Group
802.8	Fiber-Optic Technical Advisory Group
802.9	Integrated Voice/Data Networks
802.10	Network Security
802.11	Wireless Networks
802.12	Demand Priority Access LAN, 100 BaseVG-AnyLAN

CH
3

Key Concept

For the exam, you should know that 802.3 signifies an Ethernet LAN, 802.4 signifies a Token Bus, 802.5 signifies a Token-Ring LAN, and 802.2 specifies Logical Link Control.

Both the ISO and IEEE projects were developed simultaneously, and both sets of committees exchanged information. The IEEE 802 specifications focused on the two lowest levels of the OSI Reference Model, the physical and data link layers, and have become the primary standards for those levels.

The IEEE made one major enhancement to the OSI model. The engineers felt that the data link layer needed further clarification and divided the layer into two sublayers (see Figure 3.5):

- Logical Link Control (LLC)
- Media Access Control (MAC)

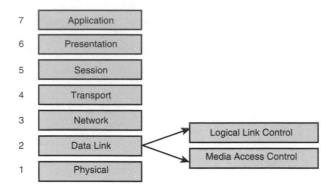

Figure 3.5
The IEEE Project 802 divided the OSI data link layer into two sublayers.

Logical Link Control Sublayer

The Logical Link Control sublayer is responsible for maintaining the link between two computers when they are sending data across the physical network connection. It does this by establishing a series of interface points, known as *Service Access Points (SAPs)*, that other computers can use to communicate with the upper levels of the network protocol stack. The primary specification for this sublayer is 802.2.

Media Access Control Sublayer

Basically, the MAC sublayer allows the computers on a network to take turns sending data on the physical network medium. This sublayer specifies the method whereby a computer determines if it can send a packet out onto the network. It is also responsible for ensuring that the data reaches the other computer without any errors.

The major IEEE 802 specifications for this sublayer include those listed in Table 3.2.

Table 3.2   Media Access Control 802 Categories

Number	Category
802.3	Carrier-Sense Multiple Access with Collision Detection LAN (CSMA/CD or Ethernet)
802.4	Token-Bus LAN
802.5	Token-Ring LAN
802.12	Demand Priority

These categories will be discussed in further detail in Chapter 7.

Real-World Application of the OSI Reference Model

Although the OSI Reference Model provides a theoretical framework for discussion of computer networks, in reality most protocol stacks do not fit into seven neat, orderly layers. The layered concept is still present, but the lines dividing the layers might be in different locations. Some protocol stacks might take the functions of a single OSI layer and divide them between multiple protocols. There are also protocols that might provide the functions of a single OSI layer, whereas other protocols might provide the functions of multiple OSI layers.

For instance, in the Novell NetWare protocol suite, the NetWare Core Protocol (NCP) operates at the OSI Application, presentation, and session layers. In the TCP/IP protocol suite, the Transmission Control Protocol (TCP) provides the services of the OSI transport layer and some of the services of the session layer, whereas the Internet Protocol (IP) provides the remainder of the transport layer services and most of the network layer services.

In truth, no one model can be applied to all computer networks. The OSI Reference Model is useful in that it defines all the functions that should occur within a network protocol stack. In general, however, most network protocol stacks fit into a four-layer model, as shown in Figure 3.6.

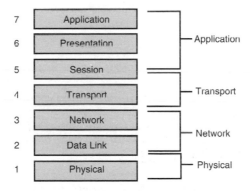

Figure 3.6
Real-world protocols might provide the functions of several layers of the OSI model.

Within the four-layer model, application protocols are concerned with the user interaction and data interchange. Transport protocols establish sessions between computers and provide for the exchange of error-free and properly sequenced data. Network protocols deal with routing and addressing issues. Finally, the physical layer, as in the OSI model, defines the physical connection and transmission of bits between computers.

Network protocols will be discussed in detail in Chapter 9, "Network Protocols," but if you have some previous experience with network protocols, Table 3.3 might help you understand how various networks fit broadly into the OSI model. (The physical layer does not appear in the table because it is essentially the same in all networks.)

Table 3.3   Comparison of Network Protocols and the OSI Model

Layer	TCP/IP	Novell NetWare	Microsoft	Apple
Application	Telnet, FTP, SMTP	NCP	SMB	Apple Share, AFP
Transport	TCP	SPX, IPX	NetBEUI	ATP
Network	IP	IPX	NetBEUI	DDP

The question you might be asking now is, "If network protocols generally fit into four layers, why does the OSI Reference Model have to have seven layers?"

To answer this, look back at the model for a computer that was outlined in the section "The Need for a Conceptual Framework" at the beginning of the chapter. It lists 11 items that could define a computer. But do all computers have all 11 items? Does every computer have a sound card or CD-ROM? In reality, you could collapse that model to six categories:

- Processor
- Memory
- Storage Devices (hard-disk drive, diskette drive, CD-ROM)
- Input Devices (keyboard, mouse)
- Monitor
- Peripherals (printer, modem, sound card)

Now, this model will work for almost every computer. With the exception of some servers and diskless workstations, you should be able to say that every computer you know of has at least the first five categories and possibly the sixth. But if you said to someone, "Yes, my computer has a processor, memory, storage devices, input devices, a monitor, and some peripherals," what would their next question be? Probably, "What type of storage devices?" This reduced model simply doesn't provide enough descriptive detail.

Likewise, although most network protocol stacks can fit into the four-layer reduced model, those four layers alone really don't fully describe what is involved with network communication. The larger OSI Reference Model (with the IEEE 802 enhancements) provides this higher level of descriptive detail.

Summary

The OSI Reference Model provides a framework in which to describe computer networks and compare the functions of different protocol stacks used in networking. The OSI model divides network communication into seven layers:

- *Application.* Provides connections to a network for user applications.
- *Presentation.* Prepares data for network transmission.
- *Session.* Establishes a session between two computers.
- *Transport.* Ensures error-free and properly sequenced transportation of data.
- *Network.* Addresses packets and determines best route to destination.
- *Data link.* Packages data into frames and establishes an error-free link between two computers.
- *Physical.* Defines the actual physical connection method between computers.

The IEEE 802 project further breaks down the OSI data link layer into two sublayers:

- *Logical Link Control.* Maintains the link between two computers.
- *Media Access Control.* Controls which computer on a network can be transmitting data at any given time.

The IEEE 802 project also defines a number of categories that relate both to the Media Access Control sublayer as well as to the physical layer. The most important categories to remember are:

- *802.3* Carrier-Sense Multiple Access with Collision Detection (Ethernet)
- *802.4* Token-Bus LAN
- *802.5* Token-Ring LAN

CH
3

QUESTIONS AND ANSWERS

1. Why should you care about the OSI Reference Model?

   A: It provides a framework for discussing network operations and design.

2. What are the seven layers of the OSI Reference Model?

   A: Application, presentation, session, transport, network, data link, and physical.

3. True or false. The transport layer handles the actual transmission of data between two computers.

   A: False. The transport layer ensures error-free and sequenced transmission of data. The physical layer actually transmits data.

4. How did the IEEE enhance the OSI model? What are the names of the sublayers?

   A: They defined two sublayers in the data link layer: Logical Link Control and Media Access Control.

5. What is the role of the network layer?

   A: The network layer is responsible for addressing and routing packets of information.

6. What does the Media Access Control sublayer do?

   A: The Media Access Control sublayer controls which computer or network device can send data out on the network media at any given time.

7. What does the IEEE 802.3 specification define?

   A: Ethernet (Carrier-Sense Multiple Access with Collision Detection—CSMA/CD)

8. What does the IEEE 802.5 specification define?

   A: Token ring

PRACTICE TEST

1. The IEEE 802.3 specification defines which network architecture?

   a. Novell NetWare

   b. Ethernet

   c. Token Ring

   d. ArcNet

Answer a is incorrect because there is no IEEE specification for NetWare. **Answer b is correct.** Answer c is incorrect because Token Ring is specified by IEEE 802.5. Answer d is incorrect because ArcNet does not have a specific IEEE designation.

2. The IEEE 802 specification divides which layer of the OSI Reference Model into two sublayers?

   a. Data link layer

   b. Physical layer

   c. Network layer

   d. Transport layer

Answer a is correct.

3. Email programs, file transfer requests, and database queries occur at what layer of the OSI Reference Model?

   a. Transport

   b. User

   c. Application

   d. Presentation

Answer a is incorrect. Answer b is incorrect because it is not an OSI layer. **Answer c is correct.** Answer d is incorrect.

4. The data link layer of the OSI Reference Model is responsible for what function?

   a. Establishing a session between two computers.

   b. Ensuring error-free and properly sequenced movement of the data.

   c. Routing messages to the appropriate address by the best available path.

   d. Packaging data into frames and providing an error-free link between two computers.

Answer a is incorrect because it defines the session layer. Answer b is incorrect because it defines the transport layer. Answer c is incorrect because it defines the network layer. **Answer d is correct.**

CH
3

5. Devices that operate at the data link layer to combine different segments of a network into one large network are called what?

a. Routers

b. Linkers

c. Bridges

d. Hubs

Answer a is incorrect because routers work at the network layer. Answer b is incorrect because "linkers" is a fictitious device. **Answer c is correct; bridges work at the data link layer.** Answer d is incorrect because hubs work at the physical layer.

6. A program operating at the application layer of the OSI Reference Model can communicate directly with an application layer program on another computer without using any other layer of the Reference Model.

a. True

b. False

Answer a is incorrect. **Answer b is correct; data must travel down through the other layers on the sending computer, across the network, and then up through the layers on the receiving computer. Two layers cannot communicate directly without going through the lower layers.**

7. A token ring LAN is defined by which IEEE 802 specification?

a. 802.3

b. 802.12

c. 802.5

d. 802.4

Answer a is incorrect because 802.3 specifies Ethernet. Answer b is incorrect because 802.12 defines demand priority (100VG-AnyLAN). **Answer c is correct; IEEE 802.5 specifies how a token ring network would operate.** Answer d is incorrect because 802.4 defines a token bus network.

8. The IEEE 802 Project divided one of the OSI layers into two sublayers. What are they called? (Choose two.)

a. Data Link Control

b. Logical Link Control

c. Network Link

d. Media Access Control

Answer a is incorrect. **Answer b is correct.** Answer c is incorrect. **Answer d is correct.**

9. As data is sent across a network, checkpoints are placed in the data stream so that in the event of failure, only the data after the last checkpoint needs to be retransmitted. At which layer of the OSI Reference Model are these checkpoints inserted?

   a. Data link

   b. Network

   c. Transport

   d. Session

Answer d is correct.

10. In addition to header information, the data link layer typically also includes a trailing _____ that provides a mechanism to ensure that the data frame was delivered without errors.

   a. Error Link Control

   b. Logical Data Check

   c. Cyclical Redundancy Check

   d. Checksum

Answer a is incorrect. Answer b is incorrect. **Answer c is correct; the Cyclical Redundancy Check (CRC) is used on Ethernet networks to verify that the data was transmitted correctly.** Answer d is incorrect.

CH
3

Network Topology

— WHILE YOU READ —

1. What are the three major topologies in use today?

2. What are the advantages of a bus network?

3. What are the advantages of a star network?

4. What are the advantages of a ring network?

5. What is a token?

6. True or False. Given that they are a simple line, bus networks are very easy to troubleshoot.

7. What is a mesh network?

8. Which topology is the easiest to reconfigure?

9. Which topology is the simplest and least expensive to install for a small network?

10. Which topology provides equal access to the media to all computers?

What Is a Topology?

As you begin to design your network, one of the first choices you must make is that of the physical layout, or topology, of your network. This choice can depend on a number of factors, including cost, equipment that you currently possess, architecture, and operating systems.

The term *topology* describes the physical layout of computers, cables, routers, and other equipment on the network. If you were to sketch your office computer network on a piece of paper, complete with which computers were connected to each other, you would be sketching the *topology* of the network. The topology is quite simply the physical layout of your network.

It is important to understand that there can be a subtle difference between the *physical* and the *logical* topology of a network. The *physical topology* of a network describes the physical layout of a computer network. The major types of physical topologies include the *bus, star,* and *ring.* The *logical topology* of a network refers to the logical path that a signal takes as it traverses the network. As an example, in many Token-Ring networks, the signal travels *logically* from computer to computer in a *ring,* even though it might *physically* appear as a star. The following sections will discuss each topology in detail.

Bus Topology

Imagine that you work in a small company where everyone has a small office connected to a long hallway. There is no receptionist, and everyone must share the responsibility of answering the phone. There is also no intercom system. When a call comes in that is not for you, you must first put the person on hold and then shout the recipient's name and the number of the phone line down the hall. The individual being called then picks up the phone on the correct line to answer the call. In addition to helping answer the phone, you are also continuously listening for your name to be called, signifying a call for you.

Although this system is simple, it is not without problems. Everyone has to be constantly listening. As more calls come in, the noise level in the hallway increases. If two people try to yell at the same time, you can't determine who said what; people have to take turns. As more people are added and the hallway gets longer, it becomes harder to hear what people are saying all the way down at the other end of the hall.

This is essentially how a computer network using a bus topology—sometimes called a *linear bus*—works. All the computers are connected to a *backbone* or *trunk.* As shown in Figure 4.1, this backbone links all the computers.

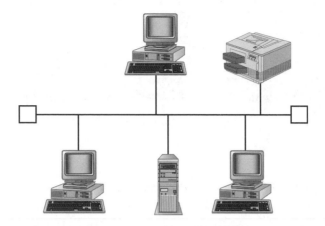

Figure 4.1
In a bus topology, all computers are connected in a line.

When a computer wants to communicate, it sends a signal out onto the cable. Just as your voice carries in all directions in a hallway, the computer's signal travels in both directions through a cable. All the other computers receive that signal and determine whether the data packet is meant for them. Whichever computer is the destination accepts the information and begins processing the data. All the others simply ignore the signal. A bus is referred to as a *passive* topology because the computers (or *nodes*) on the network simply listen and receive the signal. They do not amplify the signal or manipulate it in any way.

In the hallway scenario, if two people shouted out names at the same time, your ears are probably sophisticated enough that you could determine what each person was saying. Computers are not this smart, though, and only one computer at a time can transmit a signal on the cable. If two or more computers transmit data packets at the same time, the resulting collision of their packets renders the signal unusable. (Note that the issue of determining when a computer can transmit data is a subject in and of itself and will be covered in detail in Chapter 7, "Data Transmission.")

Another difference from the physical world is the duration of the signal. If you yell out into a hallway, the sound of your voice will fade rapidly after you are finished speaking.

However, with the efficiency of copper wire, an electrical signal can continue for a long time and will just bounce back toward the other direction when it reaches one end of a cable. Because this bouncing signal will stop other computers from transmitting, the cable used in a bus network must have a *terminator* on each end to absorb the signal and prevent it from bouncing. If a bus network is not terminated properly, no communication can take place on the network. Figure 4.2 shows an example of a terminator.

BNC terminator

Figure 4.2
In a bus network, a terminator is required on the ends of the cable to absorb the signal.

The greatest advantage of bus networks lies in the sheer simplicity of the physical layout. When using thinnet cable, no additional hardware is needed beyond the network cabling and network interface cards. The thinnet cable is very flexible, inexpensive, and easy to install. A bus network can be set up between computers within a few minutes. Additionally, a bus network can be extended easily using a *barrel connector* (see Figure 4.3). Bus networks using other media such as thicknet are simple to understand, but do require a bit more work for installation.

BNC barrel connector

Figure 4.3
A barrel connector can be used to extend a bus network.

However, bus networks are not without their disadvantages. As previously mentioned, if a network cable is not properly terminated, all communication will cease. Additionally, communication will stop if there is a break anywhere in the cable. This is much like a string of holiday lights where if one bulb fails, all the others go out, too. If a user goes to move his or her computer and inadvertently disconnects the network cable, all network traffic will cease until that cable is reconnected. For this reason, failure of a bus network can be extremely difficult to troubleshoot—just like finding that *one* bulb in the holiday light string. Each and every connection might need to be checked to find the problem. The circuit must be complete between all computers for communication to work.

Another downside to a bus network is the number of computers that can be connected to the network. As more computers are added, more transmissions are made on the cable. Each signal sent must be reviewed by every other computer. Also, every time one computer sends a signal, it prevents all the others from sending signals. If one computer interrupts another, they both have to try to retransmit their signals. As the network traffic increases, the performance decreases.

Reconfiguring bus networks can also be troublesome. The network cable must be disconnected at some junction so that another length of cable can be added. All network traffic will stop while the cable is disconnected.

Finally, the signal in a bus network can only travel so far. If the hallway in our hypothetical office was extended several times, it would eventually reach the point where the sound of someone's voice would not carry all the way from one end of the hall to the other. Likewise, the signal in a cable can only travel so far before quality of the signal will degrade to the point where it is unusable. It is possible to extend the transmission distance through the use of a *repeater*, which simply amplifies the signal before passing it along, but even these extensions can hit a physical limit. For example, in an Ethernet bus network using thinnet cable, each segment of the network cannot exceed 185 meters (607 feet). Repeaters can be used to extend the signal, but the total network length cannot exceed 925 meters (3,035 feet). (Chapter 5, "The Physical Connection," will discuss the length a cable can physically cover, and Chapter 8, "Network Architecture," will address other issues that can limit the length of a bus network.)

CH
4

 Key Concept

In a bus topology, each computer is connected directly to the primary network cable in a single line.

Advantages of the Bus Topology

A network based on the bus topology has many advantages, including the following:

- The cable and hardware used are very inexpensive.
- Installation can be both easy and rapid.
- The topology is simple to understand. (The cable runs from one computer to the next—can it be any simpler?)
- A bus network can be easily extended.

Disadvantages of the Bus Topology

Although simple to install and configure, bus networks suffer from the following disadvantages:

- They can be painfully difficult to troubleshoot. Because a break in the network *anywhere* can bring down the entire network, each and every connection might have to be checked to find the problem.
- Increased network traffic can significantly decrease the network performance.
- The overall physical length of the network is limited.

Star Topology

Back in the fictitious company, more employees have been added, and the company has moved to a new office location. Now, all employee offices are located around a central room, but still without an intercom. When you receive a call, you simply shout it out into the central room. Like before, everyone must constantly keep listening, but now everyone is located closer together. Additionally, management planned ahead and left many vacant offices available so expansion will not be a problem.

Computer networks using a star topology work roughly in this fashion. As shown in Figure 4.4, all computers on a network are connected into a central *hub*. When a computer sends a signal, it travels into the hub and then out to all the other computers connected to the hub.

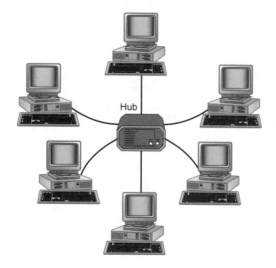

Figure 4.4
A network using a star topology uses a central hub to connect all the computers.

There are two types of hubs: *passive* and *active*. In networks using a passive hub, the signal is simply passed on to all other computers. Passive hubs are seldom used anymore, and when they are, it is primarily for very small networks because passive hubs rely solely on the power of the computers to transmit the signal. If computers are located far apart, the data signal from one computer may degrade before reaching the others. (This is similar to the bus topology, where signals can only travel so far before the quality of the signal starts to degrade.)

On the other hand, active hubs, sometimes referred to as *multiport repeaters*, use electrical power to amplify the data signal, allowing the signal to travel farther and with better clarity. Almost all hubs in use today are active hubs.

The star topology shares some similarities with the bus topology in the transmission of data. In both, only one computer can transmit data signals at a time. Also, each computer receives all data packets and must review the destination address of each individual packet. When a computer identifies a packet addressed to the computer's address, it passes that packet onto the upper layers of the OSI model. The computer simply ignores all packets that it identifies as being for other computers. However, unlike the bus topology, a break in any one network connection will *not* bring the network down. The computer with the broken cable will not be able to communicate with the others, but communication between the other computers will continue uninterrupted. For this reason, star networks are usually easy to troubleshoot. Obviously, if the central hub fails, the network will fail, but other than that, star networks are quite reliable.

Star networks are also easy to reconfigure. To add a new computer, you simply connect a new cable between the hub and the new computer. If you want to move a cable from one jack in the hub to another, you can do so without disturbing the rest of the network. A computer can be disconnected at any time by simply removing its plug. If you eventually run out of room in your hub, you can purchase a larger hub and easily transfer the cables.

In a small network, a star topology can be fairly inexpensive. Because the cable used is primarily the inexpensive *unshielded twisted pair (UTP)*, the most expensive component is the hub. However, as a star network expands, the cost of cabling can grow rapidly. Whereas cable in a bus topology runs from one computer to the next, all cables in a star run from each computer back to the central hub. If you have several computers located a significant distance from the hub, you will need to stretch a separate cable for each computer all the way from the hub to its location.

This need for individual cables can impose a distance barrier as well. Generally, most network media used in star networks limit all computers to being 100 meters (328 feet) from the hub.

CH
4

Key Concept

In a star topology, all computers are connected using a central hub. A separate cable runs from each computer back to the hub.

Advantages of the Star Topology

Networks based on a star topology have several advantages:

- Failure of a single computer will not stop communication between other computers.
- Because the connections are between the hub and individual computers, troubleshooting can be relatively easy.
- It is easy to add computers to the network and reconfigure connections.

Disadvantages of the Star Topology

Disadvantages of the star topology include the following:

- Cabling can be expensive due to the need for a separate cable between the hub and each computer.
- Failure of the hub will terminate all network communication.
- Distance can be limited due to the need for separate cables.

Ring Topology

Go back to the office scenario. Shouting phone messages into the hallway or center room has become tiring and unproductive. Additionally, you found that the people with the loudest voices tended to dominate over those with softer voices.

Now, your company has decided to hire a messenger to go around to all the offices to check for messages. This messenger spends her day circling the office, retrieving and delivering messages. Whenever you get a message for someone, you write it on a piece of paper and put it out for the messenger. The messenger picks it up, delivers it to the appropriate person, checks for messages there, and continues on to the next office. In this fashion, messages do get delivered without any shouting. Additionally, because no one can deliver a message until the messenger comes around to pick it up, no one person can interrupt the delivery of someone else's message. Finally, because the messenger stops at each office, everyone is assured that he will get a chance to pass along a message.

Although this might not actually occur in the physical world, this is essentially how networks based on the ring topology function. As shown in Figure 4.5, all the computers on a network are connected in a single circle. The signal travels in one direction around the loop.

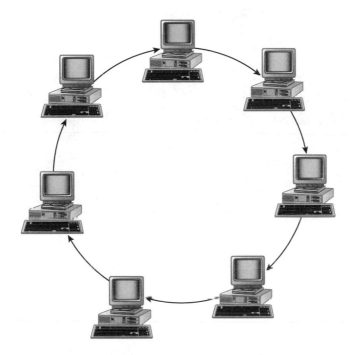

Figure 4.5
A ring topology connects all computers in a loop.

CH
4

The ring is an example of an *active* topology in that each computer does more than just receive the information. After receiving the packet, each computer amplifies the signal and sends it on to the next computer. Because of this, ring networks do not suffer the same signal degradation experienced in bus and star networks as the signal travels farther.

In some implementations, such as FDDI, the ring might involve an actual circle of cable, whereas many others, such as Token Ring, might use a device similar to a hub to connect all the computers in a *physical* star network while maintaining a *logical* ring. In Figure 4.6, you can see that the hub is wired differently internally so that the signal goes from one computer to the next in a ring. This provides the same ease of configuration as a star network while maintaining the advantages of a ring network. Such a network topology is sometimes referred to as a *star ring* or a *star-wired ring*. (Both Token Ring and FDDI will be described in more detail in Chapter 8, "Network Architecture.")

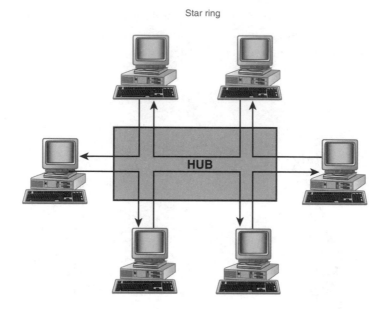

Figure 4.6
Many implementations of ring networks use a special type of hub that is wired internally as a ring.

Key Concept

In a ring topology, all computers are connected in loop.

Many rings implement a system of *token passing*, which, like the messenger in the office message analogy, ensures that every computer gets an equal opportunity to communicate on the network.

Key Concept

A *token* is a small data packet that is continually passed around the ring between computers. Each computer can only transmit a message when it has the token.

Advantages of the Ring Topology

The advantages of the ring topology include the following:

- The mechanism for fair access (token passing) can provide equal opportunities for all computers to communicate.
- Installation can be simple.
- Because the signal is regenerated at each computer, signals do not degrade as much as in other topologies.

Disadvantages of the Ring Topology

Disadvantages include the following:

- Like a bus, the failure of any one connection can bring the network down. (Note that some ring networks, such as those using FDDI, might incorporate a second ring to minimize network failures.)
- Reconfiguration can be difficult because the network might need to be brought down while the new connection is added.
- Distance can be limited due to the physical media limitations.

Hybrid Networks

Although these are the three basic topologies, many variations are possible. Elements of different topologies can be found in most networks. Three of the most common variations are discussed in the following sections.

Star Bus

The star bus topology, as shown in Figure 4.7, essentially consists of several star networks connected by a bus network. A company might implement a star network at first with one hub. When the network grows to the point where that hub is filled, a second hub is added and linked via a cable to the first hub. At the point when a third hub is added, it will simply be connected to the second hub, and so on.

This configuration might also be found in an office building with several floors. Each floor might have a hub (or hubs) that would be connected by a bus that runs from floor to floor.

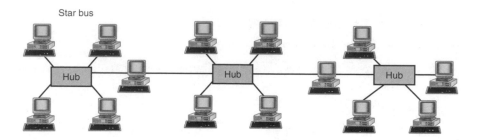

Figure 4.7
In a star bus topology, multiple hubs are connected by a bus network.

The star bus topology has the advantages of a star topology in that no one computer will bring the whole network down and that it is easy to reconfigure. Like a star topology, if a hub fails, all computers on that hub will be unable to communicate. Similar to a bus topology, if the connection between hubs breaks, computers will be able to communicate with other computers on a hub, but not with those on other hubs.

Mesh

If you worked with three other people and you all sat around a single table, communication would be quite simple. You could simply look directly at the person with whom you wanted to communicate and start speaking. There would be no need to wait for everyone else to stop talking or for a messenger. Each of you would have direct access to each other.

A true *mesh network* is one in which every computer has a link to every other computer on the network as shown in Figure 4.8. This has the advantage that you can be almost certain that your communication will always get through. Even if your direct link with another computer goes down, your message can be transmitted from your computer to another and from there to your original destination. Mesh networks are said to be highly *fault-tolerant*.

However, mesh networks are not practical for most situations. The cost of having multiple connections quickly becomes prohibitive. Additionally, installing and reconfiguring mesh networks can be a nightmare.

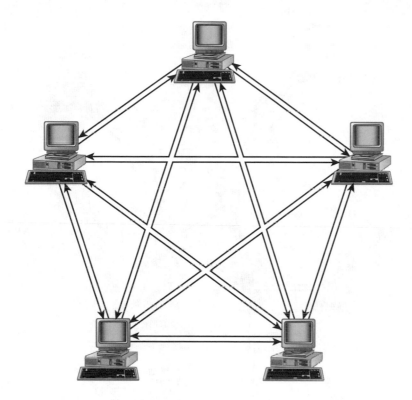

Figure 4.8
In a true mesh network, each computer has a connection to every other computer.

Hybrid mesh networks can be found, though, where some of the links have redundant connections. For example, a company might have multiple connections over a WAN between offices so that if one connection fails, they will still be able to communicate. A company doing extensive work over the Internet might have multiple connections to its Internet service provider so that Internet access will still be available. Hybrid networks such as these (see Figure 4.9) provide some degree of fault-tolerance without the huge cost of a true mesh.

CH
4

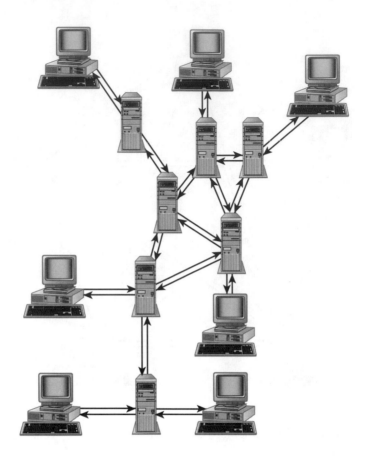

Figure 4.9
A hybrid mesh network contains redundant connections between some nodes on the network.

Choosing the Appropriate Topology

The topology you use depends on several factors, including cost, distance, installation timeframe, and physical environment. Factors to consider include the following:

- If you are installing a small network in a room or office and are looking for an inexpensive mechanism to do so, a *bus* or *star* will probably provide the best solution.

- If you know that you will be adding and reconfiguring your network, a *star* topology is by far the easiest to reconfigure.

- If you have a large number of users in a relatively confined area, a *star bus* might provide you with all the expansion that you need.

- If you are looking for a mechanism that will provide equal access to the network media even under conditions of high network traffic, choose a *ring* topology.

- If you want an extremely fault-tolerant network, choose a *mesh* topology.

Summary

The *topology* of a network describes the physical layout of a computer network. The major types of topologies include the *bus*, *star*, and *ring*. Note that there can be a difference between the *physical* and the *logical* topology of a network. For example, a Token Ring network might logically be a *ring*, even though it is physically wired as a star.

In a network based on a bus topology, all computers are connected in a single line. A bus network is very inexpensive and simple to implement. Its major drawback is that any break in the cable can cause the entire network to fail.

A star topology uses a device called a *hub* to provide a central gathering point for all network connections. A cable runs directly from each computer back to the central hub. This makes it easy to troubleshoot and reconfigure. Each computer is independent, so failure of one network connection will not jeopardize the entire network. The disadvantages to star networks include that they can be quite expensive due to the amount of cable needed and that the failure of a hub can be critical.

Computers in a true ring topology are all connected in a single loop of cable. Most rings use some type of *token passing* to provide each computer with equal access to the cable. As with bus networks, failure of one computer can bring down the whole network. Because of the difficulty in physically implementing a ring network, most ring networks are actually implemented as star-wired rings.

Variations exist including the star bus, star ring, and mesh networks. These hybrid networks include elements of the other topologies.

CH

4

QUESTIONS AND ANSWERS

1. What are the three major topologies in use today?

    A: Bus, star, and ring.

2. What are the advantages of a bus network?

    A: Inexpensive, easy to install, simple to understand, and easy to extend.

3. What are the advantages of a star network?

    A: Can be inexpensive, easy to install and reconfigure, and easy to troubleshoot physical problems.

4. What are the advantages of a ring network?

    A: All computers have equal access to the network media, installation can be simple, and signal does not degrade as much as in other topologies because it is regenerated by each computer.

5. What is a token?

    A: A small data packet that is continually transmitted around a ring network. A computer can only transmit data onto the network when it receives the token.

6. True or False. Given that they are a simple line, bus networks are very easy to troubleshoot.

    A: False. Bus networks can be *extremely* difficult to troubleshoot.

7. What is a mesh network?

    A: A network in which there are multiple network links between computers to provide multiple paths for data to travel.

8. Which topology is the easiest to reconfigure?

    A: Star.

9. Which topology is the simplest and least expensive to install for a small network?

    A: Either a bus or a star. Both are about the same in pricing. It used to be that hubs were expensive and a bus network was cheaper, but today the price of hubs has dropped so dramatically that a star network might in some instances be cheaper than a bus.

10. Which topology provides equal access to the media to all computers?

    A: Ring.

PRACTICE TEST

1. You are in charge of the computer systems for a small nonprofit organization. Your manager recently attended a trade show and came back raving about networks. She now wants you to quickly connect all the computers in the office, but she imposes some financial constraints.

REQUIRED RESULT: Your network should be as inexpensive as possible.

OPTIONAL DESIRED RESULTS: Your network should be easily reconfigurable. Your network should be easy to install.

PROPOSED SOLUTION: You suggest installing a bus network using thinnet cable. Which results does the proposed solution produce?

   a. The proposed solution produces the required result and both of the optional desired results.

   b. The proposed solution produces the required result and only *one* of the optional desired results.

   c. The proposed solution produces the required result but does *not* produce any of the optional desired results.

   d. The proposed solution does *not* produce the required result.

Answer b is correct. A bus network meets the required result because it is very inexpensive. Because it is also easy to install, it meets one of the optional results. However, a bus network is typically not easy to reconfigure, so it does not meet the second optional result.

2. The purpose of a terminator is what?

   a. To enable you to easily determine the end of the network cable

   b. To amplify the electrical signal, which allows the signal to travel over longer distances

   c. To create a wall allowing the signal to bounce back down the cable when it has reached the end

   d. To absorb the signal so that it does not bounce back when it has reached the end of the cable

Answer a is incorrect, although it *is* a side effect of having a terminator on the cable. Answer b is incorrect. Answer c is incorrect and is actually the exact thing that a terminator stops. **Answer d is correct.**

3. In a bus network, a _____ amplifies a signal so that it can travel over a longer distance. (Choose all that apply.)
   a. Repeater
   b. Hub
   c. Terminator
   d. Barrel connector

Answer a is correct. Answer b is correct because a hub is essentially a multi-port repeater. With the exception of passive hubs, which are hardly ever found anymore, the signal coming into one hub port is regenerated out all other ports. Answer c is incorrect because terminators end the signal. Answer d is incorrect because barrel connectors provide no amplification.

4. You work for a small real-estate company where several people need to share files and a printer. Your manager has indicated that he is willing to invest in a network to link all the computers. His major concern is that it should be easy to fix because you are frequently out on the road.

   REQUIRED RESULT: If problems occur, it should take a minimal amount of time to diagnose and fix the problem.

   OPTIONAL DESIRED RESULTS: Your network should be inexpensive. Your network should be easy to install.

   PROPOSED SOLUTION: You suggest installing a bus network using thinnet cable. Which results does the proposed solution produce?
   a. The proposed solution produces the required result and both of the optional desired results.
   b. The proposed solution produces the required result and only *one* of the optional desired results.
   c. The proposed solution produces the required result but does *not* produce any of the optional desired results.
   d. The proposed solution does *not* produce the required result.

Answer d is correct. Although the proposed solution meets *both* of the optional results (inexpensive and easy to install), a bus network fails the required result of needing only a minimal amount of time to diagnose and fix problems. Troubleshooting a bus network can be problematic and can require a great deal of time.

5. You are the manager of a financial firm with several branch offices. One of the branch offices has been complaining that it needs a network to be able to work productively. This particular office is small but is growing rapidly and will be moving to new office space later this year. You send several people from your Information Systems department to evaluate what type of network should be installed.

REQUIRED RESULT: Your network should be as inexpensive as possible.

OPTIONAL DESIRED RESULTS: Your network should be easily reconfigurable. Your network should be easy to install.

PROPOSED SOLUTION: Your IS department suggests implementing a star network with unshielded twisted-pair cable. Which results does the proposed solution produce?

   a. The proposed solution produces the required result and both of the optional desired results.

   b. The proposed solution produces the required result and only *one* of the optional desired results.

   c. The proposed solution produces the required result but does *not* produce any of the optional desired results.

   d. The proposed solution does *not* produce the required result.

Answer a is correct. Because a star network will be inexpensive, easy to reconfigure, and easy to install, the proposed solution meets the required result and both of the optional results.

6. To ensure equal access to the network cable among all computers, ring networks use a _____ to determine which computer can transmit.

   a. Key
   b. Token
   c. Messenger
   d. Password

Answer a is incorrect. **Answer b is correct.** Answer c is incorrect. Answer d is incorrect.

7. Within a star network, failure of any one network connection will bring the entire network down.

   a. True
   b. False

Answer a is incorrect. **Answer b is correct because the failure of any one network connection in a star network will only disrupt communication to and from a single station.** All other systems will continue to have access to the network.

CH
4

8. Multiple computers can transmit at the same time in a star network.

   a. True
   b. False

Answer a is incorrect. **Answer b is correct because only one computer can transmit in almost all star network configurations.**

9. You would like to link the computers in your Sales office to share information. Due to rapid expansion, you are adding several new salespeople each week. Over the next few months, you will be connecting new computers to your network as you add new salespeople. You do not want to disrupt the network as you add each person. You also want to minimize the cost of your network. What network topology should you use?

   a. Star
   b. Bus
   c. Ring
   d. Mesh

Answer a is correct because a star network will allow for the network to be easily reconfigured and is also inexpensive. Answers b and c are incorrect because reconfiguring a bus or ring network does involve temporarily disrupting the flow of network traffic. Answer d is incorrect because although a mesh network would provide a means to have no disruptions, it would be much more expensive than a star network.

10. Within a bus network, a _____ links all computers together.

   a. Hub
   b. Repeater
   c. Terminator
   d. Backbone

Answer a is incorrect because there are no hubs in the bus networks discussed here. Answer b is incorrect because a repeater links two or more cable segments, but it does not connect computers. Answer c is incorrect because a terminator ends the signal on the cable. **Answer d is correct because the term _backbone_ is another name for the cable used to connect all computers on a bus network.**

CHAPTER PREREQUISITE

Before reading this chapter, you should understand the basic concepts and terminology of computer networks as described in Chapter 2, "Introduction to Networks." You should also understand the functions of the Physical Layer of the OSI Reference Model as described in Chapter 3, "The OSI Reference Model."

The Physical Connection

— WHILE YOU READ —

1. What is the difference between baseband and broadband transmission?

2. What are the three main categories of cable?

3. Why and where do you use plenum cable?

4. True or false. Category 5 UTP is the minimum required cable for 10Mbps ethernet networks.

5. Explain why you might want to use shielded cable.

6. Compare the distance that can be covered between UTP and thinnet coaxial cable.

7. How is a node connected to a thicknet cable?

8. When working with thicknet, what is the port called on the computer's NIC?

9. Why is fiber-optic cable less susceptible to interference and eavesdropping?

10. Why do fiber-optic cables consist of two separate fiber-optic strands?

Making the Connection

Eventually, communication across a computer network comes down to the transmission of a signal across a medium. In most networks, this transmission takes the form of an electric signal sent across a copper wire. In some instances, light will be used across a glass strand. However, the issue, in both cases, remains the same: How do you represent the electronic data as impulses across a cable?

Most LANs use *baseband transmission,* where the 1s and 0s of the data bits are defined as discrete changes in the flow of electricity or light. This would be similar to communicating at night with someone else by flashlight. The light is either on or off.

As shown in Figure 5.1, there are only two conditions—on or off—and the entire communication cable is occupied by the transmission of one channel of data. One advantage to baseband transmission is that connected devices can both transmit and receive at the same time.

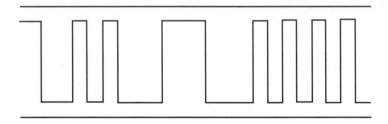

Figure 5.1
In baseband transmission, bits of data are defined by discrete changes in the signal.

In contrast, *broadband transmission* uses analog communication to divide the cable into a series of channels, as shown in Figure 5.2. Each channel has its own frequency, and all devices listening at that frequency can obtain the data. Cable TV uses this technology to bring many channels into your home using one cable. Cable similar to that used for cable TV could be used in some situations to allow both voice and network data to occupy the same physical cable.

Broadband transmission, although more versatile, normally costs more for the connection equipment. Additionally, each channel on a broadband line can only transmit in one direction. For bidirectional communication (such as that needed in a LAN environment), a separate channel must be used for each direction of network traffic.

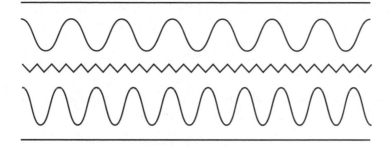

Figure 5.2
Several data channels occupy the same cable when using broadband transmission.

Key Concept

A full discussion of electronic signaling is beyond the realm of discussion in this book and could easily be another book in and of itself. Just remember that *base-band* communication uses digital technology and is used by most LANs. *Broadband* technology uses analog information to allow multiple uses of a single cable.

Regardless of the type of transmission you choose, you can use several types of physical media. Although there are literally thousands of different types of network cables, they can be broadly divided into three main categories:

- Twisted-pair
- Coaxial
- Fiber optic

Each of these media has its own advantages and disadvantages. Some are appropriate for certain networks, whereas others clearly are not.

Before I discuss the individual media types, there are a few terms you should understand:

- *Attenuation.* Sending signals across a medium requires energy. If you are driving in your car and listening to a radio station, you will begin to lose the station as you move farther away from the location of the transmitter. Eventually, the station will fade out entirely. Likewise in the networking world, energy is required to transmit data down a cable. As the signal travels down the cable, it weakens as part of the

CH
5

signal is absorbed by the media. This process, referred to as *attenuation,* imposes limits on the physical length of the cable. Media such as copper attenuate rapidly and can only be used for relatively short distances. Fiber-optic media, on the other hand, hardly suffer any attenuation at all and can be used to transmit information over large distances.

■ *Bandwidth.* In network media, the *bandwidth* of a connection refers to the number of bits that can be sent across the cable at any given time. It is usually measured in *megabits-per-second (Mbps),* where 1Mbps means that one million bits would be transmitted each second. Most ethernet networks operate with a transmission speed of around 10Mbps, although many newer ethernet networks now operate around 100Mbps. Token Ring networks operate typically at either 4Mbps or 16Mbps. Fiber-optic networks are so fast that they've introduced the term *gigabits-per-second (Gbps),* or billions of bits per second. Some fiber-optic connections can operate at a speed of 2–200Gbps.

■ *Impedance.* Impedance is the resistance of a wire to the transmission of an electric signal. The higher the impedance, the greater the energy needed to transmit a signal through the wire. Impedance is measured in ohms.

■ *Interference* (also known as *electromagnetic interference* or *EMI*). If you have traveled along a highway and heard your radio station fading out when you drove underneath some power lines, you have experienced interference. As an electric signal travels down a wire, some of its energy is absorbed by the wire itself and some of that energy radiates out from the wire. This radiating energy, also called *noise,* can interfere with the signals of other wires and devices. Likewise, the signal from other nearby devices or wires can interfere with the electric signal in a wire. Too much interference can cause the signal in a wire to degrade to the point where it is no longer recognizable.

A specific type of interference known as *crosstalk* occurs when two wires are placed next to each other inside a cable. In this instance, the noise from each line can ruin the signal in the other line.

Interference can also be a corporate security issue. The energy radiating from a cable not only can interfere with other devices, but it can also be intercepted by someone trying to eavesdrop on your transmissions. If security is of utmost importance, a fiber-optic medium that is not susceptible to EMI might be the best choice for your network.

■ *Plenum.* In most modern office buildings, there is a false ceiling, above which many of the cables (electrical, phone, and network) needed for office work are run. This space, called the *plenum,* is also used to circulate air throughout the building.

In the case of fire, the type of cable in this airspace is of crucial importance. Most cables have a very inexpensive and flexible outer layer of *polyvinyl chloride (PVC)*. The problem with PVC is that when it burns it gives off extremely noxious and deadly gases, which could easily spread throughout a building through the plenum. For this reason, almost all fire codes require the use of *plenum cabling* in false ceilings and other spaces tied to air circulation. Plenum cables are more resistant to fire and do not produce as many fumes. However, the drawback is that they are more expensive to install.

■ *Shielding.* To minimize interference to an electrical signal in a cable, some type of *shielding* is wrapped around the cable. It might take the form of foil or woven steel mesh. Although shielding reduces the interference to a cable, it increases the cost of the cable and decreases the flexibility, thereby making it harder to install.

Now that you've reviewed cabling terminology, you're ready to proceed to discussing the media categories.

Twisted-Pair Cable

Have you ever bought an extension cable for your telephone? If so, you were probably using a twisted-pair cable. Ultimately, the bulk of networks today are run on cables that resemble our regular phone lines.

Inside a twisted-pair cable, you will find multiple pairs of copper wire, as depicted in Figure 5.3. Each individual wire is wrapped in its own color-coded plastic insulation. If the wires were just placed inside the cable parallel to each other, the *crosstalk* between the wires would degrade the signal so much that the wire would be useless. Instead, the wires are twisted around each other. This twisting action has the effect of canceling out the interference of one wire by the other. Twisted-pair cables are available in two variations: unshielded and shielded.

CH
5

Insulation

Copper wire
conductor

Figure 5.3
A twisted-pair cable consists of two copper wires wrapped around each other.

Unshielded Twisted-Pair

Unshielded twisted-pair, commonly known as *UTP*, is probably the most used network medium in today's office environment. UTP is inexpensive, very flexible, and very easy to install and maintain. Because UTP is also used for telephone installations, the equipment configured for use with UTP is very readily available.

As depicted in Figure 5.4, UTP used for traditional home telephone systems contains four wires (two pairs) and has connections on either end using *RJ-11* connectors. This type of UTP is generally not used in computer networking. Instead, most networks use UTP with eight wires (four pairs) and a slightly larger *RJ-45* connector on each end.

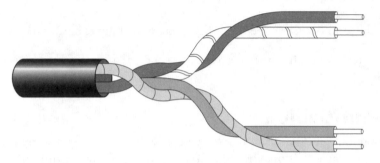

Figure 5.4
Unshielded twisted-pair cable can consist of two or more pairs of twisted copper wire.

UTP cables are usually connected directly from the network interface card on a computer to a jack in the wall. From there, UTP cable runs to a *patch panel*, where additional *patch cords* connect the signal into a *hub* or other similar device.

UTP cables are broken into categories by a standard produced by the Telecommunications Industries Association and the Electronics Industries Association (TIA/EIA). The TIA/EIA 568 Commercial Building Wiring Standard specifies information such as the data transmission speed and the number of twists per foot. Table 5.1 lists the categories of UTP commonly available.

Table 5.1   TIA/EIA568 UTP Cable Categories

Category	Data Transmission Speed	Notes
1	None	Primarily used in older telephone systems.
2	4Mbps	
3	10Mbps	The minimum required for data networks.
4	16Mbps	
5	100Mbps	Most new installations go directly for Cat 5.

 Key Concept

When taking the exam, remember that Category 3 UTP is the *minimum* required for most networks.

Note that as mentioned previously, UTP is used for telephone installations. However, this does not necessarily mean that if you have extra jacks on your existing phone system, you can simply use them for data communication. Voice communication does not have as rigorous quality demands as data communication. Before you use any existing wiring, make sure to have it tested for data communication use.

Unshielded twisted-pair cable provides an easy and inexpensive medium for networks. The major downfall is that it is highly susceptible to interference and attenuation, which means that the distance you can cover with a UTP cable is severely limited.

To aid in your exam preparation, Table 5.2 provides a summary of the characteristics of UTP cable.

Table 5.2   Summary of Information for UTP

Topic	Characteristics
Maximum cable length	100 meters (328 feet).
Transmission speed	Usually 10Mbps, can be 4–100Mbps.
Installation/maintenance	Easy to install and maintain. Very flexible. Components readily available.
Interference	Highly susceptible to interference.
Cost	Least expensive of all media.

CH
5

Shielded Twisted-Pair

Shielded twisted-pair cable (STP) differs from UTP primarily in that it contains shielding inside the cable, as shown in Figure 5.5. This shielding generally involves a woven mesh (often copper) between the wires and the plastic casing, but it might also include a foil wrap around the individual pairs. Normally, the woven mesh is grounded electrically, which further reduces the amount of interference coming in or out of the wire. Because of this need for electrical grounding, most STP cables require special connectors.

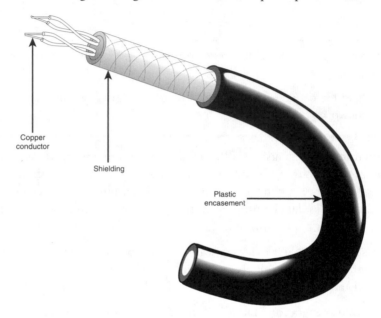

Figure 5.5
Shielded twisted-pair cable includes a layer of shielding around the central twisted-pair wires.

Examples of networks using STP include IBM's Token Ring and Apple's AppleTalk. Both types of networks have distinct specifications for the cables used.

Although STP provides a more reliable network cable than UTP, it suffers the same attenuation effects as UTP and generally can't be used for distances over 100 meters. STP is also more expensive and, because of its rigidity and special connectors, can be more difficult to install.

To aid in your exam preparation, Table 5.3 provides a summary of the characteristics of STP cable.

Table 5.3 Summary of Information for STP	
Topic	Characteristics
Maximum cable length	100 meters (328 feet) (identical to UTP).
Transmission speed	Usually 16Mbps, can be up to 155Mbps.
Installation/maintenance	Moderately easy, although cables can require special connectors. The cable is also generally quite rigid.
Interference	Resistant to interference.
Cost	More expensive than UTP or thinnet, but less than thicknet or fiber-optic.

Coaxial Cable

Early networks began with coaxial cable, commonly known as *coax*. Relatively inexpensive and easy to install, coax was the predominant cable used in computer networks until UTP became readily available. Today, coax can still be found in many computer networks.

As depicted in Figure 5.6, coaxial cable essentially consists of two conductors separated by a layer of insulation. The central core is normally either a solid copper wire or several strands of copper twisted together. Wrapped around the core is usually plastic foam insulation followed by a second conductor in the form of a woven metal mesh or foil. An outer casing, most often of plastic, encloses the entire cable.

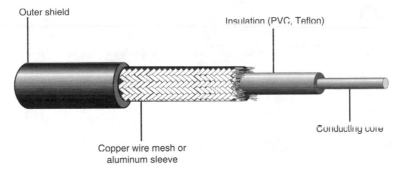

Figure 5.6
Coaxial cable consists of two conductors separated by a layer of insulation.

CH
5

The actual data is transmitted through the central core. The outer conductor is electrically grounded and provides shielding from interference and crosstalk. Because of this shielding, coaxial cable is a good choice for environments with heavy electrical interference.

Additionally, because the core wire of coaxial cable is thicker than that of twisted-pair, the electrical signal does not attenuate as much, which means that data can be carried over longer distances. Whereas twisted-pair is limited to cable lengths of 100 meters, coaxial cables can have maximum lengths of 185–500 meters.

There are two types of coaxial cable available:

- Thinnet
- Thicknet

Thinnet

Outside of UTP, thinnet is probably the most widely used network medium. Very lightweight and flexible, thinnet can be easily used to rapidly set up a network. In many ethernet configurations, thinnet is simply strung directly from computer to computer in a bus topology, without the need for a hub or other similar device. Thinnet cables generally use a *BNC (British Naval Connector)* connector on each end, as shown in Figure 5.7.

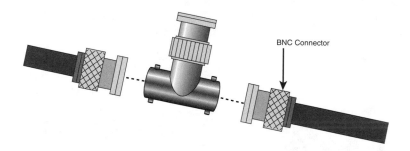

Figure 5.7
Thinnet cables usually have a BNC connector on each end.

Thinnet cables are classified as part of the *RG-58* family of cables. This classification, outlined in Table 5.4, was developed by cable manufacturers and specifies the thickness of the cable and the cable's *impedance,* or resistance to current.

Table 5.4   Common Coaxial Cables

Cable	Description
RG-58 /U	50 ohm, solid copper core
RG-58 A/U	50 ohm, stranded wire core
RG-58 C/U	Military specification of RG-58 A/U
RG-59	75 ohm, broadband transmission such as cable TV
RG-62	93 ohm, used primarily in ArcNet

When purchasing network cables, pay close attention to the difference between RG-58 and RG-59 cables. Although they look quite similar, their behavior is quite different.

Key Concept

When taking the exam, remember that only RG-58 is used for thinnet within network LANs. Furthermore, you will learn in Chapter 8, "Network Architecture," that only RG-58A/U and RG-58C/U are part of the IEEE specification for ethernet networks. Exam questions have been known to ask about thinnet cable types.

To aid in your exam preparation, Table 5.5 provides a summary of the characteristics of thinnet coaxial cable.

Table 5.5   Summary of Information for Thinnet Coaxial Cable

Topic	Characteristics
Maximum cable length	185 meters (607 feet)
Transmission speed	10Mbps.
Installation/maintenance	Easy to install. Very flexible.
Interference	Resistant to interference.
Cost	Inexpensive.

CH
5

Thicknet

Thicknet originated in the early days of the ethernet network architecture. Consisting of a half-inch rigid cable, its thick central core allows it to carry signals over distances as long as 500 meters (about 1,640 feet). Although still available, it is not commonly used due to its rigidity and expense.

Unlike the other media discussed, thicknet cables (of type *RG-11* or *RG-8*) do not connect from computer to computer. Instead, a thicknet cable would run throughout an office. Wherever a connection is needed, a *transceiver* with a *vampire tap* (also called a *piercing tap*) is attached to the cable as shown in Figure 5.8. Approximately 100 connections can be made to a single thicknet cable in this fashion.

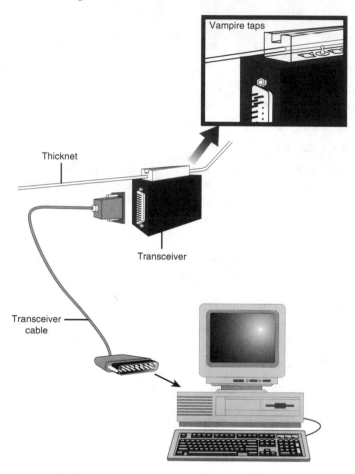

Figure 5.8

In a network using thicknet media, computers connect to the thicknet backbone using a vampire tap and drop cable.

The vampire tap actually pierces the cable insulation and makes direct contact with the central core. A *drop cable* then connects the transceiver to the *attachment unit interface (AUI)* port on the computer's network interface card. The AUI port is a 15-pin connector, also referred to as a *DB-15* connector.

Note that although thicknet cabling might not be used as much anymore, you will still find AUI ports on many network interface cards. You will also find this connection port referred to as a *DIX port*, after its inventors: Digital Equipment Corporation, Intel, and Xerox.

As mentioned previously, thicknet is no longer commonly used in LANs, but in very rare cases, you might find thicknet still serving as a backbone linking several thinnet networks.

To aid in your exam preparation, Table 5.6 provides a summary of the characteristics of thicknet coaxial cable.

Table 5.6   Summary of Information for Thicknet Coaxial Cable

Topic	Characteristics
Maximum cable length	500 meters (1,640 feet).
Transmission speed	10Mbps.
Installation/maintenance	Rigid structure makes it difficult to install in tight spaces.
Interference	Resistant to interference.
Cost	More expensive than all other media except fiber-optic cable.

Fiber-Optic Cable

In contrast to the other cable types discussed, data on a fiber-optic cable is transmitted in the form of light rather than electrical signals. For this reason, fiber-optic cables are not susceptible at all to the electromagnetic interference that degrades copper wires. Likewise, because fiber-optic cables do not generate any electromagnetic interference themselves, it is virtually impossible for an outsider to eavesdrop and listen to the signal on the cable. Although fiber-optic cables are highly secure and extremely fast, they are also very expensive.

Fiber-optic cables are constructed with a central fiber of glass, surrounded by a layer of glass called *cladding* and a protective outer casing of plastic, as shown in Figure 5.9. As light travels down the fiber, it wants to travel in all directions. The purpose of the cladding is to reflect the light back into the central fiber.

CH
5

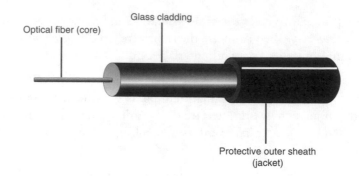

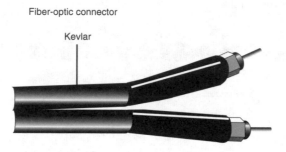

Figure 5.9
In a fiber-optic cable, a central glass core is wrapped in another layer of glass called cladding.

Do realize that although the core of a fiber-optic cable is usually glass, it is possible to reduce the expense of the cable by using a plastic fiber. However, a plastic core cannot transmit data as far as a glass core.

Because each fiber can only transmit light in one direction, fiber-optic cables normally consist of two fibers, each with its own cladding and protective jacket. One fiber sends data from the computer to the network. The other receives data sent from the network to the computer.

Installation of fiber-optic networks can be quite difficult due to the need to align cables exactly and the extremely rigid nature of the cables.

To aid in your exam preparation, Table 5.7 provides a summary of the characteristics of fiber-optic cable.

Table 5.7   Summary of Information for Fiber-Optic Cable

Topic	Characteristics
Maximum cable length	2 kilometers (6,562 feet).
Transmission speed	Usually 100Mbps, although speeds have been demonstrated up to 2Gbps.
Installation/maintenance	Difficult.
Interference	Not subject at all to electromagnetic interference.
Cost	Most expensive of all cable media.

Choosing the Right Cable

With so many options, choosing the correct cable can be difficult. Some questions to consider include the following:

- What type of cost constraints are you under?
- How many computers will you be connecting?
- How long do your cables need to be?
- What level of network traffic do you expect to have?
- How concerned are you about the security of your network?
- What type of installation issues (tight spaces and so on) will you be facing?
- How fast do you want your network to be?

In a world where cost isn't an issue and everyone's computer and office is easy to wire, fiber-optic cables certainly provide the highest level of speed and security. However, such worlds are few and far between.

If you are looking for an inexpensive, easy, and quick network, a solution using UTP and a hub or thinnet alone will get you rapidly connected.

A common configuration in today's office environment is to find UTP used throughout an office LAN. It is also typical to find fiber-optic cables operating as backbones connecting these UTP office LANs into a wide area network.

To aid in your exam preparation, Table 5.8 summarizes the characteristics of the physical network media described in this chapter.

CH

5

Table 5.8   Comparison of Different Network Media

Medium	Maximum Cable Length	Transmission Speed	Install-ation	Inter-ference	Cost
UTP	100 meters (328 feet)	10–100Mbps	Easy	High	Least expensive
STP	100 meters (328 feet)	16–155Mbps	Moderately easy	Low	Moderate
Thinnet	185 meters (607 feet)	10Mbps	Easy	Low	In expensive
Thicknet	500 meters (1,640 feet)	10Mbps	Difficult	Low	High
Fiber-optic	2 kilometers (6,562 feet)	100Mbps–2Gbps	Difficult	None	Most expensive

Key Concept

For the exam, pay especially careful attention to the distances over which data can be transmitted: UTP—100 meters, thinnet—185 meters, thicknet—500 meters, and fiber-optic—2 kilometers. You will certainly be tested on the other factors in cable selection, but distance is one means by which you can easily rule out which cables can *not* be used in a given scenario.

Summary

At the physical layer of the OSI Reference Model, the physical media are involved with the actual transmission of data between computers. This data is encoded into either a digital signal (*baseband* transmission) or an analog signal (*broadband* transmission) and sent across the network media.

Most cables are subject to some type of *attenuation*, where the signal degrades as it travels farther down the cable. This attenuation is affected by the *impedance*, or resistance, of the cable. Cables generate *interference*, which can disrupt other nearby cables or devices. A special type of interference called *crosstalk* occurs when two cables are placed in very close proximity to each other. To minimize interference, some cable types use a layer of *shielding*.

Network media are broadly classified in three categories: twisted-pair, coaxial, and fiber-optic.

Twisted-pair cables consist of several pairs of copper wire bound together. In each pair, the individual wires are twisted together in such a way that crosstalk is reduced. Twisted-pair cables are available in two varieties: unshielded and shielded.

Unshielded twisted-pair, commonly known as UTP, is the most widespread and easiest cable medium to use. Also used for telephone systems, UTP is very flexible, and its components are readily available. UTP is classified into five categories, with Category 3 being the minimum necessary for computer networking and Category 5 allowing the highest speed of data transmission. UTP is highly susceptible to interference and attenuation and has a maximum cable length of 100 meters.

Shielded twisted-pair, or STP, includes a layer of woven mesh shielding that reduces interference and allows a slightly higher transmission speed than UTP. STP is not as flexible and easy to install as UTP, but it does have the same cable-length restriction of 100 meters. IBM's Token Ring and Apple's AppleTalk networks are examples of STP.

Coaxial cable, or coax, consists of an inner core that transmits the data and an outer layer of electrically conductive shielding to reduce interference. With a thicker core than twisted-pair, coaxial cable is less subject to attenuation and can transmit data over longer distances. Coaxial cable has two types: thinnet and thicknet.

Like UTP, thinnet is easy to install and relatively inexpensive. It transmits data at 10Mbps and has a maximum length of 185 meters. Connection to thinnet cables is primarily through the use of BNC connectors.

Thicknet was the original cable used in ethernet networks and has a thicker core that allows it to transmit data up to 500 meters. When connecting to a thicknet cable, you use a vampire tap to actually pierce the cable and connect to the inner core.

Fiber-optic cables use light instead of electric signals to transmit data. Fiber-optic cables can carry data up to 2 kilometers and at extremely high speeds. This power comes at a price since fiber-optic cables are the most expensive type of cable and are more difficult to install than other media.

Finally, with all cable types that you install in the ceiling or wall space, it is important that the cables be *plenum*-grade for fire protection. In all cases, you should check with local fire codes before installing cables.

CH
5

QUESTIONS AND ANSWERS

1. What is the difference between baseband and broadband transmission?

   A: In *baseband* transmission, the entire bandwidth of the cable is consumed by a single signal. In *broadband* transmission, signals are sent on multiple frequencies, allowing multiple signals to be sent simultaneously. Because of its relative simplicity, baseband transmission equipment is significantly cheaper. Almost all LANs use baseband. Cable modems typically use broadband.

2. What are the three main categories of cable?

   A: Twisted-pair, coaxial, and fiber-optic.

3. Why and where do you use plenum cable?

   A: The *plenum* is the air space above a false ceiling in most modern office buildings that is used as an air return for the heating/cooling system. Plenum cable is used here because it is more fire-resistant and does not emit as many noxious fumes in a fire, which would be spread throughout the building by the heating/cooling system.

4. True or false. Category 5 UTP is the minimum required cable for 10Mbps ethernet networks.

   A: False. Category 3 is the minimum for 10Mbps ethernet.

5. Explain why you might want to use shielded cable.

   A: Shielding makes a cable more resistant to electrical interference. For example, you might use shielded cable in an environment where cables need to be run near large electrical motors.

6. Compare the distance that can be covered between UTP and thinnet coaxial cable.

   A: UTP can go a maximum of 100 meters, whereas thinnet can go 185 meters.

7. How is a node connected to a thicknet cable?

   A: With a transceiver that has a vampire tap (also called a "piercing tap").

8. When working with thicknet, what is the port called on the computer's NIC?

   A: An AUI port.

…continues

...*continued*

> **9.** Why is fiber-optic cable less susceptible to interference and eavesdropping?
>
> A: Because the signal is sent in a beam of light, it is not susceptible to external sources of electrical interference. Likewise, it generates no electrical signal itself that could be picked up by someone trying to eavesdrop. The only way to intercept the signal would somehow be to get in the path of the light.
>
> **10.** Why do fiber-optic cables consist of two separate fiber-optic strands?
>
> A: Because unlike electrical signals, a beam of light travels only in one direction. Therefore, two fiber-optic cables are necessary to have bidirectional communication.

PRACTICE TEST

1. You want to connect the networks in two different office buildings. The buildings are located 600 meters apart. What type of cable should you use?

- **a.** Thicknet coaxial
- **b.** Category 5 UTP
- **c.** Fiber-optic
- **d.** Shielded twisted-pair

Answer a is incorrect because thicknet can only go 500 meters. Answer b is incorrect because UTP can only go 100 meters. **Answer c is correct because fiber-optic cable can go up to 2 kilometers.** Answer d is incorrect because STP has generally the same constraints as UTP and can typically go no farther than 100 meters.

2. When the development company constructed your office building, it installed a sophisticated telephone system with extra jacks at every desk. You would like to use these extra jacks for your network. The building manager believes the system used UTP and would support data. What should you do?

- **a.** Do nothing. The UTP wires will support your network.
- **b.** Install transceivers in all jacks to convert the cables to Category 5 UTP.
- **c.** Arrange to have someone test the data transmission capability of the lines.

Answer a is incorrect because you don't know for certain that the cables are Category 5 UTP. Answer b is incorrect because this simply can't be done. **Answer c is correct; you need to test the cables before you start using them for data.**

CH
5

3. As your company's network has grown rapidly in size, users have begun complaining about the network's slow speed. Your network is currently operating at 10Mbps. You would like to upgrade it to 100Mbps. Which media could you use? (Choose all that apply.)

   a. Thicknet

   b. Category 5 UTP

   c. Fiber-optic

   d. Thinnet

Answer a is incorrect because thicknet can only support 10Mbps. **Answer b is correct as Category 5 UTP can support 100Mbps. Answer c is correct because fiber-optic can support 100Mbps.** Answer d is incorrect because thinnet can only support 10Mbps.

4. When two wires are placed side by side, the electrical noise from each wire will interfere with the signal of the other wire. What is this called?

   a. Attenuation

   b. Plenum

   c. Crosstalk

   d. Impedance

Answer a is incorrect because attenuation is the decay of a signal over distance. Answer b is incorrect because the plenum is the air space above a false ceiling. **Answer c is correct; crosstalk is the interference between two wires adjacent to each other.** Answer d is incorrect because impedance is essentially the resistance in a cable to an electrical signal.

5. The transformation of data into electrical impulses occurs at what layer of the OSI Reference Model?

   a. Data Link

   b. Network

   c. Physical

   d. Logical Link Control

Answer a is incorrect. Answer b is incorrect. **Answer c is correct.** Answer d is incorrect.

6. You have two separate office buildings, each with its own LAN operating at 10Mbps. The two buildings are located 125 meters apart. To connect the two LANs, you will need to dig a conduit and run cable under the parking lot. Your cost-conscious boss wants to use thinnet, but you would like to use fiber-optic cable instead. What would be the major reason for using the fiber-optic cable?

    a. Fiber-optic cable is easier to install and will link your networks in a much shorter time.

    b. Thinnet cable can only have a maximum length of 100 meters, and, therefore, it will not reach between the two offices.

    c. Fiber-optic cable will give you plenty of room for growth so that as your offices start to communicate more, you will not need to run more cables through the conduit.

    d. Thinnet cable cannot be used to connect two different LANs.

Answer a is incorrect because fiber-optic cable is in fact harder to install than thinnet. Answer b is incorrect because thinnet can actually go 185 meters. **Answer c is correct because fiber-optic cable provides much more capacity and also allows you to grow to using 100Mbps.** Answer d is just plain wrong.

  7. Your organization is moving to a new location where offices will be spread throughout a campus consisting of four office buildings. You are in charge of installing the computer network and linking all four buildings. The maximum distance between the buildings is 50 meters. Your company is remodeling the entire interior, so you will have plenty of space for cable.

    REQUIRED RESULT: The network must be capable of operating at speeds up to 100Mbps.

    OPTIONAL DESIRED RESULTS: You would like the network to be as secure as possible from electronic eavesdropping. You would like the network to be as inexpensive as possible.

    SOLUTION: Your IS department has suggested using fiber-optic cable to link all four buildings. Which results does the proposed solution produce?

    a. The proposed solution produces the required result and both of the optional desired results.

    b. The proposed solution produces the required result and only *one* of the optional desired results.

    c. The proposed solution produces the required result but does *not* produce any of the optional desired results.

    d. The proposed solution does *not* produce the required result.

Answer a is incorrect. **Answer b is correct.** Fiber-optic cable achieves the required result of being able to function at 100Mbps and achieves one of the optional required results regarding protection from eavesdropping. However, it fails the second required result of being as inexpensive as possible due to the fact that Cat 5 UTP could also meet the required result and would be substantially cheaper. Answer c is incorrect. Answer d is incorrect.

CH
5

8. You have two computers at home and would like to link them as inexpensively as possible. You purchase network cards and now need to choose the appropriate medium. Which of the following would be an appropriate choice? (Choose all that apply.)

    a. Thinnet

    b. STP

    c. Thicknet

    d. RG-59

Answer a is correct because thinnet could do this inexpensively. Answer b and c are incorrect because of the high expense of the associated networking equipment. Answer d is incorrect because RG-59 is not used for data networking (it's for cable TV).

9. The insurance agency for which you work has decided to install a new network that will link the computers of all the agents throughout the office. Because the company will be using some client/server database applications and expects to make heavy use of messaging and groupware products, you are very concerned about the speed of the network.

    REQUIRED RESULT: The network must be capable of operating at speeds up to 100Mbps.

    OPTIONAL DESIRED RESULTS: You would like the cabling to be as inexpensive as possible. Additionally, it must be easy to install.

    PROPOSED SOLUTION: You propose using Category 3 UTP and hubs to link all the cubicles. Which results does the proposed solution produce?

    a. The proposed solution produces the required result and both of the optional desired results.

    b. The proposed solution produces the required result and only *one* of the optional desired results.

    c. The proposed solution produces the required result but does *not* produce any of the optional desired results.

    d. The proposed solution does *not* produce the required result.

Answers a, b and c are incorrect. **Answer d is correct because Category 3 UTP fails to meet the required result of operating at 100Mbps because it can only operate at 10Mbps. (Note that it *does* meet all the optional results.)**

10. Whenever you want to connect a computer to a thicknet cable, a _____ is attached to the cable.

    a. Vampire cable

    b. Cladding

    c. Transceiver

    d. Attachment Unit Interface

Answer a is incorrect because there is no such thing. Answer b is incorrect because it's the layer inside of a fiber-optic cable. **Answer c is correct; a transceiver (which includes a vampire tap) is attached to a thicknet cable.** Answer d is incorrect because the AUI port is on the computer's NIC.

Wireless Connections

— WHILE YOU READ

1. What are the different categories of wireless transmission?

2. What are three types of radio communication used in LANs?

3. How does spread-spectrum transmission differ from other radio
    transmission methods?

4. Explain how frequency-hopping works?

5. What is the main limitation of microwave links?

6. What are two types of infrared communication?

7. What is a wireless bridge?

The Lure of Wireless Media

Imagine that you are a salesperson who works most of the time from a laptop computer. Whenever you go into the office, you would like to just go in, sit down, and start sharing data from the network. You don't want to have to mess around with any cables. You just want to start communicating. Beyond the office, you would like to remain in contact with your network as you travel throughout your sales region in your car.

Or suppose that your organization has grown to the point where you cannot possibly fit any more people into your current building. There is a beautiful building where you would like to rent some space located directly across the highway. However, you would need to connect the two buildings with a computer network, and there is no possible way you could run a cable under the highway.

Or imagine that you are the primary technical support person for your company. Because of some current high-profile projects, your management wants you to be immediately available should something go wrong with the programs. You have a laptop and can dial in from home to troubleshoot problems. But you wish there was some way that you could use email to access the network from other locations such as the beach, your boat, or a remote cabin in the mountains.

Breaking the physical connection has long been a dream of many a network designer. Today, the technology exists to make that dream a reality. Wireless media can now provide the capability for providing remote network connections and also for connecting networks over large distances.

Wireless media falls broadly into three categories:

- Radio
- Microwave
- Infrared

Each will be explained in detail in the following sections, but first you should be sure you understand the electromagnetic spectrum.

The Electromagnetic Spectrum

All transmission of energy takes place in the form of waves in the *electromagnetic (EM) spectrum*. As shown in Figure 6.1, the electromagnetic spectrum ranges from electrical power and telephone at the low end to X-rays and gamma rays at the high end. *Electromagnetic frequency* is the number of wave cycles per second and is measured primarily in terms of *hertz (Hz)*. When electromagnetic frequencies enter the range of light, the unit of measurement becomes the *hertz volt (ev)*.

Please note that for the exam, you will not need to memorize the electromagnetic spectrum. It is shown in Figure 6.1 to provide a framework for discussion of wireless media.

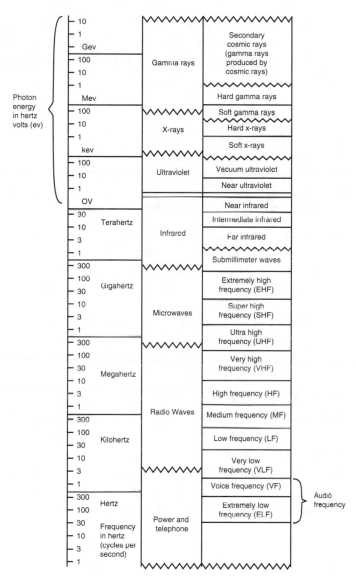

Figure 6.1

The electromagnetic spectrum defines frequencies from power and voice to x-rays and gamma rays.

You are probably most familiar with this type of measurement from the dial on your car radio. AM radio stations operate in the frequency range of 530–1,600 kilohertz (1KHz = 1,000Hz), whereas FM radio stations use 88–108 megahertz (1MHz = 1,000,000Hz). Additionally, if you look at almost any home electrical product or appliance, you will usually find that it is designed to operate at 60Hz, the frequency of most electrical power in the United States. Lastly, you can generally hear sounds between 30Hz and 20KHz.

The frequency of the transmission medium affects both the amount of data that can be transmitted and the speed at which the transmission occurs. Low frequencies can travel for very long distances and through many obstructions, but the amount of data that can be sent is very limited. You have probably noticed that you sometimes can receive AM radio stations from other parts of the country. Likewise, short-wave (ham) radio operators routinely communicate with other users on the other side of the world. Another example is the use by military organizations of Very Low Frequency (VLF) radio signals to communicate with submarines located deep in the ocean.

As the frequency of a signal increases, the amount of data that can be transmitted also increases. The sound quality of an FM station is much better than that of an AM station. However, that quality comes at the price of the distance the signal can travel. Although you can tune in an AM station over long distances, you can usually only tune in an FM radio station while you are in the vicinity of the station's transmission tower. After that tower disappears beyond the horizon, you rapidly lose the signal. As the frequency continues to increase and you begin using microwave sources or laser communication, you can send a large amount of data, but you are restricted to *line-of-sight* communication (meaning that your transmitter and receiver are within sight of each other).

As important as it is, frequency is not the only factor affecting the speed and quality of transmission. The power of the transmission source also plays a large role. A radio station with transmitters broadcasting at 100,000 watts will be received over a much larger area than a station transmitting at 25,000 watts.

Most computers transmitting over a cable LAN operate at the low end of the spectrum, using either simple electrical signals or radio frequency (RF) signals. Fiber-optic cables operate at the other end of the spectrum, using the high frequencies of infrared or visible light.

Radio

The *radio frequency (RF)* portion of the electromagnetic spectrum occupies the range of frequencies from 10KHz to 1 gigahertz (GHz). This range is broken into numerous *bands* of frequencies designated for specific purposes. Both AM and FM radio are examples, as well as television signals in the VHF (normally, TV channels 2–13) and *Ultra High Frequency (UHF)* bands.

The use of almost all radio frequencies is regulated by government agencies. In the United States, this responsibility is assigned to the *Federal Communications Commission (FCC)*. The FCC licenses organizations to use specific frequencies and also specifies regulations for the equipment used in the process of communication. Although obtaining a license can be a difficult and time-consuming process, when obtained, it virtually guarantees you a clear communications channel.

However, because many organizations do not want to pursue licensing a frequency, the FCC does make several frequencies available for unregulated use. They are the following:

- 902–928MHz
- 2.4GHz
- 5.72–5.85GHz

If you have ever used a cordless phone or remote control toy, it was probably operating in the 902–928MHz range. Because that frequency range has been available for quite some time and is now used by many devices, the 2.4GHz range is becoming increasingly used. Because the cost of equipment also increases with higher frequencies, the 5.72GHz range is seldom used at this time.

Using radio frequencies within a computer network to transmit data requires that each device must have both an *antenna* and a *transceiver*. Depending on the distance and frequencies being used, the antenna might resemble that on a typical radio, cellular phone, or TV set. The transceiver is a device that can both transmit and receive data.

Radio communication used by computer LANs fall into three categories:

- Low-power, single-frequency
- High-power, single-frequency
- Spread-spectrum

These different categories will be discussed in the following sections.

Low-Power, Single-Frequency

In this scenario, both the transmitter and receiver are effectively tuned in to the same frequency through which all data communication occurs. The low power of these systems usually means that the signal attenuates rapidly and can only be used in a confined area. Depending on the frequency used, walls and other obstructions can block these signals and prohibit communication. Interference from other devices can easily occur, especially in the heavily used 902MHz range. LANs based on these technologies are also highly susceptible to eavesdropping, although the low power limits the range at which someone could pick up the signal.

CH
6

To aid in your exam preparation, Table 6.1 provides a summary of the characteristics of low-power, single-frequency radio networks.

Table 6.1 Summary of Information for Low-Power, Single-Frequency Radio Networks	
Topic	*Characteristics*
Frequencies	All possible, but generally low GHz.
Maximum distance	10s of meters.
Transmission speed	Can be 1–10Mbps.
Installation/maintenance	Relatively easy to install.
Interference	Highly susceptible to interference.
Cost	Moderate.
Security	Highly susceptible to eavesdropping, although due to low power, the signal is generally limited to the immediate building.

High-Power, Single-Frequency

As the name implies, these networks operate at a higher power that can transmit over a larger area. Typically, networks of this type might transmit as far as the horizon or over the horizon through the use of repeaters and/or bouncing the signal off the atmosphere. Although this can be quite suitable for communication with mobile users, it comes at a price. High-power, single-frequency networks generally require more expensive transmission equipment, especially with antennas and repeaters, and also require FCC licensing for communication. Operators of the equipment must be FCC-licensed and must maintain all equipment in accordance with FCC regulations.

Security is also a strong concern in this type of network. With the signal being broadcast over a large area, it could conceivably be intercepted by others wanting to eavesdrop on your network.

To aid in your exam preparation, Table 6.2 provides a summary of the characteristics of high-power, single-frequency radio networks.

Table 6.2   Summary of Information for High-Power, Single-Frequency Radio Networks

Topic	Characteristics
Frequencies	All possible, but generally low GHz.
Maximum distance	A function of power and frequency of transmitters. Can be line-of-sight or over the horizon.
Transmission speed	Can be 1–10Mbps.
Installation/maintenance	Difficult. Requires licensing.
Interference	Highly susceptible to interference.
Cost	Moderate to very expensive.
Security	Highly susceptible to eavesdropping, especially as the signal is broadcast over a large area.

Spread-Spectrum

Spread-spectrum communication was developed to address the many downsides to single-frequency communication (both high- and low-power). Instead of using just one frequency, spread-spectrum networks use several frequencies simultaneously. This improves reliability and increases resistance to interference. Although the use of multiple frequencies makes eavesdropping difficult, security can be tightened even further by encrypting the data communication.

There are two main types of spread-spectrum transmissions:

- Direct-sequence modulation
- Frequency-hopping

Direct-sequence modulation breaks data into parts (called *chips*) and transmits that data on several different frequencies (see Figure 6.2). The receiving station knows what frequencies to monitor and reassembles the arriving chips into packets of data. Security can be tightened by transmitting decoy data along with the real data and by transmitting fake data on other decoy frequencies. The receiving station knows which frequencies are valid and how to determine which chips are valid. Someone wanting to eavesdrop would need to find all the frequencies and would have to differentiate between the real and fake data.

Networks of this type typically operate in the unregulated frequencies and can achieve transmission speeds of up to 2–6Mbps.

CH
6

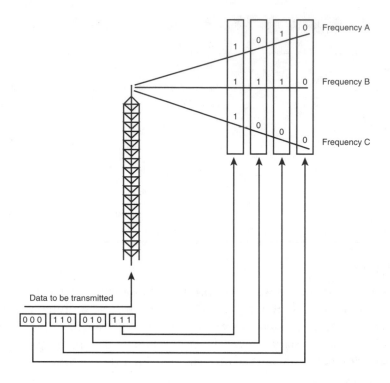

Figure 6.2
Direct-sequence modulation involves the simultaneous transmission of data over several frequencies.

Frequency-hopping, as shown in Figure 6.3, switches data between multiple frequencies. Both the transmitter and receiver are synchronized to use the same predetermined frequencies and time slots. Timing is crucial, and both sides must be exactly in sync for communication to occur. For this reason, it is difficult for an outsider to eavesdrop on this type of network. To do so, she would need to know the predetermined information.

Frequency-hopping networks do provide more security than direct-sequence modulation networks, but at the price of speed. Although they can achieve speeds of up to 2Mbps, frequency-hopping networks are generally limited to slower speeds.

Key Concept

Spread-spectrum radio systems transmit data on multiple frequencies and are more secure than single-frequency radio systems.

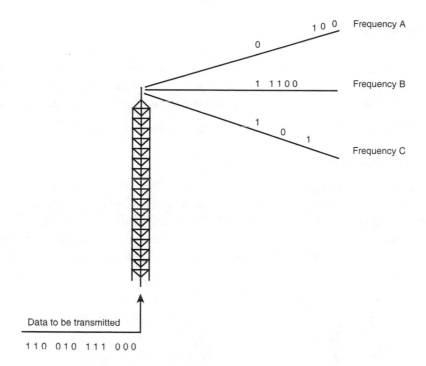

Figure 6.3
In frequency-hopping, data is transmitted on different frequencies using a predetermined schedule.

To aid in your exam preparation, Table 6.3 provides a summary of the characteristics of spread-spectrum radio networks.

Topic	Characteristics
Table 6.3 Spread-Spectrum Radio Networks	
Frequencies	Typically 902–928MHz. Some at 2.4GHz.
Maximum distance	Depends on power and frequency. Often limited, but can be over several miles.
Transmission speed	Direct-sequence 902MHz systems offer 2–6Mbps. GHz systems offer higher rates. Frequency-hopping typically lower (under 1Mbps).
Installation/maintenance	Depends on design. Can range from simple to complex.
Interference	Resistant to interference.
Cost	Relatively inexpensive.
Security	Highly resistant to eavesdropping.

CH
6

Microwave

Using the higher frequencies of the low gigahertz range, *microwave communication systems* can offer higher data transmission rates. However, to accomplish this, both the transmitter and receiver must be within sight of each other. Microwave communication usually requires use of a licensed frequency and therefore is more costly than radio systems.

There are two types of microwave communication: *terrestrial* and *satellite*.

Terrestrial Microwave

If while traveling along a highway you have noticed towers with conical satellite dishes, you have seen terrestrial microwave communication systems. These systems use a tightly focused high-frequency signal to link two sites. Each site must use a *directional parabolic antenna* and must be within the line of sight of the other antenna, as shown in Figure 6.4. *Relay towers* can be used to extend the signal across great distances.

Figure 6.4
Terrestrial microwave communication can occur between two buildings.

Terrestrial microwave systems are typically used to link networks over long distances where cables are not practical or are cost-prohibitive. Because of the line-of-sight requirement, finding suitable locations for relay towers can be quite problematic.

Installation of terrestrial microwave systems is moderately difficult, primarily due to the fact that the antennas must be carefully aligned to receive the signal. Additionally, the use of licensed frequencies imposes requirements on the equipment used and the personnel operating the equipment.

Low-power microwave systems can also be used in some small LAN environments. Each computer would have a small transmitter that would communicate with a microwave hub located in some high, centralized location such as a ceiling. For this to work, there still must be a line-of-sight between each transmitter and the hub.

Key Concept

Although terrestrial microwave systems allow communication over great distances, the sending and receiving stations must have a clear line-of-sight between them.

To aid in your exam preparation, Table 6.4 provides a summary of the characteristics of terrestrial microwave communication.

Table 6.4 Summary of Information for Terrestrial Microwave Communication

Topic	Characteristics
Frequencies	Typically 4–6GHz or 21–23GHz.
Maximum distance	Depends on power and frequency. Often limited, but can be over several miles.
Transmission speed	Depends on frequency, but often 1–10Mbps.
Installation/maintenance	Moderately difficult.
Interference	Varies with power, antenna size, and frequency used. Over short distances, interference is usually not a problem. However, atmospheric conditions (rain, fog, and so on) can affect longer-distance or higher-frequency systems.
Cost	Moderate to high.
Security	Susceptible to eavesdropping. Signal usually encrypted.

CH 6

Satellite Microwave

Like terrestrial microwave systems, *satellite communication systems* use directional parabolic antennas and must be within the line of sight of the other antenna. The primary difference is that one antenna is on the ground and the other is orbiting on a *geosynchronous* satellite at 50,000 km (22,300 miles) above the earth. These satellites orbit at an altitude and speed where they stay fixed in the same position. This is the method used for transmitting television images from around the world.

For network communications, the signal from your LAN would be transmitted to a satellite and from there back to a specified region of the earth (see Figure 6.5). At the receiving end, another antenna would translate the signal from the satellite and transmit the data onto the LAN at the other site. If the two regions are close together, the transmission might be handled by one satellite. If you are transmitting to a location somewhere far away, the signal might be received by one satellite and then transmitted to another satellite for transmission back to the ground.

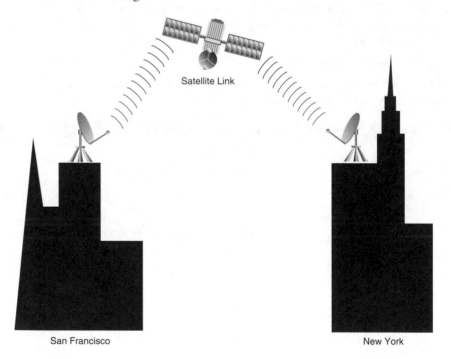

Satellite Link

San Francisco

New York

Figure 6.5
Satellite microwave communication provides communication over large distances.

Because of the large distance from the ground to the satellite and back, *propagation delays* of between 0.5 and 5 seconds are not uncommon. This is true regardless of whether you are transmitting to a nearby location or halfway across the globe.

Installing a satellite communication system to link two networks is a highly complex and involved process. Obviously, launching your own satellite is beyond the reach of all but the wealthiest organizations, but even leasing frequencies on existing satellites is extremely expensive. After frequencies have been obtained, the configuration of both the satellite and the ground stations is a highly technical matter best left to those trained in the subject.

As the signal transmitted from a satellite can cover a large geographic area, eavesdropping is relatively easy. For this reason, most satellite transmissions are encrypted in some manner.

To aid in your exam preparation, Table 6.5 provides a summary of the characteristics of satellite microwave communication.

Table 6.5   Satellite Microwave Communication

Topic	Characteristics
Frequencies	Typically 11–14GHz.
Maximum distance	Worldwide.
Transmission speed	Depends on frequency, but typically 1–10Mbps.
Installation/maintenance	Highly to extremely difficult.
Interference	Vulnerable to EM interference, jamming, and atmospheric conditions.
Cost	Very expensive.
Security	Highly susceptible to eavesdropping, but the signal is usually encrypted.

Infrared

Moving up the electromagnetic spectrum, *infrared (IR)* frequencies occupy the range from 100GHz–1,000THz (terahertz), just below the range of visible light. The technology used for wireless networking is very similar to the infrared technologies used for remote control units for television or stereo systems. Either a *light-emitting diode (LED)* or a laser is used as the light source to send a beam of light between the transmitter and receiver.

Infrared technologies operate at high frequencies that allow high data-transmission speeds. However, because they are close to visual light frequencies, they have many of the same transmission issues as regular light sources. Just as you cannot watch a TV through a wall, infrared signals cannot travel through walls or other large objects. When you have a bright light close to your TV, it can interfere with your ability to see the picture. Likewise, an infrared signal can be degraded by the presence of another light source.

You might wonder how this interference could occur without another specific infrared light source in the area. However, even normal incandescent lighting fixtures can interfere with infrared communications. This is due to the fact that normal light fixtures also emit infrared in addition to the visible light you see.

One advantage to infrared networks is that they are not susceptible to the types of electro-magnetic interference that plague other media types such as coaxial cable. Like fiber-optic cable, infrared systems can be used in environments with interference such as electrical motors or power lines.

Infrared communication technologies take two forms: *point-to-point* and *broadcast*.

Point-to-Point Infrared

Point-to-point infrared systems use a highly focused narrow beam of energy to connect two sites at high data-transmission speeds. Within a LAN environment, many laptop computers and *personal digital assistants (PDAs)* now have infrared ports for docking with desktop systems or other peripherals. Although the process requires precise alignment of the infrared ports on the laptop and docking unit, the procedure can alleviate the need to attach cables to plug in to the network. Infrared adapters can also be added to regular PCs as shown in Figure 6.6.

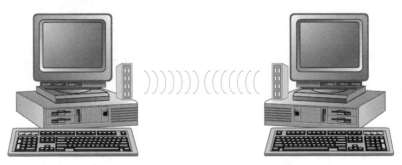

Figure 6.6
Point-to-point infrared communication provides communication between two computers in close proximity to each other.

Laser technologies operating in the infrared range have emerged as a viable alternative to terrestrial microwave systems. Where a line of sight is available, laser-based systems can link buildings over several thousand meters. Unlike terrestrial microwave systems, laser-based solutions do not require FCC licenses, and therefore can be easier to install and maintain than comparable microwave systems.

Regarding security, point-to-point infrared transmissions are quite difficult to intercept. The beam of energy is so tightly focused that someone would essentially need to interrupt the data stream to eavesdrop on communication. That interruption would be noticeable on the receiving end.

To aid in your exam preparation, Table 6.6 provides a summary of the characteristics of point-to-point infrared systems.

Table 6.6   Summary of Information for Point-to-Point Infrared Communication

Topic	Characteristics
Frequencies	100GHz–1,000THz.
Maximum distance	Limited to line of sight. Some laser technologies can send a signal over thousands of meters.
Transmission speed	100Kbps–16Mbps.
Installation/maintenance	Moderate. Requires precise alignment of transmitter and receiver.
Interference	Highly resistant to EM interference. Bright light sources can cause problems.
Cost	Ranges from inexpensive for LED technology to highly expensive for laser solutions.
Security	Very resistant to eavesdropping due to line-of-sight requirement and narrow focus of energy beam.

Broadcast Infrared

Broadcast infrared systems use some method of dispersing the signal so that multiple units can receive the transmission. In the example shown in Figure 6.7, transmitter units on each computer aim their signal in the general vicinity of the transceiver on the ceiling. This unit, sometimes called an *active transmitter*, amplifies the signal and retransmits it out over the entire area. An alternative method of providing this dispersion is to place reflective material on the ceiling that can bounce the infrared light from a transmitter back down to all other stations.

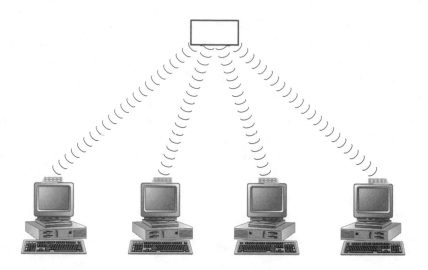

Figure 6.7
Broadcast infrared communication systems can replace the wiring of a LAN.

 Key Concept

Note that most television and stereo systems use this type of transmission. You can usually use the remote control unit from most positions within the room. Units with more power can bounce their signal off the walls or windows.

Systems using broadcast infrared are generally easy to install and configure because precise alignment is not required. The major disadvantage to these systems is their lack of data-transmission speed. Because they are not as narrowly focused as point-to-point systems, they usually cannot transmit at speeds of more than 1Mbps. Although this limits their usefulness in most network environments, they can be an attractive solution for situations where mobility is needed and data-transmission speed is not critical.

To aid in your exam preparation, Table 6.7 provides a summary of the characteristics of broadcast infrared communication.

Table 6.7   Summary of Information for Broadcast Infrared Communication

Topic	Characteristics
Frequencies	100GHz–1,000THz.
Maximum distance	10s of meters.
Transmission speed	Usually 1Mbps or less.
Installation/maintenance	Easy.
Interference	Resistant to EM interference, but bright light can interfere with signal.
Cost	Inexpensive, though more than a comparable network using cable.
Security	More susceptible than point-to-point due to wide broadcast area. However, broadcast IR networks are usually limited to a confined area.

Applications for Wireless Media

Although wireless networks are usually more expensive than comparable cable networks, there are several circumstances where their characteristics can be ideal.

Extending the LAN

One of the places where wireless connections can be ideal is when you have two buildings that are located in close proximity but a cable connection is not an option. There might be a major highway or some natural obstruction such as a river or canyon between the buildings. In these instances, a *wireless bridge* (see Figure 6.8) can be established using one of the media described earlier. For short-range connections, a spread-spectrum radio connection can provide an inexpensive option. However, a terrestrial microwave or laser-based (infrared) solution might provide the highest level of data transmission speed and security.

Key Concept

A *wireless bridge* can be used to connect two networks in situations where it is impossible to use traditional cable media.

CH
6

There might be some cases, too, where wireless solutions might actually prove to be less expensive than comparable cable solutions requiring leased lines from the telephone company. If you needed a 10Mbps connection between two offices that were within sight of each other, the one-time investment in wireless media might turn out to be less expensive in the long run than the monthly fees for leased lines between the offices.

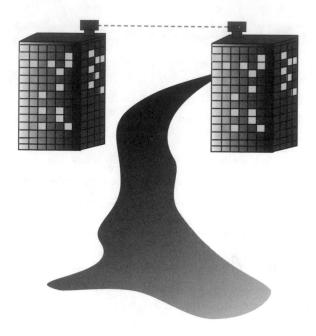

Figure 6.8
A wireless bridge can be established using infrared (laser) communication.

When you are looking to extend your network over a larger geographical area, your wireless options are primarily microwave networks. Terrestrial microwave systems using a series of relay towers might provide the connection you need. Beyond that, you enter the high-priced realm of satellite microwave. If you need to communicate with an office in some remote part of the world, satellite might be your only option.

High-power, single-frequency radio links could also work in some circumstances. Given the appropriate power levels and frequencies, radio signals can be bounced off the atmosphere and cover great distances. These radio systems also provide effective *multipoint* connectivity and can allow remote users to access your network from outside the confines of your office building. This can work for extending access to your LAN from vehicles, boats, or aircraft.

Mobile Computing

In some instances, you might want to completely replace the cable LAN. For instance, a sales office might have employees working primarily on laptops that they carry in and out of the office. A shipping company might want its employees to be mobile throughout the warehouse area without being tied down to a desk. Within a hospital, doctors or other staff might want network access from wherever they are in the building.

The exact type of wireless LAN used for these different situations will depend on the situation, especially such factors as bandwidth requirements, cost issues, and the distance needed to be covered. Spread-spectrum radio solutions can provide true mobility. Low-power, single-frequency systems can also provide an effective alternative. In the example of the sales office, if the employees' laptops will be relatively stationary, a point-to-point infrared solution would provide the highest transmission speed. Low-power microwave systems are also possible in some environments.

Looking to the Future

Wireless technology continues to evolve rapidly, and new technologies might provide even more methods of breaking the physical connection. Most paging services now support email and other services through their radio-based paging networks. Standards have also evolved for digital transmission over cellular-phone networks. *Cellular Digital Packet Data (CDPD)* might soon provide another mechanism for easy network connection for mobile users. Several large satellite ventures are under way that could result in entire rings of satellites circling the globe and expanding the bandwidth available for satellite communication. Now that more people are finding the benefits of wireless media, the costs are dropping, and you will only see more technologies coming out within the years ahead.

Summary

Wireless media can provide an alternative to regular physical cable. Wireless technologies operate at different electromagnetic frequencies. The higher the frequency you use, the more data you can transmit. As frequencies get higher, however, the transmission distance decreases due to attenuation and interference. Equipment and operating costs also increase as the frequency increases.

Wireless technologies fall into three main categories: radio, microwave, and infrared.

Radio technologies operate on either a single frequency or multiple frequencies. *Single-frequency systems* can exist in low-power forms for local use or in a high-power form for use over a larger distance. *Spread-spectrum systems* transmit data on multiple frequencies, either by breaking data into parts and transmitting different parts on different frequencies or by rapidly hopping between frequencies. Spread-spectrum systems are more resistant to eavesdropping than single-frequency systems.

Microwave communication operates at higher frequencies but requires that each end of the connection be within the line of sight of each other. *Terrestrial* microwave systems use parabolic antennas to create a point-to-point link between two sites. This link can be extended through the use of relay towers. *Satellite* microwave also establishes a point-to-point link, but it does so by bouncing the signal off a geosynchronous satellite.

CH
6

Infrared communication systems operate at still higher frequencies close to the range of visible light. Infrared systems using light-emitting diodes (LEDs) can function at high data rates in a *point-to-point* system or provide lower data rates but higher mobility in a *broadcast* system. Laser technologies can also be used to establish a point-to-point connection.

A common application of wireless connections is to establish a *wireless bridge* between two buildings where running a cable is not feasible or desirable. This connection might be made through terrestrial microwave or laser communication systems. Another application would be to replace the cables of a regular LAN. LAN systems usually involve spread-spectrum radio, low-power, single-frequency radio, or infrared systems.

QUESTIONS AND ANSWERS

1. What are the different categories of wireless transmission?

   A: Radio, microwave, and infrared.

2. What are three types of radio communication used in LANs?

   A: Low-power, single-frequency; high-power, single-frequency; spread-spectrum.

3. How does spread-spectrum transmission differ from other radio transmission methods?

   A: Spread-spectrum uses a signal sent out on multiple frequencies.

4. Explain how frequency-hopping works?

   A: Data is transmitted on a series of frequencies according to a predetermined pattern and timing known only to the transmitter and the receiver.

5. What is the main limitation of microwave links?

   A: The transmitter and receiver must be within a line of sight.

6. What are two types of infrared communication?

   A: Point-to-point and broadcast.

7. What is a wireless bridge?

   A: A situation in which two networks are linked across some distance by a wireless technology (typically microwave or infrared). Often used when laying a cable connection would be prohibitively expensive.

PRACTICE TEST

1. Which wireless radio technology provides the highest level of security from eaves-dropping?

    a. Spread-spectrum radio

    b. High-power, single-frequency radio

    c. Low-power, single-frequency radio

    d. Multi-phase radio

Answer a is correct. Answers b and c are incorrect because they provide little security. Answer d is incorrect because it is a fictitious answer.

2. If you want to connect networks in two buildings without using cable connections, which wireless media could you use? (Choose all that apply.)

    a. Terrestrial microwave

    b. Broadcast infrared

    c. Point-to-point infrared

    d. High-power, single-frequency radio

Answers a, c, and d are all correct because they could be used to link two buildings. Answer b is incorrect because broadcast infrared only works within a small area and could not be used between two buildings.

3. What are the two main types of spread-spectrum radio communication?

    a. High-power, single-frequency

    b. Multi-phase

    c. Direct-sequence modulation

    d. Frequency hopping

Answer a is incorrect. Answer b is incorrect. **Answers c and d are correct.**

4. When a signal is sent from one site to another using a satellite, there might be a _____ of up to 5 seconds.

    a. Synchronization delay

    b. Geosynchronous feedback

    c. Propagation delay

    d. Feedback loop

Answers a, b, and d are incorrect. **Answer c is correct.**

CH 6

5. A _____ connects two adjacent buildings without using cable.

    a. Wireless gateway

    b. Wireless bridge

    c. Point-to-point link

    d. Spread-spectrum

Answer a is incorrect because that is not the common term used. **Answer b is correct; a wireless bridge can connect two adjacent buildings.** Answers c and d are really terms for two technologies that could be used to create a wireless bridge.

6. Which of these statements are true about point-to-point infrared communications? (Choose all that apply.)

    a. Bright lights can interfere with the signal.

    b. Point-to-point systems can communicate over thousands of meters.

    c. Point-to-point systems do not require line-of-sight. One reflected bounce is possible before signal degradation.

    d. These systems are highly resistant to eavesdropping.

Answer a is correct; bright lights *can* interfere. Answer b is correct, given some of the laser technologies available today. Answer c is incorrect because point-to-point systems *do* require line-of-sight. **Answer d is correct because the only way to eavesdrop on the signal would be to get right in the path of the signal, which would definitely be noticed by the receiver.**

7. Your company has two 20-story office buildings separated by a river. There is a bridge across the river, but a cabling company has given you an outrageous price quote for running a cable between buildings. As a result, you would like to explore wireless solutions.

    REQUIRED RESULT: Computers on the LAN in one office building must be able to communicate with computers on the LAN in the other building.

    OPTIONAL DESIRED RESULTS: The wireless media should be highly secure from potential eavesdroppers. Due to some power lines in the area, a solution should also be resistant to electromagnetic interference.

    PROPOSED SOLUTION: You suggest installing a point-to-point infrared link from the roof of each building through laser technology. Which results does the proposed solution produce?

    a. The proposed solution produces the required result and both of the optional desired results.

    b. The proposed solution produces the required result and only *one* of the optional desired results.

   c. The proposed solution produces the required result but does *not* produce any of the optional desired results.

   d. The proposed solution does *not* produce the required result.

Answer a is correct. The point-to-point link will allow computers to communicate, will be secure, and will not be affected by electromagnetic interference. Answers b, c, and d are incorrect.

  8. If you want to provide an environment within your office where users can move around with their computers, which wireless media can you use?

    a. Spread-spectrum radio

    b. Satellite microwave

    c. Point-to-point infrared

    d. High-power, single-frequency

Answers a and d are correct because users can move around with both spread-spectrum and high-power, single-frequency solutions. Answers b and c are incorrect because computers would need to be stationary for communication to occur.

  9. What two types of transmission devices are used in infrared communication?

    a. Incandescent lights

    b. Light-emitting diodes

    c. Phasers

    d. Lasers

Answer a is incorrect as incandescent lights do not provide the necessary focus. **Answer b is correct; most low-power infrared solutions use LEDs.** Answer c is incorrect as phasers are really only found in Star Trek. **Answer d is correct; infrared solutions for point-to-point links, especially over great distances, usually use lasers.**

  10. Which of the following statements are *not* true about low-power, single-frequency radio networks?

    a. Maximum distance covered is usually in the tens of meters

    b. Susceptible to eavesdropping

    c. Highly susceptible to electromagnetic interference

    d. Can support data transmission rates up to 100Mbps

Answer a is incorrect because it is true. Answer b is incorrect because it is true. Answer c is incorrect because it is true. **Answer d is correct because it is a false statement. Low-power, single-frequency radio networks can typically operate at no more than 10Mbps.**

CH
6

CHAPTER

7

CHAPTER PREREQUISITE

Before reading this chapter, you should understand the functions performed by the data link layer of the OSI Reference Model, as described in Chapter 3, "The OSI Reference Model." You should also understand the types of physical network media described in Chapter 5, "The Physical Connection."

Data Transmission

WHILE YOU READ

1. Where do network interface cards fit into the OSI Reference Model?

2. When data flows between the different components of your computer, it flows along a _____.

3. What is a MAC address?

4. Identity the two most common settings you need to configure on a NIC.

5. What is the role of an IRQ?

6. What does a driver do?

7. What are the four primary methods of allowing access onto the network media?

8. Explain the difference between CSMA/CD and CSMA/CA.

9. What is the primary advantage of token passing?

10. _____ is the most common implementation of CSMA/CD.

Network Interface Cards

When you want to send information across the network, your computer transmits that information using a *network interface card (NIC)*, also known as a network adapter or network card. In addition to preparing and sending the data, the network interface card also provides the physical connection to the network media.

Key Concept

Looking back at the OSI Reference Model, network interface cards not only provide the physical layer connection, but also provide the functionality of the data link layer. In doing so, network interface cards implement the Logical Link Control and Media Access Control sublayers defined by the IEEE 802 project.

One of the fundamental issues with which the network adapter must grapple is the translation of data from *parallel* transmission to *serial* transmission. When data flows between different components of your computer, it flows along a data *bus*. For instance, when the central processor needs information from the hard drive, that information must travel from the hard drive to the computer's motherboard across a bus. This bus consists of several parallel wires, allowing multiple bits of data to move simultaneously from one place to the other. Most of the first generation of personal computers used 8-bit buses, meaning that 8 bits of data could move at one time. With the arrival of the IBM PC/AT and all the IBM-compatible clones in the mid-1980s, the 16-bit bus came into use. Today, most new computers are using 32-bit buses, and 64-bit buses are slowly becoming available.

Think of a data bus like an auto highway. Cars and trucks can travel in several different lanes. The wider the highway, the more cars that can travel simultaneously. A four-lane highway can accommodate more traffic than a two-lane highway. An eight-lane highway can accommodate even more!

Unfortunately, whereas data inside the computer travels along highways, travel across a network medium is like travel along a single-lane road. All bits have to go single file. As depicted in Figure 7.1, resolving this dilemma of receiving information from a 16- or 32-lane data highway (parallel) and sending it out a single-lane network road (serial) is the network adapter's primary task. The NIC packages all the bits into data *packets* and then transmits each packet serially onto the network media.

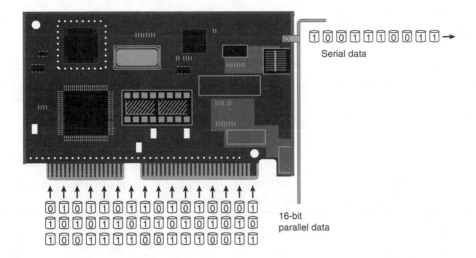

Figure 7.1
The primary function of the NIC is to convert the parallel data from the computer's data bus to serial data for transmission on the network media.

 Key Concept

One way to optimize network communications is to install a network card that optimizes the full width of your computer's bus. For example, use a 32-bit NIC in a computer supporting a 32-bit bus.

To actually send this data across the network media, the network interface card must include a *transceiver (trans*mitter/re*ceiver)* appropriate for the network medium being used. For instance, in most Ethernet networks, the card will have a connector for Thinnet or UTP cables and will translate the data into electrical signals. In a network using fiber-optic cable, the network interface card will have the appropriate connectors for fiber-optic cable and will translate the data into light signals.

In addition to sending data from your computer onto the network, the network interface card also receives all data packets transmitted on the network media and determines which packets are for your computer. Those packets are then converted from the network's serial data flow into the parallel data flow appropriate for your computer.

CH
7

To determine which packets belong to your computer, your network interface card needs to have an address. The Institute for Electrical and Electronics Engineers (IEEE) developed an addressing scheme and assigned blocks of addresses to manufacturers of network interface cards. Each manufacturer "burns" a unique address into chips on each individual network interface card. Therefore, your computer will have a unique address on the network. Your network interface card simply looks for packets containing its address and begins the translation process.

Key Concept

The hardware address of the network interface card is commonly known as the *MAC address* because of the Media Access Control sublayer of the OSI Reference Model. For example, the address for an Ethernet NIC has the form 08-40-06-24-A2-5A.

You will not be tested on it, but for your information, the hardware address of your network interface card, or NIC, is expressed as six bytes. The first three bytes, known as the vendor code or Organizational Unique Identifier (OUI), are given to the manufacturer by the IEEE. The IEEE regulates the OUI, so there aren't any duplicate hardware addresses floating around. The second three bytes are made up by the manufacturer and are generally part of the serial number of the card. The full hardware address is commonly known as the MAC address because it is used to uniquely identify a network node at the Media Access Control sublayer of the OSI reference model. An Ethernet NIC with the hardware address of 00-10-4B-66-E1-81 uniquely identifies a NIC made by 3Com. This is because the OUI of 00-10-4B was assigned by the IEEE to 3Com.

You now understand that your network interface card is responsible for sending and receiving data from the network. When you choose a network interface card, you will need to configure several settings appropriate for your computer, such as the interrupt and I/O port address. Although these configuration settings will be discussed later in the chapter, you first need to be sure you have the right type of card.

Types of Buses

In the early days of the personal computer industry, there was only one bus design, and purchasing expansion cards, such as network interface cards, was relatively simple. However, as the technology evolved, other standards for buses were created. Today, there are four main types of *bus architecture*: ISA, EISA, Micro Channel, and PCI. Because each of these types is physically different, your network interface card must use the same bus architecture as your computer. As shown in Figure 7.2, the physical profile of each card makes differentiating between the bus types relatively simple. (Note that although you should know the different bus types for the exam, you will not be tested on the order of the evolution of different bus types.)

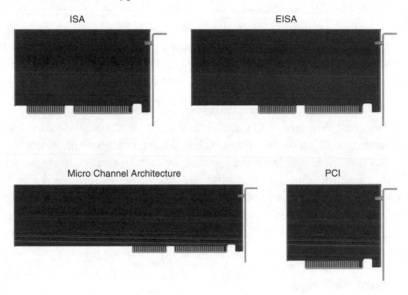

Figure 7.2
The physical profile of the network interface card is one simple method of determining for what type of data bus it is designed.

- *ISA (Industry Standard Architecture)*. The ISA bus was first used in the original IBM PC and all subsequent clones. Originally an 8-bit bus, it was expanded in 1984 to 16-bits. ISA was the standard in PCs until the EISA bus was introduced in 1988.

- *EISA (Extended Industry Standard Architecture)*. In 1988, a consortium of nine computer manufacturers led by Compaq introduced the EISA bus. The EISA bus delivered a 32-bit data flow. It was also compatible with the ISA bus, meaning that a card developed for an EISA bus could also fit into an ISA slot on an older computer. In that case, it would only provide a 16-bit data flow.

- *MCA (Micro Channel Architecture)*. In 1988, IBM introduced the PS/2 computer as the first of what IBM believed would be the next generation of PCs. One of the differences was the introduction of a new bus called Micro Channel Architecture. This bus is capable of working as either a 16- or 32-bit bus. However, because it was physically and electrically different from the ISA bus, new cards were required for these PCs.

CH
7

■ *PCI (Peripheral Component Interconnect).* As faster processors became available, the need for a faster data bus became apparent. Manufacturers developed the concept of the *local bus*, where the same high-speed connection used by the CPU to communicate with onboard devices is extended to communicate with peripherals. Several local bus standards evolved, but the 32-bit PCI bus developed by Intel has now emerged as the *de facto* standard. You will find it incorporated into most Pentium- or PowerPC-based computers. The PCI bus is also the first to incorporate the plug-and-play features discussed later in this chapter.

Beyond these four, there are other standards such as NuBUS (used in Apple Macintosh systems), VESA Local Bus, and "PC Card" (PCMCIA) that can be found on some computers. The important thing to remember is that the type of network interface card you use must match the bus available in your computer. It is, in fact, possible for your computer to support multiple data buses. A different type of expansion slot is simply needed for each data bus. For instance, today most new server computers provide several PCI expansion slots and several EISA expansion slots, whereas most client computers will have both PCI and ISA expansion slots. Note the exception that EISA slots are backwards-compatible and will work with ISA cards.

Configuration Settings

When you have the appropriate type of network interface card for your computer, you need to configure it for use within your computer.

In the ideal world, all you should have to do is open up your computer, insert the network interface card, close the computer, and turn the computer on. When the computer powers up, everything should be working fine, and you should immediately be able to communicate with the network. Unfortunately, the real world is usually quite different.

In the past couple of years, manufacturers have improved their equipment and gotten closer to the ideal previously described. With the Windows 95 operating system, Microsoft introduced the concept of *Plug and Play*. In theory, if your computer motherboard, operating system (currently only Windows 95/98), and expansion cards all support Plug and Play functionality, you should just be able to insert the card, turn on the computer, and have everything work properly. When the computer goes through its initial *Power-On Self-Test* (often referred to as "POST"), it will identify all the Plug and Play components and automatically configure the devices appropriately. This works fairly well if all components conform to the Plug and Play requirements. If some of your devices are not Plug and Play or if a device does not exactly conform to Plug and Play standards, you might have to manually configure some portions of your system.

For all older computer systems, and for any operating systems other than Windows 95/98, you will have to manually configure your network interface card before it can work with your system. Configuration of a card involves changing three settings:

- Interrupt Request (IRQ)
- Base I/O port
- Base memory address

Most of the time, these settings are configurable through software. However, with older NICs, you might need to change a *jumper* or *DIP switch* (see Figure 7.3). A jumper is a small connector that essentially connects two pins together and completes a circuit. A DIP (dual inline package) switch is a small assembly with plastic switches that can be turned on or off using a small screwdriver or fingernail.

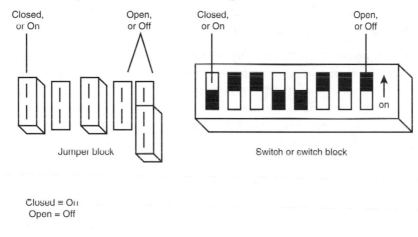

Figure 7.3
Older NICs are configured with either a jumper or a DIP switch.

Interrupt Request (IRQ)

Inside your computer, you normally have only one central microprocessor chip, also known as a central processing unit (CPU). However, connected to that one chip through a data bus, you have many devices such as your keyboard, mouse, disk drives, printers, serial ports, sound card, and network interface card. With many different devices accessing it through the data bus, the microprocessor chip inside your computer needs to know when a device needs attention. For instance, when a user clicks the button on the mouse, the mouse needs some way to alert the processor that the user has initiated a mouse action (a button press). Likewise, if your network interface card receives data from the

CH
7

network, the NIC needs some mechanism to alert the processor that it has data to be processed.

In the realm of computer hardware, this mechanism is known as an *interrupt request,* or *IRQ.* Your computer has a number of built-in *interrupt request lines* that allow all your devices to alert the microprocessor that they need service. Because each device must use a unique IRQ setting, you need to determine what IRQs are available before you install your network interface card. If you insert your card with a conflicting IRQ, you will find that you cannot communicate with the network and that the conflicting IRQ might interfere with the proper functioning of some other device.

On machines using Microsoft DOS, Windows 3.*x*, or Windows 95/98, you can issue the DOS command MSD.EXE to run the Microsoft System Diagnostics tool to find out what IRQs are available. In Windows NT, you need to go into the Windows NT Diagnostics tool, found in the Administrative Tools program group or menu. Alternatively, in Windows NT you can issue the command WINMSD.EXE.

The interrupt request mechanism has been around since the earliest days of PCs, and most IRQs have been assigned a common use, as shown in Table 7.1. Because network interface cards came on the scene later, they must be set to use one of the unassigned IRQs. Because most computers don't have a second printer (LPT2) or a sound card, network interface cards are often set to use IRQ5. IRQ3 is often a second alternative if a second serial port is not being used. If neither IRQ3 or IRQ5 are available, you should consult Table 7.1 to find an IRQ setting that is available on your system.

Key Concept

For the exam, you *must* know that each hardware device needs a unique IRQ and that IRQs are available for a NIC. It would be wise to memorize the IRQ list in Table 7.1.

Table 7.1   Standard IRQ Settings

IRQ	Typical Usage
0	System timer
1	Keyboard
2	Secondary IRQ controller or video adapter
3	Unassigned (unless used for COM2, COM4, or bus mouse)
4	Serial ports COM1 and COM3
5	Unassigned (unless used for LPT2 or sound card)

IRQ	Typical Usage
6	Floppy disk controller
7	Parallel port LPT1
8	Real-time clock
9	Unassigned, redirected IRQ2, sound card, or third IRQ controller
10	Unassigned or primary SCSI controller
11	Unassigned or secondary SCSI controller
12	PS/2 Mouse
13	Math coprocessor (if installed)
14	Primary hard-drive controller
15	Unassigned or secondary hard-drive controller.

Note that the exact assignment of IRQs 2 and 9 will depend on the actual hardware in your computer. In the early days of PCs, the interrupts were controlled by one integrated circuit (IC) chip with only eight available IRQs (IRQs 0–7). When this proved inadequate, a second interrupt controller chip was added to handle IRQs 8–15. However, because the actual microprocessor could only accept interrupts from one IC, the second IC was "cascaded" onto the first. When a device connected to the second IC needed service, the second IC would trigger IRQ 2 on the first IC, which then would interrupt the microprocessor. Devices formerly using IRQ 2 were usually redirected to use IRQ 9. If additional interrupts were necessary, a third IC (IRQs 16–23) would be cascaded onto the second IC, with its output driving IRQ 9 on the second chip (which, in turn, would trigger IRQ 2 on the first IC and interrupt the microprocessor). This arrangement continues to exist in most computers today.

Base I/O Port

After a device has obtained the attention of the microprocessor, it needs to send its data to the microprocessor. The microprocessor, in turn, needs to send data back to the device. Because almost all devices share the same data buses on the motherboard, there needs to be some method of determining the destination device for data sent from the microprocessor. To accomplish this, each device is assigned a *base input/output (I/O) port* that essentially serves as the address the processor uses when communicating with that device. Like the IRQ, the base I/O port of a device must be unique.

Port numbers are written in hexadecimal notation and are often expressed in terms of a 16-bit range (300-30F). You will often see them written with a trailing "h," as in "300h," or a prefix of "0x," as in "0x300." Network interface cards are typically assigned the base

I/O port of 300h. Other common values are 280h or 310h. If none of those are available, consult Table 7.2 to find a value not assigned to existing hardware.

You can use MSD.EXE or Windows NT Diagnostics again to determine the port numbers currently assigned on your computer.

Table 7.2   Base I/O Port Assignments

Port	Device	Port	Device
200	Game port	300	Network interface card
210		310	Network interface card
220		320	
230	Bus mouse	330	
240		340	
250		350	
260		360	
270	LPT3	370	LPT2
280		380	
290		390	
2A0		3A0	
2B0		3B0	LPT1
2C0		3C0	EGA/VGA video adapter
2D0		3D0	CGA video adapter
2E0		3E0	
2F0	COM2	3F0	COM1, Floppy-disk controller

Base Memory Address

To cope with the flood of information coming in on the parallel data bus, your network interface card establishes a *buffer* area in the computer's memory (RAM) where the data is temporarily stored while being converted to serial data and sent out to the network media. The starting address of this buffer area is known as the *base memory address* or *upper memory address* for the network interface card.

Like the IRQ and base I/O port, the base memory address must be unique for each device. However, because most devices do not use upper memory areas, competition for addresses is very limited. Many network interface cards use a base memory address of D8000, and you generally do not need to adjust this.

Note that for reasons understood only to themselves, some manufacturers abbreviate the base memory setting by removing the final 0. So, a NIC with the memory address of "D8000" would be set with a value of "D800."

Performance Enhancements

Beyond configuration issues and bus types, there are several other factors to consider when choosing a network interface card. As mentioned at the beginning of the chapter, the NIC needs to convert data from the parallel stream of the computer's data bus to the serial stream of the actual network media. Because the data bus can operate at much higher speeds than the network media, your NIC can become a performance bottleneck that will slow down your entire system. It is in your best interest to have the fastest possible flow of data through your NIC. (This data flow is often referred to as *throughput.*) Such enhancements include the following:

- *RAM buffering.* Many network adapter cards now include RAM chips on the actual card. As data flows at a high speed from the computer's data bus, the information can be temporarily held in a RAM *buffer* while awaiting transmission out onto the network media. This process can greatly increase the speed of the network adapter.

- *Direct Memory Access (DMA).* Without DMA, your computer's microprocessor is involved with transferring all information from the network interface card into system memory. A DMA controller inside your computer takes this activity away from the processor and deals directly with all data transfer. If your NIC and computer support DMA, the DMA controller will transfer data directly from your NIC's buffer into system memory, eliminating the processor's involvement and allowing it to focus on other operations.

- *Bus mastering.* Similar to DMA, bus mastering is a technique where your NIC takes control of the computer's data bus and transfers data directly into system memory without involving the microprocessor. Although they can produce great speed increases, cards with bus mastering are expensive.

- *Onboard microprocessor.* Many network interface cards further speed up data throughput by having a separate microprocessor on the NIC to handle data transfer. This removes the computer's central processor from actually processing the incoming network data.

- *Shared memory.* In some cases, the NIC can contain RAM that is shared with the computer. Because the computer treats this memory as if it was directly installed into the computer, the microprocessor can read and write data directly into the shared memory. Because that shared memory is already on the NIC, the NIC can rapidly transfer data to and from the network media.

CH

7

All these techniques can help speed up data transfer between the computer's data bus and the network media. Many NICs will implement one or more of these enhancements. The NIC performance speed will increase with more enhancements, but so will the price. It is important to choose a network interface card appropriate to the level of network communication you will be using. Your servers should use NICs with the best possible performance that you can afford. If your client computers will not be using network-intensive applications, almost any NIC will do. However, if they will be heavily using the network, they, too, should be equipped with high-performance network interface cards.

Drivers

Before you can use your network interface card, you need to install a *driver* for the card. Because there are a large number of NIC manufacturers, it would be extremely difficult for every operating system vendor to know about the exact hardware configuration of every available NIC.

Instead, operating system vendors developed the system of using *device drivers* for communication between the operating system and the actual hardware devices installed in your computer. A *driver* is simply a small piece of software that is installed into your operating system to allow it to use a specific device. For example, if you have installed printers onto your system, you will remember installing printer drivers in order to use the printer.

Installing a driver for a network interface card is usually a simple procedure. Modern operating systems such as Windows 95/98 and Windows NT already include drivers for a wide range of network interface cards. Additionally, most NIC manufacturers supply a disk with drivers for different operating systems. Each operating system has a slightly different method of actually installing the driver. However, most rely on some type of graphical interface to accomplish the task. Figure 7.4 shows how the installation of a driver is accomplished within Windows NT 4.0.

Although most manufacturers provide drivers for all popular operating systems, before purchasing a NIC make sure to check that a driver is available for your operating system. Additionally, if your operating system vendor provides a Hardware Compatibility List (HCL), choosing a NIC and driver from the HCL provides the highest level of confidence that the NIC will work with your system.

As you install the driver, you will typically be asked to provide configuration information such as the IRQ of the network interface card.

Figure 7.4
Windows NT 4.0 provides a graphical installation tool for installing drivers.

Key Concept

If configuration information is required by your software driver, you must enter the exact same configuration information you used when installing your network interface card. For example, if your NIC is set to use IRQ 5 and port 300h, you need to make sure your driver is also set to use those values. If not, the driver will not be able to communicate with the NIC, and you will not be able to use the network.

Be aware that over time most manufacturers update their drivers to increase the performance of their network interface cards. These updated drivers are usually available from the manufacturer's Web site or from Microsoft's Web site. If an updated driver becomes available, you typically download the appropriate file and install it through the same mechanism that you used to install the original driver. This capability to easily upgrade drivers is another advantage to the mechanism of using drivers. If communication between your computer and your NIC was coded into the actual operating system, you would not be able to improve your NIC performance until the next release of your operating system.

CH

7

Getting Data on the Network

Beyond simply converting data from your computer's bus to the network media, your network interface card also provides the crucial function of determining *when* your computer can transmit data on the network media. If any two computers transmit data at the same time, their packets will *collide*, and the electrical signal of the data will be corrupted to the point where the information will be lost.

Key Concept

A *collision* is when two computers transmit data simultaneously.

Avoiding these collisions and organizing data transfer are the primary tasks of devices that function at the Media Access Control sublayer of the OSI data link layer. There are four primary methods of allowing access onto the network media:

- Contention
- Token passing
- Demand priority
- Polling

Contention

Do you have multiple phone extensions inside your house for one phone line? If so, you have probably experienced *contention-based* access control. Basically, everyone in your house competes for access to that one phone line.

In a "pure" contention-based system, any computer could transmit at any time. This would be similar to all residents of your house just picking up the phone and starting to dial. If no one else was on the line, it might work. If someone was on the line, your call wouldn't go through, and you would interrupt the other call. As people started to make more calls, this system would break down. Likewise, in the computer world, a "pure" contention access method would not work well at all. To bring some order to the system, two methods are used:

- Carrier-Sense Multiple Access with Collision Detection
- Carrier-Sense Multiple Access with Collision Avoidance

Both methods provide a means of limiting the number of collisions on the network.

Carrier-Sense Multiple Access with Collision Detection (CSMA/CD)

CSMA/CD is essentially how you usually work with your home telephone. Generally, you pick up a phone and listen to see if you get a dial tone. If so, you dial your number and make your call. As long as you are using the phone line, no one else can call out. If you do not get a dial tone and you hear someone else on the phone, you have to wait. You can keep checking, but as long as the line is in use, you can't do anything.

It might happen that you pick up the phone at the same time as someone else in your house, hear the dial tone, and start dialing at the same time (or close to the same time) as that other person. Because you both dial simultaneously, the numbers you transmit interfere with each other, and you can't connect. At this point, one of you will have to let the other go first and wait for the other to complete her call.

In a nutshell, the previous example demonstrates how computer networks using CSMA/CD operate. As shown in Figure 7.5, multiple computers have access to the network media. Before sending data, each computer senses whether the cable is free. If so, the computer sends its data. If not, the computer waits until the network media is free. If two or more computers happen to transmit at the same time, they detect the collision of their data with another computer's data. At this point, each computer waits a random period of time and then starts the process all over again. With these random intervals between retransmission, the chances that multiple computers would both transmit at the same time are greatly reduced.

Although this might seem unworkable in a networked environment, CSMA/CD is, in fact, quite fast and forms the basis for the extremely popular Ethernet network architecture. It does not require sophisticated equipment and can be implemented very inexpensively. However, the disadvantages of CSMA/CD include the following:

- *More users means more collisions.* With the addition of more users to the network, more computers are trying to transmit their data. As the data transmissions increase, the number of collisions greatly increases. In very heavy network traffic, this method can dramatically slow the speed of network data.

- *Unequal access to network media.* If one computer repeatedly transmitted information, it could "hog" the network media and not give other computers the opportunity to transmit.

- *No means to prioritize traffic.* All computers are equal in that all network traffic appears the same to all other computers. There is no way to indicate that traffic from the network server, for instance, should have a higher priority.

- *Distance restrictions.* Because of the attenuation of the network media, as your network becomes longer, computers at one end are unable to sense when a computer at the other end has begun transmission. CSMA/CD networks are generally limited to 2,500 meters (1.5 miles) or less.

CH
7

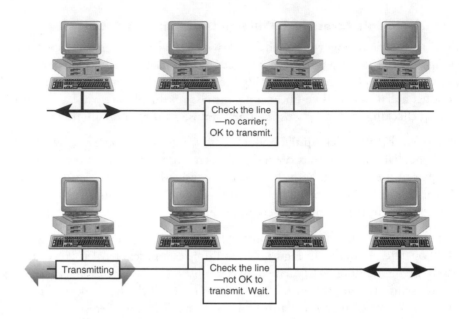

Figure 7.5
Computers on a network using Carrier-Sense Multiple Access with Collision Detection
check the network media before transmitting to see whether it is being used.

 Key Concept

In Carrier-Sense Multiple Access with Collision Detection, a computer checks the
media to see whether it is clear to transmit. If the media is free, the computer
transmits. If two computers simultaneously transmit, they will detect the ensuing
collision of data and will wait a random period of time before attempting to
retransmit. The most popular implementation of CSMA/CD is Ethernet.

Carrier-Sense Multiple Access with Collision Avoidance (CSMA/CA)

Carrier-Sense Multiple Access with Collision Avoidance is very similar to CSMA/CD,
with one crucial difference: Computers transmit their intention to send data before they
actually do so. Imagine in your household if, before using the phone, everyone had to yell
out to let everyone know that they were about to make a phone call. Although this would
probably avoid many instances of two people picking up the phone and dialing at the
same time, it would make for a noisy household.

As on CSMA/CD networks, a computer on a network using CSMA/CA, such as an AppleTalk network, first checks the network media to see if the cable is in use. However, unlike CSMA/CD, if the cable is not in use, the computer attempts to avoid collisions by first transmitting a signal on the network indicating that it is about to transmit data. After that signal has gone out, the computer transmits the actual data. Any other computers that were getting ready to transmit data will pause when they receive the first signal and wait until after the data has been sent.

The major issue with this access method is that each signal of transmission intent is broadcast to the entire network. Although such signals might avoid many data collisions, the increased use of the network to transmit these signals will greatly slow down the transmission speed of data across the network. For this reason, CSMA/CA is not used nearly as much as CSMA/CD.

Key Concept

Carrier-Sense Multiple-Access with Collision Avoidance is similar to CMSA/CD except that a computer on a CSMA/CA network first transmits a packet signaling the computer's intent to transmit prior to actually transmitting data. The original LocalTalk version of AppleTalk used CSMA/CA.

Token Passing

Imagine that you are attending a group seminar on some topic. When you arrive, you find all the chairs placed in a circle. After everyone is seated, the instructor states that as an icebreaker exercise, he is going to pass an object around the circle. When you receive this object, you can introduce yourself and tell the group something about who you are. No one else can speak while you have the object, and you can speak for a certain period of time. When you finish, you pass the object to the person next to you. If you don't want to say anything, you do have the option of simply passing along the object to the next person.

Networks using a token-passing access method function in this manner. As shown in Figure 7.6, a special packet called a *token* travels continually around the network in a circle. When a computer receives the token, it can transmit data to any other computer. After it finishes or if it has nothing to transmit, it passes the token to the next computer. Because of the circular nature of this method, token-passing networks are most often implemented using a ring topology.

CH

7

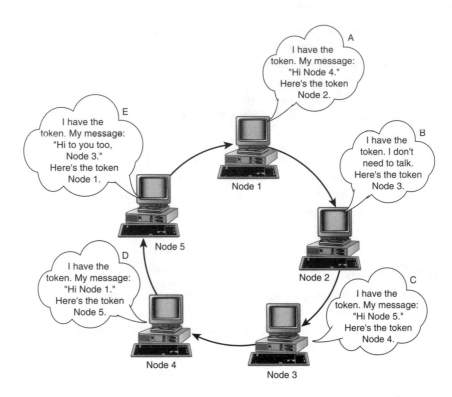

Figure 7.6
A network-utilizing token passing provides equal access to the network media for all computers.

The strength of this approach is that because computers can only transmit when they have the token, there are no collisions. Access to the network media is guaranteed. In networks with a high volume of traffic, token-passing networks can provide a high level of performance because computers are not blocked waiting for collisions to be resolved. Additionally, because the time the token can spend at each computer can be set to a specified interval, token-passing networks can be very appropriate for environments where data is time-critical, such as automated manufacturing facilities.

The primary disadvantage of token-passing networks is that the token must always circulate around the network. If there is very low network traffic and only one computer on the network wants to transmit, it still must wait for its turn.

Another disadvantage is that the process of passing the token around requires more complicated and more expensive equipment (network interface cards, hubs, and so on) than the equipment required for a contention-based network.

Key Concept

In token passing, a small data frame called a token passes from computer to computer. A computer can only transmit when it receives the token. This ensures that all computers have equal access to the network media.

Key Concept

Another way to remember these access methods is to think about driving through an intersection. *Contention*-based networks resemble approaching an intersection without a stoplight. If you look and see no one coming, you can turn. It works great when there aren't many people around. On the other hand, if a long line of traffic is coming, you could be sitting there for a very long time. *Token passing* is like the intersection with a stoplight. Everyone is guaranteed a chance to enter the intersection. However, if you have a red light and no one else is visible at all, you still have to wait for the light to turn green.

Several network architectures utilize token passing, including Token Ring (IEEE 802.5), Token Bus (IEEE 802.4), and FDDI. Token Ring and FDDI will be discussed in more detail in the next chapter.

Demand Priority

In newer networks using the 100Mbps standard 100VG-AnyLAN (also known as IEEE 802.12), intelligent hubs are used in a star-bus network, as shown in Figure 7.7. The hubs control which computers can transmit data on the network. A computer sends a signal, called a *demand*, to the hub indicating that it wants to transmit. The hub responds with an acknowledgment that the computer can start transmitting packets of data. The hub then cycles between whichever computers have made demands, allowing each of them to transmit one packet in turn.

Collisions are not an issue because the hub controls access to the network. If multiple computers make simultaneous demands, the hub will determine whether one of those computers is configured to be a higher priority than the other. If so, it will let that computer transmit data first. If they are of equal priority, the hub will cycle between all computers.

CH
7

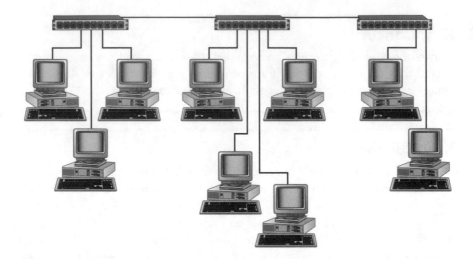

Figure 7.7
Demand priority uses intelligent hubs to determine which computers need to access the network.

Demand priority also makes more efficient use of the network media. Unlike token-passing networks, computers that do not have information to transmit are simply ignored until they signal the hub for service. Additionally, packets are transmitted between a computer and the hub and from the hub to the destination; they are not broadcast all over the network as they are in CSMA/CD and CSMA/CA networks.

The efficiency of this access method comes at a price. The major disadvantage to demand priority is the current high cost of the specialized hubs and other equipment needed for this to work.

Polling

Polling is an older access method that utilizes a central controller to determine which computer can transmit data on the network (see Figure 7.8). This central controller, referred to as the *primary* device, continually *polls* all the *secondary* devices (the computers) to determine whether they have data to transmit. If they do, the primary device allows them to transmit for a limited time before moving on to the next device. No device can transmit until it is polled.

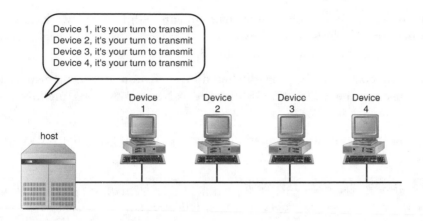

Figure 7.8
Polling relies on a central controller to determine network access.

The polling access method shares many of the same advantages as token passing. Access to the network media is guaranteed, and no one computer can dominate the network media. Additionally, the central controller can provide a single point to manage the network. The controller can also assign certain computers, such as a server, a higher priority and allow them to transmit for a slightly longer time.

However, like token passing, polling does not make efficient use of the network media and is constantly generating network traffic. Also, although the central controller can be an advantage for network management, if it fails, the entire network will be brought down. (If a computer fails in a token-passing network, the token can continue to circulate.)

Comparison of Different Access Methods

When you purchase a network interface card, that card will need to provide the type of network access method used on your network. Most NICs will be identified as *Ethernet cards* or *Token-Ring cards*. The differences between the different access methods are summarized in Table 7.3.

The most common type of local area network in use today is the contention-based (CSMA/CD) architecture of Ethernet. It is fast in low-traffic environments and requires only simple software and inexpensive hardware. CSMA/CA networks are primarily found in AppleTalk environments.

CH
7

Token-passing networks are common in environments with heavy network traffic or time-critical information. Token-passing networks are also viewed as more reliable because you are guaranteed that the data will be transmitted.

Networks using polling can be primarily found in an environment using mainframe computers. For instance, networks using IBM's Systems Network Architecture (SNA) utilize polling.

Demand-priority systems will be found in newer networks utilizing the 100VG-AnyLAN architecture.

Table 7.3   A Comparison of Different Access Methods

Access Method	Advantages	Disadvantages	Example Architectures
Contention	Fast in low traffic Inexpensive	Slow in high traffic No access guarantee No priority mechanism	Ethernet (CSMA/CD) LocalTalk (CSMA/CA)
Token passing	Fast in high traffic Guaranteed access Time-critical	Slow in low traffic More expensive	Token Ring, ARCNet
Demand	Fast priority access Can set priority	Expensive Guaranteed	100VG-AnyLAN
Polling	Guaranteed access	Inefficient use of network	IBM's SNA

Summary

The process of connecting your computer to the physical media for your network involves obtaining the appropriate *network interface card (NIC)* and software *driver*. The network interface card, also called a *network adapter card*, translates information coming from the parallel *data bus* used by the computer into a serial stream of bits that can be sent out over the network medium. The card also includes a *transceiver* that physically connects the card to the network media, translates the bits of data into electrical or optical signals, and sends it out onto the media. The transceiver also receives information from the media and passes it on to the other components of the NIC.

Before purchasing a NIC, you must know what type of data bus is used by your computer. The four primary buses in use today are *ISA, EISA, PCI,* and *Micro Channel Architecture.*

When you have a NIC, it must be configured properly before being installed into your machine. If your NIC and operating system support the *Plug and Play* architecture, all you should have to do is open up your computer, insert the card, close your computer, and turn it on. All configuration will occur automatically. Currently, this functionality is only supported by the Windows 95/98 operating system.

However, if your NIC and operating system do not support Plug and Play, you will need to manually configure the card. This usually involves the *interrupt request (IRQ)* setting and *base I/O port.* These two settings are usually configured with software but on older cards might be configured with a *DIP switch* or *jumper.* Each device that is connected to your computer's processor must use a unique IRQ and base I/O port. For NICs, you might also need to configure the *base memory address* of the card.

After you have the NIC configured and installed, you will need a *device driver* for it to work correctly. Because there are so many different possible NIC configurations, vendors of operating systems required NIC manufacturers to supply a *driver* that allows the operating system to communicate with the NIC. The driver is a small software program that is usually installed through a graphical interface.

Finally, in learning about how networks function, you need to understand how the NIC knows when to transmit data onto the network media. The four primary *access methods* used today are *contention, token passing, demand priority,* and *polling.*

Contention-based networks, such as Ethernet or AppleTalk, essentially allow any computer to transmit at any time. If two or more computers transmit at the same time, *collisions* occur, and data must be retransmitted. Token-passing networks, such as Token Ring, eliminate collisions and guarantee access to the network media by continually circulating a packet called a *token* and only allowing computers to transmit when they have the token. Demand-priority networks using the new standard of 100VG-AnyLAN put all the access control in the hands of intelligent hubs. Computers send a *demand* for service to the hub, which then allows the computer to transmit data. Polling networks use a central controller that continually *polls* each device on the network. A computer can only transmit data when it is polled.

CH

7

QUESTIONS AND ANSWERS

1. Where do network interface cards fit into the OSI Reference Model?

   A: At the physical and data link layers.

2. When data flows between the different components of your computer, it flows along a _____.

   A: Bus

3. What is a MAC address?

   A: The hardware address burned into the NIC. "MAC" comes from the IEEE Data Link sublayer Media Access Control.

4. Identify the two most common settings you need to configure on a NIC.

   A: IRQ and base I/O port

5. What is the role of an IRQ?

   A: To signal the CPU that a given device needs service from the CPU.

6. What does a driver do?

   A: A driver allows an operating system to use a specific device.

7. What are the four primary methods of allowing access onto the network media?

   A: Contention, token-passing, demand priority, and polling

8. Explain the difference between CSMA/CD and CSMA/CA.

   A: In both, computers listen to see if the media is free before transmitting, but in CSMA/CA, a computer next sends a small packet alerting all other computers that it is going to transmit. The computer then transmits the actual data. In CSMA/CD, if the media is free, the computer just starts transmitting data.

9. What is the primary advantage of token passing?

   A: Equal access to the media for all computers.

10. _____ is the most common implementation of CSMA/CD.

    A: Ethernet

PRACTICE TEST

1. What is an example of a type of network utilizing contention to control access?

   a. Token Ring
   b. ARCNet
   c. Ethernet
   d. SNA

Answer a is incorrect because Token Ring uses token passing. Answer b is incorrect because ARCNet uses token passing. **Answer c is correct because Ethernet uses contention.** Answer d is incorrect because SNA uses polling.

2. You need to install a network card into your PC. You currently have a serial mouse on COM1, a modem using COM2, a printer on LPT1, one hard drive, and a sound card using IRQ 5 connected to your computer. Which of the following IRQs can you use for your network card? (Choose all that apply.)

   a. IRQ 3
   b. IRQ 7
   c. IRQ 11
   d. IRQ 15

Answer a is incorrect because COM2 uses IRQ 3. Answer b is incorrect because LPT1 uses IRQ 7. **Answers c and d are correct because both are available.**

3. Which of the following statements is true? (Choose all that apply.)

   a. A driver is a small piece of software that allows your operating system to communicate with a hardware device.
   b. Only one driver is needed by your operating system to communicate with all installed devices.
   c. Operating system vendors supply drivers that will work with all network interface cards.
   d. A driver is only necessary if you do not use a Plug and Play network interface card.

Answer a is correct. Answer b is incorrect because a system usually needs a separate driver for each installed device. Answer c is incorrect because the OS vendors only provide common drivers, whereas the NIC manufacturers provide drivers for their cards. Answer d is incorrect and just plain wrong.

CH
7

4. You have a new computer that will function as a server for your network. It has a serial mouse, a modem on COM2, two hard drives (each on its own controller), and a SCSI controller for additional SCSI drives. Which of the following IRQs can you use for the network interface card? (Choose all that apply.)

   a. IRQ 3

   b. IRQ 9

   c. IRQ 10

   d. IRQ 15

Answer a is incorrect because COM2 uses IRQ 3. **Answer b is correct because IRQ 9 is available.** Answer c is incorrect because the SCSI controller will default to IRQ 10. Answer d is incorrect because the second hard drive controller will use IRQ 15.

5. An example of a network using demand-priority access control is what?

   a. Ethernet

   b. System Network Architecture (SNA)

   c. LocalTalk

   d. 100VG-AnyLAN

Answer a is incorrect because Ethernet uses contention. Answer b is incorrect because SNA uses polling. Answer c is incorrect because LocalTalk uses contention. **Answer d is correct; 100VG-AnyLAN uses demand priority.**

6. Which of the following are *not* advantages of the access method Carrier-Sense Multiple Access with Collision Detection? (Choose all that apply.)

   a. Network interface cards are inexpensive.

   b. Collision detection mechanism means that all computers are guaranteed access to the network media.

   c. Fast data transmission in environments with heavy network traffic.

   d. Transmissions can be prioritized based on which computer is sending the data.

Answer a is incorrect because it *is* an advantage of CSMA/CD. **Answer b is correct because it is *not* true of CSMA/CD; no computers are guaranteed access. Answer c is correct because it is *not* true of CSMA/CD; with heavy network traffic, transmission speed goes down. Answer d is correct because it is *not* true of CSMA/CD; there is no prioritization of data.**

7. Your company is moving into a new building, and you have been asked to develop a plan for installing a new network in the building. Due to the heavy traffic load on your current network, your management has asked you to consider all options.

REQUIRED RESULT: The network must be capable of fast data transmission under conditions of very heavy network traffic.

OPTIONAL DESIRED RESULTS: Because some parts of your manufacturing process require data in a timely manner, your network should be able to ensure on-time delivery of information. Due to recent revenue shortfalls, your proposal should be extremely inexpensive to implement.

PROPOSED SOLUTION: You suggest installing a Token-Ring network using a token-passing access method. Which results does the proposed solution produce?

a. The proposed solution produces the required result and both of the optional desired results.

b. The proposed solution produces the required result and only *one* of the optional desired results.

c. The proposed solution produces the required result but does *not* produce any of the optional desired results.

d. The proposed solution does *not* produce the required result.

Answer b is correct because although Token Ring meets the required result and the optional result related to timing, it will be rather expensive and will therefore fail the second optional result.

8. On each network interface card, a _____ connects the NIC to the physical medium and translates the data into a signal appropriate for the network media.

a. Transmitter

b. Converter

c. Data translator

d. Transceiver

Answer a is incorrect; a transmitter is usually used with radio. Answers b and c are incorrect and refer to nothing associated with NICs. **Answer d is correct.**

9. You need to install a network interface card into a basic PC in your office. The PC is not connected to a printer and has only a serial mouse on COM1 and one hard drive. Which of the following IRQs can you use? (Choose all that apply.)

a. IRQ 3

b. IRQ 4

c. IRQ 11

d. IRQ 15

Answer a is correct because LPT1 is not being used. Answer b is incorrect because COM1 uses IRQ 4. **Answer c is correct because no SCSI controllers are being used. Answer d is correct because the second hard drive controller is not being used.**

CH
7

10. Which of the following are *not* disadvantages to networks using the token-passing access method? (Choose all that apply.)

   a. In environments with low network traffic, the network media is used inefficiently because the token packet must still circulate.

   b. The equipment necessary for this type of network can be more expensive than other network types.

   c. Access to the network media is not guaranteed.

   d. Collisions will slow network traffic under heavy usage.

Answer a is incorrect because it *is* a disadvantage of token-passing networks. Answer b is incorrect because it *is* a disadvantage. **Answer c is correct because access *is* guaranteed. Answer d is correct because there are no collisions in a token-passing network.**

CHAPTER PREREQUISITE

Before reading this chapter, you should understand physical network media from Chapter 5, "The Physical Connection," and media access methods from Chapter 7, "Data Transmission." You should also be familiar with Chapter 3, "The OSI Reference Model," and Chapter 4, "Network Topology".

Network Architecture

WHILE YOU READ

1. What is the primary difference between 10BASE2 and 10BASE5?

2. Explain the 5-4-3 rule.

3. In a 10BASE2 network, what is the maximum distance between any two points on the network?

4. Name 3 Ethernet frame types.

5. Explain the difference in frame size between Token-Ring and Ethernet.

6. In Token-Ring, what you think of as a hub is called a _____.

7. How does beaconing help in a network?

8. What is the normal speed of an ARCNet network?

9. What is LocalTalk?

10. How is FDDI different from Token-Ring?

Earlier in this book, you learned about network media, the concepts of network topologies, network access methods, and how data gets transmitted onto the network media. You discovered that different physical media could be used for many different types of networks and how network interface cards interact with the physical media. You were also exposed to bus, star, and ring networks and how traffic flows throughout a network. Further, you learned about the OSI Reference Model and how an ideal network should function.

Now, you're going to build on that information and see how those topics are integrated into what is referred to as a *network architecture*. The architecture of a network refers not only to the topology of the network, but also to the physical media and the data access method. Although the OSI Reference Model addresses the ideal network, the network architectures discussed in this chapter will relate to how real-world networks function.

Ethernet

In the late 1960s and early 1970s, many organizations were trying to find ways to connect several computer systems to share resources. Early experiments led to the development of Ethernet in 1972 by Robert Metcalfe and David Boggs, two researchers at Xerox's Palo Alto Research Center (PARC). Xerox's first commercial version of Ethernet, released in 1975, enabled users to transmit data at approximately 3Mbps between 100 computers over a distance approaching 1 km.

This technology proved to be so successful that Xerox, Intel, and Digital Equipment Corporation developed a new standard for Ethernet operating at a speed of 10Mbps. The IEEE later used this standard as the basis for its 802.3 network specification, which defined how Ethernet networks operate at the physical and data link layers of the OSI Reference Model.

Today, Ethernet has emerged as the most popular network architecture in general use. It has the advantage of typically being inexpensive and also easy to install and configure.

There are actually several different types of networks defined under the umbrella of Ethernet. They all share a similar method for packaging data into *frames*, use baseband signaling for data transmission, and most use *carrier-sense multiple-access with collision detection (CSMA/CD)* for controlling access to the network media. The majority of the Ethernet networks can transmit data at up to 10Mbps, but two newer specifications have emerged providing transmission at 100Mbps.

With all Ethernet implementations, computers use an address that is "burned in" to read-only memory (ROM) on the network interface card (NIC) to communicate at the packet level. The addresses of both the computer sending the information and the destination computer are incorporated into the data frame sent onto the network media.

In this chapter, the Ethernet specifications discussed are grouped into two broad categories: 10Mbps and 100Mbps. The specific types of networks you'll learn about include the following:

- 10BASE-T
- 10BASE2
- 10BASE5
- 10BASE-F
- 100BASE-T
- 100VG-AnyLAN

You might find it helpful to understand the IEEE naming convention for Ethernet networks. As originally conceived, the naming convention had three components:

- Data transmission speed in megabits-per-second (Mbps), rounded to the nearest hundred.
- Type of signal transmission (baseband versus broadband).
- Maximum distance the network could cover in hundreds of meters.

In this manner, 10BASE5 indicated a network architecture that would allow baseband transmission of data at 10Mbps over a distance of 500 meters. Similarly, 10BASE2 allowed transmission up to 185 meters (rounded to 200 for the sake of simplicity).

As time went on, the naming convention changed, and Ethernet over twisted-pair became 10BASE-T and over fiber-optic became 10BASE-F.

10Mbps

When Ethernet was first established, it was defined as a standard at 10Mbps. Today, there are four common forms in use:

- *10BASE5.* Ethernet using thicknet coaxial cable.
- *10BASE2.* Ethernet on thinnet coaxial cable.
- *10BASE-T.* Ethernet over unshielded twisted pair (UTP).
- *10BASE-F.* Ethernet using fiber optic cable.

They all use similar data frame formats and CSMA/CD for controlling data access.

10BASE5

The original Ethernet networks formed the basis for the IEEE's 10BASE 5 specification. This specification defined a network using thicknet coaxial cable to interconnect up to 100 computers in a bus topology with segments up to 500 meters (1,640 feet).

As mentioned in Chapter 5, "The Physical Connection," thicknet makes use of a trans-ceiver that is connected to the network cable by way of a *piercing tap* (also called a *vam-pire tap*). This tap pierces the outer cable covering and makes direct contact with the interior conductor. A *drop cable* extends from the transceiver to the *Attachment Unit Interface (AUI)* or *DIX* port on your computer's NIC. In a pure 10BASE5 environment, there must be a separate transceiver for each network connection, as shown in Figure 8.1.

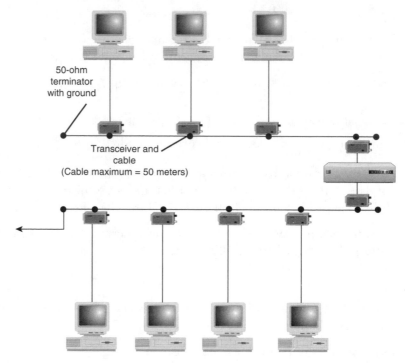

Figure 8.1
Ethernet 10BASE5 networks use transceivers attached to the thicknet cable.

Note that what is now commonly called the *AUI connector* or *AUI port* was originally referred to as the *DIX connector* because of the creators of the protocol: Digital Equipment Corporation, Intel, and Xerox.

10BASE5 has a number of distinct distance requirements. Transceivers must be a mini-mum of 2.5 meters (8 feet) apart. Each cable segment can be a maximum of 500 meters long. Up to five segments can be connected using *repeaters* for a total network length between any two points of 2,500 meters. Finally, the drop cable connecting the computer and the transceiver can be no longer than 50 meters (164 feet).

Key Concept

On the exam, you will probably find some question asking you about network lengths using 10BASE5. It is important to know that the lengths of the drop cables are *not* used in calculating the overall length of the network. The 500-meter segment length only includes the backbone thicknet cable. Drop cable lengths are irrelevant.

CH
8

10BASE5 is also subject to the *5-4-3 rule* for planning coaxial Ethernet networks. As shown in Figure 8.2, a 10BASE5 network can have five segments connected by four repeaters (*hubs*) for a maximum network length of 2,500 meters (8,200 feet). However, due to attenuation, only three of the segments can actually contain more network connections than the start and end points. The other two segments can be used to connect the network over long distances.

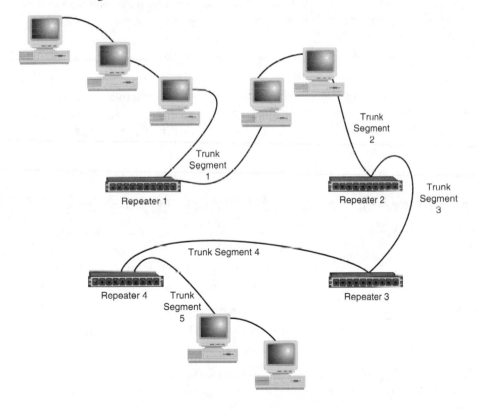

Figure 8.2
The 5-4-3 rule states that coaxial Ethernet networks can have five network segments connected by four repeaters with only three of the segments being populated.

Note that the 5-4-3 rule applies between *any two points* on the network. Your first instinct might be to say that because there are only 100 connections allowed per segment and a maximum segment length of 500 meters, then per the 5-4-3 rule, you can have a maximum network distance of 2,500 meters and a maximum number of nodes of 300.

However, what if some of the connections on one of the middle segments were repeaters themselves? What if they, in turn, had other segments connected to them? The 5-4-3 rule simply says that this limitation is between *any* two points. The trick in analyzing Ethernet network design is to make sure that from any point on the network there are no more than five segments with four repeaters and only three of the segments are populated.

Key Concept

The 5-4-3 rule in Ethernet says that between any two points on an Ethernet network there can be no more than five network segments connected by four repeaters with no more than three of those segments being populated (where being populated means having more connections that just the start and end points).

10BASE5 networks were the original Ethernet networks. If they are even used today, they are generally relegated to serving as the backbone for other Ethernet networks. For instance, you might find thicknet running between buildings with a transceiver at either end connected to a hub with 10BASE2 connections flowing from the hub throughout the building.

Table 8.1 summarizes information about the 10BASE5 network architecture.

Table 8.1   Summary of 10BASE5 Information

Information Category	10BASE5 Specifics
Advantage	Long distances
Disadvantages	High cost, difficult to install
Topology	Bus
Cable type	50-ohm thicknet
Connector type	Vampire tap transceiver, AUI/DIX connector
Media access method	CSMA/CD
Maximum segment length	500 meters (1,640 feet)
Maximum length between any two points	2,500 meters (8,200 feet)

Information Category	10BASE5 Specifics
Minimum length between nodes	2.5 meters (8 feet)
Maximum # of connected segments	5, with only 3 populated
Maximum # of nodes per segment	100
Maximum # of nodes for network	1,024
Transmission speed	10Mbps
IEEE specification	802.3

CH 8

10BASE2

The next evolution of Ethernet involved the use of *thinnet cable*. Thinnet is very flexible and simple to install. Unlike thicknet, the transceiver is part of the NIC, and the thinnet cable connects directly to the NIC. As mentioned in Chapter 5, thinnet uses a BNC connector in a bus topology and requires a terminator at both ends of the cable. One of the terminators should be grounded—for instance, with a grounding strap or wire running from the terminator to a ground point such as the screw on an electrical outlet.

The IEEE specification for 10BASE2 requires the use of RG-58A/U or RG-58C/U cable. This cable has an impedance of 50 ohms and a central core consisting of multiple strands.

Key Concept

Test questions will try to trip you up on the specific cable types used in 10BASE2. Remember that the only types specified by the IEEE are RG-58A/U and RG-58C/U. RG-58U (or RG-58/U) is *not* acceptable. Likewise, RG-59, the 75-ohm cable used for cable TV, will not work.

Similar to 10BASE5, 10BASE2 networks are restricted by the 5-4-3 rule to five 185-meter segments connected by four repeaters, with only three of the segments being populated with network connections. Within each 185-meter segment, smaller pieces of cable can be linked using *barrel connectors*; however, each barrel connector reduces the quality of the signal on the cable.

Just as with 10BASE5, do realize that the 5-4-3 rule allows repeaters to be connected to one of the middle segments and that the measurement is between any two points in a 10BASE2 network.

Because 10BASE2 networks were significantly cheaper to implement than thicknet networks, they entered widespread use and are still found in some network installations today. However, this cost benefit was eliminated by the development of 10BASE-T networks based on the even less costly media of UTP. The development of 10BASE-T networks using a star topology also overcame the troubleshooting difficulties of the bus topology used by 10BASE2.

Table 8.2 summarizes information about the 10BASE2 network architecture.

Table 8.2 Summary of 10BASE2 Information	
Information Category	*10BASE2 Specifics*
Advantages	Simple to install, relatively inexpensive
Disadvantage	Bus topology is difficult to troubleshoot
Topology	Bus
Cable type	50-ohm thinnet—RG-58A/U and RG-58C/U
Connector type	BNC
Media access method	CSMA/CD
Maximum segment length	185 meters (607 feet)
Maximum distance between two points	925 meters (3,035 feet)
Minimum length between nodes	0.5 meters (20 inches)
Maximum # of connected segments	5, with only 3 populated
Maximum # of nodes per segment	30
Maximum # of nodes for network	1,024
Transmission speed	10Mbps
IEEE specification	802.3

10BASE-T

10BASE-T networks are based on UTP and are by far the most popular type of Ethernet network in use today. Using a star topology as depicted in Figure 8.3, 10BASE-T networks are not subject to the same troubleshooting difficulties as 10BASE2 and 10BASE5. The UTP media is very inexpensive, as is most of the other 10BASE-T hardware including NICs and hubs. Similar to 10BASE2, the transceiver is usually included as part of the NIC. UTP cables plug directly into the RJ-45 jack (see Figure 8.4) on the card.

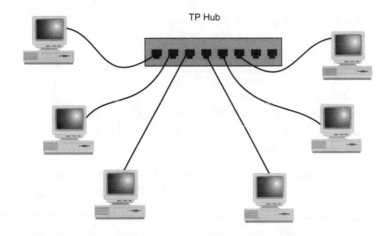

Figure 8.3
10BASE-T networks use UTP cable in a star topology.

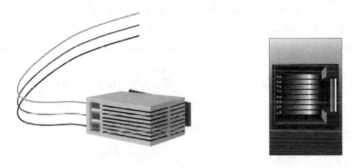

Figure 8.4
UTP cables plug into the RJ-45 jack on a NIC.

Key Concept

On the test, remember that the IEEE specification for 10BASE-T requires UTP. *Shielded twisted-pair (STP)* is *not* part of the specification.

10BASE-T networks are still subject to the 5-4-3 rule, but with one important difference. Recall that in the previous discussions, a "populated" network segment was one in which there were more connections in the segment than just the start and end points. Although this can be true with coaxial cables, twisted-pair cables can *only* have a start and end connection and therefore can never be considered as "populated."

In a pure 10BASE-T network you could think of the rule almost as the "5-4" rule: Between any two points on the network there can be no more than five network segments connected by four repeaters. The "3" part of the rule simply doesn't apply if all the segments are UTP cable because *none* of the segments have more than the start and end point connections.

It is worth remembering the entire 5-4-3 rule, however, because if you get into mixed networks, that is, networks involving both 10BASE-T and either 10BASE2 or 10BASE5, the "3" part of the rule *does* apply.

Although 10BASE-T networks perform effectively using UTP cable of Categories 3, 4, and 5, most new installations will use Category 5 UTP because it can handle a future capacity of 100Mbps.

Key Concept

For the test, remember that Category 3 is the *minimum* required for 10BASE-T. Also, remember from Chapter 5 that cables running in the ceilings and walls of most modern buildings must be *plenum*-rated.

The primary disadvantage of 10BASE-T is the comparatively short distances that UTP can cover (100 meters). To get around this, you might find 10BASE-T running from hubs interconnected over some distance by a 10BASE2 or 10BASE-F connection.

Note that if you want to connect two 10BASE-T hubs together, you cannot simply connect a 10BASE-T (UTP) cable from one hub to the other. The problem is that each hub is expecting to receive data on one pair in the UTP cable and to transmit data on another pair. With a regular UTP cable, both transmit and receive pairs will be connected to each other, and no data will be transmitted.

To solve this problem, you must connect the transmit pair on one hub to the receive pair on the other and vice versa. There are two methods of doing this. First, you can use a *crossover* cable, which is a UTP cable where the transmit and receive pairs are swapped from one end of the cable to the other. Second, most 10BASE-T hubs have one hub port that is designated as an "uplink" port. (Other terms are used depending on the manufacturer's marketing department!) This port will function normally when connected to a regular computer. However, there is usually a button next to the port that will swap the transmit and receive pairs and allow it to be connected *with a regular UTP cable* to another hub. Note that you only need to use this uplink port on *one* of the hubs (not on both) to solve the problem.

Table 8.3 summarizes information about the 10BASE-T network architecture.

Table 8.3 Summary of 10BASE-T Information	
Information Category	*10BASE-T Specifics*
Advantages	Very inexpensive, simple to connect, easy to troubleshoot
Disadvantage	Limited distance
Topology	Star
Cable type	Unshielded twisted-pair (Categories 3–5)
Connector type	RJ-45
Media access method	CSMA/CD
Maximum segment length	100 meters (328 feet)
Maximum distance between any two points	500 meters
Minimum length between nodes	0.5 meters (1.5 feet)
Maximum # of connected segments	1,024
Maximum # of nodes per segment	1
Maximum # of nodes for network	1,024
Transmission speed	10Mbps
IEEE specification	802.3

10BASE-F

The IEEE specification for 10Mbps Ethernet running across fiber-optic cables is known generally as *10BASE-F* and encompasses several variations.

All variations use a star topology with data sent using light signals instead of electrical signals. Similar to 10BASE-T, up to 1,024 network nodes can be connected using hubs. However, because of the high cost of the fiber-optic cable and equipment, 10BASE-F is generally not used in a LAN environment. You might find it used for a LAN in situations where high electrical interference or heightened security concerns warrant the use of a medium that is not subject to electromagnetic interference. However, more often you will find it as a backbone connecting different 10BASE-T networks.

Although fiber-optic cables can operate at speeds much higher than the 10Mbps defined in the 10BASE-F specification, their primary disadvantage is their extremely high cost and the difficulty in installation.

Table 8.4 summarizes information about the 10BASE-F network architecture.

Table 8.4 Summary of 10BASE-F Information	
Information Category	*10BASE-F Specifics*
Advantage	Long distances
Disadvantages	Very expensive, difficult to install
Topology	Star
Cable type	Fiber-optic
Connector type	Specialized
Media access method	CSMA/CD
Maximum segment length	2,000 meters (6,561 feet)
Maximum overall network length	N/A
Minimum length between nodes	N/A
Maximum # of connected segments	1,024
Maximum # of nodes per segment	1
Maximum # of nodes for network	1,024
Transmission speed	10Mbps
IEEE specification	802.3

100Mbps

As the need for higher network speed has increased, vendors have created two competing standards for 100Mbps Ethernet: 100VG-AnyLAN and 100BASE-T. 100BASE-T is further subdivided into three categories: 100BASE-TX, 100BASE-T4, and 100BASE-FX. Both standards will be discussed further, but some points of comparison are useful ahead of time:

- 100VG-AnyLAN and 100BASE-T both require users to replace all network interface cards with 100VG-AnyLAN or 100BASE-T NICs.
- Even though both standards use UTP cable, 100BASE-TX requires Category 5 cable, whereas 100VG-AnyLAN and 100BASE-T4 can use any Category 3, 4, or 5 cable provided that it has four pairs of wire. In either case, some users might have to upgrade their installed cable.

- With 100BASE-TX and 100BASE-T4, communication is restricted to a range of 100 meters. 100VG-AnyLAN networks using Category 3 or 4 UTP are also subject to this 100 meter restriction. However, 100VG-AnyLAN can reach distances of 150 meters using Category 5 UTP.

- Both 100VG-AnyLAN and 100BASE-FX can use fiber-optic cable to transmit over distances as far as 2,000 meters.

- Vendors have created NICs for both standards that enable network administrators to easily migrate from 10BASE-T networks. Users can install the new NIC and continue to use it with 10BASE-T until they are ready to switch over to the higher-speed network.

- 100BASE-T networks can transmit only Ethernet frame types, while 100VG-AnyLAN can transmit both Ethernet and Token-Ring packets, allowing it to be easily integrated with both architectures.

- 100BASE-T is covered under the IEEE's 802.3 specification, while 100VG-AnyLAN is under the new IEEE 802.12 specification.

100BASE-T

100BASE-T, also called *Fast Ethernet* or *100BASEX*, is essentially an outgrowth of efforts to increase the capacity of 10BASE-T networks. Originally developed by Grand Junction Networks, 3Com, Intel, and others, it modifies the 802.3 Ethernet standard to support 100Mbps data transmission rates primarily over Category 5 UTP cables. To do this, 100BASE-T networks use shorter cable lengths and link multiple hubs as shown in Figure 8.5.

The 100BASE-T standard actually defines three cable types:

- *100BASE-T4*. Four-pair Category 3, 4, or 5 UTP.
- *100BASE-TX*. Two-pair Category 5 UTP.
- *100BASE-FX*. Two-strand fiber-optic cable.

One important factor about 100BASE-TX networks is that they *require* Category 5 UTP cable. Many 10BASE-T networks will operate using existing voice-grade Category 3 UTP such as that installed with most phone systems. This cable will have to be upgraded before such a network can upgrade to 100BASE-TX.

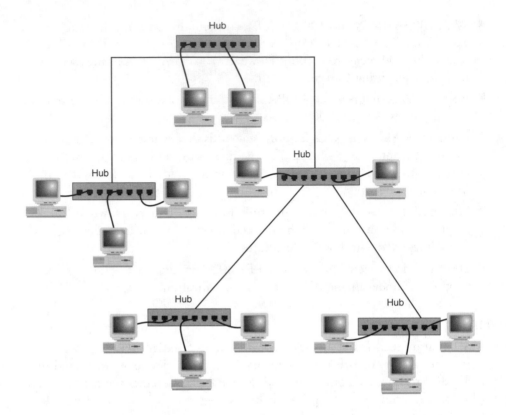

Figure 8.5
100BASE-T networks use a star topology similar to 10BASE-T networks.

100BASE-T4 can support 100Mbps over Category 3, 4, or 5 UTP. However, it requires all four twisted-pairs of wire in a UTP cable to be available. Because 10BASE-T only requires two pairs of wire, some current installations of UTP might allocate two wire pairs for data and use another pair for voice phone. If so, additional UTP cable will need to be installed with all four pairs available before 100BASE-T4 can operate.

Although there are three cable standards available, 100BASE-TX has become the most popular and is usually what people are referencing when they refer to *100BASE-T* or *Fast Ethernet.*

Table 8.5 summarizes information about the 100BASE-T network architecture.

Table 8.5 Summary of 100BASE-T Information	
Information Category	*100BASE-T Specifics*
Advantages	Fast, simple to connect, easy to troubleshoot
Disadvantages	Limited distance, expensive hardware
Topology	Star
Cable type	Category 5 UTP—100BASE-TX; Category 3, 4, 5 UTP—100BASE-T4; Fiber-optic cable—100BASE-FX
Connector type	RJ-45
Media access method	CSMA/CD
Maximum segment length	100 meters (328 feet)—100BASE-TX, 100BASE-T4; 2000 meters (6,561 feet)—100BASE-FX
Maximum overall network length	N/A
Minimum length between nodes	2.5 meters (8 feet)
Maximum # of connected segments	1,024
Maximum # of nodes per segment	1
Maximum # of nodes for network	1,024
Transmission speed	100Mbps
IEEE specification	802.3

100VG-AnyLAN

Originally developed by Hewlett-Packard and AT&T, 100VG-AnyLAN uses the *demand priority* media access method rather than CSMA/CD. In this situation, intelligent hubs receive *demands* for service from computers and allow those computers to transmit to their destination computer. 100VG-AnyLAN networks use a star topology similar to 10BASE-T with a series of cascading hubs interlinked, as shown in Figure 8.6. A central "root" hub is connected to multiple hubs, each of which can be connected to other hubs.

100VG-AnyLAN is designed to work with any "voice-grade" UTP and can be used with many existing 10BASE-T UTP installations of Category 3 or higher. The only caveat is that 100VG-AnyLAN requires all four pairs of wires in a UTP cable, whereas 10BASE-T only requires two pairs (one to transmit and one to receive). In some existing 10BASE-T installations, two pairs of wire in a UTP cable might be used for the network, while another pair might be used for a phone. If this is so, the cable will need to be upgraded to support data use of all four wire pairs before it can be used with 100VG-AnyLAN.

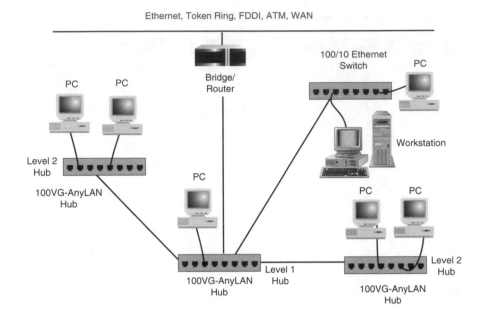

Figure 8.6
Hubs are interconnected in a 100VG-AnyLAN network to form a star topology.

You might also hear 100VG-AnyLAN referred to as any of the following: 100BASEVG, 100VG, VG, or AnyLAN.

With demand priority, 100VG-AnyLAN offers several distinct performance advantages. Because the hubs provide all access control, data packets are not broadcast throughout the entire network. Data is routed through the hub(s) from the source to the destination. This has the added benefit of ensuring a higher degree of privacy because all computers are not receiving the data packets. Another feature is that incoming service demands can be prioritized by the hubs and items needing time-sensitive transmission can be given a higher priority.

The 100VG-AnyLAN architecture also has an advantage in that it is not limited to use with Ethernet. By using the appropriate NIC drivers, 100VG-AnyLAN can be configured to use Token-Ring frames instead of Ethernet frames, allowing it to be integrated into an existing Token-Ring network. Through the use of a device called a *bridge* and the appropriate frame type, a 100VG-AnyLAN network can coexist and exchange information with either a Token-Ring or Ethernet network.

Like 10BASE-T, 100VG-AnyLAN has a maximum distance of 100 meters over Category 3 UTP between a hub and a computer. Unlike other UTP architectures, in 100VG-AnyLAN networks with Category 5 UTP, this distance can be extended to 150 meters. 100VG-AnyLAN is also defined for use with fiber-optic cable at distances up to 2,000 meters.

Table 8.6 summarizes information about the 100VG-AnyLAN network architecture.

Table 8.6   Summary of 100VG-AnyLAN Information

Information Category	100VG-AnyLAN Specifics
Advantages	Fast, simple to connect, easy to troubleshoot, can be used with either Ethernet or Token-Ring packets.
Disadvantages	Limited distance (UTP), expensive hardware
Topology	Star
Cable type	Unshielded twisted-pair (Categories 3–5), shielded-twisted-pair, fiber-optic
Connector type	RJ-45
Media access method	Demand priority
Maximum segment length	100 meters (328 feet) if using Category 3 UTP or STP 150 meters (492 feet) if using Category 5 UTP 2000 meters (6,562 feet) if using fiber-optic
Maximum overall network length	N/A
Minimum length between nodes	2.5 meters (8 feet)
Maximum # of connected segments	1,024
Maximum # of nodes per segment	1
Maximum # of nodes for network	1,024
Transmission speed	100Mbps
IEEE specification	802.12

Ethernet Frame Types

Before you explore other architectures, you need to understand one final aspect of Ethernet. Regardless of which of the previously described Ethernet architectures you use, your data will be packaged by the network driver and NIC into a *frame* and sent out onto the network media. There are, however, four different frame types, each of which is incompatible with the others:

- *Ethernet 802.3*. Used primarily in Novell NetWare 2.x and 3.x networks.
- *Ethernet 802.2*. Used in Novell NetWare 4.x networks by default.
- *Ethernet SNAP*. Used in some AppleTalk networks.
- *Ethernet II*. Used in TCP/IP networks.

Key Concept

For communication to occur between two computers on an Ethernet network, they both must use the *identical* frame type.

All frame types use a packet size between 64 and 1,518 bytes and can work with the network architectures mentioned previously. Generally, your network will only use one of the frame types, but it is possible that certain computers, such as your servers, might use multiple frame types to communicate with different segments of your network.

Ethernet 802.3

Also known as *raw Ethernet*, this frame type was developed before the actual IEEE 802.3 Ethernet specification was finished. As such, it is actually not in full compliance with the IEEE 802.3 specification and today is found primarily in Novell NetWare 2.2 and 3.x networks.

As depicted in Figure 8.7, an Ethernet 802.3 data frame begins with a preamble and a one-byte *Start Frame Delimiter (SFD)* field that indicates the beginning of the frame. The destination and source addresses are next, followed by a field for the length of the data and the actual data. The packet is concluded with a four-byte *Cyclical Redundancy Check (CRC)* that ensures that the data was not corrupted in transit.

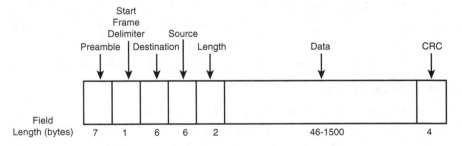

Figure 8.7
Ethernet 802.3 frames contain addressing information and the length of the data.

Ethernet 802.2

Ethernet 802.2 frames are in full compliance with the IEEE 802.3 standard and are the default frame type for Novell NetWare 3.12 and 4.x networks. Ethernet 802.2 frames contain similar fields to the Ethernet 802.3 frames, with the addition of three *Logical Link Control (LLC)* fields.

Ethernet SNAP

Ethernet *SNAP (SubNetwork Address Protocol)* frames offer enhancements to the Ethernet 802.2 frame type, including the addition of a *type* field to indicate which network protocol is used in the data portion of the frame. Ethernet SNAP frames are primarily used in AppleTalk Phase II networks (discussed in the section, "AppleTalk," later in this chapter).

Ethernet II

TCP/IP networks and networks using multiple network protocols generally use Ethernet II frames. As shown in Figure 8.8, Ethernet II frames differ from Ethernet 802.3 frames in that they combine the preamble and SFD fields and include a protocol type field where the Ethernet 802.3 frames have a length field.

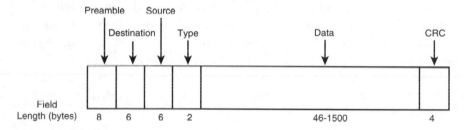

Figure 8.8
Ethernet II frames include a type field to indicate what network protocol is used.

Token-Ring

In the mid-1980s, IBM developed the Token-Ring network architecture to provide users with a fast and reliable network. Later standardized as IEEE 802.5, a Token-Ring network is physically wired using a star topology, as are 10BASE-T Ethernet networks. However, as shown in Figure 8.9, the network is implemented as a *logical ring*, meaning that the hub is wired so that the signal travels in a ring.

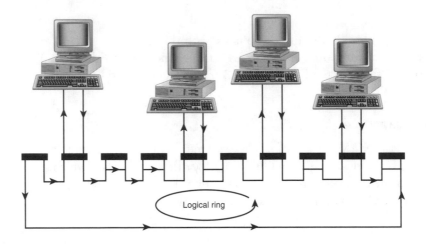

Figure 8.9
Token-Ring networks are wired in a physical star, but implement a logical ring.

Token-Ring networks use a token-passing media access method to ensure that each computer on the network gets a chance to transmit data. A small data frame called a *token* is passed around the ring. Each computer on the network receives the token from its *nearest active upstream neighbor (NAUN)*. If the token is free and the computer has data to transmit, the computer attaches its data to the token and sends it on to its *nearest active downstream neighbor (NADN)*. Each subsequent computer receives the token, determines that the token is in use, and repeats the transmission of the token and data, exactly as they were received, on to its NADN.

Eventually, the data reaches the destination computer, which copies the data and passes it to upper layer protocols for processing. The destination computer then toggles two bits in the data packet and passes the token and data again out onto the ring. Finally, the token and data return to the source computer, which verifies that the data was sent successfully (by noticing the two toggled bits) and then frees up the token and passes it to its NADN.

Although this process might seem cumbersome, it actually allows for fast transmission of information. Because there are no collisions to worry about, computers normally do not need to retransmit information. As network traffic increases, the token still circulates, allowing each computer to transmit information.

As originally conceived, IBM Token-Ring networks operated at a speed of 4Mbps. Later improvements increased that speed to 16Mbps. Token-Ring data frames can be 4,000 to 17,800 bytes in length, in contrast to a maximum frame size of 1,500 bytes in an Ethernet data frame.

Similar to Ethernet networks, each computer on a Token-Ring network uses the address burned into its NIC card.

Key Concept

For the exam, remember that Token-Ring networks use a larger data frame size than Ethernet. This allows for the more rapid transmission of large blocks of data.

Token-Ring Hubs

Within a Token-Ring network, each hub is known as a *Multistation Access Unit (MAU)* and is wired as a logical ring as shown previously in Figure 8.9.

Key Concept

A Token-Ring hub can also be referred to as an MSAU *(MultiStation Access Unit)* or SMAU *(Smart Multistation Access Unit)*.

A typical IBM MAU might have ten connection ports, eight of which are used for connections to computers. The other two ports are *Ring In (RI)* and *Ring Out (RO)*, allowing Token-Ring MAUs to be linked. Figure 8.10 shows how two MAUs would be linked to provide access for up to 16 workstations.

If additional hubs are needed, each MAU would be added in such a manner that the logical ring would be preserved. The IBM specification for Token-Ring states that up to 33 hubs can be connected in this fashion. Although the original Token-Ring MAUs could only accommodate eight network connections, IBM and other vendors now manufacture hubs with sixteen or more ports.

Cables in a Token-Ring Network

Token-Ring networks can use either UTP or STP cables. In 1984, IBM outlined a comprehensive cabling system that defined cable types, connectors, and all other components necessary for computer networking. When Token-Ring was introduced, it used this IBM cabling system.

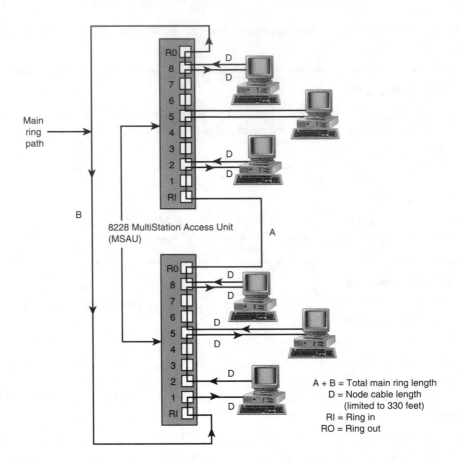

Main ring path

8228 MultiStation Access Unit (MSAU)

A + B = Total main ring length
D = Node cable length (limited to 330 feet)
RI = Ring in
RO = Ring out

Figure 8.10
Token-Ring MAUs (hubs) are linked in such a manner that the logical ring is preserved.

The IBM cabling system breaks out cables into different types. Cables are defined based on *American Wire Gauge (AWG)* standards that specify wire diameters. AWG numbers are inversely assigned to diameters, meaning that larger AWG numbers indicate smaller diameters. As a reference, standard telephone wire has a thickness of 22 AWG. Thicknet coaxial cable is rated at 12 AWG, whereas thinnet coaxial cable is 20 AWG. A cable rated at 26 AWG would be smaller than regular telephone wire.

The IBM cable types are as follows:

- *Type 1.* STP cable with two twisted pairs of 22 AWG solid-core wire surrounded by a braided shield and casing. This is the typical cable used between computers and MAUs.

- *Type 2.* STP cable with two twisted pairs of 22 AWG solid-core wire for data and four twisted pairs of 26 AWG wire for voice. Used in situations where you want both voice and data to be carried over one cable.

- *Type 3.* UTP voice-grade cable with four twisted pairs of 22 or 24 AWG cable. Used as a cheaper alternative to Type 1, but cannot transmit at more than 4Mbps.

- *Type 4.* Not defined.

- *Type 5.* Fiber-optic cable used primarily for linking MAUs over distance.

- *Type 6.* STP cable with two twisted pairs of 26 AWG stranded-core wire surrounded by a braided shield and casing. Similar to Type 1, except that the stranded-core allows more flexibility. The stranded-core also limits the distance to two-thirds that of Type 1. This cable type is primarily used as a *patch cable* in wiring closets to connect hubs.

- *Type 7.* Not defined.

- *Type 8.* STP cable for use under carpets. It is essentially Type 6 cable with a flat casing.

- *Type 9.* Plenum-rated version of Type 6 cable.

Traditionally, most Token-Ring networks used Type 1 or Type 3 cable. However, the IEEE developed a specification called *UTP/TR* that defines the use of regular Category 5 UTP within a Token-Ring environment. Today, many Token-Ring installations will use regular UTP instead of the more costly IBM STP cables. However, in environments where electrical interference is an issue, Type 1 STP might be favored because the shielding reduces susceptibility to interference.

Key Concept

Most Token-Ring networks today will use either IBM Type 3 UTP or IBM Type 1 STP. Newer networks might use standard Category 5 UTP.

When UTP cables are used to connect computers to hubs, they use the standard RJ-45 connection. Type 1 STP cables, however, have a 9-pin connector on one end for the NIC and a special *IBM data connector* or *Type A connector* on the other end for the MAU.

Beaconing

One feature of Token-Ring networks is their capability to self-repair network problems through a process called *beaconing.* On a Token-Ring network, the first computer to be powered on becomes the *Active Monitor* responsible for ensuring that data can travel around the ring. All other computers become *Standby Monitors* when they are turned on.

The role of the Active Monitor is really quite simple. Every seven seconds, it sends out a special frame to its nearest active downstream neighbor. This packet announces the address of the Active Monitor and the fact that the Active Monitor is the upstream neighbor. The neighboring station examines that packet and passes it along to the next station after changing the upstream address. This third station now has a packet listing the address of the Active Monitor as well as the address of its upstream neighbor. It then fashions a packet to send on to its neighbor. In this manner, the packet travels around the ring and back to the Active Monitor. When it has completed the ring, the Active Monitor knows that the network is intact, and all the stations on the network know the address of their upstream neighbor.

As depicted in Figure 8.11, if a computer has not heard from its upstream neighbor after seven seconds, it sends a packet on to the ring announcing three items: its address, the address of its NAUN (which has not communicated), and a beacon type. This packet travels around the network, forcing all computers to check their configuration. If there is no answer from the NAUN, the ring can reconfigure itself to route around the problem area. In this manner, a level of *fault tolerance* (for example, the capability to continue functioning in spite of problems) can be created that ensures a high level of network reliability.

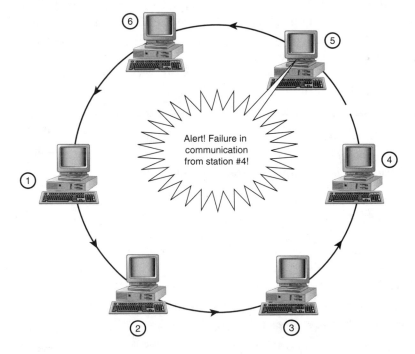

Figure 8.11
Beaconing is the process where computers on a Token-Ring network detect a problem and attempt to fix it.

Key Concept

Beaconing is a process where computers on a ring can detect that there is a potential failure of the ring and reconfigure the ring to bypass the problem station.

Table 8.7 summarizes information about the Token-Ring network architecture.

Table 8.7 Summary of Token-Ring Information

Information Category	Token-Ring Specifics
Advantages	Fast and reliable
Disadvantages	More expensive than compa-rable Ethernet solutions; can be difficult to troubleshoot
Topology	Ring
Cable type	IBM cable types, typically Types 1 (STP) and 3 (UTP)
Connector type	RJ-45 or IBM Type A
Media access method	Token passing
Maximum cable length	45 meters (150 feet) with UTP, 101 meters (330 feet) with STP
Maximum overall network length	N/A
Minimum length between nodes	2.5 meters (8 feet)
Maximum # of connected segments	33 hubs
Maximum # of nodes per segment	Depends on hub
Maximum # of nodes for network	72 nodes with UTP; 260 nodes with STP
Transmission speed	4 or 16Mbps
IEEE specification	802.5

ARCnet

The *Attached Resource Computer Network (ARCnet)* is the oldest network architecture discussed in this book. Created in 1977 by Datapoint Corporation, ARCnet provides network transmission speed up to 2.5Mbps using a token-passing media access method. Like Token-Ring, ARCnet implements a *logical ring* topology but, as shown in Figure 8.12, can physically structure the network as either a bus, star, or a mixture of both. Additionally, a single network can incorporate multiple media such as UTP, coaxial cable, and fiber-optic cable.

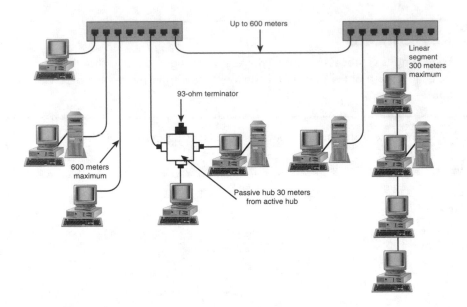

Figure 8.12
ARCnet can use both star and bus topologies in the same network.

Data transmission in ARCnet is similar to Ethernet in that signals are broadcast across the entire network. Each computer on the network listens for signals directed to its address and processes those signals while ignoring all others. Hubs in an ARCnet environment are wired in a similar manner to Ethernet star networks, *not* as logical rings in the way that Token-Ring hubs are wired.

ARCnet's token-passing mechanism is quite different from that of Token-Ring networks. In Token-Ring, the token passes from station to station, related to proximity. For example, when the token enters the hub from one computer, it travels through the hub to the next connected port and from there to the connected computer. When that computer is finished with the token, it goes back to the hub and on to the next nearest computer.

In contrast, the ARCnet token travels from computer to computer based on the *station identifier (SID)*. ARCnet NICs do not use a burned-in address like Ethernet and Token-Ring. Instead, each NIC simply has a DIP switch on it that is used to set the SID for each computer. This address can be from 1 to 255 and is set at the time that you install an ARCnet NIC into a computer. Essentially, the token passes from the computer with a SID of 1 to a computer with a SID of 2, from 2 to 3, from 3 to 4, and on numerically until a computer with a SID of 255 passes it back to the computer with a SID of 1.

Because most ARCnet networks do not have 255 nodes, computers on an ARCnet network learn their *next station identifier (NID)* to avoid passing the token to non-existent nodes. When a computer is added or removed from the network or when the network is first started, the station with the lowest SID (usually 1) identifies itself as the station with the token and sends a query on the network for a station with a SID one number greater than itself. If it gets no answer, it keeps incrementing the number until it finally gets a response. It sets its NID to the SID of the computer that responded and then passes the token on to that computer. This second computer then begins its own query process to find the next highest station. Ultimately, some machine reaches 255 during its query and continues querying at 1. When this process is over, the network has been reconfigured, and each station knows the address of the next station, as shown in Figure 8.13.

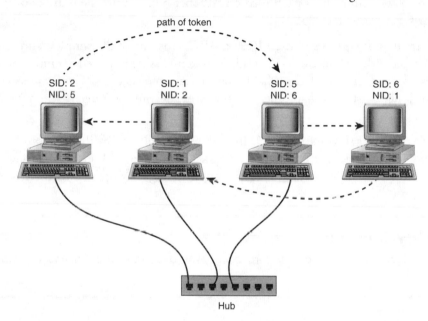

Figure 8.13
The token in an ARCnet network is passed from one computer to the next in numerical order.

Note that within ARCnet, the acronym *SID* is used for a station identifier. However, within the Windows NT and Windows 95 operating systems, a SID refers to the *security identifier* (or *security identification number*) assigned to a user or group.

Although this token-passing arrangement is easy to understand and works quite well, it has several drawbacks. To start with, care needs to be taken with the order in which addresses are assigned. The token will pass from one station to the next highest numerical station, regardless of whether the two stations are next to each other or far apart. If you assign addresses based on proximity, the flow of your network traffic will be more efficient and faster. The token also travels at a fixed speed, which limits the overall speed of the network.

Another drawback to ARCnet is the manual configuration process. Each computer must have a unique address and must be configured by hand. The network administrator must keep track of these addresses and ensure that any new installations use new numbers. Additionally, the 8-bit DIP switch used on ARCnet NICs limits the number of stations on an ARCnet network to 255.

There were definite reasons to use ARCnet. ARCnet is one of the simplest and least expensive network architectures to install. Its token-passing scheme guarantees access to the network media and provides reliable transportation of data. ARCnet can also transmit data over longer distances than other architectures and can use a diverse mixture of physical media.

However, ARCnet's slow speed of 2.5Mbps and its inability to easily interconnect with other network architectures has limited its appeal. Today, even though some vendors have released *ARCnet Plus* with operating speeds approaching 20Mbps, ARCnet networks are fading from use.

Key Concept

ARCnet is a network architecture using token passing with a maximum speed of 2.5Mbps.

ARCnet Hubs

ARCnet hubs provide a star topology and are produced in two variations. *Active hubs* provide the majority of connections in an ARCnet network. As a signal enters an active hub, its strength is amplified and is sent on to all other ports. Active hubs typically contain eight ports, although more might be possible. Active hubs can be linked in a distributed star topology. When linked in such a manner, two active hubs can be no farther than 600 meters (2,000 feet) apart.

Passive hubs usually have four ports and exist only to pass the signal from one port to the other. They do not have a power supply and must be connected to active devices such as active hubs and NICs. Therefore, a passive hub cannot be connected to another passive hub. A typical configuration would be for three computers to be connected to a passive hub, with the fourth port connecting the passive hub to an active hub. In ARCnet, it is required that all unused ports on a passive hub be terminated with an appropriate terminator. Additionally, passive hubs have distance limitations and can be no more than 30 meters (100 feet) from an active hub.

ARCnet Cables

As mentioned in the previous section, ARCnet networks can use many different types of cable. The most common type in use is RG-62 A/U 93-ohm coaxial cable with a BNC connector on either end. When used in a bus topology, BNC *T-connectors* are used in a similar fashion to Ethernet 10BASE2 networks. In a star configuration, the BNC connectors are plugged directly into the hub or NIC without a T-connector.

Table 8.8 summarizes information about the ARCnet network architecture.

Table 8.8   Summary of ARCnet Information

Information Category	ARCnet Specifics
Advantages	Inexpensive, easy to install, reliable
Disadvantages	Slow, does not interconnect well with other systems
Topology	Star and bus
Cable type	RG-62 A/U coaxial (93 ohm), UTP, fiber-optic
Connector type	BNC, RJ-45, others
Media access method	Token-passing
Maximum segment length	600 meters (2,000 feet) -RG-62 A/U
	121 meters (400 feet)- UTP
	3485 meters (11,500 feet) - fiber-optic
	30 meters (100 feet) from a passive hub
Maximum overall network length	6060 meters (20,000 feet)
Minimum length between nodes	Varies
Maximum # of connected segments	Varies
Maximum # of nodes per segment	Varies
Maximum # of nodes for network	255
Transmission speed	2.5Mbps
IEEE specification	No IEEE specification, but ANSI 878.1

AppleTalk

AppleTalk is a simple and easy-to-use network architecture used by Apple Macintosh computers. Because all Macintosh computers come equipped with a built-in NIC, setting up an AppleTalk network is a simple matter of connecting cables between Macintosh computers. For this reason, AppleTalk networks are extremely popular within Macintosh environments.

When first introduced in 1983, the term *AppleTalk* referred to the networking protocols and the actual hardware used to connect computers. In 1989, Apple Computer changed the definition of AppleTalk to refer to the overall architecture and added the term *LocalTalk* to refer to the cabling system.

AppleTalk uses a dynamic addressing system to determine each computer's address. When a computer is powered up, it can choose a numerical address it used previously or pick an address at random. The computer then broadcasts that address to the network to determine whether any other computer is using that address. If the address is not taken, the computer starts using the network with that address. If it is, the computer chooses another address at random and broadcasts that address to determine whether it is in use. This process continues until a valid address is found.

In the original AppleTalk implementation, now called *AppleTalk Phase 1*, only 32 computers could be connected on a network, and only LocalTalk cabling was supported. With the use of hubs, the overall network could be increased to 254 computers. In 1989, Apple delivered *AppleTalk Phase 2*, which introduced *EtherTalk* and *TokenTalk*, allowing use of AppleTalk network protocols on top of Ethernet and Token-Ring architectures. AppleTalk Phase 2 extended the theoretical number of computers that could be on a network to 16 million for EtherTalk and TokenTalk (although that number is still subject to the limitations of the Ethernet and Token-Ring architectures). However, even with AppleTalk Phase 2, LocalTalk networks are still limited to 254 nodes.

LocalTalk

As the capability to use LocalTalk cabling is built in to every Macintosh computer, it is very common to find LocalTalk networks in small Macintosh-only environments. LocalTalk uses STP cable in a bus topology. This configuration was originally intended to make it easy for users to share expensive peripherals such as laser printers and was primarily designed for small environments such as that depicted in Figure 8.14.

CH
8

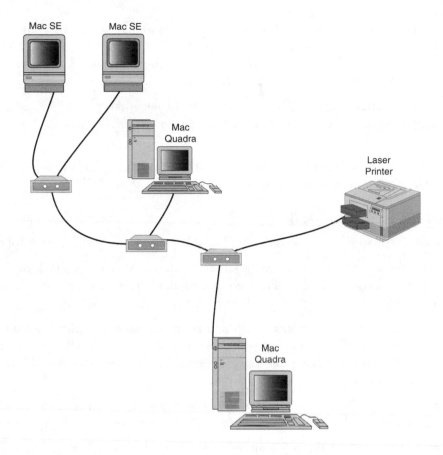

Figure 8.14
LocalTalk networks can use a bus topology that might actually resemble a tree.

Note that previous discussion of the bus topology focused on media such as thinnet, which connects all computers in a straight line. LocalTalk connectors, however, can accept connections from both other Macintosh systems and other connectors. This can result in a physical layout that resembles a tree more than a line. However, it still functions as a bus.

LocalTalk uses the media access method of CSMA/CA. Before transmitting on the network, a computer listens to determine whether anyone else is transmitting. If not, the computer transmits a packet signaling that it will be sending data onto the network media. Other computers receive this alert and know not to start transmitting data. The original computer then sends its data onto the network to its destination. Through this mechanism, most collisions are avoided.

The problem with this approach, however, is that the speed of the network suffers greatly from all these packets. The maximum speed of a LocalTalk network is a mere 230.4Kbps! When you compare this to the 10Mbps speed of an Ethernet network, it is easy to see why LocalTalk is not used in networks with heavy traffic.

One major advantage to LocalTalk is that because the networking hardware and software are already built in to each Macintosh, setting up a simple LocalTalk network is very inexpensive.

Although simple to install and easy to use, LocalTalk cabling is generally only found in small Macintosh-only environments due to its speed limitations.

EtherTalk and TokenTalk

To overcome the speed limitations of LocalTalk, Apple created EtherTalk and TokenTalk.

EtherTalk allows a network to use AppleTalk network protocols over a 10Mbps IEEE 802.3 Ethernet network. TokenTalk allows AppleTalk network protocols to be transmitted over a 4 or 16Mbps IEEE 802.5 Token-Ring network.

In both cases, you must add a separate NIC to your Macintosh computer to use the network. Similar to installing a NIC into a PC, vendors of Macintosh NICs provide the necessary EtherTalk or TokenTalk protocols. Both protocols support AppleTalk Phase 2 and its extended addressing.

Both EtherTalk and TokenTalk can also be used with additional software to provide connectivity between a Macintosh computer and a PC Ethernet or Token-Ring environment.

Note that EtherTalk and TokenTalk are subject to the same limitations as Ethernet and Token-Ring.

Table 8.9 summarizes information about the LocalTalk network architecture.

Table 8.9 Summary of LocalTalk Information	
Information Category	*LocalTalk Specifics*
Advantages	Simple, easy to install
Disadvantages	Slow, limited size
Topology	Bus
Cable type	STP
Connector type	Specialized
Media access method	CSMA/CA
Maximum segment length	300 meters (1,000 feet)

Information Category	LocalTalk Specifics
Maximum overall network length	300 meters (1,000 feet)
Minimum length between nodes	N/A
Maximum # of connected segments	8
Maximum # of nodes per segment	32
Maximum # of nodes for network	254
Transmission speed	230.4Kbps
IEEE specification	None

FDDI

Fiber Distributed Data Interface (FDDI), pronounced as "fiddy," uses fiber-optic cable and token-passing to create a very fast and reliable network operating at speeds of 100Mbps. It can include up to 500 nodes over a distance of 100 km (60 miles). FDDI has two different configurations: Class A and Class B. A Class A FDDI network uses two counter-rotating rings as shown in Figure 8.15. A Class B FDDI network uses only one ring to transmit data. Although Token-Ring networks are a logical ring but are wired as a physical star topology, FDDI networks are implemented as a true physical ring. There are no hubs, although devices called *concentrators* provide similar functionality.

Token passing in an FDDI network operates differently from in Token-Ring networks. Similar to Token-Ring networks, a token frame circulates around the ring. However, after transmitting one data frame, the possessor of the FDDI token can transmit more data frames before waiting for the first data frame to return around the ring. Furthermore, when the token holder has complete transmitting frames, it can immediately pass the token to the next station where that station can begin transmitting frames. In this manner, multiple frames can be circling around the ring.

FDDI also supports the capability to set the priority level of a data frame and token. For instance, servers can be given the capability to send more data frames onto the network than other stations. Likewise, video transmissions or time-sensitive data can be given a higher priority so that the packets will be delivered on time.

In a Token-Ring network, all computers communicate through hubs. If there is a cable break, the other stations can recognize this through the beaconing process and reroute the packets around the port in the hub causing the problem. With FDDI, all data is transmitted on the *primary ring*, while the *secondary ring* provides a method for compensating for breaks in the cable. When a computer determines that it cannot transmit data to its downstream neighbor, it transfers the data to the secondary ring and sends the data back around the network in the opposite direction. When the packet reaches the other end of the ring where the break is, it is transferred back to the primary ring and continues on as before. As shown in Figure 8.16, this mechanism allows data to be reliably transmitted throughout the network.

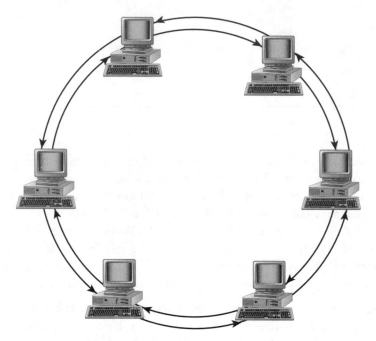

Figure 8.15
Class A FDDI networks use dual counter-rotating rings to provide reliable connections at 100Mbps.

There are two types of FDDI NICs called *Dual Attachment Stations (DAS)* and *Single Attachment Stations (SAS)*. Dual Attachment Stations are attached to both rings and are intended primarily for servers, concentrators, and other devices that need the reliability afforded by the dual-ring structure. Single Attachment Stations are intended for individual workstations to be attached to a concentrator. They implement only one ring connection, but because the concentrator into which they are connected is usually connected to both rings, the reliability of the network can be ensured.

Concentrators are similar to the hubs used in other architectures. *Dual attachment concentrators* are connected to both rings and have ports allowing the connection of workstations. *Single attachment concentrators* may be connected to dual attachment concentrators as a method of allowing more workstations to be connected to the network.

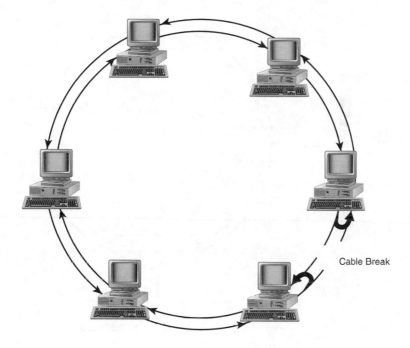

Cable Break

Figure 8.16
A break in a FDDI network results in packets being sent back on the second ring.

Figure 8.17 depicts how a typical FDDI network might be implemented. As the diagram indicates, it is common to have a device such as a *router* or *switch* linking the FDDI network to a LAN. In fact, the common use of FDDI is as a backbone network connecting multiple LANs. The fiber-optic technology used for FDDI is simply too expensive to be used in most LAN environments. However, its speed, reliability, and capability to cover long distances make it an excellent choice for a backbone network.

For your information, because FDDI uses fiber-optic cable, it is also a choice in environments with heavy electromagnetic interference. Networks requiring high security might also choose FDDI due to the inability of outsiders to eavesdrop on fiber-optic transmissions.

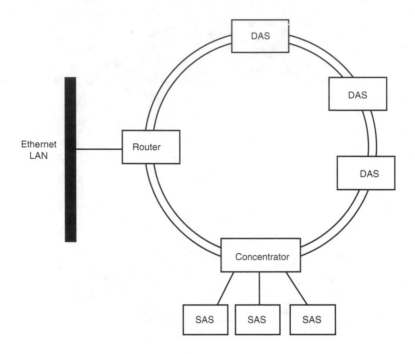

Figure 8.17
A typical FDDI network can include servers, concentrators, and links to other networks.

Table 8.10 summarizes information about FDDI network architecture.

Table 8.10 Summary of FDDI Information	
Information Category	*FDDI Specifics*
Advantages	Very fast, long distances, highly secure, resistant to EMI
Disadvantages	Very expensive, difficult to install
Topology	Ring
Cable type	Fiber-optic
Connector type	Specialized
Media access method	Token-passing
Maximum segment length	N/A
Maximum overall network length	100 km (60 miles)
Minimum length between nodes	N/A
Maximum # of connected segments	N/A

Information Category	FDDI Specifics
Maximum # of nodes per segment	N/A
Maximum # of nodes for network	500
Transmission speed	100Mbps
IEEE specification	No IEEE specification, but ANSI X3T9.5

Summary

The most popular network architecture in use today is the IEEE 802.3 Ethernet standard, operating at 10Mbps using one of four architectures: 10BASE-T, 10BASE2, 10BASE5, or 10BASE-F. 10BASE-T implements a star topology using unshielded twisted-pair (UTP) cable. 10BASE2 and 10BASE5 implement a bus topology using thinnet and thicknet coaxial cable. 10BASE-F is a fiber-optic standard that is usually used as a backbone to connect other Ethernet LANs together.

The design of Ethernet networks is subject to the 5-4-3 rule, which specifies that between any two points on an Ethernet network, there can be no more than five network segments connected by four repeaters with no more than three of those segments being populated. A *populated* segment is one in which there are more connections to the cable than just the start and end points. Note that a segment can only be populated if it is a coaxial cable because twisted-pair cable never has more than the start and end points.

All 10Mbps Ethernet networks use carrier-sense multiple-access with collision detection (CSMA/CD) for media access control. They also all use one of four Ethernet frame types: Ethernet 802.3, Ethernet 802.2, Ethernet SNAP, or Ethernet II. For two devices to be able to communicate on an Ethernet network, they both must be using the same frame type.

100Mbps Ethernet networks are now available in two forms: 100BASE-T and 100VG-AnyLAN. 100BASE-T builds upon existing Ethernet networks and requires Category 5 UTP. It uses CSMA/CD for media access and needs special NICs and hubs. 100VG-AnyLAN is designed to operate over any voice-grade (Category 3) or higher UTP cables that have four twisted-pairs of wire. It, too, requires users to upgrade their NICs and hubs. 100VG-AnyLAN attains 100Mbps speeds by using a new access method called *demand priority,* where intelligent hubs control which nodes can transmit at any time.

In all Ethernet networks based on a star topology, if you want to connect two hubs together, you need to cross the data from the transmit pair on one hub to the receive pair on the opposite hub and vice versa. One solution is to use a *crossover cable,* and the other is to use a special port on one of the hubs.

Ethernet networks have attained such high popularity primarily because they are inexpensive, easy to implement, and fast enough for most modern networks. Their main downfall is in situations with heavy network traffic, where the contention-based media access method becomes inefficient.

Beyond Ethernet, another popular network architecture is IBM's Token-Ring. Token-Ring networks use a constantly circulating token to determine which computer can transmit information. A computer cannot transmit data frames onto the network unless it has the token. Token-Ring networks are implemented as a *logical ring*, but are in fact wired physically with a star topology. To accomplish this, Token-Ring hubs, referred to as Multistation Access Units (MAUs), are wired internally as a ring. Multiple hubs can be cascaded together to create a larger ring.

Token-Ring networks primarily use Type 1 (STP) and Type 3 (UTP) cables as defined by the IBM cabling system. Another feature of Token-Ring networks is the capability to self-repair the network through a process called *beaconing*, where stations let others on the ring know when they are not receiving transmissions from other stations.

Token-Ring networks are popular in situations with heavy network traffic or where reliability is of great concern.

ARCnet is an older network architecture that implements a token-passing system using numerical addresses manually configured on NICs. The topology can be a star, bus, or a mixture of both, whereas the media can be coaxial, UTP, fiber-optic, or a combination of all media. ARCnet is a very flexible and easy architecture, but it is limited by its 2.5Mbps data transmission speed and restriction to 255 nodes. Although higher-speed versions of ARCnet are becoming available, the network architecture is fading from use.

AppleTalk refers to both a network architecture and a suite of protocols used by Apple Macintosh computers. Macintosh systems come with a NIC already built in and can use LocalTalk cabling with no extra hardware. LocalTalk is a cabling system using shielded twisted-pair (STP) in a bus topology. Because it uses CSMA/CA for a media-access method, it is restricted to speeds of 230Kbps. For this reason, LocalTalk is primarily used in very small, Macintosh-only networks.

Macintosh systems can now also use EtherTalk and TokenTalk to use AppleTalk network protocols over Ethernet and Token-Ring networks.

Finally, Fiber Distributed Data Interface (FDDI) is a newer network architecture based on fiber-optic cables that can provide data transmission speeds of up to 100Mbps over a distance as great as 100 km (60 miles). It uses token-passing, but unlike Token-Ring, a computer with the token can transmit multiple frames before the first frame has traveled completely around the ring. Also unlike Token-Ring, FDDI does not use hubs but instead implements a true physical ring topology.

FDDI has two different configurations: Class A and Class B. A Class A FDDI network uses two counter-rotating rings. A Class B FDDI network uses only one ring to transmit data. On a Class A FDDI network, data is transmitted on the primary ring, and the secondary is used for backup purposes. If a computer detects a break in the line, the data is sent back around the ring in the opposite direction on the secondary ring. In this manner, a reliable connection can be maintained between sites on the ring.

Because of the high cost of fiber-optic cable and accessories, FDDI is used primarily as a backbone linking other networks.

QUESTIONS AND ANSWERS

1. What is the primary difference between 10BASE2 and 10BASE5?

    A: 10BASE2 uses thinnet, and 10BASE5 uses thicknet coaxial cable.

2. Explain the 5-4-3 rule.

    A: In an Ethernet network, between any two points on the network, there can be no more than five network segments or four repeaters, and of those five segments only three of the segments can be populated (meaning having more than the start and end connections of the segment).

3. In a pure 10BASE2 network, what is the maximum distance between any two points on the network?

    A: 925 meters (5 segments at 185 meters each)

4. Name three Ethernet frame types.

    A: Possible choices include: 802.3, 802.2, SNAP, Ethernet II

5. Explain the difference in frame size between Token-Ring and Ethernet.

    A: In Ethernet, the frame size is essentially 1,500 bytes, whereas in Token-Ring, It can have the much larger range from 4K to 17K..

6. In Token-Ring, what you think of as a hub is called a _____.

    A: Multistation Access Unit (MAU)

7. How does beaconing help in a network?

    A: Beaconing is a process where computers on a ring can detect that there is a potential failure of the ring and reconfigure the ring to bypass the problem station.

...continues

…continued

> **8.** What is the normal speed of an ARCNet network?
>
> A: 2.5Mbps
>
> **9.** What is LocalTalk?
>
> A: LocalTalk was the original Apple Macintosh cabling system that was based on CSMA/CA.
>
> **10.** How is FDDI different from Token-Ring?
>
> A: Several answers: FDDI uses two counter-rotating rings, is implemented as a physical ring, can have multiple frames transmitting simultaneously, operates at 100Mbps, and allows the setting of a priority level on a data frame.

PRACTICE TEST

1. Which of these network architectures are *not* capable of transmitting data at 100Mbps? (Choose all that apply.)

  a. Token-Ring
  b. Ethernet
  c. FDDI
  d. ARCnet

Answer a is correct because Token-Ring has a current maximum of 16Mbps. Answers b and c are incorrect because both Ethernet and FDDI can do 100Mbps. **Answer d is correct because ARCnet can only do 2.5Mbps.**

2. Which of the following Ethernet architectures use a bus topology? (Choose all that apply.)

  a. 100VG-AnyLAN
  b. 10BASE2
  c. 10BASE5
  d. 10BASE-T

Answers a and d are incorrect because they use a star topology. **Answers b and c are correct.**

3. In a Token-Ring network, what is the name of the process whereby network nodes become aware that one of the nodes has failed and are able to reroute traffic around the failed node?

   a. Fault-tolerance
   b. Token correction
   c. Fault domain
   d. Beaconing

Answers a, b and c are incorrect. **Answer d is correct.**

4. You currently have a 10Mbps 10BASE-T Ethernet network. Your users have a mixture of 486 and Pentium PCs running Windows 95 and Windows for Workgroups. All computers are connected to the network over Category 5 UTP. You plan to migrate the network to 100Mbps using a 100BASE-T network architecture. What steps will you need to take? (Choose all that apply.)

   a. Replace all cable with cable that supports 100Mbps.
   b. Replace all network interface cards.
   c. Replace all 486 computers with Pentiums.
   d. Replace all network hubs.

Answer a is incorrect because all the cabling is currently Category 5 UTP. **Answer b is correct; all NICs will need to be replaced.** Answer c is incorrect because the 486s should work fine. **Answer d is correct; all hubs will need to be replaced.**

5. Your company is moving to a new office building and will be installing a new 10BASE-T network. While the contractors are building the walls, you would like them to install data cables that will allow you to upgrade the network to 100Mbps at some future date. What type of cable should you specify?

   a. Category 5 UTP
   b. Category 1 UTP
   c. Type 1 UTP
   d. Type 5 UTP

Answer a is correct; Category 5 UTP will support 100Mbps. Answers b, c, and d are incorrect.

6. TCP/IP-based Ethernet networks use which of the following Ethernet frame types?

   a. Ethernet 802.3
   b. Ethernet 802.2
   c. Ethernet II
   d. Ethernet SNAP

Answers a and b are incorrect because they are used primarily in NetWare networks. **Answer c is correct; TCP/IP networks use the Ethernet II frame.** Answer d is incorrect because Ethernet SNAP is used in some AppleTalk networks.

7. Which of the following frame types are the default types used in Novell NetWare networks? (Choose all that apply.)

   a. Ethernet 802.3
   b. Ethernet 802.2
   c. Ethernet II
   d. Ethernet SNAP

Answers a and b are correct; they are used primarily in NetWare networks. Answer c is incorrect because TCP/IP networks use the Ethernet II frame. Answer d is incorrect because Ethernet SNAP is used in some AppleTalk networks.

8. Which Ethernet architecture requires that each end of the bus be terminated? (Choose all that apply.)

   a. 10BASE2
   b. 10BASE5
   c. 10BASE-T
   d. 10BASE-F

Answers a and b are correct because both need terminators. Answers c and d are incorrect because they do not use a bus topology.

9. What is the IEEE specification for Token-Ring?

   a. 802.2
   b. 802.3
   c. 802.5
   d. 802.12

Answer a is incorrect because it is for Logical Link Control. Answer b is incorrect because it is for Ethernet. **Answer c is correct; 802.5 is for Token-Ring.** Answer d is incorrect because it is for demand priority.

10. Which of the following do *not* use CSMA/CD?

   a. 100VG-AnyLAN
   b. 100BASE-T
   c. FDDI
   d. ARCNet

Answer a is correct because 100VG-AnyLAN uses demand priority. Answer b is incorrect because 100BASE-T *does* use CSMA/CD. **Answer c is correct because FDDI uses token passing. Answer d is correct because ARCNet uses token passing.**

CHAPTER PREREQUISITE

Before reading this chapter, you should understand the layers of the OSI Model (see Chapter 3, "The OSI Reference Model"), methods of transmitting data (see Chapter 7, "Data Transmission"), and network architectures (see Chapter 8, "Network Architecture").

Network Protocols

WHILE YOU READ

1. What is the difference between a connectionless and connection-oriented protocol?

2. Name two nonroutable protocols.

3. Differentiate between TCP and IP.

4. What is the role of a subnet mask?

5. How does DHCP simplify network administration?

6. Why is the frame type an issue in NetWare networks?

7. Explain the difference between NetBIOS and NetBEUI.

8. In Windows NT, how do you configure the network protocols?

9. What is the role of NDIS and ODI?

10. List the order in which NetBIOS name resolution occurs.

The Role of Protocols

When two world leaders meet face-to-face, they are very concerned about the protocols used for communication. Should they shake hands? Should they give each other a hug or kiss a cheek? How close should they be to each other? How should they sit at a table? What language should be spoken? All these factors can make a huge difference in the success or failure of an international, political, communication session. If the wrong protocols are used, communication will not occur.

Likewise in the realm of computer networks, communication protocols are vital to the flow of network traffic. For two computers to communicate, they must use the same protocols.

As you know by now, the actual operations of a network involve many functions. Because protocols have been developed to address all types of network functions, they are usually grouped together into *protocol stacks* or *protocol suites*. Two of the most popular protocol suites are TCP/IP, used on the Internet and in many large networks, and IPX/SPX, used within Novell NetWare networks.

Although the remainder of this chapter will discuss different protocol suites in detail, it is important now to differentiate between types of protocols that will be included within the protocol suites. There are two major distinctions between protocols:

- Connectionless versus connection-oriented protocols
- Routable versus nonroutable protocols

Each of these distinctions will be discussed in the following sections.

Connectionless Versus Connection-Oriented Protocols

When you send someone a letter in the mail, you simply drop the letter in a postal box. You have no idea whether or when the letter will ever arrive, nor do you receive any acknowledgement that it was received. You have no guarantee that the letter will get there at all.

On the other hand, when you call someone on the phone, there is a small delay while a connection is established between you and the person you are calling. After you have spoken for some time, you hang up and the connection is terminated.

Within a computer network, *connectionless* communication occurs much like the letter in the mail. Protocols using connectionless communications require no initial connection and simply assume that the data will get through. Connectionless services are fast because they do not require any overhead, nor do they provide any sequencing of packets. As data is just transmitted, sorting out the sequence of the packets is left to higher-level protocols. Packets of data in connectionless communication are often referred to as *datagrams*.

Connectionless services are often used on LANs when packets need to be sent to multiple computers (such as broadcasts searching for a particular computer) or when the data stream is a service such as audio or video where data needs to be transmitted at the highest possible speed. The UDP protocol of the TCP/IP protocol suite is an example of connectionless communication.

Key Concept

Connectionless communication involves the simple transmission of data where there is no guarantee that it will be received by the recipient.

In contrast, *connection-oriented* communication resembles a phone call. A connection is established between two machines before communication can begin. After the connection is established, data is transmitted in a sequenced, orderly fashion. As each packet reaches the recipient, an acknowledgement is sent back to the sender. If there are any errors, the data is retransmitted. When all the data has been transmitted, the connection is terminated. Connection-oriented communication is also referred to as *reliable* communication because the successful transmission of data is guaranteed.

Connection-oriented communication protocols are used when you want to ensure reliable transmission of data. They are especially used across WAN connections where the physical media might introduce errors into connectionless transmissions. The TCP protocol is an example of connection-oriented communication.

Key Concept

Connection-oriented communication involves the establishment of a reliable connection between two computers. Data is transmitted in a sequential fashion with the successful receipt of each packet acknowledged by the recipient.

Microsoft operating systems require that networking protocols and drivers must be able to provide both connectionless and connection-oriented communication.

Routable Versus Nonroutable Protocols

Another major distinction between protocol suites is their suitability for large-scale, or *enterprise*, networks. As you will learn in Chapter 13, "Creating Larger Networks," devices called *routers* enable you to connect several LANs together into a larger network. Some network protocols, such as TCP/IP and IPX/SPX, can be used with routers to build large networks and are referred to as *routable* protocols. In contrast, *nonroutable* protocols, such as NetBEUI, were designed for small networks and cannot be scaled for use with routers in building large networks. One of the factors influencing your choice of what protocol to use on your network will be whether you anticipate building a larger network.

Key Concept

Routable protocols can work with a router and can be used to build large networks. Examples include TCP/IP and IPX/SPX. *Nonroutable* protocols are designed to work on small, local networks and cannot be used with a router. Examples include NetBEUI and DLC.

Protocols

In PC computer networks, there are three primary protocol stacks in use:

- TCP/IP
- IPX/SPX (Novell NetWare)
- NetBEUI

Due primarily to interest in Internet connectivity, TCP/IP's use has grown dramatically over the past few years. Still, large installations using both IPX/SPX and NetBEUI are quite common. These three protocols will be discussed later in the chapter, followed by a brief mention of other networking protocols that are commonly available.

For the exam, you should thoroughly understand TCP/IP, IPX/SPX, and NetBEUI, and you should at least know about the other protocols mentioned in this chapter.

TCP/IP

The TCP/IP protocol suite is often referred to as the *Internet protocol suite* because it was created during the development of the Internet (see Chapter 15, "The Internet"). As it later became integrated into all UNIX servers, TCP/IP entered wide use with large networks (often referred to as enterprise networks). TCP/IP's scalability from small to large networks and the current heavy interest in connecting LANs to the Internet has enabled TCP/IP to evolve into the most widely used network protocol today.

Because TCP/IP was created before the OSI Reference Model, TCP/IP protocols do not map exactly to OSI layers. However, the equivalent functionality is included. As shown in Figure 9.1, the TCP/IP protocol suite includes the following protocols:

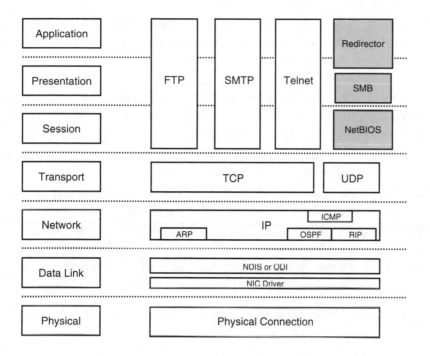

Figure 9.1
The TCP/IP protocol suite shown in this figure is used throughout the Internet.

- *FTP (File Transfer Protocol).* FTP provides a method for transferring files between computers.
- *Telnet.* With Telnet, users can log on to remote systems across a network.
- *SMTP (Simple Mail Transport Protocol).* SMTP defines the standard for all email sent across the Internet.
- *TCP (Transmission Control Protocol).* TCP is the primary transport layer protocol used within TCP/IP. It provides a reliable, connection-oriented data transportation service in conjunction with IP (defined in the following section). When establishing a connection, TCP uses a *port* address to determine to which connection a packet is destined. TCP also provides the capability to fragment messages and reassemble packets through sequencing.
- *UDP (User Datagram Protocol).* UDP provides a connectionless transportation service on top of IP.

- *IP (Internet Protocol).* All network addressing and routing in TCP/IP network is handled by IP. IP provides a connectionless datagram service for fast, but unreliable, communication between network nodes.
- *ARP (Address Resolution Protocol).* ARP is a network layer protocol that maps hardware addresses to IP addresses for delivery of packets on the local network segment.
- *ICMP (Internet Control Message Protocol).* ICMP is a protocol used in conjunction with IP to provide error control. ICMP can detect network error conditions and warn IP to avoid certain network areas.
- *RIP (Routing Information Protocol).* RIP is a distance-vector routing protocol that determines the shortest path between two locations by counting the number of *hops* that a packet has to make. It is similar but not identical to the RIP protocol used in IPX/SPX networks.
- *OSPF (Open Shortest Path First).* OSPF is a newer link-state routing protocol that is more efficient and needs less overhead than RIP.

Note that routing protocols such as RIP and OSPF will be discussed in more detail in Chapter 13.

TCP/IP is now the default protocol suite used within Windows NT. TCP/IP is also incorporated into all other current Microsoft operating systems. For your information, the TCP/IP protocols are defined through a series of RFC (Request For Comments) documents developed by the community of Internet users. You can obtain more information about TCP/IP and other Internet-related protocols by browsing an RFC database found at sites such as `http://www.ietf.org/rfc.html`.

IP Addressing

Within TCP/IP networks, each computer is assigned a 32-bit *IP address* that resembles the following:

192.168.24.123

The 32-bit address is divided into four groups of eight bits, called *octets*, with each octet written as a decimal number from 0 to 255 separated by a period (referred to as a *dot*). Part of the IP address will define the *network ID* of your network, and the remainder of the address provides the *host ID* of the individual computer. For instance, 24.123 in the preceding address might identify a specific computer within the TCP/IP network that has the address 192.168. (Think of this network/host division like a phone number. A phone number has an area code and/or country code and then a local number.)

Note that within TCP/IP networking, the term *host* is used to refer to a computer on the network.

Key Concept

To allow data to be properly delivered, each IP address must be unique within your entire TCP/IP network. Additionally, if you are connected to the global Internet, each IP address you use must be unique within the entire Internet.

When operating your own internal network, you can really choose any range of IP addresses. However, when you connect your network to the Internet, your Internet Service Provider (ISP) will provide you with a valid range of IP addresses.

For the Networking Essentials, you do not need to be a TCP/IP expert (although it would not hurt!) because there is an entire exam focusing on TCP/IP. However, you should understand what IP addresses are, the function of subnets, and DHCP. The addressing information included in the following text is provided so that you can better understand IP addressing. However, this material will not be tested in depth on the Networking Essentials exam.

Originally, the Internet community divided IP address space into different classes and provided for address allocation through a central registry. The three classes available for normal use were the following:

- *Class A.* These addresses were intended for extremely large networks, used the first octet to identify the network, and allowed over 16 million hosts per network. Class A addresses begin with network IDs between 1 and 126.

- *Class B.* These addresses were intended for medium sized networks, used the first two octets to identify the network, and supported over 65,000 hosts per network. Class B addresses begin with network IDs between 129 and 191.

- *Class C.* These addresses were intended for small networks and used the first 3 octets to identify the network, providing a total of 254 hosts per network. Class C addresses begin with network IDs between 192 and 223.

Today, the method of allocating addresses has changed slightly. However, the idea of address classes is still commonly used when discussing TCP/IP networks, and it provides a framework for discussing IP addressing.

Subnet Masks

When you prepare to call someone on the telephone, how do you know whether you need to dial the area code first or you can just dial the local number? In the U.S., the answer lies in the use of the three-digit area code. Assuming you know your area code, if someone gives you a phone number with an area code matching your own, you know that you (usually) do not have to dial the area code. On the other hand, if someone gives you a number using an area code different from your own, you know you always need to dial the area code first to connect to that phone number.

Within TCP/IP networks, computers work in a similar manner. However, although you know that the first three digits of a phone number will be the area code, computers do not immediately know how many of the 32 bits in an IP address represent the network and how many represent the host portion of the address. To make this distinction between network and host, computers use a *subnet mask* that tells them how to read an address (see Table 9.1).

Table 9.1 Typical Subnet Masks	
Subnet Mask	*IP Address Class*
255.0.0.0	Class A
255.255.0.0	Class B
255.255.255.0	Class C

Key Concept

When sending a packet to another computer on a TCP/IP network, a computer uses a subnet mask to determine the network and host portions of the destination address and to determine whether the destination address is local or remote.

For instance, the subnet mask for a Class A address tells the computer to use the first octet for the network address and the remaining three octets for the host address. In contrast, the Class C subnet mask of 255.255.255.0 tells the computer to use the first three octets for the network address and only the final octet for the host address.

To understand how this works, consider an example. When Computer X (192.168.24.100) goes to send a message to Computer Y (192.168.25.200), Computer X uses its subnet mask to determine whether Computer Y's address is local or remote. If Computer X is on a Class B network, it compares the first two octets (192.168), determines that Computer Y is local, and sends the packet out on the local network. However, if Computer X is on a Class C network, it compares the first three octets, determines that the network portions are different (192.168.24 and 192.168.25), and forwards the packet to a network router for delivery to the network containing Computer Y.

Although this works fine, consider what would happen if Computers X and Y in the preceding example are on separate Class C networks separated by a router, but Computer X is misconfigured with a Class B subnet mask. When Computer X examines Computer Y's address, it looks only at the first two octets, concludes Computer Y is local, and sends the packet out on the local network. However, because Computer Y is in fact on another network, the message never gets through. For this reason, computers on TCP/IP networks must be using the correct subnet masks for communication to be successful.

Key Concept

On the exam, you might get questions asking about why two TCP/IP computers might not be able to communicate with each other. If everything else is working fine, it might be that they have different subnet masks.

Dynamic Host Configuration Protocol (DHCP)

As larger networks began using TCP/IP, the process of manually assigning an IP address to each individual computer became quite cumbersome. Keeping track of what IP addresses were already assigned became more difficult as computers were moved around within an organization. To simplify the task of assigning IP addresses, engineers on the Internet developed the *Dynamic Host Configuration Protocol (DHCP)*.

To use DHCP, you set up a software program called a DHCP server somewhere on the network and provide the DHCP server with a block of IP addresses that it can assign. You then must go to all client computers on the network and configure them to request an IP address from the DHCP server. When those computers are restarted (and for every future time they are powered on), they send a broadcast message on the local network requesting an IP address from a DHCP server. The DHCP server then assigns IP addresses to each request until the server no longer has IP addresses available. Each address is *leased* to a client computer for a specific period of time and can be renewed if the client computer still needs the address.

One of the strengths of DHCP is that computers can be easily moved around within an organization. When a computer is connected to a different network segment and powered on, the computer sends out a broadcast request on the new network segment and gets an IP address from the DHCP server on that network segment. This process enables network administrators to centrally allocate blocks of IP addresses to DHCP servers and more easily keep track of which addresses are already allocated.

Key Concept

For the exam, remember that DHCP provides a mechanism for dynamically assigning IP addresses.

IPX/SPX

Like TCP/IP, the IPX/SPX protocol suite used in Novell NetWare networks can be used for both small networks and large enterprise networks. As shown in Figure 9.2, the IPX/SPX protocol suite consists of the following protocols:

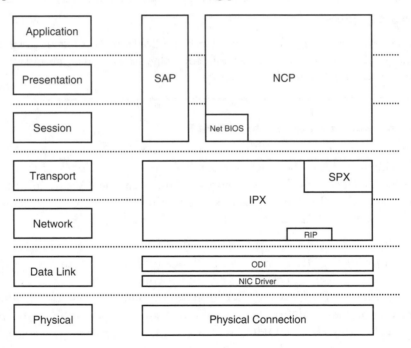

Figure 9.2
The IPX/SPX protocol suite shown in this figure is used by Novell NetWare networks.

- *SAP (Service Advertising Protocol).* File servers and print servers periodically broadcast SAP packets to advertise the address of the server and the services available.
- *NCP (NetWare Core Protocol).* NCP functions at transport, session, presentation, and application layers to handle all client/server interactions, such as printing and file sharing.

- *SPX (Sequenced Packet Exchange).* SPX provides connection-oriented communication on top of IPX.

- *RIP (Routing Information Protocol).* RIP is the default routing protocol for IPX/SPX networks and uses a distance-vector algorithm to calculate the best route for a packet. It is similar to the RIP protocol used in TCP/IP networks.

- *IPX (Internetwork Packet Exchange).* All network addressing and routing in an IPX/SPX network is handled by IPX. IPX provides a connectionless datagram service for fast, but unreliable, communication with network nodes.

- *ODI (Open Data-link Interface).* ODI allows IPX to work with any network interface card.

Within Microsoft networks, *NWLINK* is Microsoft's implementation of IPX/SPX. NWLINK also provides support for NetBIOS names discussed in the following section (which is why NetBIOS appears in Figure 9.2).

One concern when using IPX/SPX within Ethernet networks is that all computers need to use the identical *frame type.* If you recall from Chapter 8, "Network Architecture," there are four possible Ethernet data frame types: Ethernet 802.2, Ethernet 802.3, Ethernet SNAP, and Ethernet II. In Novell NetWare 2.x and 3.x networks, the default frame type is Ethernet 802.3, whereas the default frame type is Ethernet 802.2 in Novell NetWare 4.x networks. If communication does not occur between two computers, you should check to make sure that the frame types match.

Microsoft Networking (NetBIOS/NetBEUI/SMB)

IBM and Microsoft jointly developed the *Network Basic Input Output System (NetBIOS)* and *NetBIOS Extended User Interface (NetBEUI)* protocols to support network communication within small- to medium-sized networks. NetBIOS and NetBEUI are two separate protocols that are constantly confused with each other. As shown in Figure 9.3, both protocols are members of a protocol suite found in Microsoft operating systems. The Microsoft networking components include the following:

- *Redirector.* Makes network resources appear as if they are local resources. Directs requests for network resources to the appropriate network server.

- *Server Message Block (SMB).* Provides peer-to-peer communication between the redirector on a client and the server software on a file server.

- *NetBIOS.* Establishes sessions between computers and maintains those connections.

- *NetBEUI.* Provides data transportation.

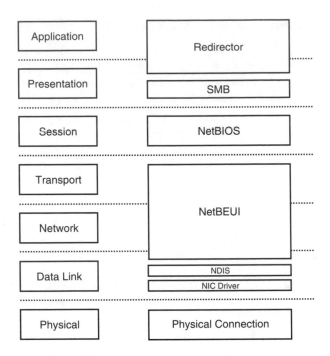

Figure 9.3
Microsoft operating systems use several networking protocols, including NetBIOS and possibly NetBEUI.

NetBIOS

NetBIOS is a Session Layer protocol that allows computers to communicate over a small LAN. NetBIOS provides an application programming interface (API) that applications can use to communicate with network resources. Some characteristics of NetBIOS include the following:

- Each computer on a NetBIOS network uses a unique 15- character name to identify itself. (NetBIOS names actually include a 16th character that uses a hexadecimal number to identify the service that created the name. However, the user can only set the first 15 characters of the name.)
- To transfer data between systems, NetBIOS establishes a connection-oriented session between computers. NetBIOS is responsible for establishing, maintaining, and terminating the connection, as well as ensuring that all data is correctly delivered.

- Connectionless communication is also possible through NetBIOS.
- NetBIOS uses broadcast packets to identify other computers on the local network. Computers periodically broadcast their names so that others can find them and access network resources.

NetBIOS is nonroutable and relies on an underlying protocol (such as TCP/IP, IPX/SPX, or NetBEUI) to provide network transportation. Although primarily designed to be carried over NetBEUI, NetBIOS can be carried over TCP/IP using *NetBIOS over TCP/IP (NBT)* packets.

Because all Microsoft operating systems use NetBIOS for upper-layer network communication, you need to understand how NetBIOS fits into network layers. Even more importantly for the exam, you need to understand how NetBIOS names are resolved to computer addresses. Because NetBIOS name resolution is important, regardless of what network protocol suite is used, a special section focusing on name resolution can be found at the end of this chapter.

Key Concept

NetBIOS is a session layer protocol that provides an application programming interface that allows applications to communicate over the network. Although originally designed to work with NetBEUI, NetBIOS can now also be used with TCP/IP and IPX/SPX.

NetBEUI

NetBEUI is a small, fast, and efficient transport and network layer protocol designed to be used with NetBIOS in small workgroups. Because NetBEUI is incorporated into all Microsoft operating systems, you will find it frequently used in small environments to provide fast network communication. NetBEUI does not require much system memory, which is a great advantage when it is necessary to include DOS computers in your network.

However, because NetBEUI is nonroutable, it is difficult to use for large installations and is usually replaced by TCP/IP or IPX/SPX as a network grows larger.

Key Concept

NetBEUI is a small, fast, nonroutable transport protocol used in small workgroup settings.

SMB

The *Server Message Block (SMB)* protocol is a presentation layer protocol used within Microsoft networks for communication, primarily between the redirector and the server software. For instance, if you want to use your File Manager or Windows Explorer to view a list of files on a Windows NT Server computer, your computer would first establish a network connection to the file server using a network protocol such as NetBEUI or TCP/IP. On top of that connection, a NetBIOS session would be created between your workstation's redirector and the server process on the file server. After that session is established, the two computers would transmit SMB packets back and forth for you to view the list of files.

SMB also allows Windows computers to interconnect with file servers running Microsoft's older *LAN Manager* protocol.

 Key Concept

The Server Message Block (SMB) protocol is a presentation layer protocol that provides communication between Windows redirectors and file servers.

Redirector

The *redirector* is a piece of software that enables users to access network resources as if they were local resources. Redirectors will be discussed in more detail in Chapter 10, "Network Operating Systems."

Other Protocols

Although TCP/IP, IPX/SPX, and NetBEUI are the primary protocols used within PC networks today, you should be aware of a number of other protocols that might be mentioned on exam questions. The remainder of this section briefly describes the other networking protocols available.

AppleTalk

You learned in Chapter 8 that AppleTalk defined the network architecture used in many Macintosh networks. AppleTalk also defines a comprehensive suite of protocols for networking within the Macintosh environment. Several of the protocols included in the AppleTalk suite are the following:

- *AppleShare.* Provides application layer services.
- *AppleTalk Filing Protocol (AFP).* Manages file sharing.

- *AppleTalk Transaction Protocol (ATP)*. Provides a transport layer connection between computers.
- *Datagram Delivery Protocol (DDP)*. Provides network layer transportation of packets across a network similar to the IP and IPX protocols.

AppleTalk combines computers into logical groups, called *zones,* that are similar to *workgroups* within a Windows environment.

DECnet

DECnet is Digital Equipment Corporation's implementation of its *Digital Network Architecture (DNA)*. DECnet is a comprehensive suite of protocols that, in its current version known as "Phase V," closely resembles the OSI Reference Model. DECnet is routable and, although not typically found in PC networks, can be found in larger networks integrating with digital mainframe and minicomputer systems.

DLC

Data Link Control (DLC) is a nonroutable protocol designed for data link layer communication with IBM mainframes and Hewlett-Packard network printers. Because it is a low-level protocol that has no interaction with the Windows redirector or other upper-layer services, DLC is not commonly used within PC networks.

Note that with HP network printers, DLC only needs to be installed on the computer functioning as a print server and communicating directly with the HP printer. Client computers printing to the printer by way of the print server do not need to have DLC installed.

As a tip, for whatever reason, exam questions seem to frequently include DLC as a protocol choice. Just remember that it is nonroutable and only used for low-level communication with IBM mainframes and network printers.

NFS

Network File System (NFS) is a protocol used primarily on UNIX and Linux computers to provide the same functionality as the Windows redirector. Originally developed by Sun Microsystems, NFS makes remote file systems appear to be local file systems. You might need to use NFS within a PC network if you want to connect PCs to a UNIX/Linux file server or have UNIX/Linux workstations access a PC file server.

CH
9

OSI

When the International Standards Organization (ISO) developed the *Open Systems Interconnect (OSI)* Reference Model, the organization also developed a suite of protocols that correlate exactly to individual layers of the OSI Model. OSI protocols provide all layers of functionality, with a number of application layer protocols for different purposes. Although it is not commonly used in PC networks, you might need to interconnect to larger systems using OSI protocol stacks.

SNA

IBM's *System Network Architecture (SNA)*, similar to DECnet and OSI, is in fact an entire suite of protocols used widely in the world of IBM mainframe and AS/400 computers. Two of the protocols included within SNA are the following:

- *Advanced Peer-to-Peer Communications (APPC)*. Provides transport and session layer services to allow peer-to-peer networking.
- *Advanced Peer-to-Peer Networking (APPN)*. Provides network and transport layer connections between computers. Designed to be used in conjunction with APPC.

For your information, Microsoft *SNA Server* is a product designed to interconnect PC networks with SNA networks, such as those using IBM mainframes or AS/400 computers.

X-Windows

X-Windows is a set of protocols developed by MIT to provide a graphical user interface for UNIX and Linux workstations. Widely adopted within the UNIX/Linux world, you might need to install X-Windows client software on PCs if you want to run UNIX/Linux applications on a PC client.

Configuring Protocols

As you first configure your computer for networking, either when you first install the operating system or when you later install a network interface card, you will be prompted to install network protocols. Some operating systems, such as Windows NT, automatically install network protocols for you. If you want to install additional protocols later, you usually can use a graphical interface such as that shown in Figure 9.4. In Microsoft operating systems, this capability is found in the Network portion of the Control Panel.

This graphical interface also provides a mechanism for removing protocols and for configuration. In Microsoft operating systems, you can usually double-click the name of the network protocol to enter additional configuration options (see Figure 9.5).

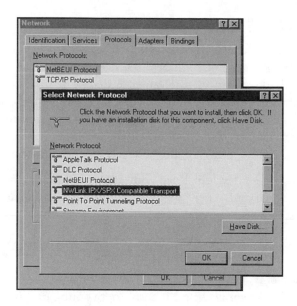

Figure 9.4
Windows NT enables you to easily install additional network protocols through the
Select Network Protocol dialog box.

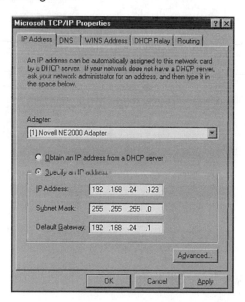

Figure 9.5
The Network Control Panel enables you to configure network protocols through specific
dialog boxes, as shown in this Microsoft TCP/IP Properties dialog box example.

The Role of NDIS and ODI

When computer networks were first developed, each network driver and network interface card could only be bound to one protocol stack. Although this worked fine in early networks that used only one protocol, a solution needed to be found as networks expanded and started to involve multiple protocols. This issue of only one protocol binding to one NIC especially affected servers that needed to communicate with all client workstations. Although the problem could be solved by installing multiple NICs and binding each one to a separate protocol, this solution was not desirable.

Instead, *driver interfaces* were developed that allowed multiple protocols to be bound to the same network interface card. There are two incompatible driver interface standards in use today. They are as follows:

- *Open Driver Interface (ODI)*. Developed by Novell and Apple, ODI is found primarily in Novell NetWare networks.
- *Network Driver Interface Specification (NDIS)*. Developed by Microsoft, NDIS is used primarily in networks using Microsoft networking products.

As shown in Figure 9.6, NDIS defines the interface between protocol stacks and network interface cards. Multiple protocol stacks such as TCP/IP and IPX/SPX can use the same network interface card, provided an NDIS-compatible NIC driver is available. Note that NDIS also allows a protocol to use multiple network interface cards, so for example, one computer could use TCP/IP with two separate NICs, each of which could be connected to a different network.

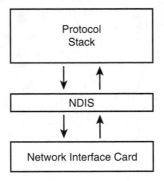

Figure 9.6
NDIS allows multiple protocols to work with the same network interface card.

Key Concept

NDIS and ODI allow multiple protocol stacks to use the same network interface card and allow multiple NICs to use the same protocol.

NetBIOS Name Resolution

As mentioned earlier in this chapter, NetBIOS provides an upper-layer application programming interface (API) for applications to use to communicate with network resources. Because most Windows applications use the NetBIOS API, it is critical that you understand how NetBIOS names are resolved to network addresses.

As mentioned previously, NetBIOS identifies each computer on the network by a unique 15-character name, with a 16th character used to provide additional system information about the name. The NetBIOS name is usually created when the operating system is first installed onto a computer or when the networking software is activated. When a computer is first powered on, it broadcasts its name onto the network. If a duplicate name is found, the user or administrator will need to change its NetBIOS name before the computer can utilize network resources.

Key Concept

For the exam, know that a NetBIOS name is 16 characters long, but you can only configure 15 characters and that each NetBIOS name must be unique within a network. Furthermore, NetBIOS names cannot contain spaces or back slash (\) characters.

As an illustration, if you would like to see all the NetBIOS names that are assigned to a Windows NT or Windows 95/98 computer, type in the command nbtstat n from the command prompt. Your computer must be using TCP/IP as a network protocol for this command to function properly.

When a computer wants to connect to another computer on a network using NetBEUI, NetBIOS first checks a local name cache to see if the hardware address is known. If not, NetBIOS sends out a connectionless broadcast to all computers searching for the computer with a given name. When the destination computer responds with its hardware address, a NetBIOS session is established between the two computers.

However, on a network using TCP/IP, finding other computers is not quite so easy. Because TCP/IP networks use network addresses (IP addresses) for network connections, NetBIOS must encapsulate resource requests in TCP/IP packets using the *NetBIOS over TCP/IP (NBT)* protocol. Furthermore, TCP/IP networks typically involve several network segments connected together by routers. Because NetBIOS primarily uses broadcast packets for name resolution and because most routers drop broadcast packets, alternative methods of name resolution are necessary.

In TCP/IP networks, NetBIOS uses the following hierarchy to resolve names to network (IP) addresses (also shown in Figure 9.7):

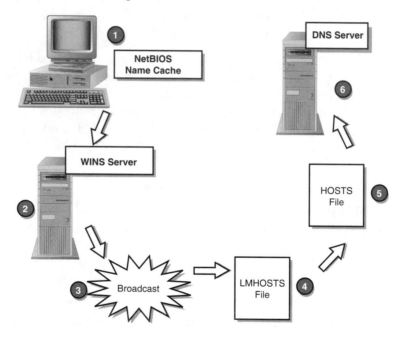

Figure 9.7
Microsoft operating systems resolve NetBIOS names using several different methods.

1. NetBIOS name cache
2. WINS server (if configured)
3. NetBIOS broadcast
4. LMHOSTS file (if enabled)
5. HOSTS file (if found)
6. DNS server (if configured)

Although the NetBIOS name cache and NetBIOS broadcast are the same methods mentioned earlier, the other methods deserve further explanation.

WINS

Windows Internet Name System (WINS) is a Windows NT service that provides dynamic resolution of NetBIOS names to IP addresses. When a computer configured to use WINS is powered up, the computer contacts the WINS server with the computer's NetBIOS name and IP address. The WINS server adds the name/address combination to its database and possibly replicates the data to other WINS servers within your LAN. When a WINS-enabled computer needs to contact another computer on the network, NetBIOS contacts the WINS server to determine the network address of the destination computer.

Because NetBIOS is nonroutable, NetBIOS broadcast requests only reach computers on the local network. For this reason, when a computer without WINS attempts to connect to a network resource, NetBIOS will only see the computers on the local network. However, after a computer is configured to use WINS, NetBIOS will see the names and network addresses of all other computers that have registered with a WINS server, regardless of on what network segment the computers are located. In this manner, a WINS server can be used to let all computers see other computers as if they were on the local network.

LMHOSTS and *HOSTS* Files

Before WINS was available, the primary method of resolving NetBIOS names to IP addresses was through entries in either an LMHOSTS or HOSTS file. These files are simple text files listing IP addresses followed by NetBIOS names and must be maintained by hand. Although these files could be used for name resolution today, in practice a combination of WINS and DNS provides the name resolution necessary.

DNS

The *Domain Name System (DNS)* uses a distributed system of name servers to map Internet-style *domain names* such as microsoft.com into valid IP addresses. If NetBIOS cannot find the IP address for a network name by any other means, NetBIOS will query a DNS server. (A full discussion of DNS can be found in Chapter 15.)

Summary

Just as international protocols define how communication should occur between people in foreign relations, network protocols define how communication should occur between computers.

Computer communication protocols are usually grouped together in a *protocol stack* or *protocol suite* and are installed onto a computer before it can connect to a network. Two of the most common protocol stacks are TCP/IP used on the Internet and Novell's IPX/SPX used in Novell NetWare networks.

Protocols have many characteristics, but two that differentiate protocols from each other are the connection type and the capability to be routed. *Connection-oriented* protocols provide a reliable point-to-point connection that guarantees that data will be sent correctly, whereas *connectionless* protocols merely send the data to the recipient with no guarantee of delivery. *Routable* protocols are suitable for networks, from small office networks to large enterprise-wide networks, whereas *nonroutable* protocols are designed primarily for small networks.

There are primarily three protocol stacks in wide use within networks using Microsoft operating systems: TCP/IP, IPX/SPX, and NetBEUI.

The TCP/IP protocol suite evolved as the Internet was developed and is widely used throughout networks of all sizes today. The suite consists of several protocols, the most important of which include the *Internet Protocol (IP)*, which provides data transportation, and the *Transmission Control Protocol (TCP)*, which provides reliable connection-oriented data transportation on top of IP.

To communicate within TCP/IP networks, all computers are assigned a unique 32-bit *IP address* consisting of a portion identifying the network and a portion identifying the individual computers, referred to as *hosts*. Computers use a *subnet mask* to determine which part of the IP address refers to the network and which part refers to an individual computer. IP addresses are either assigned manually or provided dynamically using the *Dynamic Host Configuration Protocol (DHCP)*. DHCP eases network administration and allows computers to be easily moved around within an organization.

The IPX/SPX protocol suite is used primarily within Novell NetWare networks. Like TCP/IP, the suite consists of a number of protocols. Similar to IP, *Internetwork Packet Exchange (IPX)* provides basic data transmission across a network, and *Sequenced Packet Exchange (SPX)*, like TCP, provides reliable connection-oriented communication.

Microsoft and IBM jointly developed the *Network Basic Input Output System (NetBIOS)* and *NetBIOS Extended User Interface (NetBEUI)* to support communication over small- to medium-sized networks. Although NetBIOS and NetBEUI were developed to work together, they have now been separated, and NetBIOS can work with a variety of protocols. NetBIOS provides a session layer application programming interface that PC applications can use to access network resources. NetBIOS can now be used on top of TCP/IP and IPX/SPX networks. NetBEUI is a small, fast, nonroutable protocol designed to carry NetBIOS and found primarily in small PC networks.

Although TCP/IP, IPX/SPX, and NetBEUI are the primary protocols used within PC networks, there are a large number of additional protocols in use, including DECnet, DLC, NFS, OSI, and SNA.

In most current operating systems, installation of protocols is usually accomplished through a graphical user interface. The ease of installation is aided by the existence of two driver interfaces, *Network Driver Interface Specification (NDIS)* and *Open Driver Interface (ODI)*, that allow multiple protocols to be bound to the same network interface card.

Finally, because most PC applications use NetBIOS to access network resources, you must have some method of translating, or *resolving*, 15-character NetBIOS computer names into valid network addresses. On a local network segment, NetBIOS uses simple broadcast packets to identify other computers. However, because NetBIOS is non-routable, some mechanism must be used to allow computers on different network segments to know about each other. The primary mechanism used within Microsoft networks is the *Windows Internet Name System (WINS)*, which operates on a TCP/IP network to allow all network segments to see NetBIOS names as if they were on one large network. It is also possible to manually configure NetBIOS addresses through host files or through using the *Domain Name System (DNS)*.

CH
9

QUESTIONS AND ANSWERS ─────

1. What is the difference between a connectionless and connection-oriented protocol?

   A: With a connectionless protocol, data is simply transmitted with no guarantee it will reach its destination. With a connection-oriented protocol, a reliable channel of communication is established between the two endpoints and the data is guaranteed to reach the destination.

2. Name two nonroutable protocols.

   A: NetBEUI, DLC

3. Differentiate between TCP and IP.

   A: TCP is a transport layer protocol providing connection-oriented communication and sequencing. IP is a network layer protocol providing addressing and routing.

4. What is the role of a subnet mask?

   A: A subnet mask is used to divide an IP address into a network and host portion and to determine whether a destination address is local or remote.

...*continues*

...continued

> **5.** How does DHCP simplify network administration?
>
> A: DHCP dynamically allocates IP addresses so that no one has to keep track of which computer has which IP address.
>
> **6.** Why is the frame type an issue in NetWare networks?
>
> A: Because NetWare (IPX/SPX) networks can use different Ethernet frame types, two computers must be using the same frame type in order to communicate successfully.
>
> **7.** Explain the difference between NetBIOS and NetBEUI.
>
> A: NetBIOS is a session layer protocol that provides an application programming interface that allows applications to communicate over the network. NetBEUI is a small, fast, nonroutable transport protocol on top of which NetBIOS can operate.
>
> **8.** In Windows NT, how do you configure the network protocols?
>
> A: In the Network Control Panel.
>
> **9.** What is the role of NDIS and ODI?
>
> A: To allow multiple protocols to bind to a single network interface card and to allow multiple NICs to use the same protocol.
>
> **10.** List the order in which NetBIOS name resolution occurs.
>
> A: NetBIOS name cache, WINS server, broadcast, LMHOSTS file, HOSTS file, DNS

PRACTICE TEST

1. What role does a subnet mask play?
   a. It identifies which network a computer is on within an IPX/SPX network.
   b. It identifies an individual machine on a TCP/IP network.
   c. It is appended to the end of an IP address to provide a distinct network address.
   d. It differentiates between the network and host portions of an IP address.

Answer a is incorrect because subnet masks have nothing to do with IPX/SPX. Answer b is incorrect because that would be the IP address. Answer c is incorrect and just plain wrong. **Answer d is correct.**

2. You want to run some audio applications over your network and need the maximum amount of speed possible. What type of communication protocol should you use?

   a. Connection-oriented
   b. Connectionless

Answer a is incorrect. **Answer b is correct; because there is no overhead established with setting up the connection and checking that the data reached the destination, connectionless protocols are the fastest.**

3. Your organization has 5 Windows NT servers, 10 UNIX servers, and 25 PC clients running Windows 95. What network protocol should you use for easy communication between all clients and servers?

   a. NetBEUI
   b. TCP/IP
   c. IPX/SPX
   d. SNA

Answer a is incorrect because the UNIX boxes can't use NetBEUI. **Answer b is correct because TCP/IP will work for all computers.** Answer c is incorrect because it will not work with the UNIX computers. Answer d is incorrect because it will not work for any of the systems.

4. Your office has 2 Windows NT Servers and 5 Novell NetWare servers. Because you do not want to add any additional software to your computers, what network protocol should you use?

   a. TCP/IP
   b. NetBEUI
   c. IPX/SPX
   d. NFS

Answers a and b are incorrect because the NetWare servers cannot use either protocol. **Answer c is correct; all computers can use IPX/SPX.** Answer d is incorrect because NFS is a UNIX file-sharing protocol.

5. Your company has a diverse network consisting of multiple network segments connected together. On each network segment there are multiple servers. Users' PCs are connected to different segments, and each PC uses resources from one of the servers on its network segment. You have been charged with developing a NetBIOS naming scheme that will easily identify individual computers.

   REQUIRED RESULT: The NetBIOS names must uniquely identify each computer.

OPTIONAL DESIRED RESULTS: Within the name, you must be able to identify which network segment each computer is on. You must also be able to identify the server with which the computer primarily communicates.

PROPOSED SOLUTION: You propose a naming scheme using an eighteen-character NetBIOS name for each PC. The first eight characters will identify the PC's network segment, the next seven will identify the server used, and the last three will be a unique number identifying the PC. Which results does the proposed solution produce?

   a. The proposed solution produces the required result and both of the optional desired results.

   b. The proposed solution produces the required result and only *one* of the optional desired results.

   c. The proposed solution produces the required result but does *not* produce any of the optional desired results.

   d. The proposed solution does *not* produce the required result.

Answers a, b, and c are incorrect. **Answer d is correct because each unique NetBIOS name can only be 15 characters long, and the proposed scheme would create an 18-character name.**

   6. As more users have been added to your TCP/IP network, you are losing track of which IP addresses you have assigned to individual workstations. You want to simplify the task of assigning IP addresses. What type of server should you establish on your network?

     a. DHCP

     b. WINS

     c. DNS

     d. BOOTP

Answer a is correct; a DHCP server would simplify the process of assigning IP addresses. Answers b and c are incorrect because WINS and DNS have to do with name resolution. Answer d is incorrect because BOOTP works with diskless machines that boot remotely.

   7. You have two computers on a Novell NetWare network that cannot communicate with each other. You have checked the hardware, and both computers appear to be communicating properly with the network. What is the most likely problem?

     a. One computer is using NDIS, while the other is using ODI.

     b. Both computers have identical IP addresses.

     c. The two computers are using different frame types.

     d. The two computers are using different subnet masks.

Answer a is incorrect because the choice of NDIS versus ODI makes no difference in communication. Answer b is incorrect because you are in an IPX/SPX network with no IP addresses. **Answer c is correct; different frame types can make two machines unable to communicate.** Answer d is incorrect because subnet masks are for TCP/IP and not NetWare.

8. Within your office TCP/IP computer network, Computer A is on one network segment, and Computer B is on another network segment. The two segments are interconnected by a router. From Computer A, you can connect to other computers on both network segments, with the exception of Computer B. From Computer B, you can only communicate with other computers on the same network segment. What is the probable cause of the problem?

   a. Computer A has the wrong subnet mask.
   b. Computer B has the wrong subnet mask.
   c. Computers A and B have the identical IP address.
   d. Computer B has an invalid IP address.

Answer a is incorrect because Computer A can get to all computers on both networks. **Answer b is correct; remember that a subnet mask is used to determine if a destination address is local or remote. If the wrong address is used, the computer will think that remote addresses are local and try to find them on the local network. That is the case here because Computer B can only communicate locally.** Answer c is incorrect because both machines *are* communicating with other machines. Answer d is incorrect because Computer B *is* able to communicate with other computers on its local network.

9. What is the primary function of NDIS and ODI within a network?

   a. They increase the network throughput in routers in which they are installed.
   b. They allow data to be interchanged between different network protocols.
   c. They allow multiple protocol stacks to use the same network interface card.
   d. They convert parallel data into serial data.

Answers a, b, and d are incorrect. **Answer c is correct.**

10. You have a network of Windows NT computers, Novell NetWare servers, and Apple Macintosh computers. At a minimum, what protocols will you have present on your network?

    a. IPX/SPX, AppleTalk
    b. AppleTalk, TCP/IP
    c. NetBEUI, AppleTalk
    d. AppleTalk, NetBEUI, IPX/SPX

CH
9

Answer a is correct; your Windows NT and Novell NetWare machines can communicate with IPX/SPX and your Apples can use AppleTalk. Answers b and c are incorrect because in neither case would your NetWare servers be able to use TCP/IP or NetBEUI. Answer d is incorrect because the question asked for the minimum number of protocols necessary, and NetBEUI is not necessary in this situation.

CHAPTER PREREQUISITE

This chapter requires a basic understanding of how networks function (see Chapter 2, "Introduction to Networks"), knowledge of the OSI Reference Model (see Chapter 3, "The OSI Reference Model"), and a familiarity with the basic functioning of a personal computer.

Network Operating Systems

WHILE YOU READ

1. What are the primary functions of a network operating system?

2. What does a redirector do?

3. A name in the format \\servername\pathname is called what?

4. In Microsoft networks, the term for making a folder accessible to others on the network is what?

5. When someone prints to a network printer, the print job is put into a _____ on the print server.

6. True or False: Network printer drivers for Windows NT 4.0 will also work for Windows NT 3.51.

Functions of a Network Operating System

Within a personal computer, the *operating system* handles the interaction between you and the hardware and software. Although traditional operating systems such as DOS and Windows 3.1 provide this functionality for standalone computers, they were not designed with any networking capabilities. Over time, some minimal networking functions have been added, but both DOS and Windows 3.1 are still designed to be used primarily on standalone PCs.

In contrast, a *network operating system (NOS)* is designed to provide the networking capabilities necessary for network operation. Typically, a network operating system, such as Novell NetWare or Windows NT Server, runs on a server computer, whereas a regular operating system, such as Windows or DOS, runs on client computers. Today, this distinction has blurred with operating systems such as Windows NT Workstation and Windows 95/98, all of which are designed for client computers, yet provide enough networking functionality that they can be called network operating systems.

A network operating system provides several functions:

- File and printer sharing
- User account administration
- Network security

For these functions to occur, software needs to be installed on both the client computers and the network servers.

Note that user account administration and network security will be addressed in Chapter 16, "Network Administration."

Software Components

Within a computer network, there are two software components that need to be installed:

- *Client software*, which enables users to access and utilize network resources such as file servers and printers.
- *Server software,* which allows the computer to make network resources available for others to share in addition to performing other administrative functions.

The two different types of software will be described in the following sections.

Client Software

On a standalone computer, requests for file or print resources are handled by the computer's CPU. For example, when a user on a standalone computer types in a request to see a directory listing, as shown in Figure 10.1, that request is handled by the local computer. (Note that Windows NT 4.0 and Windows 95/98 use the term *folder* instead of the term *directory* used in DOS, Windows 3.x, and Windows NT 3.51. The two terms will be used interchangeably within the text.)

Figure 10.1
On a standalone computer, a user's request for a directory listing is handled by the local computer.

However, when networking software has been installed on the computer, a program called a *redirector* enters the picture. The redirector intercepts all requests for file or printer resources and determines whether those requests are for the local machine or for a network resource. If the requests are for local resources, the redirector passes the request on to the CPU for processing. If the requests are for a network resource, the redirector passes the request to the appropriate network server, as depicted in Figure 10.2.

The advantage of this approach is that the location of resources is transparent to your applications. When you are in an application and save a file to a particular drive, the application does not need to know whether that drive is on your local system or on some network file server. The redirector makes it appear as if all drives are local. Likewise, when you choose to print a file, your application sends a print request to the printer you have chosen. The redirector intercepts that request and sends it to the appropriate local or network printer.

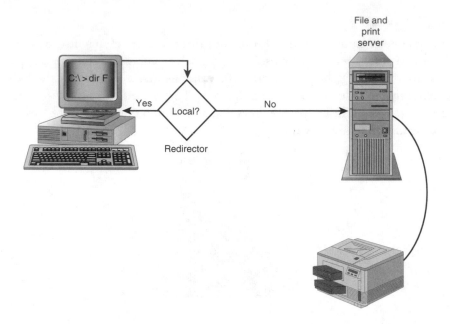

Figure 10.2
A user's request for a directory listing on a networked computer is handled by a redirector.

Within a PC environment, part of the task of a redirector is to keep track of *drive designators* that label each network file resource. For instance, most computers have a floppy drive known as A: and a hard disk drive known as C:. When you want to routinely access information from a directory on a network file server, you *map* the remote directory to a drive designator such as F: or G:. The redirector remembers what mappings you have created and enables you to treat them as if they are local drives.

Today, some operating systems such as Windows NT 3.51, Windows for Workgroups, and DOS require you to map a drive to a shared folder before you can access files in that folder. However, newer operating systems such as Windows 95/98 and Windows NT 4.0 enable you to reference shared network resources by using a *universal naming convention (UNC)* pathname. A UNC name takes the form *servername**pathname*. Note that although it is called "universal," the UNC is really a Microsoft naming convention.

For instance, if a shared folder named MARKETING is located on a server called SALESSRVR, the UNC name for that folder would be \\SALESSRVR\MARKETING. (Note that UNC names are *not* case-sensitive.) If a file REPORT.DOC exists in that folder, the UNC name for that file would be \\SALESSRVR\MARKETING\ REPORT.DOC.

With both Windows 95/98 and Windows NT 4.0, you can use a UNC name wherever you would normally use a drive letter and regular pathname. The redirector interprets the UNC name and directly accesses the shared resources.

Key Concept

A *universal naming convention (UNC)* pathname is a method of referencing shared network resources. The format of a UNC name is *servername**pathname*.

Because operating systems have evolved over time, some client operating systems now include the redirector software as part of the regular operating system. Examples within the Microsoft environment include Windows NT Workstation, Windows 95/98, and Windows for Workgroups. With older operating systems such as DOS or Windows 3.1, you will need to manually add the redirector software.

Note that in the theoretical framework of the OSI Reference Model, the redirector works primarily at the presentation layer and also at the application layer. One way to think of it is that the redirector presents resource requests from applications to the networking protocols and presents the network resources to the applications as if they were local.

Key Concept

Network client software involves a *redirector* that functions primarily at the OSI presentation layer and also at the application layer to allow applications access to network resources. The redirector intercepts resource requests from applications and determines whether they are for local or network resources and forwards the request to the appropriate resource.

Note that although the term *redirector* is used for the network client software with Microsoft networks, the term *requestor* is used within Novell networks.

Server Software

Whereas network clients typically need only the redirector software to access network resources, network servers require more complex software to perform their tasks. The necessary software is usually all bundled into the *network operating system* and is managed through a variety of administrative tools that are supplied with the NOS (see Figure 10.3).

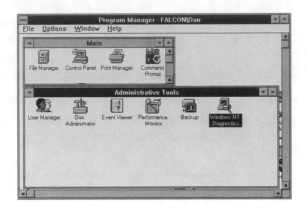

Figure 10.3
Windows NT includes tools to accomplish administrative tasks.

For instance, the network operating system will provide software that allows folders (also called directories) to be *shared* on the network. This software manages such things as which users can have access to the folder, how many users can access the folder at the same time, and what permission each user will have to modify items inside the folder.

As part of this process, server software handles incoming resource requests from redirectors on client computers and sends those requests to the appropriate resource.

Server software also provides tools to manage user accounts and provides network security. Before connecting to network resources, the user must *log on* (or *log in*) to the network. The network operating system manages this logon process and determines whether the user will be able to access network resources. Administrative tools are provided that enable network administrators to add or delete users and to specify the level of network access that each user will be allowed.

Because servers are typically used to store important data, network operating systems usually incorporate backup software that enables you to easily protect your data. Many times this software is used in conjunction with *fault-tolerant* disk drives that provide an extra level of hardware protection. Additionally, most network operating systems provide software for monitoring network performance.

You should note that some network operating systems, such as Windows NT Server and Novell NetWare, allow a computer to function as a server in a complex environment. These NOSs are designed to allow your computer to process network requests at high speed and to provide data protection and network security.

However, some components of server software are also incorporated into client operating systems such as Windows 95/98 and Windows NT Workstation. With these operating systems, a computer can both access network resources as a client and share resources as a server. When operating in such a fashion, a computer is referred to as a *peer*. Although client operating systems might provide some server functions, they usually lack the more sophisticated tools found in a network operating system.

Network Services

For the certification exam, you should understand all the services provided by a network operating system. Although later chapters will discuss services such as adding users and backing up data, you should at this point become familiar with two basic NOS services:

- Sharing files
- Sharing printers

These will be discussed later in the context of Microsoft networks.

If at all possible, you should try out these skills on a computer that is connected to an actual network. Appendix I, "Lab Exercises," provides several exercises focusing on file sharing.

File Sharing

Within a Microsoft network, files can be shared by using a server operating system such as Windows NT Server or by using one of the following client operating systems: Windows NT Workstation, Windows 95/98, or Windows for Workgroups. File sharing can be accomplished from the command line or through using a graphical tool such as the File Manager or Windows Explorer. Note that you cannot share an individual file, but you must instead share the folder/directory that contains that file.

Key Concept

In Microsoft networks, a folder is *shared* out onto the network for others to use.

Using the File Manager within Windows for Workgroups or Windows NT 3.51 (Workstation or Server), you click the folder you want to share, go to the Disk menu, and choose Share As. The resulting dialog box will resemble Figure 10.4. You can enter a share name of up to 15 characters (with no spaces), a descriptive comment, and the maximum number of users able to access this directory at the same time.

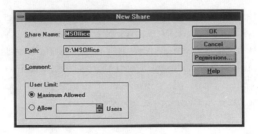

Figure 10.4
Within Windows NT 3.51, you share a directory by using the New Share dialog box.

Before leaving this dialog box, you need to set the permissions for who can access this directory. Press the Permissions button, and you will see an Access Through Share Permissions dialog box, similar to Figure 10.5. You can now choose which users or groups can access the files in this directory. Note that in setting the permissions for the directory, you are applying those permissions by default to all files within a directory. With Windows NT, it is possible to override those default settings and apply more restrictive permissions, but that is done through the properties for the specific file and not through this Permissions dialog box.

Figure 10.5
When sharing a directory, you can assign certain permission levels to individual users in the Access Through Share Permissions dialog box.

File sharing in Windows 95/98 and Windows NT 4.0 is similar. However, you click an object with the secondary mouse button (also referred to as *right-clicking*) and choose Sharing from the context menu, as shown in Figure 10.6.

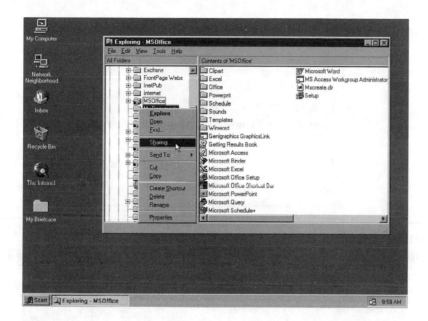

Figure 10.6
In Windows 95/98, you right-click to bring up a menu from which you can open the Sharing dialog box.

Accessing shared resources is also slightly different between Microsoft operating systems. Again, using the File Manager within Windows NT 3.51 and Windows for Workgroups, you choose Connect Network Drive from the Disk menu (or use a toolbar icon) and then *browse* the list of network resources as shown in Figure 10.7. Choose a folder to which to connect, and it will be mapped to a drive letter on your system (assuming that you have the correct access permissions). Then, you can simply begin using files in that directory.

Windows NT 4.0 and Windows 95/98 provide this same dialog box, but they also provide you with the Network Neighborhood, as shown in Figure 10.8. You can browse the Network Neighborhood and use files directly from within the Network Neighborhood window, or you can browse to find a resource and then map a drive letter to that resource.

CH
IO

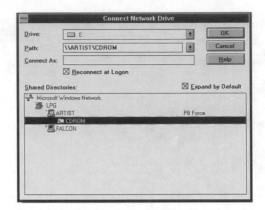

Figure 10.7
When mapping a network drive in Windows NT 3.51, you browse through a list of shared resources in the Connect Network Drive dialog box.

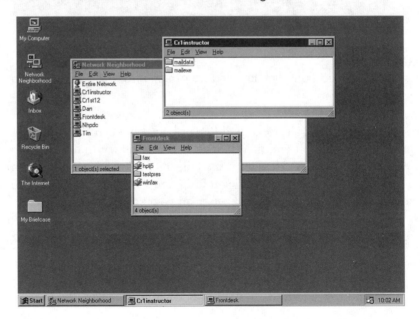

Figure 10.8
Windows NT 4.0 and Windows 95/98 provide a Network Neighborhood window for browsing network resources.

After you connect to a network resource, the redirector on your computer keeps track of your connection and directs requests to save or retrieve files to the appropriate network resource.

On Microsoft networks, computers share files using the *Server Message Block (SMB)* protocol. In Novell NetWare networks, file sharing is through the *NetWare Core Protocol (NCP)*. In UNIX/Linux networks, file sharing is through the *Network File System (NFS)* protocol. Note that UNIX/Linux computers can also use a program called Samba to use SMB to participate in Microsoft file sharing.

Key Concept

Microsoft computers share files using the Server Message Block (SMB) protocol. UNIX/Linux computers share files using the Network File System (NFS) protocol. On the exam, be sure not to confuse these file sharing protocols with network protocols such as TCP/IP and IPX/SPX.

CH
10

Network Printing

Network printing involves a bit more complexity than does sharing files, although the actual process of sharing a printer or connecting to a shared printer occurs in much the same manner as the process of sharing files or connecting to shared folders. As you can when sharing a folder, you can name a shared printer and assign appropriate permissions. The major difference is that instead of using the File Manager or Network Neighborhood, you use the Print Manager or the Printers icon in the Control Panel. For connecting to a printer, Windows 95/98 even includes the Add Printer Wizard, shown in Figure 10.9, which greatly simplifies the process.

Figure 10.9
The Windows 95/98 Add Printer Wizard simplifies the task of connecting to network printers.

When you have connected as a client to a network printer, your computer's redirector will send all appropriate print requests to that printer, just as the redirector sends all file requests to the appropriate shared folder.

The complexity of network printing occurs on the server end. When a request arrives for a file in a shared folder, the server's task is fairly minimal. All the server needs to do is determine whether the file is in use by someone else and whether the requestor has permission to access the file. If there is no problem, the server returns the requested file. If there is a problem, the server returns an error message.

Likewise, when the server receives a request to print a file, it determines whether the requestor has permission to use the printer, and if not, it returns an error message. However, even if it is okay for the user to print the file, the server does not immediately send it to the printer. Instead, it *spools* the *print job* into the *print queue*, where the file will sit until the printer is ready to start printing it (see Figure 10.10). A program called a *spooler* monitors the queues and the status of the printers and manages the process of actually printing the documents on the printer.

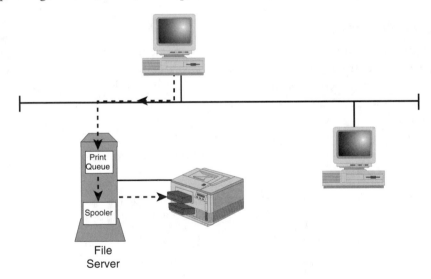

Figure 10.10
When a file is printed to a network printer, it is spooled into a print queue, where it sits until the printer is ready to print it.

This process enables multiple users to print to a network printer without interfering with each other's printouts. As each print job arrives, it is placed in the queue until the spooler lets it proceed to the actual printer. A computer functioning as a dedicated print server might have several printers attached to it, each of which would have its own print queue.

One feature of a network operating system is that users can usually manage a print queue remotely. If a user wants to cancel a print job he has sent to a printer, he can open up the Print Manager or the specific printer window and cancel the printing of the file. Although users are typically limited to managing only their own print jobs, network administrators can remotely manage the entire queue and can cancel anyone's print jobs or modify the printing order of print jobs.

Printer drivers are the final element of complexity within network printing. As with network interface cards, the operating system uses printer drivers to communicate with printers. The issue is that each operating system uses different drivers for specific printers. Therefore, a problem arises when you share a printer from a Windows NT 3.51 computer and a user on a Windows 95/98 computer wants to print to that printer. Because the printer drivers for Windows NT 3.51 and Windows 95/98 are different, the Windows 95/98 user will not be able to print to your computer.

There are two possible solutions to this problem. First, on the server computer, you can load the print drivers for all the operating systems that will be using your printer. So, in a typical Microsoft environment today, you might load the printer drivers for Windows NT 3.51, Windows NT 4.0, Windows 95/98, and Windows 3.x. As a result, any user can connect to that printer, and the redirector and spooler software will be able to use the appropriate drivers. The other alternative is to install the appropriate printer drivers on the client machines. Using this method, when the user goes to print, the redirector processes the print file before sending it on to the print server.

Summary

Although a normal operating system handles interactions between a user and the hardware and software in a computer, a network operating system provides additional functionality that enables users to share files and printers on the network, administer user accounts, and provide network security. Network operating systems common in the PC world include Windows NT Server and Novell NetWare.

Beyond the physical components, connecting a computer to a network involves some additional software components. On the client side, a *redirector* enables users to map network resources to additional drive letters and use those network resources as if they were local disk drives. The redirector essentially intercepts any requests to save or retrieve files, determines whether the file is local or on the network, and sends it to the appropriate resource. Some operating systems such as Windows NT and Windows 95/98 already include a redirector. For others, such as DOS and Windows 3.1, the redirector must be installed later.

CH
10

Server software involves a number of services and administrative tools that are bundled into network operating systems such as Windows NT Server. Server software typically includes tools to manage user accounts, back up and protect data, and monitor network performance.

Network operating systems commonly provide the services of sharing files and sharing printers. To share files within a Microsoft environment, you can use the command line, File Manager, or Windows Explorer. Permissions can be set to restrict which network users can access the shared information.

Although sharing printers is accomplished in a similar manner, the server process involves several steps. When the user submits a print job, it is spooled into a print queue, where a spooler monitors the status of printers and permits the print job to be printed when a printer is available. Printers can typically be managed remotely, and network administrators are usually able to cancel or reprioritize queued print jobs.

QUESTIONS AND ANSWERS

1. What are the primary functions of a network operating system?

    A: File and printer sharing, user account administration, and network security.

2. What does a redirector do?

    A: Intercepts requests for files located on a network server and redirects those requests to the server.

3. A name in the format `\\servername\pathname` is called what?

    A: A Universal Naming Convention (UNC) pathname.

4. In Microsoft networks, the term for making a folder accessible to others on the network is what?

    A: Sharing.

5. When someone prints to a network printer, the print job is put into a _____ on the print server.

    A: print queue.

6. True or False: Network printer drivers for Windows NT 4.0 will also work for Windows NT 3.51.

    A: False. Each operating system needs its own printer drivers.

PRACTICE TEST

1. What is the name of the piece of software that allows a network client PC to use network resources just as if those resources were directly connected to the PC?

  a. Spooler

  b. Redirector

  c. Network driver

  d. Network protocol

Answer a is incorrect because a spooler works with printing. **Answer b is correct.** Answer c is incorrect because a network driver is usually what is used with a NIC. Answer d is incorrect because it is a protocol used for networking, as opposed to a piece of software.

2. Which of the following operating systems enable users to share files on a network? (Choose all that apply.)

  a. Windows 95

  b. Windows 3.1

  c. Windows for Workgroups

  d. Windows NT Workstation

Answers a, c, and d are correct. Answer b is incorrect because Windows 3.1 does not enable users to share files automatically. It is possible to add the appropriate software to Windows 3.1 so that it could share files, but this is not included by default.

3. When you want to make a network resource readily accessible on your client computer, you can _____ a drive letter to that resource.

  a. Redirect

  b. Map

  c. Spool

  d. Hard-wire

Answers a, c, and d are incorrect. **Answer b is correct.**

4. What is the name of the software program on a print server that manages print queues and allows files to actually be printed?

  a. Redirector

  b. Print redirector

  c. Print job

  d. Spooler

Answer a is incorrect because the redirector is on the client computer. Answer b is incorrect because it is vague and makes no sense in this situation. Answer c is incorrect; a print job is the actual print output waiting to be sent to the printer. **Answer d is correct; a print *spooler* is the program that actually sends the print jobs to the printers.**

5. Within a Microsoft network, the process of making a folder available to everyone else on a network is called what?

   a. Sharing

   b. Redirecting

   c. Publishing

   d. Spooling

Answer a is correct. Answers b, c, and d are incorrect.

6. When a document is sent to a network printer, it is received by the print server and immediately sent directly to the printer.

   a. True

   b. False

Answer a is incorrect. **Answer b is correct; the document goes into a print queue.**

7. Which of the following are *not* functions of a network operating system? (Choose all that apply.)

   a. Providing file and printer sharing.

   b. Handling user interactions on client machines.

   c. Administering user accounts.

   d. Providing network security.

Answers a, c, and d are all incorrect because they *are* functions of a network operating system. **Answer b is correct because this is *not* something handled by a network operating system.**

8. When sharing a printer on a network, which of the following properties can you configure? (Choose all that apply.)

   a. Shared printer name.

   b. Fonts and typefaces that can be used on the printer.

   c. Permissions of who can use the printer.

   d. Speed at which the client computer can connect with the printer.

Answers a and c are correct and are configured at the time you share the printer (and can be changed later). Answers b and c are incorrect as they are dependent on the client computer configuration.

9. Within Windows NT, which of the following are *not* options that you can configure when sharing a folder on the network? (Choose all that apply.)

   a. Share name.

   b. Maximum number of users that can simultaneously connect to the shared folder.

   c. Restrictions on which computers (as compared to users) can access the shared folder.

   d. Permission settings for individual users to access the folder.

Answers a, b, and d are all incorrect because they *are* settings that can be configured on a share. **Answer c is correct because a Windows NT computer uses user-level security and bases all share permissions on user accounts.**

10. You install a laser printer onto a Windows NT 3.51 Server computer and verify that you can print correctly from your machine. A user on a Windows NT 3.51 Workstation machine can also print to the printer across the network. However, one of your users on a Windows 95 computer cannot print to the new printer across the network, but he can print to other network printers connected to the same Windows NT 3.51 Server. You have not denied him permission to use the new printer. What could explain the problem?

   a. The user has mistakenly configured his redirector to deny him access to the printer.

   b. The user's print spooler will not send print jobs to the server.

   c. The appropriate Windows 95 printer driver is not installed on the printer server or the user's computer.

   d. Windows 95 redirectors cannot communicate with Windows NT print servers.

Answers a and b are incorrect because the user *is* printing to other printers on the same machine. **Answer c is correct; the problem will be fixed with the right printer driver.** Answer d is incorrect because Windows 95 redirectors *do* communicate with Windows NT servers.

CH
10

Network Applications

WHILE YOU READ

1. Explain the difference between a standalone application and a network version of a standalone application.

2. Why do people install the network versions of standalone applications?

3. List three examples of applications that require a network to function properly.

4. Differentiate between a shared-file system and a client/server application.

5. What is a Mail Transfer Agent?

6. What is the difference between SMTP and POP3?

7. What do LDAP and X.500 do?

8. True or False: SMTP is a routable protocol.

9. What are two protocols used to transfer mail between systems?

10. At which layer of the OSI Reference Model do databases and email systems operate?

Applications in a Network Environment

Whenever you are working on a computer, you are using some type of program, or *application*, to accomplish whatever it is you are doing. For instance, you might be using a word processor, spreadsheet, database, game, or other application.

On a network, each of these applications can have different levels of interaction with the network itself and can be classified in one of three broad categories:

- Standalone applications
- Network versions of standalone applications
- Network-only applications

Standalone Application

Standalone applications are designed to be operated on a single computer *without* requiring a network. Examples would be traditional word processors, such as Microsoft Word and WordPerfect, or spreadsheets, such as Microsoft Excel or Lotus 1-2-3.

Network interaction for this type of application is usually limited to using files from a file server. For instance, a directory on a file server could be *mounted* or *attached* to a local computer and would simply show up as an additional drive letter such as F:. Users of standalone applications on that computer could save files to the F: drive just as if they were saving them to the C: or A: drives. As far as they would be concerned, the network drive would be no different than local drives. This enables administrators to efficiently manage computer resources by making large disk drives available to all users.

Standalone applications could also be located on a file or application server, and individual users could run the program from the network drive. For example, if a company had one copy of a database program and wanted several people to use it, the company might locate it on a server. Multiple users could then run that program from the file server. However, using the application in this fashion might violate the license agreement that came with the software and put your company in legal peril. You will also find that some standalone applications will not function in this manner and will not enable multiple users to access the software.

If you want to allow your users to be able to run an application over the network, you really need to be using the network version of the standalone application.

Network Versions of Standalone Applications

Network versions of standalone applications are basically identical to their standalone counterparts, with the exception that they are designed to be compatible with networking software, are able to take advantage of networking functions, and are usually licensed for multiple concurrent users. After you have installed an application of this type, your users might not even notice the difference from a previously installed standalone application. In a Windows environment, they will just double-click an icon and open the application as they always have done.

Although users might not notice, shared applications can be a great benefit for network administrators. Some of the advantages include the following:

- *Easier setup and administration.* Only one version of the software has to be installed rather than going around installing it on each user's workstation. Upgrades involve upgrading only the version on the server. Users do not have to be involved with the installation programs, but instead can simply work with the programs and leave the administration to the administrators.

- *Version control.* Installing an application on a server means that all users will be using the same version of an application. You do not have to worry about whether some users are using version 4.0 of a product while others are using version 7.0.

- *Disk space.* With the applications stored on the server, the client machines do not need as much disk space locally.

- *Cost.* Most network versions of an application allow for *site licensing* that enables you to use the application for a certain number of users. A site license for 200 users is usually substantially cheaper than purchasing 200 individual copies of the software.

Regarding licensing, most applications require you to purchase some type of license for the number of users who will be using the application. This usually takes the form of a site license, as mentioned previously, although it might also be in the form of you purchasing a number of *client-access-licenses* equal to the number of people who will be using the application.

In either case, licensing is often on an "honor system." For example, if you have a site license for 50 users and a 51st user goes to open the application, she will often be able to do so. However, at that point you are violating your license agreement and placing your company in legal jeopardy should it be audited in the future. In the past, software companies have gone after violators with penalties ranging from extra fees to confiscation of equipment by police.

Some applications actually do have the capability to control the number of users sharing the application. These types of applications offer licenses in a manner similar to a librarian offering books. For example, you can keep checking out books until they are all gone, and when you are finished with a book, you return it. If this were the case in the previous example, the 51st user would actually be denied access and would be forced to wait until another user stopped using the application and returned her license.

Installing a network version of an application on a server sometimes merely involves installing the application into a directory and then sharing that directory for others to access. Often, it requires installing a few system files onto the local workstation, with the bulk of the files remaining on the server. Typically, applications are installed on a file server along with directories containing data. In some instances, an *application server* might be set up for the sole purpose of sharing applications.

Although sharing applications can be a great benefit, it is not without disadvantages, including the following:

- *Network speed.* Shared applications require more network bandwidth than standalone applications. When users have standalone applications, the only network traffic they generate is from retrieving files across the network. However, when accessing network versions of the software, all the components of the software that actually make up the application need to be pulled across the network as well as the actual data files. Heavy application usage can slow down the network.

- *Unusable in case of network failure.* With standalone applications, if the network fails, users will not be able to access files stored on a file server but will still be able to use their application with files stored locally. However, with shared applications, failure of the network means that users will not be able to use the application at all.

Network-Only Applications

Although sharing typical office applications such as word processors from a central server is a common use of a network, there is also an entire class of applications that will function only in a networked environment. The network-only applications are quite numerous, but some examples include the following:

- Shared databases
- Electronic mail
- Group scheduling
- Groupware

Before I discuss these examples, you need to understand that there are several different models for how these network applications can function:

- Centralized applications
- Shared–file system applications
- Client/server applications

Understanding these different models is crucial to understanding how network applications function and how to troubleshoot problems with applications.

Centralized Applications

With a centralized application environment as shown in Figure 11.1, users connect into a central host computer such as a mainframe either by using a dedicated *terminal* or by opening a *terminal session* on their PCs. In either case, users essentially have a screen or window that displays information from the mainframe. The mainframe handles all the processing, and the users interact with the program through their one window. Generally, programs of this nature are character-based and include minimal graphics.

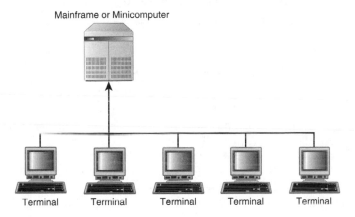

Figure 11.1
Centralized applications rely on a central host computer to provide all the processing power.

As an example, consider how many of the traditional mainframe database programs work. Users have a terminal window that enables them to type in requests for information. When a user types in information, all the individual keystrokes are sent to the mainframe computer for processing. The user then completes a form and submits a request. The mainframe processes that request, finds the required information, formats all the information for display in the terminal window, and sends it back to the user. Take note that the user's PC or terminal does essentially nothing during the entire transaction process.

Older dial-up electronic mail services or bulletin board systems are other examples. To use one of these services, you launch a terminal program on your PC, dial in to the service, and send/receive email using a text-based interface. Again, the only thing your PC does is display a window on your screen and provide basic connection services. Everything else happens on the host system.

Although this computing model is the manner in which most traditional mainframe applications operate, centralized applications generate a lot of network traffic and do not efficiently use the capabilities of desktop PCs available today. For these reasons, pure centralized applications have generally been replaced by client/server applications.

Key Concept

In *centralized* applications, all the processing occurs on the server, and the client is used only as a terminal to connect to the server.

Shared–File System Applications

In stark contrast to centralized applications, *shared–file system applications* perform all the processing on the client PC and use the server only for file storage. An example of this would be popular PC electronic mail programs such as Microsoft Mail or cc:Mail. Many general-purpose PC database programs, personal information managers (PIMs), and scheduling programs also work on this model.

For example, in most PC electronic mail programs, there is a central location where a "post office" is stored. As depicted in Figure 11.2, PC users use a mail program to reach across the network and retrieve information from a special directory on a file server.

Although this computing model makes more efficient use of the power available in desktop PCs, it does not necessarily solve the issue of network traffic. When a user starts the mail program and goes to access his inbox, the mail program must transfer that portion of the mail post office file from the file server to (usually) a temporary file on the PC. The mail program must then keep that local copy synchronized with the main part of the file, usually through constant checks of the main file on the file server. Even if the user only occasionally gets email, the mail program must keep checking. The process of constantly checking for mail is often referred to as *polling*. This polling process and the general transfer of mail messages and temporary files across the network can generate quite a bit of network traffic.

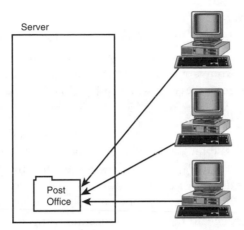

Figure 11.2
With email programs using the shared–file system model, PC clients access a shared folder on a file server.

Shared–file system applications also introduce a number of security issues. With a centralized application, security concerns are essentially limited to the host system and can be addressed there. However, for a shared–file system application to work, all PC clients must have the capability to read and write information where the shared data resides. Additionally, all PC clients must also cooperate to ensure that the data files are not corrupted by multiple users accessing the files at the same time. This is often accomplished by some type of *file-locking* or *record-locking* mechanism, which can add extra overhead to the processing time.

As networks evolved and started to shift from mainframe-based systems to PC-based systems, shared–file system applications developed to allow alternatives to centralized applications. Although they have their place, especially in small offices and organizations, in many environments, shared–file system applications, like the centralized applications, are being replaced with client/server applications.

 Key Concept

In *shared–file system* applications, all the processing is performed on the client end with the server only being used for file storage.

Client/Server Applications

Whenever you use the World Wide Web, you are seeing client/server computing in action. For example, when you want to view a Web site, you type its address into your Web browser (or choose it from a bookmark list or existing Web page). Your browser sends your request for a page to the Web server responsible for that site. The Web server receives your request and sends back the HTML file for the requested page.

Your browser receives the HTML file, formats it for your screen, determines whether it needs to request additional graphics, and shows the page to you. There is no further connection with the Web server. Your browser enables you to view the page in addition to managing all issues such as showing you more of the page when you scroll down. When you click a link to view another page, your browser then sends off a request to a Web server for the appropriate page and repeats the procedure with the new page.

Processing is sometimes split between the browser and the server. If you fill out a Web form and press a button to submit the form data, your browser takes all the information you entered, reformats it into a compressed package, and sends that package in a short burst to a Web server. The server extracts the data, passes it to a script or program for processing, and sends some type of response back to the browser in the form of an HTML or text file, which, again, the browser reformats and presents to the user.

Client/server applications combine the advantages of both centralized applications and shared–file system applications. Client programs handle user interaction and display, whereas server programs perform extensive data processing. This computing model also makes more efficient use of computing resources. Desktop PCs have more than enough computing power to handle window manipulation and user input; however, they might not have the processing power to perform large database indexing and searching operations. Instead, a server can be equipped with enough resources (processors, RAM, and so on) to easily accomplish large-scale data manipulation. The server can also enable many people to simultaneously access a data resource, regardless of whether it is a Web site, database, or email system. (The processing performed by the server in the background, out of view of the user, is sometimes referred to as *back-end processing*.)

For example, consider how the email example from the previous section would work in a client/server environment. As shown in Figure 11.3, the PC client mail programs now interact with a mail server program. The mail server, in turn, interacts with the actual post office, often referred to as an *information store* or *message store* in the world of messaging programs.

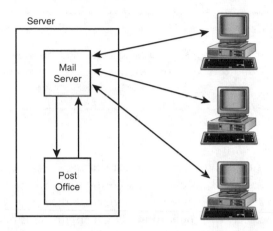

Server

Mail
Server

Post
Office

Figure 11.3
Client/server applications divide the processing between the client PCs and the server.

This arrangement offers a number of significant advantages over the shared–file system approach. First, client mail programs do not have to get involved with the structure of the post office. Instead of actually delivering the message, they just pass it off to the mail server to deliver.

Second, the client mail programs do not have to be continually checking the status of the mail file on the server. The mail server notices when new mail arrives for a user and alerts that user's client that a message has arrived. Because communication can occur in both directions, network traffic is reduced by eliminating the constant polling for messages.

Finally, security is greatly increased in this scenario. Client mail programs are not directly accessing the message store, so they do not need to have read/write permission to that directory on the file server, nor do you need to be concerned about file-locking issues. The mail server is the only program accessing the message store. Client/server applications can be found throughout the world of networks today. Beyond the Web and email systems, client/server applications have also revolutionized the way databases are accessed on a network. While making more efficient use of both client and server components, the only major disadvantage to client/server applications is that they can often be more difficult to configure than shared-file system or host-based applications.

Key Concept

With client/server applications, processing is divided between a client that inter-acts with the user and a server that performs back-end data manipulations and processing.

Electronic Mail

Although networks might first have been used for sharing files, it wasn't long until pro-grammers figured out that networks could be a great communication medium. Soon, vendors began to offer *electronic mail (email) applications* that could run on a variety of systems. Like most other network applications, email applications began in the centralized host-based environment of mainframe computers and evolved over time to the PC shared–file system and client/server applications of today.

Because sending and receiving electronic mail usually involves a number of different applications, you will often hear reference to *email systems* or *messaging systems*. Most email systems enable users to send and receive messages to one or many users and to attach files to messages. Email systems usually provide the capability of enabling users remote access to their messages. Return receipts and delivery notification alerts are also common features.

There are many different email systems available today for PC networks, including the following examples:

- *Microsoft Mail.* A simple and easy-to-use shared–file system email system. It is widely used, both as a separate product and also through the "Exchange" client (now called Windows Messaging) provided with Microsoft Windows 95.
- *Microsoft Exchange Server.* A powerful client/server messaging/groupware system.
- *cc:Mail.* Another simple and easy-to-use shared–file system email application from Lotus and IBM.
- *Lotus Notes.* A client/server messaging/groupware system.
- *Novell GroupWise.* A client/server messaging/groupware system.
- *SMTP/POP3 systems.* Email systems implemented using clients and servers based on common Internet protocols such as SMTP and POP3. An example of a client would be *Outlook Express*, a client provided for free as part of Microsoft's Internet Explorer 5.

As shown in Figure 11.4, the Microsoft Exchange (or Windows Messaging) client is one email application available to users of Windows-based PCs.

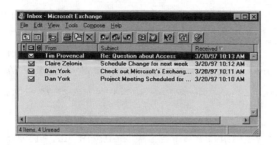

Figure 11.4
Microsoft Exchange (also known as Windows Messaging) enables users to send and receive electronic mail.

Care should be taken to differentiate the Windows 95 Inbox, called *Microsoft Exchange*, from the actual Microsoft Exchange client used with Microsoft Exchange Server. Both products use the same graphical interface, but the Windows 95 version lacks the capability to actually work with Exchange Server. The Windows 95 Inbox can be used only with an Internet mail account, a Microsoft Mail Post Office, or Microsoft Fax. When you want to start using Exchange Server, you have to actually upgrade the Windows 95 Inbox client.

With Windows NT 4.0 and the latest release of Windows 95 (OSR2), Microsoft has addressed this confusion by changing the name of the application launched by the Inbox from *Exchange* to *Windows Messaging System*. With Windows 98, Microsoft has gone away from the Windows Messaging System and now includes *Outlook Express* as the standard email client.

Entire books are written about email systems, but the following sections will summarize three different areas:

- Components of an email system
- Email protocols
- Connecting email systems

Components of an Email System

The exact features of an email system might vary widely, but generally include the following components:

- *Email client.* Also called a *User Agent (UA)* or *Mail User Agent (MUA),* the email client is responsible for all user interaction such as reading and composing messages.

- *Message Transfer Agent (MTA).* The MTA is responsible for transporting messages from one user's mailbox to another or to other MTAs for delivery.

- *Directory services.* Email systems provide a list of users on their systems. In Microsoft products, there is a *Personal Address Book* and a *Global Address List.*

- *Post office.* Also called an *information store* or *message store*, this is the location of all user messages.

Some of the terminology in this list, such as User Agent and Message Transfer Agent, originates with the X.400 protocols. They are mentioned because Microsoft uses the terminology with Exchange Server and other messaging components of its operating systems. X.400 is defined later in this chapter.

Email Protocols

Because electronic mail applications have their own standards for communication, you should be familiar with the protocols mentioned in this section. These protocols define addressing, attaching files, and how messages are sent between users. Some email applications still use proprietary protocols, but today, most support nonproprietary (or *open*) protocols such as those used on the Internet.

Key Concept

For the exam, make certain that you do not confuse any of these email communication protocols (for example, SMTP and X.400) with other networking protocols. Exam questions asking about networking protocols have sometimes thrown in a few email protocols just to confuse you.

Electronic mail protocols can be broken into three different categories:

- Transport/delivery protocols
- Directory services
- Messaging application programming interfaces

Transport/Delivery Protocols

There are several protocols involved with the actual transportation and delivery of electronic mail. They include the following:

- *SMTP.* Simple Mail Transport Protocol (SMTP) is the standard for communication between email servers on the Internet. It essentially describes how email servers should send and receive messages. The Internet style of addressing (user@domain) originates with SMTP.

- *POP3* and *IMAP4*. The problem with SMTP is that computers need to constantly be online to use it. If the computer is not online, messages can be rejected. Email servers are usually always online, so transferring messages with SMTP works fine. However, because most PCs are not always connected to the Internet, another mechanism was developed for transferring messages. Currently, SMTP is used to deliver a message to your mailbox on an email server. When you dial in with your PC, you then receive the messages from the server using *Post Office Protocol version 3 (POP3)*. Although POP3 has been adequate, it is in the process of being upgraded to *Internet Mail Access Protocol version 4 (IMAP4)*.

- *MIME*. The *Multipurpose Internet Mail Extension* standard defines the method in which files are attached to SMTP messages.

- *X.400*. The International Telecommunication Union's X.400 standards define a whole range of protocols for transferring mail between email servers. X.400 standards cover topics such as addressing, user interfaces, transport protocols, and delivery instructions. X.400 is often used on corporate backbones between email servers.

- *MHS*. Novell's *Message Handling Service (MHS)* is the *de facto* standard for transporting email within Novell NetWare environments. It is similar to SMTP and X.400 in that it typically works in the background while transporting messages.

X.400 was actually developed by the CCITT (Comité Consultatif Internationale de Télégraphie et Téléphonie or International Telegraph and Telephone Consultative Committee), a committee of the International Telecommunications Union, and it can be referred to as a *CCITT standard*. However, the trend now is to refer to CCITT standards as *ITU standards*.

Directory Services

One of the issues within an email system is finding the address for someone with whom you want to communicate. Most email applications have a directory of some type, but two standards are becoming increasingly used:

- *LDAP*. *Lightweight Directory Access Protocol (LDAP)* is an emerging standard that is now being widely adopted by Internet email vendors. With an LDAP-equipped email client, a user can query an email server (assuming the server supports LDAP) and find email addresses for users on that server.

- *X.500*. Developed by the CCITT/ITU, X.500 is a standard for directory services that is widely used for organizing email addresses.

CH
II

Key Concept

For the exam, remember that X.500 and LDAP are directory services protocols and operate at the upper layers of the OSI Model. Do not confuse X.500 and LDAP with network protocols.

Messaging APIs

As email systems began to proliferate, vendors of desktop applications wanted a mechanism that would allow their desktop applications to work with any underlying email system. Messaging application programming interfaces (APIs) were developed to meet this need. Essentially, they enable any application developer to integrate email support into her application. For instance, many word processors now include a Send menu choice that enables you to quickly send a document through email. The word processors call the messaging API, which communicates with the user's email system.

Although a number of messaging APIs were proposed, two are primarily in use today:

- *MAPI.* Microsoft defined its Messaging API and incorporated MAPI throughout all its office products.
- *VIM.* Lotus created its *Vendor-Independent Messaging* protocol with the support of many other (non-Microsoft) application vendors.

Even though both messaging APIs are used, Microsoft's sheer dominance of the desktop application market has led to the widespread support and use of MAPI.

Connecting Email Systems

Because most email systems are designed to accommodate a large number of users, a single email system might meet the needs of your organization. However, at some point you might encounter the need to communicate with other email systems. It might be that, as a result of a merger, you need to integrate two different systems or that your users might be clamoring for the capability to send email to Internet users. In any case, most email systems now have the capability to exchange messages with other systems.

Some messaging systems, such as Microsoft Exchange, already come with several connectors that enable you to easily link with other systems. However, other messaging systems such as Microsoft Mail usually require you to purchase and install a separate *gateway* program. The gateway software sometimes can run on an existing PC, but it might need a separate, dedicated PC. Many companies today are using the Internet as a way to connect multiple systems.

Scheduling

Applications for scheduling an individual's time have been available for most of the history of PCs. Such applications typically enable you to view your schedule for the next day, week, month, or year and enable you to quickly make changes to that schedule. Events can be scheduled over multiple days and at different times. You can usually set alerts to notify you in some manner before the appointment occurs. If you attempt to schedule an appointment when you already have something scheduled, the scheduling program can alert you to the conflict and let you resolve the conflict. Microsoft Outlook, shown in Figure 11.5, is an example of a program that includes a scheduling component. Other examples include Microsoft Schedule+ and Lotus Organizer.

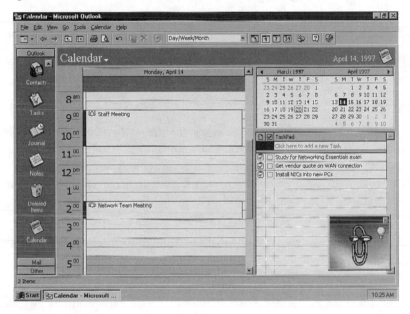

Figure 11.5
Microsoft Outlook provides individual and group scheduling capabilities.

Although all this might be useful to an individual, scheduling on a network enables a group to work together. If you want to schedule a meeting with several people, rather than contacting each person to ask if he is free for a meeting at a particular time, you can use the scheduling application to query his electronic calendar to see if he is free. Most network scheduling applications have the capability of enabling you to view multiple calendars at once, determine the best time to meet, actually insert the new appointment into the users' calendars, and even notify the users through an email message. The exact capabilities vary by product and might also depend on the permission settings for users' calendars.

Whereas most network scheduling programs enable you to view another user's calendar to determine where she is scheduled to be, depending on the application, that user might need to give you specific permission to view her calendar. If this function exists, there is usually the capability to schedule a "private" appointment that is only viewable to you for items that you do not want everyone else to know about. Most applications also enable you to designate someone else who is able to maintain your schedule. For instance, an executive might give his assistant permission to modify and update the executive's calendar.

Network scheduling applications can be a great benefit to organizations to enable users to more effectively and efficiently schedule employees' time. Of course, for them to be effective, all users within a group or company need to actually *use* the schedule application!

Groupware

Groupware applications, also referred to as *workgroup applications*, are similar to email systems in that people can use them for electronic communication. However, groupware applications also provide additional services that are designed to enable a group of people to work better together. Some groupware systems, such as *Microsoft Exchange* and *Lotus Notes*, provide both email and workgroup functions. Other groupware products might focus on one particular aspect of working together.

Uses for groupware applications are continually evolving, but include such possibilities as the following:

- *Group discussions*. Most systems have some capacity for discussions that are shared between many users. Names typically used by groupware products include bulletin boards, news-groups, forums, conferences, and public folders.

- *Workflow automation*. Routine business tasks and business processes can be automated. For instance, expense report submission could be accomplished through a form that would be submitted to one person who would automatically forward it on to someone else. Groupware programs can provide a mechanism to track this process.

- *Help Desk*. Corporations might provide an online database where users could search for resolutions to problems similar to what they are experiencing. If no matches are found, a form could be submitted to which the technical staff would follow up. The results would then be included in the online database.

- *Collective document creation.* Many groupware products provide a mechanism where multiple people can work together to create a document.
- *Internal publishing.* Companies might provide online employee manuals, newsletters, and other information that could be accessed by employees throughout the company.
- *Forms.* Groupware applications typically include the capability to design forms that can be used to automate business processes.

As networks play an even more crucial role within the business operations of organizations, groupware applications will continue to evolve and include many more functions. With Microsoft's release of Office 97 and then Office 2000, especially its Outlook product (see Figure 11.6), workgroup functionality is now integrated into all its desktop products.

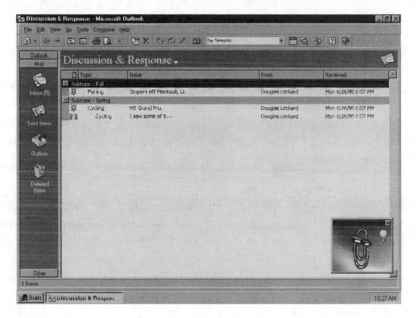

CH
11

Figure 11.6
Microsoft Outlook displays an online discussion forum.

Shared Databases

From the beginning, computer networks have been used to give users access to large database systems. Centralized and later client/server *Database Management Systems (DBMS)* were developed to share data across a network. Although centralized applications were once the norm, today most networks use some type of client/server application. The *DBMS engine* runs on a server and provides fast access to information. Client applications on PCs send *queries* to the engine. Network traffic is limited to the requests from the client and the pieces of data sent back from the server. DBMS examples within typical Microsoft networks include *Microsoft SQL Server* and *Microsoft Access.*

Like email applications, DBMS applications also have a number of different standards. However, the DBMS community has united behind only a couple of major standards:

- *SQL. Structured Query Language (SQL)* is a *data access language* that is used by almost all client/server database applications. The queries sent by the client to the server are composed of SQL statements.

- *ODBC.* Microsoft's *Open Database Connectivity (ODBC)* is an application programming interface that enables Windows application developers to integrate database connections into their applications. Just as network interface card (NIC) drivers allow a computer to communicate with any NIC, ODBC drivers allow an application to communicate with any database. When the application makes a data query, the ODBC drivers convert the query into SQL and send it to the appropriate database engine.

As mentioned in the discussion of shared–file system applications earlier in the chapter, it is possible to operate a database application by using a shared–file system approach. Many inexpensive database applications take this approach, which can perform adequately in a small environment. However, operating in this model, database applications consume large amounts of network bandwidth. Usually the entire database has to be copied from the file server to the client computer, where it is processed and then sent back to the file server. As a network grows in size, this high amount of network traffic rapidly makes client/server applications a much more attractive choice.

Key Concept

Again, watch out for tricky exam questions that might include SQL and ODBC about routing or network protocols. These two protocols operate at the upper layers of the OSI model and have nothing to do with the underlying network (where routing occurs).

Summary

Operating at the application layer of the OSI Reference Model, network applications provide the functionality that makes networks useful.

Applications can function at several levels within a network. Traditional standalone applications can simply save and retrieve files using file servers. Network versions of standalone applications might be located on a file server and provide network administrators with an easy means of administering the application.

There are, however, applications specifically designed for use in a networked environment, including electronic mail, scheduling, groupware, and shared databases.

True network applications can use three different models of computing. Centralized applications have all the processing power on the host computer with the client only providing a window to the host computer. Shared–file system applications, on the other hand, perform all the processing on the client end and use the server only for storing data files. Client/server applications divide the processing between the client and the computer. The client handles all user interaction and the server actually manipulates the data. Client/server applications make more efficient use of network resources and desktop computing power and are the dominant model for newer network applications.

CH
II

QUESTIONS AND ANSWERS

1. Explain the difference between a standalone application and a network version of a standalone application.

   A: A standalone application will only enable one person to use the application at a time. The network version will enable multiple people to run the program at the same time.

2. Why do people install the network versions of standalone applications?

   A: Several possible answers: easy setup and administration, ease of upgrading, cost, and saving space on the client machines.

3. List three examples of applications that require a network to function properly.

   A: Several possible answers: email, groupware, scheduling, chat, Web browsers/servers, and shared databases.

...continues

...continued

4. Differentiate between a shared–file system and a client/server application.

   A: With a shared–file system application such as a database, the clients all access the central shared database, leaving open possible security and performance holes. With a client/server application, clients only communicate with the server process, which in turn actually accesses the database. This latter approach provides more security.

5. What is a Mail Transfer Agent?

   A: An application that transfers mail between two mail systems.

6. What is the difference between SMTP and POP3?

   A: SMTP is used to send and receive mail between computers that are online all the time. POP3 is used to retrieve mail from a mailbox stored on a server. Home email users typically use POP3 to retrieve their email from a server inbox and then use SMTP to send their messages off.

7. What do LDAP and X.500 do?

   A: LDAP and X.500 provide directory services that enable people to find information in, for instance, a corporate directory.

8. True or False: SMTP is a routable protocol.

   A: False. SMTP has nothing to do with routing. Usually, SMTP runs on top of TCP/IP, which *is* routable.

9. What are two protocols used to transfer mail between systems?

   A: Three answers given in the chapter: SMTP, X.400, and MHS.

10. At which layer of the OSI Reference Model do databases and email systems operate?

    A: Application.

PRACTICE TEST

1. Email systems and database management systems operate at what layer of the OSI Reference Model?

   a. Network

   b. Presentation

   c. Application

   d. Session

Answers a, b, and d are incorrect. **Answer c is correct.**

2. What does SMTP stand for?

   a. Simple Message Transfer Protocol

   b. Simple Mail Transport Protocol

   c. Safe Message Transport Protocol

   d. Secure Mail Transport Protocol

Answers a, c, and d are incorrect. **Answer b is correct.**

3. Which type of application creates the least amount of network traffic?

   a. Centralized application

   b. Shared–file system application

   c. Network version of a standalone application

   d. Client/server application

Answers a, b, and c are incorrect. **Answer d is correct because client/server applications usually involve only small transmissions of data between the client and server.**

4. Which of the following are *not* advantages of installing the network version of a standalone application? (Choose all that apply.)

   a. All users will be using the same version of the application.

   b. Network bandwidth will be conserved because only a small amount of network traffic will be generated.

   c. Users will still be able to work in the event of a network failure.

   d. The cost of a site license is usually substantially less than that of individual copies of software.

Answer a is incorrect because it *is* an advantage of network versions. **Answer b is correct because it is *not* an advantage; network traffic will be *higher*. Answer c is correct because it is *not* an advantage; users will *not* be able to work in the event of a network failure.** Answer d is incorrect because it *is* an advantage.

CH
II

5. Any desktop application can be installed on a file server and used across a network by multiple users.

    a. True

    b. False

Answer a is incorrect. **Answer b is correct because an application cannot simply be installed on a file server. It usually must be the network version of an application.**

6. Which of the following are protocols involved with electronic mail? (Choose all that apply.)

    a. SMTP

    b. X.400

    c. TCP/IP

    d. MHS

Answer a is correct; Simple Mail Transport Protocol is the primary email protocol used on the Internet. Answer b is correct; X.400 is involved with email. Answer c is incorrect; TCP/IP does not directly do anything with email. **Answer d is correct; Message Handling Service is Novell's email protocol.**

7. Which of the following protocols are *not* involved with electronic mail? (Choose all that apply.)

    a. X.500

    b. NFS

    c. MIME

    d. POP3

Answer a is incorrect because X.500 provides directory services for email delivery. **Answer b is correct; the Network File System protocol deals with sharing files across a network.** Answer c is incorrect because MIME is used in the handling of email attachments. Answer d is incorrect because Post Office Protocol version 3 is used for email retrieval.

8. A database application utilizes a component on a user's PC that handles all user interaction and a component on a server that deals with data processing. This is an example of which model of computing?

    a. Standalone applications

    b. Shared–file system applications

    c. Client/server applications

    d. Centralized applications

Answers a, b, and d are incorrect. **Answer c is correct because there is a component on both the client and server that work together.**

9. SQL and ODBC are protocols used by what?

   a. Network operating systems
   b. Email systems
   c. Groupware applications
   d. Database management systems

Answers a, b, and c are incorrect. **Answer d is correct; SQL and ODBC are used by database systems.**

10. Your manager has complained that only you can use the new standalone graphics application that he recently purchased. He insists that you move it to a file server so that others can use it. After doing so, which two statements are true?

   a. Because the application was not designed for network use, it will probably not function properly.
   b. You are most likely in violation of your license agreement.
   c. Due to the fact that this application was not designed to use network resources, running this application from the network will not slow the network down at all.
   d. All users will be able to use the program without any problems and with no additional installation work required.

Answer a is correct because the application will probably not work at its full potential, perhaps locking out users or simply not performing at its normal speed. Answer b is correct because the license agreement usually says that an application can be used only on a single machine. Answer c is incorrect because if it does work, it *will* consume network bandwidth. Answer d is incorrect because it is most likely a false statement.

CH
II

CHAPTER PREREQUISITE

Before reading this chapter, you should understand the fundamentals of networking (see Chapter 2, "Introduction to Networks"), data transmission (see Chapter 7, "Data Transmission"), network protocols (see Chapter 9), and network operating systems (see Chapter 10).

Remote Access

WHILE YOU READ

1. At a data signal level, what does a modem do?

2. What are the two different types of modems?

3. What is the PSTN?

4. What speed can Basic Rate ISDN provide?

5. The service in Windows NT that allows dial-up clients to connect to the computer is what?

6. In Windows 95/98 or Windows NT 4.0, the dial-out client is called what?

7. Explain the difference between SLIP and PPP.

8. Which protocols can Windows NT Server RAS support for clients connecting to it?

9. Which protocols can Windows NT support when dialing out to a remote machine?

10. List three security options Windows NT Server provides when accepting dial-in connections.

Modems

Over time, as networks become more critical to the operations of your organization, users will desire access to network resources when they are out of the main office. Whether they are at home, at a remote office, or in a hotel room while on a business trip, they will want to connect back into the office network. The simplest answer is to have those users connect back to the office network using a telephone line. However, because computers use digital signals (bits) and telephone lines use analog signals (sound), you cannot simply plug a computer into a phone line.

To accomplish the task of communicating over a phone line, you need to use a *modem*. As shown in Figure 12.1, the primary task of a modem is to convert the 1s and 0s of a digital signal into an analog sound wave to be transmitted across a phone line. At the receiving end, another modem converts the analog signal back into a digital signal.

Figure 12.1
A modem converts the computer's digital signal into an analog signal for transmission over a phone line.

Key Concept

A *modem* is a device that MOdulates a data signal from digital to analog and DEModulates a signal from analog back to digital.

Modems are generally available for either internal or external connections to a computer. An internal modem plugs into an expansion slot on the motherboard of your computer and provides an *RJ-11* jack (a four-wire telephone jack) from which you can connect a standard telephone cable between the modem and your wall telephone jack.

An external modem is a separate box that is connected to your computer by way of a serial cable (known as an RS-232 cable). External modems have an RJ-11 jack for your connection to your telephone and normally have lights to indicate various status conditions.

Modem speed is measured in terms of the number of *bits per second (bps)* that can travel across the phone line. As shown in Table 12.1, the International Telecommunications Union has developed the so-called *V-series* of standards for modem speed. Note that some standard designations contain the words *bis* or *terbo*. These designations have nothing to do with speed and are merely the French words for "second" and "third," indicating that these are revisions of earlier standards.

Table 12.1 ITU Standards for Modems		
Standard	*Bps*	*Year Introduced*
V.22bis	2400	1984
V.32	9600	1984
V.32bis	14,400	1991
V.32terbo	19,200	1993
V.FastClass (V.FC)	28,800	1993
V.34	28,800	1994
V.42	57,600	1995
V.90	57,600	1997

There is some confusion between the *bps* rate and the *baud* rate of a modem. Baud is an older term that refers to the oscillation of a sound wave on which one bit of data is carried, whereas bps refers to the actual number of bits transmitted each second. In early modems, the baud rate and the bps rate were equivalent. For instance, an early 300bps modem did, in fact, have 300 oscillations of sound waves each second. However, as technology evolved, engineers developed methods to compress information and manipulate analog signals to send multiple bits with each sound wave oscillation. These improvements rendered the baud rate obsolete as a measurement of speed. For instance, a modem transmitting at 28,800bps might in fact be transmitting at only 9,600 baud.

You might also hear modems described as *Hayes-compatible*. In the early 1980s, Hayes Microcomputer Products, Inc., introduced a modem called the Hayes Smartmodem that included advanced features, such as the capability to automatically dial phone numbers. These features and the command set used to initiate the features were soon incorporated into modems from rival manufacturers. Over time, the Hayes-compatible command set became the *de facto* standard for all modems.

There are two types of modems in use today:

- Asynchronous
- Synchronous

CH
12

The type of modem you use will depend on what type of lines you are using for a connection.

Asynchronous Modems

Asynchronous (or *async*) modems are the type of modems widely used for most communication today. Designed to be used over a regular telephone line, asynchronous modems convert every byte of data into a stream of 1s and 0s. As shown in Figure 12.2, each byte is sandwiched between a start and stop bit.

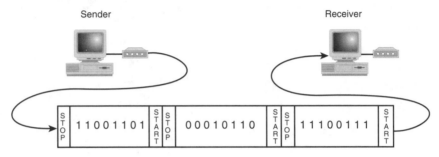

Figure 12.2
Asynchronous modems package data inside of start and stop bits.

Before communication begins, the sending and receiving modem must agree on the transmission speed and the sequence of start and stop bits. Only then can communication successfully occur.

Beyond the start and stop bits, many modems incorporate some type of error checking to ensure that the data is sent correctly across the telephone line. The simplest method of error checking involves including a *parity* bit when transmitting each byte. Essentially, parity checking works like this: The sending modem counts how many 1s are in the data stream. If the number is odd, the parity bit is set to 1. On the other end, the receiving modem also counts the number of 1s and determines whether the number is odd or even. The receiving modem then compares its results with the parity bit. If the results match, the data is probably okay and is sent on for processing. If the results do not match, the receiving modem requests a retransmittal of that data packet and will continue to do so until it successfully receives the data packet intact.

Finally, most asynchronous modems incorporate some type of data compression to achieve higher transmission speeds. One of the compression protocols in use today is referred to as V.42bis.

Although all of this error checking and compression makes the communication reliable, that reliability comes at a price. Asynchronous modems often use almost 25 percent of the transmission just for error checking and control.

Synchronous Modems

Whereas asynchronous modems depend on start and stop bits to determine where data begins and ends, synchronous modems depend on timing. Both synchronous modems must be carefully synchronized for communication to take place. As shown in Figure 12.3, synchronous modems transmit data in frames with occasional synchronization (or *sync*) bits inserted to ensure the accuracy of timing.

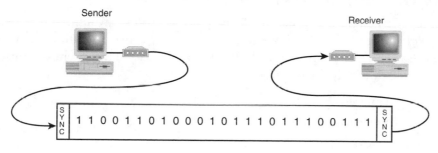

Figure 12.3
Synchronous modems depend on careful timing for the transmission of data and use synchronization bits to ensure that data is being transmitted accurately.

Because synchronous modems do not need the start and stop bits used by asynchronous modems, they can achieve much higher data transfer rates than asynchronous modems. However, because synchronous modems are not designed for communication over regular phone lines, they are generally only found in use with dedicated leased lines. Synchronous modems can also be used for remote connections to IBM mainframe computers.

Digital Modems

Digital modems are not, in fact, modems, but are a creation of the marketing departments of manufacturers of *Integrated Services Digital Network (ISDN)* communication equipment. ISDN, described later in this chapter and in more detail in Chapter 14, "Wide Area Networks (WANs)," provides an all-digital connection with speeds up to 128Kbps. The actual connection device for ISDN is comprised of a *Network Termination (NT)* device and *Terminal Adapter (TA)* equipment. Today, the two components are usually packaged in one physical box and might be referred to by either name.

CH
12

However, realizing that computer users in general are familiar with modems, ISDN manufacturers began calling the NT/TA device a *digital modem* in an attempt to make it easier to lure people toward using ISDN. Digital modems can *only* be used with ISDN and cannot be used over regular telephone lines.

Note that just as digital modems can only be used with digital phone lines such as those of ISDN, regular modems can only work with normal analog phone lines. Some users have accidentally damaged (or destroyed!) their laptop modem by inadvertently connecting it to a digital phone line!

Types of Connections

Beyond understanding what type of modems your users will use, you need to address what type of connection users will use to connect to your network. Within the world of the Public Switched Telephone Network (PSTN), as the telephone system is formally known, there are basically three options:

- Dial-up connections
- ISDN (Integrated Services Digital Network)
- Dedicated leased lines

Note that the PSTN, dedicated leased lines, and ISDN will be discussed in greater detail in Chapter 14.

Dial-up connections simply use the regular phone lines and provide a temporary connection between two sites. Because telephone connections vary in quality and reliability, communication speeds are typically limited to 56,000bps or lower. Transmission speeds of 115Kbps have also been demonstrated in experiments; however, such technology is not yet widely deployed.

Integrated Services Digital Network (ISDN) provides a dial-up means of transmitting voice and data over a digital phone line. *Basic Rate ISDN* provides two 64Kbps B-channels for voice or data and one 16Kbps D-channel for call setup and control. *Primary Rate ISDN* provides 23 B-channels and 1 D-channel and is used primarily for WAN connections. Although requiring the installation of a special digital phone line, ISDN can be very beneficial for remote access because the BRI user can combine the two 64Kbps channels together for a total speed of 128Kbps. Many organizations are finding ISDN to be a cost-effective means of linking remote sites where only occasional connections are necessary.

Dedicated leased lines involve leasing a full-time permanent telephone line between two points. Although it is possible to lease dedicated analog phone lines for use with modems, for the expense involved, there are better technologies for creating dedicated connections between offices. For more information on dedicated connections, read Chapter 14.

Remote Access Software

When your users connect into your network using a modem, there needs to be some type of software that enables them to access network resources. Within Microsoft networks, the software to handle incoming connections is usually the *Remote Access Service (RAS)* provided with Windows NT. Although the RAS software provided with Windows NT Workstation can only handle one incoming connection, RAS in Windows NT Server can handle up to 256 inbound connections. As shown in Figure 12.4, a typical scenario is to dedicate one server for RAS usage and attach multiple modems to that server.

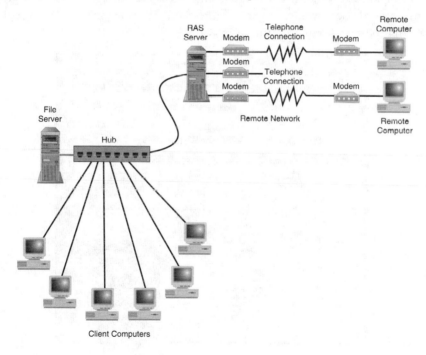

Figure 12.4
A server running Remote Access Service can provide remote access to a Microsoft network.

CH
12

Key Concept

Remote Access Service on Windows NT Workstation supports only one inbound connection, whereas RAS on Windows NT Server supports up to 256 inbound connections.

When connected, users can access network resources as if they were connected directly to the network. There will, of course, be a speed difference due to the fact that modems today generally operate at around as close to 56Kbps as the quality of their phone lines permits, whereas most networks operate around 10Mbps. Obviously, this will be less of a problem for any ISDN users connecting at 128Kbps, but it will still not give the same performance as direct LAN connections.

As shown in Figure 12.5, the RAS server software is easy to configure. When a modem is attached to a specific port, you simply configure the RAS server software to accept incoming calls to that port and start the Windows NT RAS service.

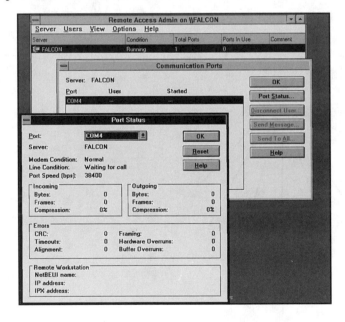

Figure 12.5
RAS server software enables remote users to connect to your computer and can be easily configured in the RAS Administration dialog box of Windows NT.

Key Concept

A *RAS server* is a Windows NT computer configured to use the RAS server software to enable remote users to connect into a network over modems.

On the client side, there are two different programs used within Microsoft networks. In Windows NT 3.51 and Windows for Workgroups, the software is referred to as a *RAS client*. As shown in Figure 12.6, you create an entry in the RAS "phone book" and then just press the Dial button.

Figure 12.6
In Windows NT 3.51, the RAS client enables a workstation to connect to a RAS server after appropriate configuration of the information in the Edit Phone Book Entry dialog box.

In Windows 95/98 and Windows NT 4.0, the remote client software is called *Dial-Up Networking (DUN)*. As shown in Figure 12.7, DUN provides an easy-to-use interface in Windows 95/98, which is similar to the RAS client interface included with Windows NT 3.51. However, as shown in Figure 12.8, DUN also includes a wizard program to help with the process of making a connection to a remote system.

CH
12

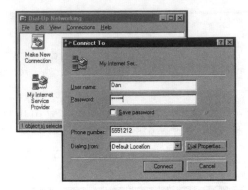

Figure 12.7
After double-clicking a connection icon in the Dial-Up Networking window of
Windows 95/98, you will see a Connect To dialog box displaying information about
the connection.

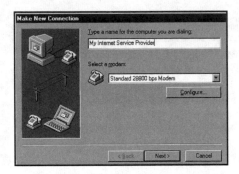

Figure 12.8
Dial-Up Networking in Windows 95/98 includes an easy Make New Connection
Wizard to make new connections.

Both the RAS and DUN clients can be used to connect to a Windows NT computer
running the RAS server software. Additionally, the programs can be used to connect
directly to Internet service providers to access the Internet.

 Key Concept

Microsoft operating systems provide either a Remote Access Service client or a
Dial-Up Networking client to enable users to connect to remote systems.

Remote Communication Protocols

When using the RAS/DUN client described earlier, you have the option of choosing the communication protocol you will use when connecting. The RAS/DUN client can support two communication protocols:

- Serial Line Internet Protocol (SLIP)
- Point-to-Point Protocol (PPP)

As shown in Figure 12.9, you can easily configure the protocol through a configuration dialog box within the RAS/DUN client.

Serial Line Internet Protocol (SLIP)

Serial Line Internet Protocol (SLIP) is an older protocol that was developed primarily to allow PCs to connect to the Internet using a modem. It essentially provides OSI Reference Model physical layer functionality by allowing data to flow across the telephone line to a remote system. SLIP provides no error checking and relies on the hardware to make any error corrections. SLIP supports connections only to TCP/IP networks and requires the use of a static IP address by the connecting machine. Although SLIP provides no data compression, there is a variation called *Compressed SLIP* (*CSLIP*) that does offer compression. Due to the superiority of PPP, SLIP is no longer in common use.

Key Concept

Serial Line Internet Protocol (SLIP) only supports one network protocol, TCP/IP, and provides no error checking or compression. A variation, Compressed Slip (CSLIP), does support compression.

CH

12

Point-to-Point Protocol (PPP)

Point-to-Point Protocol (PPP) provides a much more robust and reliable connection between computers. The greatest difference from SLIP is that PPP provides both physical layer and data link layer functionality and essentially turns your modem into a network interface card. Through this added functionality, PPP supports multiple network protocols such as IP, IPX, and NetBEUI, as shown previously in Figure 12.9. Additionally, PPP provides compression and error checking that make PPP faster and more reliable than SLIP. PPP also provides for password encryption, a major security enhancement. When using SLIP, all passwords are plain text and therefore open to interception. PPP is the only protocol in use by even moderately secure networks.

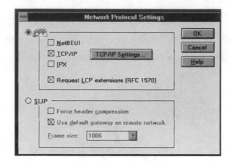

Figure 12.9
The RAS client can be used with either SLIP or PPP, which can be configured in the
Network Protocol Settings dialog box in Windows NT and Windows for Workgroups.

Note that the PPP specification itself provides for the use of a wide range of network protocols, including IP, IPX, NetBEUI, AppleTalk, and DECnet. Microsoft's implementation
of PPP, however, only supports IP, IPX, and NetBEUI.

At the Data Link Layer, PPP packages data into frames and provides error-checking
mechanisms to ensure accurate transmission of data. PPP also incorporates a protocol
called *Link Control Protocol (LCP)* that establishes the logical link control between the
two computers that will be communicating.

Although both SLIP and PPP are used to connect to TCP/IP networks, PPP offers the
added benefit of supporting the dynamic allocation of IP addresses. This dynamic IP
addressing support enables administrators to allocate a range of addresses for the RAS
modems and have users use only those addresses.

Although SLIP was originally the primary protocol used by PCs to connect to the
Internet, PPP has rapidly replaced SLIP as the protocol of choice for TCP/IP connections.

 Key Concept

PPP provides fast and reliable remote communication using multiple network protocols. Unlike SLIP, PPP provides both error correction and data compression. PPP
also supports the dynamic allocation of IP addresses when using TCP/IP and can
transmit encrypted passwords for authentication.

Choosing a Remote Communication Protocol

The choice of which protocol to use can be an easy choice to make. If you are connecting into a RAS server running on a Windows NT computer, your only choice is PPP. SLIP is provided in Microsoft operating systems only for RAS *client* connections.

Key Concept

The Windows NT RAS Server supports *only* PPP connections, not SLIP.

When connecting to other systems, your choice really depends on the capabilities of the remote system to which you are connecting. Because PPP is faster and more reliable than SLIP, PPP will always be the preferred choice. Although you might find SLIP in very limited use, perhaps within some older UNIX or hobbyist environments, most remote networks are now using PPP.

Note that at the time this book was written, there were an increasing number of Internet service providers who provide *only* PPP connections. Although SLIP had been used frequently for connecting PCs to the Internet, its use is almost entirely fading away.

Key Concept

On the exam, do not confuse PPP with PPTP. Point-to-Point Tunneling Protocol (PPTP) is a new protocol supported in Windows NT 4.0 that allows the establishment of a secure link between two network segments over a TCP/IP network such as the Internet. It is *not* the same as PPP.

Security over Remote Connections

When you allow remote connections to your network, you are opening up a security hole that an intruder could use to penetrate your system. However, when using Microsoft's Remote Access Service software, there are several options available:

- *Passwords.* When users dial in to a RAS server, the server software uses full Windows NT security to authenticate the user. If the server is part of a Windows NT domain, the user's name and password will be sent to a domain controller to be verified. If the server is a standalone workstation or part of a workgroup, the local security database will be used to validate the user.

■ *Granting Dial-In Permission.* Even before the password is validated, RAS server software can be configured to deny users the capability to connect to the RAS server. As shown in Figure 12.10, each user can be configured separately to have the capability to dial in to the network.

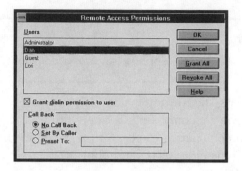

Figure 12.10
Windows NT RAS server software enables you to configure permissions for individual users through the Remote Access Permissions dialog box.

■ *Callback capability.* When a user connects into the RAS server, the RAS server can be configured to disconnect the modem and call the user back to establish the connection. As shown in Figure 12.10, this property can be set to a predetermined phone number. This way, you could allow a user to connect into the network from only her home or remote office.

■ *Encryption.* RAS/DUN clients and RAS servers are automatically set to encrypt communication over the phone lines between the client and the server. As shown in Figure 12.11, a RAS client can be configured to connect to a server with only certain levels of encryption. If an encrypted connection cannot be successfully made, the RAS client will terminate the connection attempt. Note that if the default authentication is used for allowing any authentication to occur, a password can be sent in regular (clear) text and could be easily read if intercepted.

Additionally, in Windows NT Server 4.0, RAS access permissions can be set through the User Manager for Domains.

These security options alone do not guarantee that intruders will not be able to penetrate your network, but they can at least reduce the threat.

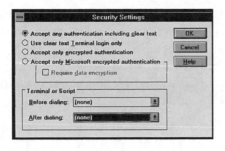

Figure 12.11
RAS clients can be configured to only connect to servers that will accept encrypted connections through entries into the Security Settings dialog box.

Summary

When providing remote access to your network, the primary mechanism is through dial-up connections using modems. Modems are devices attached to computers that translate between the digital signal from the computer and the analog signal (sound) of the telephone lines. When sending data, the modem converts the data into analog sound waves. On the receiving end, the modem converts the analog sound waves back into digital data for processing by the computer.

There are two primary types of modems: asynchronous and synchronous. Asynchronous modems are the type commonly used in personal computers and provide connections over regular telephone lines. Asynchronous modems use start and stop bits to identify where individual bytes of data begin and end. With error correction and compression, today's asynchronous modems typically operate around 56Kbps. Synchronous modems do not use start and stop bits but instead rely on exact coordination of timing between the sending and receiving computers. With less overhead than asynchronous modems, synchronous modems can attain higher speeds, but they are limited primarily to dedicated leased lines.

To connect to a remote network, users have the choice of using regular telephone lines, ISDN lines, or dedicated leased lines. Use of regular telephone lines is the most common technique for remote connection, but ISDN lines are gaining in popularity due to their higher speed. Due to their expense, dedicated leased lines are used primarily for full-time permanent connections between offices.

The modem connection alone will not do anything without the appropriate software operating at both ends of the connection. Within Microsoft operating systems,

Remote Access Service (RAS) is provided for remote connections. The RAS server software operates on Windows NT Server and provides up to 256 inbound connections. The client software comes in the form of a RAS client (Windows NT 3.51 and Windows for Workgroups) and a Dial-Up Networking (DUN) client (Windows 95/98 and Windows NT 4.0). Both RAS and DUN clients enable computers to connect to RAS servers or directly to Internet Service Providers.

One other configuration element is what communication protocol the remote client will use to communicate with the server. The RAS/DUN client provides the option of connecting to a remote network using either SLIP or PPP. Serial Line Internet Protocol (SLIP) is an older protocol that only supports TCP/IP connections to remote networks and provides no error checking or compression. PPP is the successor to SLIP and is widely used because it supports the transmission of packets using multiple network protocols. PPP also provides sophisticated error checking and compression that make PPP much faster and more reliable than SLIP. Additionally, PPP provides password encryption for secure authentication.

Although RAS/DUN clients support connections using either SLIP or PPP, the RAS server incorporated into Windows NT supports only PPP connections.

Finally, providing remote network access does introduce security threats. Microsoft RAS provides several options to reduce this threat, including the use of Windows NT user account security, user callback capability, and encryption between the RAS/DUN client and the RAS server.

QUESTIONS AND ANSWERS

1. At a data signal level, what does a modem do?

   A: A modem converts an outbound digital signal to analog (modulation) and converts an inbound analog signal to digital (demodulation).

2. What are the two different types of modems?

   A: Asynchronous and synchronous.

3. What is the PSTN?

   A: The Public Switched Telephone Network—the telephone system.

4. What speed can Basic Rate ISDN provide?

   A: Two channels of 64Kbps that can be combined for 128Kbps.

...continues

...continued

5. The service in Windows NT that allows dial-in clients to connect to the computer is what?

A: Remote Access Service (RAS).

6. In Windows 95/98 or Windows NT 4.0, the dial-out client is called what?

A: Dial-Up Networking (DUN).

7. Explain the difference between SLIP and PPP.

A: SLIP is an older protocol that supports only TCP/IP and provides no error-checking and compression. PPP is a newer protocol that supports multiple network protocols, provides error-checking and compression, and supports dynamic allocation of IP addresses.

8. Which protocols can Windows NT Server RAS support for clients connecting to it?

A: PPP.

9. Which protocols can Windows NT support when dialing out to a remote machine?

A: SLIP and PPP.

10. List three security options Windows NT Server provides when accepting dial-in connections.

A: Several possible answers, including: password, callback capability, encryption, and limiting who has dial-in permission.

CH 12

PRACTICE TEST

1. When a computer running Windows NT Server operates as an RAS server, how many inbound connections can be established?

   a. 1
   b. 128
   c. 256
   d. 1,024

Answer a is incorrect. Answer b is incorrect. **Answer c is correct; Windows NT Server can support 256 inbound connections.** Answer d is incorrect.

2. Windows NT Server, operating as an RAS server, can use which of the following communication protocols over a modem? (Choose all that apply.)

a. PPP

b. SLIP

c. CSLIP

d. DLC

Answer a is correct; Windows NT Server, operating as an RAS *server*, can only support PPP. Answers b and c are incorrect but would be supported on dial-out connections as a *client*. Answer d is incorrect because DLC is not a modem communication protocol.

3. Your company has expanded its network operations and would now like to provide employees with remote network access. The company's network is TCP/IP-based with a mixture of Windows NT, Windows 95, and UNIX workstations. Your network includes UNIX, Windows NT, and Novell NetWare servers. You have been given the assignment of implementing a remote access system.

REQUIRED RESULT: Users must be able to connect remotely using standard telephone lines.

OPTIONAL DESIRED RESULTS: Users should be able to access resources on both the Windows NT servers and the Novell NetWare servers. Additionally, remote communication should use the most reliable protocols available.

PROPOSED SOLUTION: You propose adding several modems to a UNIX server and implementing remote access using SLIP server software. Which results does the proposed solution produce?

a. The proposed solution produces the required result and both of the optional desired results.

b. The proposed solution produces the required result and only *one* of the optional desired results.

c. The proposed solution produces the required result but does *not* produce any of the optional desired results.

d. The proposed solution does *not* produce the required result.

Answers a, b, and d are incorrect. **Answer c is correct because SLIP *does* enable users to connect (meeting the required result), but it would not enable users to access the NetWare servers (SLIP only supports TCP/IP not IPX/SPX), and SLIP is not the most reliable protocol available.**

4. Which communication protocols do *not* support the use of multiple network protocols? (Choose all that apply.)

   a. SLIP
   b. PPP
   c. CSLIP

Answers a and c are correct; SLIP and CSLIP only support TCP/IP. Answer b is incorrect because PPP *does* support multiple protocols.

5. Which of the following protocols are supported by a RAS client using PPP? (Choose all that apply.)

   a. IPX
   b. IP
   c. DECnet
   d. NetBEUI

Answers a, b, and d are correct. Answer c is incorrect.

6. Which two statements are true about asynchronous modem communication?

   a. Data is separated by start and stop bits.
   b. Transmission of data relies on careful coordination of timing by both the sending and receiving computer.
   c. Error checking and data compression are provided.
   d. Data is converted from analog signals into digital signals for transmission over the telephone line.

Answer a is correct. Answer b is incorrect and is true of synchronous modems. **Answer c is correct.** Answer d is incorrect because the statement is the exact opposite of what occurs.

7. What type of communication occurs between modems where the beginning and end of bytes of data are determined by careful coordination of timing between sending and receiving computers?

   a. Asynchronous
   b. Synchronous
   c. Digital
   d. Time-Differential

Answer a is incorrect because asynchronous communication relies on start and stop bits. **Answer b is correct.** Answers c and d are both incorrect.

CH
12

8. Which two statements about PPP are *not* true?

   a. Multiple network protocols are supported.

   b. The only network protocol supported is TCP/IP.

   c. The protocol provides no error checking or compression.

   d. The protocol provides error checking and compression.

Answer a is incorrect because it *is* true about PPP. **Answer b is correct because PPP supports multiple protocols. Answer c is correct because PPP does provide error-checking and compression.**

9. Which two statements about SLIP are *not* true?

   a. Multiple network protocols are supported.

   b. The only network protocol supported is TCP/IP.

   c. The protocol provides no error checking or compression.

   d. The protocol provides error checking and compression.

Answer a is correct because SLIP supports only TCP/IP. Answer b is incorrect because it is true. Answer c is incorrect because it is true. **Answer d is correct because SLIP provides no error checking and compression.**

10. PPP operates at which layers of the OSI model? (Choose all that apply.)

   a. Session

   b. Physical

   c. Transport

   d. Data link

Answers a and c are incorrect. **Answers b and d are correct.**

CHAPTER PREREQUISITE

Before reading this chapter, you should understand the basics about the layers of the OSI Model (Chapter 3, "The OSI Reference Model"), data transmission methods (Chapter 7, "Data Transmission"), network architectures (Chapter 8, "Network Architecture"), and network protocols (Chapter 9, "Network Protocols").

Creating Larger Networks

WHILE YOU READ

1. What are the types of devices you can use to create larger networks?

2. What is attenuation?

3. At what layer of the OSI model does a repeater operate?

4. True or False Repeaters can be used to connect two dissimilar network architectures, such as Ethernet and Token Ring.

5. How does a bridge help reduce network congestion?

6. At what layer of the OSI model do bridges function?

7. Explain the difference between a bridge and a router regarding broadcast packets and packets with unknown destination addresses.

8. What types of addresses do routers work with as compared to bridges?

9. What are two types of routers?

10. At what layer of the OSI model does a router function?

11. Explain a brouter's operation.

12. How is a gateway different from a router?

When your organization expands and starts to use its network more, there comes a point when you simply outgrow your existing network capacity. It might be that you physically can no longer add extensions to your network, or it might be that the network is experiencing extremely high traffic and you need to find some way to relieve the congestion. In either case, there are several different devices you can use to expand your network.

LAN Expansion

When your organization grows, one of your first needs might be to extend your network beyond its existing range. Two devices are used to accomplish this:

- Repeaters
- Bridges

Repeaters

As you learned in Chapter 5, "The Physical Connection," when a signal passes along a cable, it encounters resistance from the cable itself, which weakens the signal. Gradually, the quality of the signal degrades to the point where the receiving station has trouble recognizing the original signal. This process, called *attenuation*, imposes real distance limits on the physical media used in networks.

Repeaters are devices that simply receive incoming signals from one cable segment and boost their signal strength before passing them on to another cable segment. Most repeaters do not just amplify the electrical signal before resending it. If they did, they would amplify not only the network signal, but also the electrical noise on the cable. Instead, repeaters receive the incoming signal, interpret it as a series of 1s and 0s, and regenerate that signal on the other cable segment. Therefore, the strength of the signal entering the second cable segment should be similar to what it was when it left the computer's NIC on the first segment. Figure 13.1 depicts this process.

Repeaters operate at the physical layer of the OSI Reference Model and have no knowledge of the type of data, packet addresses, or protocols. They do not perform any translation or filtering of the actual data. They simply retransmit signals from one cable segment to another.

Although this section focuses on physical media, repeaters are also used with wireless media. For example, repeaters can be used to extend the range of a microwave link.

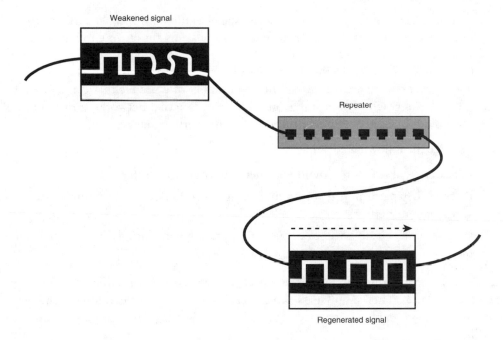

Weakened signal

Repeater

Regenerated signal

Figure 13.1
Repeaters receive a weakened signal and regenerate it before passing it along the network.

Because they deal with only electrical or optical signals, repeaters cannot be used to link two network segments using different network architectures. For instance, an Ethernet network could not be connected to a Token-Ring network using a repeater. The access method, such as CSMA/CD or token-passing, must be the same on all cable segments connected to the repeater.

Repeaters can be used, however, to connect different physical media types in the same network. For example, an Ethernet network using twisted pair might use a repeater, such as a hub, to retransmit the signal onto coaxial cable. Again, for this to work, the identical media access method must be used on all connected cable segments.

Note that you have probably been using repeaters for some time if you have used 10BASE-T Ethernet networks. Most hubs also function as repeaters, with the exception of passive hubs that do not use electrical power.

CH
13

Repeaters can transmit information at the same speed as the network, primarily because they do not process the data. However, they do require a tiny bit of time to regenerate the signal. If there are several repeaters in a row, the time needed to regenerate the signal can introduce a *propagation delay* in the signal that can affect network communication. For this reason, most network architectures limit the number of repeaters that can be used to extend a network segment. For example, in 10BASE-2 Ethernet networks, a maximum of four repeaters can be used to connect together five network segments.

Repeaters offer the following advantages:

- Repeaters enable you to extend your network over large distances.
- Because they perform little or no processing, they do not seriously impact the speed of your network.
- Some repeaters enable you to connect network segments using different physical media.

Because they know nothing about the data packet, repeaters cannot reduce or eliminate network congestion. They simply pass along every packet of data, regardless of whether the packets contain good or corrupted data. Other disadvantages of repeaters include the following:

- Repeaters do not have any knowledge of addressing or data types and cannot be used to connect network segments using different architectures.
- They do not do anything to ease network congestion problems.
- There are limits on how many repeaters can be used within a network.

Key Concept

Repeaters function at the physical layer of the OSI Reference Model to take incoming signals from one network segment, boost the signal strength, and retransmit the signal onto another network segment. Repeaters deal only with electrical and optical signals and have no knowledge of the data or any addresses. They cannot be used to connect network segments with dissimilar architectures, such as Token-Ring and Ethernet.

Bridges

Imagine you work in an office where all employees sit in cubicles in a large room. Now imagine that three or four of those employees work on projects together and are always talking back and forth about their work. Over time, this becomes a distraction to the point at which you find it difficult to get your job done. One solution would be to construct a wall that would subdivide the larger room into two smaller rooms. The individuals who are constantly talking to each other would be on one side, and you and your coworkers would be on the other. There would be a door that would enable you to go and talk to the others and enable them to come visit you, but you would not have to hear all their conversations. The wall stops all audio transmissions between the two rooms — except transmissions that are meant to be delivered to one of the rooms (for example, when someone opens the door and speaks into the other room).

On a computer network, *bridges* perform this type of segmenting. Like a repeater, bridges connect multiple network segments and receive incoming signals from all segments. However, bridges examine the destination address of the packet before simply forwarding it on to other segments. If the destination address is, in fact, on another network segment, the bridge retransmits the signal just like a repeater does. However, if the destination address is on the same network segment as the source of the address, the bridge recognizes that the packet does not need to be forwarded to other segments and simply discards the packet. As a result, a network can be divided so that a particular portion of the network does not congest the entire network.

As an example, consider the network shown in Figure 13.2. Computers D and E are both file servers but are located in two different departments: Research and Sales. If a repeater were used to connect the two network segments, each computer would receive the packets transmitted by *all* the other computers. As the Research users at computers A, B, and C would start to move large data files back and forth from server D, the network traffic they generate would slow down traffic on the entire network. Sales users at computers F and G would find it very slow to retrieve their own files from server E.

However, using a bridge like this one, packets flowing between computers in the Research Department would *not* be transmitted to the Sales side of the network. When computer A would request files from server D, the bridge would receive the packet just as would computers B and C. However, the bridge would recognize that A and D are on the same network segment and would just discard the packet without forwarding it. In this manner, the heavy traffic on the Research network would not impact the Sales network.

If a computer on one segment wants to communicate with a computer on the other segment, the bridge will recognize this and forward the packet. If the researcher at computer B needed information from the Sales server E, that request would be broadcast on the Research network and would also be received by the bridge. The bridge would examine the packet, determine that the destination is not on the Research network, and retransmit the packet onto the Sales network. Likewise, requests from the Sales network for resources on the Research network would be forwarded to the Research network.

CH
13

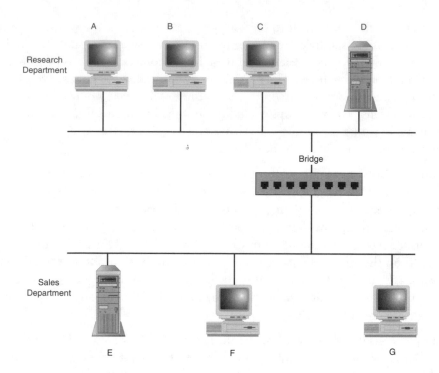

Figure 13.2
A bridge can break a network into multiple segments and ease the overall network congestion.

Key Concept

It is important to understand that a bridge checks the destination address against the addresses it knows to be on the same network as the source. If the destination is not on the same network, the bridge forwards the packet. Note that the bridge does not have to know that the destination address is, in fact, on the other segment. It only knows that the destination is *not* on the same segment as the source.

Using Hardware Addresses

To make this work, of course, the bridge has to have some understanding of which computers lie on which segment. Bridges operate at the data link layer of the OSI Reference Model and have access to the Media Access Control (MAC) addressing information in each data packet. Each computer's NIC must have a unique *MAC address*. In Ethernet and Token-Ring networks, this address is usually burned into the NIC when it is manufactured. NICs in an ARCnet network are manually assigned numeric addresses through a DIP switch on the NIC, whereas NICs on an AppleTalk network are dynamically assigned addresses when they are powered up. Through one of these mechanisms, each computer will have a unique address that can be used on the local network.

Bridges do all their work with these *MAC addresses*, which are also referred to as *hardware addresses*.

Determining the Appropriate Segment

Bridges use either *transparent bridging* or *source-route bridging* to determine which network segment includes a specified hardware address.

Transparent bridges are used throughout Ethernet networks. These bridges, also referred to as *learning bridges*, build a *bridging table* as they receive packets. When the bridge is first powered on, its bridging table is empty. As the bridge receives packets from the different network segments to which it is connected, it scans the source and destination addresses of all packets and keeps track of which packets arrived from which network segments. Over time, the bridge develops a comprehensive list of addresses.

When a packet is received by the transparent bridge, its source address and destination address are compared with the bridging table. If the two addresses are on the same network segment, the packet is discarded. If the bridging table knows that the destination address is on a different segment, the packet is forwarded *only* to the destination segment. If the destination address is unknown, the packet is forwarded to *all* segments other than the one from which it came.

You should note that some bridge vendors refer to this bridging table as a *routing table*. This gets confusing because routers do, in fact, have a *routing table* that is quite different from a bridging table.

Source-routing bridges are used primarily in IBM Token-Ring environments and rely on the source computer to provide path information within the packet. This type of bridge does not require a lot of processing power because most of the work is being done by the source computer. Source computers use *explorer packets* to determine the best path to a particular computer. That information is then included within a packet sent across the network. When a source-routing bridge receives such a packet, it makes note of the path and uses it for future packets being sent to that destination.

CH
13

Because most Microsoft networks tend to use Ethernet as a network architecture, you will probably encounter transparent bridges the most. Unless otherwise noted, you should assume any exam question about bridging deals with transparent bridges.

Regardless of the type of bridge used, bridges are slower than repeaters because they need to examine the addressing of the data packet. This should not be a problem, though, if a network is segmented properly with users who need to communicate frequently on the same side of the bridge. By filtering data packets, bridges can actually increase the overall speed of the network by reducing congestion.

However, bridges do not reduce network congestion caused by *broadcast packets*. Most of the data packets sent on a network are sent from one computer to another computer. However, there are times when a computer needs to relay information to all other computers on the network. To do this, the computer sends out a broadcast packet on the network. When all other computers on the network receive this packet, they read and process the packet as if it were addressed to them individually.

Broadcast packets can be a benefit on a network. In fact, some network protocols such as NetBEUI rely on the transmission of broadcast packets. However, excessive use of broadcast packets can dramatically slow down a network. The capability to send broadcast packets can lead to disaster, too, if a NIC malfunctions and starts to deluge the network with broadcasts. Such a condition, called a *broadcast storm*, can bring a network to its knees. Bridges are no help in this situation because they forward all broadcast packets.

Key Concept

Bridges forward all broadcast packets. Additionally, when a bridge encounters an unknown destination address, its default action is to forward the packet to all other network segments.

Bridging Between Dissimilar Networks

Like repeaters, bridges can connect network segments using different physical media. For instance, a bridge could connect an Ethernet 10BASE-T network segment to an Ethernet 10BASE-2 network segment.

Whereas repeaters operate at the physical layer of the OSI Reference Model and work with signals on the network media, bridges operate at the data link layer of the OSI Model and deal with hardware (MAC) addresses. Similar to repeaters, most bridges do not perform any type of data translation and are intended to work with only one type of data frame. For this reason, almost all bridges are designed to work with a single network architecture. Most bridges would not enable you to connect an Ethernet network with a Token-Ring network.

There are, however, *translation bridges* designed to address this issue. For instance, there are translation bridges that do enable you to link Ethernet and Token-Ring networks. They have an Ethernet port and a Token-Ring port. To Ethernet nodes, these bridges appear as transparent bridges and accept the transmission of Ethernet data frames. To Token-Ring nodes, they appear as source-routing bridges and accept Token-Ring frames. These bridges also translate Ethernet frames into Token-Ring frames and vice-versa. Similarly, there are bridges that translate frames between Ethernet and FDDI.

Key Concept

For the exam, you should remember that with the exception of translation bridges, bridges do *not* enable you to connect networks with different architectures. When asked about connecting dissimilar networks, you should assume the answer refers to a regular bridge unless an answer to an exam question specifically says "translation bridge."

Advantages and Disadvantages

Bridges offer many advantages, including the following:

- Bridges can act as repeaters and extend a network to greater distances.
- Bridges can restrict the flow of traffic between network segments and ease network congestion.
- They can connect network segments using different physical media.
- Bridges called *translation bridges* can connect networks with different architectures.

However, bridges do have some disadvantages, including the following:

- Because bridges examine hardware addresses, they are slower than repeaters.
- Broadcast packets, intended for all computers on a network, are forwarded by bridges to all network segments.
- Bridges are more expensive and complex than repeaters.

Key Concept

Bridges operate at the data link layer of the OSI Reference Model and are used primarily to segment a network to reduce network traffic.

Bridges and Multiple Paths

Bridges work fine to connect several small networks. However, as a network grows in complexity, bridges start to encounter limitations. For instance, as networks become more critical to daily operations, it is common to desire multiple paths between network segments so that information can flow between segments even if one path fails. Bridges do not work well with multiple paths and, in some cases, can create conditions where packets start to travel around the network in endless loops. Even if they could handle multiple paths, bridges do not have a mechanism in place to determine which path is the best.

Internetworking

An *internet*, or *internetwork*, is comprised of two or more independent networks that are connected, yet still continue to function separately. An example would be a Token-Ring network and an Ethernet network that are *interconnected* so that users on each network can access resources on the other network. Both networks continue to function as separate Token-Ring and Ethernet networks, yet users can exchange data between the two networks. Probably the most well-known internetwork currently in use is the global Internet, which is entirely comprised of interconnected smaller networks.

The task of connecting different networks is handled by an *internetworking* device. In this section, you will learn about three such devices:

- Routers
- Brouters
- Gateways

Routers

Routers are devices that can connect networks into a complex internetwork. Like bridges, routers can be used to simply connect network segments and filter network traffic. However, unlike bridges, this filtering process uses network addresses (instead of hardware addresses).

As shown in Figure 13.3, routers can be used to create networks with multiple paths between network segments. Each network segment, also referred to as a *subnetwork* or *subnet*, is assigned a network address. Furthermore, each node on a subnet is assigned a specific address. Using this combination of network and node addresses, a router can *route* a data packet from a source address to a destination address somewhere else on the network.

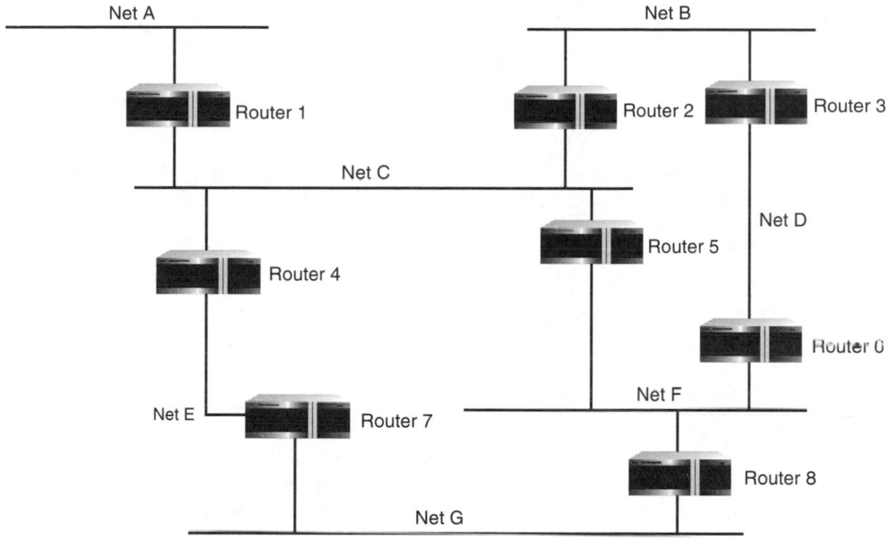

Figure 13.3
Routers can be used to create complex networks.

To accomplish this routing, a router must strip the data link layer information off of a data packet and examine the network layer addressing information enclosed inside. Each data packet transmitted contains the destination network address and node address appropriate for the network protocol being used.

After the router obtains the destination address for a given packet, it compares the address to its internal *routing table* to determine which route the packet should use. The router then repackages the data packet using data link layer information appropriate to the route it will travel.

The advantage of this approach is that routers can send information over different network architectures. For instance, a packet received from an Ethernet network can be sent out over a Token-Ring network. The router removes the Ethernet data frame, examines the packet to determine the network address, repackages the data into a Token-Ring frame, and sends it out onto the Token-Ring network.

Be aware that there can be speed differences when routing between different architectures. For example, Ethernet networks use a data frame size of approximately 1,500 bytes, whereas Token-Ring frames can range in size from 4,000 to around 18,000 bytes. Moving packets from Ethernet to Token Ring is simple: The router merely takes the data from the Ethernet packet and places it inside of a Token-Ring packet. However, due to the larger

CH
13

size of a Token-Ring frame, the router must repackage the data from one Token-Ring packet into several Ethernet packets before sending it out.

A major difference between bridges and routers lies in how they handle unknown addresses. When a bridge determines that a destination is unknown, it forwards the packet to all connected network segments other than the one from which the packet came. A router, on the other hand, expects to be able to identify the network address and only sends along packets for which it has an address. If a destination address does not match a valid entry in the routing table, the packet is discarded. In addition, packets that are corrupted are discarded by routers, even though bridges would forward them. Routers also discard broadcast packets, minimizing the effects of broadcast storms.

Key Concept

For the exam, remember the following: Upon receiving a broadcast packet or a packet with an unknown destination address, *bridges forward* the packet, whereas *routers discard* the packet.

Note that the fact that routers discard broadcast packets can have ramifications on your network structure. For instance, recall from Chapter 9, "Network Protocols," that within a TCP/IP network, addresses can be dynamically assigned by a DHCP server. When a computer is powered on, it issues a broadcast packet asking that it be assigned an IP address by a DHCP server. Because routers do not forward broadcast packets, you will need to have a DHCP server on each subnet of your network. (Note that some routers can be enabled to forward DHCP requests according to a process outlined in RFC 1542.)

It is important to understand, too, that a router's routing table is quite different from a bridging table in that a bridge keeps track of the *hardware addresses* on the segments connected to it, whereas a router deals only with *network addresses*. A bridge knows the address of the actual computers on each of its segments and conceivably the addresses of computers on remote segments, whereas a router knows only the addresses of other networks and of the routers that handle those networks.

Types of Routers

A routing table can be built in two ways: by *static routing* or *dynamic routing*.

Static routers require that a network administrator manually configure the routing table. Each individual route must be entered by hand. The router will always use the same route to send packets to a specified network address, even if it is not necessarily the shortest route. If there is no route to a network address, the packet cannot be delivered.

Dynamic routers, on the other hand, use a process of *discovery* to find out information about available routes. These routers communicate with other routers and are constantly receiving updated routing tables from other routers. If multiple routes are available between two networks, dynamic routers can choose the best route for each packet to travel. Dynamic routers choose the best route in one of two ways:

- Using a *distance-vector algorithm*, it calculates a *cost* for each route based on the number of routers (or *hops*) between two networks. The path a given packet will take is determined by which route has the cheapest cost. *RIP (routing information protocol)*, used by both TCP/IP and IPX/SPX networks, is an example of this type of algorithm.

- Using a *link-state algorithm*, the router takes into account other factors such as network traffic, connection speed, and assigned costs when calculating the best route. Routers using this type of algorithm require more processing power but provide more efficient packet delivery. OSPF (Open Shortest Path First) is a link-state algorithm used in many TCP/IP networks.

Dynamic routers are easier to maintain than static routers, but the constant updating of routing tables does generate additional network traffic.

For your information, Windows NT 4.0 and the server versions of Windows 2000 can act as either a static or dynamic router.

Routable Protocols

One disadvantage of routers is that they only work with *routable* network protocols whose network addressing mechanism supports some method of breaking the network into multiple segments. Routable protocols include the following:

- DEC/Net
- DDP (AppleTalk)
- IPX/SPX (Novell NetWare)
- OSI
- TCP/IP

Protocols that are *nonroutable* include the following:

- DLC (used with HP network printers and IBM mainframes)
- LAT (Digital Equipment Corporation)
- NetBEUI (Microsoft)

CH
13

Key Concept

For the exam, remember that both NetBEUI and DLC are *nonroutable* protocols that will not work with a router.

Be careful not to confuse the concept of *routable* protocols with the *routing* protocols, such as RIP and OSPF, mentioned in the previous section. *Routing* protocols are used by routers to determine how to route packets. *Routable* protocols are the actual network protocols, such as TCP/IP and IPX/SPX, that are used for communication by all network nodes.

Advantages and Disadvantages

Routers offer many advantages, including the following:

- Routers can interconnect networks using different network architectures and media access methods, such as Ethernet and Token-Ring.
- When there are multiple paths across a network, a router can choose the best path and make the most efficient use of network resources.
- Routers can reduce network congestion because, unlike bridges, they do not retransmit broadcast messages or corrupted data packets.

However, routers do have some disadvantages, such as the following:

- Routers are more expensive and complex than bridges or repeaters.
- Routers work only with routable network protocols.
- When using dynamic routing, continual updates of router information generate additional network traffic.
- Routers are slower than bridges because they need to perform more processing on the data packet.

Key Concept

Routers operate at the network layer of the OSI Reference Model and connect networks using network protocols, determine the best path for a data packet to travel, and send the packet to the appropriate destination. Because routers work with network protocols, they can send packets over different network architectures.

Brouters

Brouters are hybrid devices that combine aspects of both bridges and routers. When they receive data packets using routable protocols, brouters function exactly like routers and route the data packets to the appropriate destination. However, when they receive data packets using nonroutable protocols, brouters function as a bridge and forward the packet based on hardware addresses. To accomplish this, brouters maintain both a bridging table (based on hardware addresses) and routing tables for the protocols used on the network.

Brouters are typically found on networks using a mixture of routable and nonroutable protocols. For instance, if you were seeking to reduce network traffic on a large network that used both TCP/IP and NetBEUI, neither bridges nor routers would provide a solution. Bridges would enable you to break the network into several segments, but they would forward broadcast packets from one segment to all other segments. On the other hand, routers would enable you to segment the network so that TCP/IP addresses could be transmitted only on their source and destination segments, eliminating traffic on the other segments. However, because NetBEUI is nonroutable, your NetBEUI users would not be able to communicate beyond their own network segment.

Brouters enable you to solve this by routing the TCP/IP packets and bridging the NetBEUI packets. Although this still results in NetBEUI packets being transmitted to all segments, you would at least be able to reduce network traffic somewhat by eliminating the broadcast of TCP/IP packets to all segments.

Brouters can be a great tool for segmenting some networks. In addition, they can be more cost-effective in some situations than a separate bridge and router are. However, they are generally more expensive and more complex than other networking devices. For this reason, they are only found in limited use.

Key Concept

Brouters are devices that function at both the network and data link layers of the OSI Reference Model and combine elements of both bridges and routers. They route packets that use routable protocols and bridge packets that use non-routable protocols.

Gateways

A *gateway* translates information between two completely different network architectures or data formats. An example would be a gateway that allows a TCP/IP LAN to communicate with a mainframe system using IBM's SNA (Systems Network Architecture). Another example would be a gateway that converts electronic mail from Microsoft Mail to Simple Mail Transport Protocol (SMTP) for transmission across the network.

Whereas routers work at the network layer of the OSI Reference Model and can route packets using the same protocol (such as IP or IPX) across networks regardless of the underlying network architecture (Ethernet or Token Ring), gateways can route information across networks over multiple protocols. Gateways can change the format of the actual data, whereas routers can only repackage data into different data frame formats.

For example, Windows NT Server includes *Services for Macintosh*. This service allows a Microsoft Windows Network client using NetBEUI to communicate with Macintosh computers using AppleTalk via the Windows NT Server. The gateway software allows the Macintosh file servers and printers to appear to Microsoft Windows clients as if they were actually on the PC network. Likewise, the gateway allows the Macintosh computers to see the PC file servers and printers as if they were on the Macintosh network. The gateway handles all the translation of data from NetBEUI to AppleTalk and vice versa, as depicted in Figure 13.4.

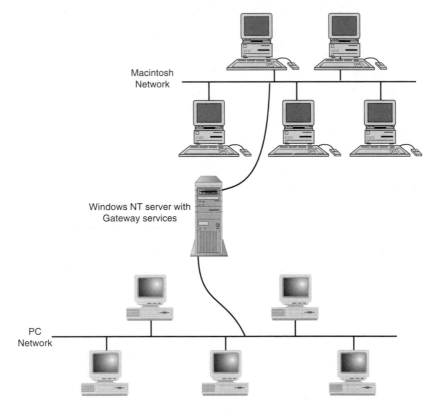

Figure 13.4
A Windows NT Server running Services for Macintosh can interconnect PC and Macintosh networks.

When packets arrive at a gateway, the gateway software strips off the networking information and continues moving the data packet up the layers of the OSI Model until it reaches the layer at which it can translate the data. After it has translated the data into the format needed for the destination, the gateway repackages the data using *the networking protocols of the destination system* and sends the data on to the destination. Figure 13.5 depicts this process.

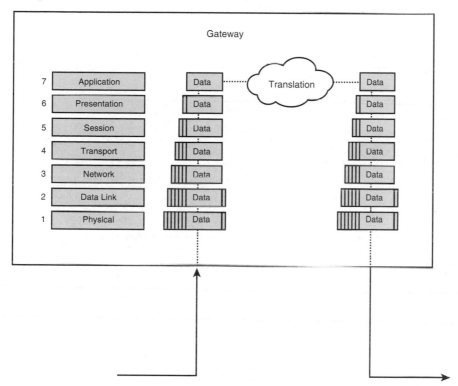

Figure 13.5
A gateway brings a data packet up through the incoming OSI layers, translates the data, and sends it back down through the outgoing OSI layers.

Because gateways are usually involved in data translation, they operate at the upper layers of the OSI Model. Some might operate at the network or session layers, but most operate at the application layer.

Gateways are normally focused on one task and often require a dedicated computer for their use. They tend to be more expensive than other internetworking devices, as well as harder to install and slower than devices such as routers.

Advantages of gateways include the following:

- Gateways can connect completely different systems.
- They specialize in one task and can do that task well.

Disadvantages of gateways include the following:

- Gateways are often more expensive than other devices.
- Gateways are frequently more difficult to install and configure.
- Because of the processing involved with data translation, gateways can be quite slow.

Be aware that some older TCP/IP documentation uses the term *gateway* to refer to a router.

Key Concept

Gateways function at the application and other upper layers of the OSI Reference Model to connect systems that use completely different protocols or data formats.

Switches

At the time this book is being updated (September 1999), Microsoft's *Networking Essentials* exam does not at all cover the network devices known as "switches." However, switches are being used extensively in networks throughout the IT industry.

Essentially, a switch physically looks like a hub. You connect computers to the switch just like a hub, and to the casual observer, it would be hard to tell that it was not a hub.

However, internally a switch is extremely different from a hub. Remember that when a signal comes into a port on a hub, that signal is regenerated out of every other port on the hub. In contrast, a switch acts like a bridge and learns the address of the computers connected to each and every port. When a signal comes in on one port, the data header is examined and then switched over to only the port connected to the destination computer.

The great advantage of this approach is that unlike a hub, in a switch, multiple computers can be transmitting simultaneously. If Computer 2 needs to send data to Computer 4, the switch will connect ports 2 and 4 together. Meanwhile, Computer 3 needs to send data to Computer 8, and Computer 1 needs to send data to Computer 5. All these data streams could be sending simultaneously because they are not using the identical ports.

Now, if Computer 7 needed to also send to Computer 4, the switch would alternate between Computer 2 and Computer 7, letting each send in turn to Computer 4.

As far as which addresses it uses, a switch will usually use either Layer 2 (hardware—for example, Ethernet or Token Ring) or Layer 3 (network—for example IP or IPX) depending on its manufacture. Switches implement all their packet examination in hardware and operate at very high speeds.

Again, this is not something on which you will be tested on the Networking Essentials exam, but *is* a subject you will face directly as you enter into the IT industry.

Summary

When extending a network or connecting several networks, several devices are available for use.

Repeaters extend the distance a network can cover. A repeater accepts an incoming signal, interprets it as a string of 1s and 0s, and retransmits it to another cable segment. Repeaters do not know anything about the data and work only with the actual signals on the network media.

Bridges can work as repeaters to extend a network and connect network segments, but they can also filter network traffic to reduce congestion. Bridges work with hardware addresses that are assigned to a NIC in some manner. A bridge reads the source and destination addresses of every incoming data packet and compares the addresses to a *bridging table*. If the source and destination address are on the same network segment, the data packet is discarded. If the addresses are on different network segments and the bridge knows which segment the destination is on, the data packet is forwarded to only the destination segment. If the destination address is unknown, the bridge forwards the data packet to all network segments other than the one from which it originated.

Bridges work at the OSI Model data link layer and, in almost all cases, require that the data access methods be the same on all network segments.

Whereas bridges work with hardware addresses, *routers* work with network-protocol addresses and can transmit packets across networks using different data access methods (Ethernet, Token Ring). When a router receives a packet, it examines the network protocol address, compares the destination address to a *routing table*, determines the best route for the data packet to take, and sends it on to the destination. Unlike a bridge, a router can examine the packet header information, and it does not transmit broadcast messages or corrupted packets.

CH
13

Routers work at the OSI Model network layer and can work only with *routable* network protocols such as TCP/IP and IPX/SPX. Packets using *nonroutable* protocols such as NetBEUI and DLC cannot be retransmitted by a router and are discarded.

Brouters are hybrid devices that combine features of both bridges and routers, and they are found only in networks using multiple protocols. When a packet is received that uses a routable protocol, a brouter acts as a router and routes the packet to the appropriate destination. When a packet is received with a nonroutable protocol, the brouter functions as a bridge and determines where to forward the packet based on hardware addresses.

Gateways are devices that translate information between completely different network architectures or data formats. Gateways operate at the upper layers of the OSI Reference Model and, unlike routers or bridges, can actually change the format of the data itself. Examples of gateways include systems used to convert messages from one email format to another and systems that allow PC LANs to communicate with mainframe systems.

Table 13.1 lists the devices discussed in this chapter, the layer of the OSI Reference Model at which each one functions, an example of the type of signal or protocol with which each works, and the typical use within a network.

Table 13.1   A Comparison of Devices Used to Extend and Interconnect Networks

Device	OSI Layer	Works with	Typical Use
Repeater	Physical	Electrical signals	Extends LAN segments.
Bridge	Data link	Hardware addresses filters network on hardware	Extends LANs; traffic-based addresses.
Router	Network	Routable protocols (IP, IPX)	Connects networks; determines best paths; sends packets based on network address.
Brouter	Network and data link	Both routable and nonroutable protocols	Functions as both a router and a bridge.
Gateway	Application and other layers above network	Dissimilar protocols, email, applications	Interconnects different systems by translating protocols and data.

QUESTIONS AND ANSWERS

1. What are the types of devices you can use to create larger networks?

A: Repeaters, bridges, routers, brouters, and gateways.

2. What is attenuation?

A: The process where the quality of a signal degrades as the signal travels farther away from its source.

3. At what layer of the OSI model does a repeater operate?

A: Physical.

4. True or False. Repeaters can be used to connect two dissimilar network architectures, such as Ethernet and Token Ring.

A: False. Repeaters can connect two *physically* dissimilar networks, such as a star and a coaxial bus, but both must be using the same network architecture.

5. How does a bridge help reduce network congestion?

A: A bridge keeps traffic where the source and destination are both on the same network from going over onto other networks.

6. At what layer of the OSI model do bridges function?

A: Data link.

7. Explain the difference between a bridge and a router regarding broadcast packets and packets with unknown destination addresses.

A: When encountering a packet with a broadcast or unknown destination address, a bridge will *forward* the packet to all the other networks to which it is connected, whereas a router will *drop* the packet and not allow it off of the source network.

8. What types of addresses do routers work with as compared to bridges?

A: Routers work with *network* addresses (such as IP addresses), whereas bridges work with *hardware* addresses (such as Ethernet addresses).

9. What are two types of routers?

A: Static and dynamic.

CH
13

...continues

…continued

> **10.** At what layer of the OSI model does a router function?
>
> A: Network.
>
> **11.** Explain a brouter's operation.
>
> A: A brouter routes packets that use routable protocols and bridges packets using nonroutable protocols.
>
> **12.** How is a gateway different from a router?
>
> A: A gateway operates at the upper levels of the OSI model and translates information between two completely different network architectures or data formats.

PRACTICE TEST

1. You are routing information between a Token-Ring and an Ethernet network. You find that information flows very quickly from your Ethernet network to your Token-Ring network, but information flows very slowly from the Token-Ring network to the Ethernet network. What could explain this behavior?

   a. Ethernet networks use a larger data frame size.
   b. Token-Ring networks use a larger data frame size.
   c. Your router is configured to give priority to Ethernet frames.
   d. There is more network traffic on the Token-Ring network.

Answer a is incorrect because Ethernet uses a *smaller* frame size. **Answer b is correct because Token Ring uses a larger frame size. For each Token Ring packet received, the router has to do extra work to split it into multiple Ethernet packets.** Answer c is incorrect, although theoretically possible. Answer d is incorrect because even if there was more traffic, the Token Ring architecture should ensure that the router would have the opportunity to transmit information onto the network.

2. As your network has grown, your users are complaining more about the slow speed of the network. Upon examination, you have found a high level of broadcast packets emanating from some parts of the network. You would like to segment the network so that these packets do not affect the overall network performance.

REQUIRED RESULT: You need to reduce network congestion and eliminate the flood of broadcast packets on your network.

OPTIONAL DESIRED RESULTS: After segmentation, the network must still be capable of transmitting data around 10Mbps. It should also be easy to administer.

PROPOSED SOLUTION: You suggest using bridges to divide the network into multiple segments and to filter data so that packets do not spread across the network. Which results does the proposed solution produce?

a. The proposed solution produces the required result and both of the optional desired results.

b. The proposed solution produces the required result and only *one* of the optional desired results.

c. The proposed solution produces the required result but does *not* produce any of the optional desired results.

d. The proposed solution does *not* produce the required result.

Answer d is correct because bridges do *not* solve problems with broadcast packets. Bridges simply forward broadcast packets to all connected networks. Note that a bridge solution *would* meet both optional results but would fail to meet the required result.

3. As your network has grown, your users are complaining more about the slow speed of the network. Upon examination, you have found a high level of broadcast packets emanating from some parts of the network. You would like to segment the network so that these packets do not affect the overall network performance. Your company has been using a Microsoft network with NetBEUI as the primary network protocol and would like to continue to do so.

REQUIRED RESULT: You need to reduce network congestion and eliminate the flood of broadcast packets on your network. All users must be able to share data and work as before.

OPTIONAL DESIRED RESULTS: After segmentation, the network must still be capable of transmitting data around 10Mbps. It should also be easy to administer.

PROPOSED SOLUTION: You propose a network using routers to divide the network into multiple segments. Which results does the proposed solution produce?

a. The proposed solution produces the required result and both of the optional desired results.

b. The proposed solution produces the required result and only *one* of the optional desired results.

c. The proposed solution produces the required result but does *not* produce any of the optional desired results.

d. The proposed solution does *not* produce the required result.

CH
13

Answer d is the correct choice because although routers will reduce the broadcast problem, they will not pass NetBEUI packets. NetBEUI is a nonroutable protocol. Be careful with situations like this where you have two *almost* identical questions right after each other on the exam. You must read very carefully because you will note that routers *would* solve the problem defined above in question 2.

4. A NIC can malfunction on a computer and start generating high levels of broadcast packets. What is the term for the resulting network condition?
   a. Broadcast storm
   b. Broadcast flood
   c. Network storm
   d. Broadcast fault

Answer a is the correct term. Answers b, c, and d are incorrect.

5. The primary purpose of a repeater is what?
   a. To interconnect different systems by translating protocols and data.
   b. To extend a LAN by linking multiple segments.
   c. To connect networks and determine the best path from one network segment to another.
   d. To extend a LAN by linking multiple segments and filtering packets based on hardware addresses.

Answer a is incorrect because it defines a gateway. **Answer b is the correct definition.** Answer c is incorrect because it is the primary purpose of a router. Answer d is incorrect because it is the primary purpose of a bridge.

6. Which of the following are routable protocols? (Choose all that apply.)
   a. IP
   b. IPX
   c. NetBEUI
   d. SMTP

Answers a and b are correct. Answer c is incorrect because NetBEUI is a nonroutable protocol. Answer d is incorrect because SMTP is an (application layer) email protocol that rides on top of a routable/nonroutable (network layer) protocol.

7. Which of the following protocols are *not* routable? (Choose all that apply)
   a. TCP/IP
   b. NetBEUI
   c. IPX
   d. DLC

Answer a is incorrect because TCP/IP (specifically IP) is routable. **Answer b is correct.** Answer c is incorrect because IPX is routable. **Answer d is correct.**

8. Your company has both a PC LAN running TCP/IP and an IBM mainframe computer using SNA. You would like to link the two systems so that PC users can more easily access the data on the mainframe. Which type of device should you use?

   a. Bridge
   b. Router
   c. Gateway
   d. Brouter

Answer c is correct; a gateway operates at the application layer and can translate between two completely different network protocols. Answers a, b, and d are incorrect because all three devices function at the lower levels of the OSI model and cannot translate between network protocols.

9. Your company has had a network in place for several years. One year ago, you upgraded the entire network to use TCP/IP and set up DHCP servers to dynamically allocate IP addresses. The company has recently merged with another company and about 200 new employees will be moving into your office building over the next several months. Because you believe that the existing network structure will not handle the additional traffic of the new users, you are considering alternatives that would segment the network.

   REQUIRED RESULT: The new network structure must have multiple segments with reduced network traffic. All users must be able to exchange data.

   OPTIONAL DESIRED RESULTS: Your solution should require minimal changes to the client computers. Due to the cost of the merger, whatever solution you propose must be very inexpensive.

   PROPOSED SOLUTION: You propose a network using routers to divide the network into multiple segments. Which results does the proposed solution produce?

   a. The proposed solution produces the required result and both of the optional desired results.
   b. The proposed solution produces the required result and only *one* of the optional desired results.
   c. The proposed solution produces the required result but does *not* produce any of the optional desired results.
   d. The proposed solution does *not* produce the required result.

**CH
13**

Answer b is correct because the proposed solution of routers *will* segment the network with reduced traffic and all users *will* still be able to exchange data. Additionally, the solution will require very little change on the client computers (a change of the default gateway might be all that's needed). However, using routers will not be inexpensive, so the solution fails on that optional result.

10. Which of the following statements are true about repeaters? (Choose all that apply.)

　　a. Repeaters regenerate the data signal.

　　b. Repeaters can filter data based on hardware addresses.

　　c. Repeaters can extend a network indefinitely.

　　d. Repeaters can link two network segments together.

Answer a is correct. Answer b is incorrect because this is a function of bridges, not repeaters. Answer c is incorrect because although repeaters can extend the network a great distance, there are some definite hard limits to how far a network can be extended. **Answer d is correct.**

CHAPTER PREREQUISITE

Before reading this chapter, you should review Chapter 3, "The OSI Reference Model," Chapter 5, "The Physical Connection," Chapter 7, "Data Transmission," and Chapter 8, "Network Architecture." You should also know how networks are interconnected (see Chapter 13, "Creating Larger Networks").

Wide Area Networks (WANs)

WHILE YOU READ

1. What is the difference between a dedicated connection and a switched network?

2. Explain circuit switching versus packet switching.

3. What is a virtual circuit?

4. With a digital leased line, what device do you connect to the line on your end?

5. At what speed does a T1 line allow you to send data?

6. When calculating fractional-T1 service, what is the interval used?

7. Why is X.25 so slow?

8. What are the advantages of frame relay?

9. ATM breaks data packets into cells with a length of _____.

10. If a line is rated as OC-3, what speed can data flow through the line?

An Overview of Wide Area Network Connectivity

Within a very small geographic area, LANs work fine. By using appropriate physical media and connectivity devices, such as routers and bridges, the LAN in your building can be extended by connecting several LANs. For example, if your organization has offices in several buildings located in close proximity, the LANs in each building could be connected as a larger LAN.

However, you eventually reach a point at which LAN media can no longer be extended. Most of the physical media discussed earlier in this book can cover, at most, a distance of 500 meters. With fiber-optic cables, the distance can be extended to approximately 2 kilometers, but the expense involved could be too prohibitive.

When you want to extend your network beyond the limit of your LAN, you have to explore technologies that enable you to create a network over a larger geographic distance. Such a network is referred to as a *wide area network (WAN)*.

A WAN may extend across a region, state, and country or around the globe. The technologies involved are basically the same regardless of the distance. In its physical construction, a WAN involves several LANs interconnected with high-speed communication links (often referred to as *WAN links*). Bridges, routers, and other connectivity devices ensure that all the data is transmitted correctly across the communication links. A properly connected WAN should enable your network users to access network resources across the WAN links with the same ease as the resources that are on the local network.

As far as the actual connections are concerned, most organizations do not own the physical WAN connections. It would simply be far too expensive for an organization to purchase all the physical cable media, connect it between offices, and then continue to maintain the physical connections. Instead, the majority of WAN links are leased from a service provider who owns and maintains all the actual physical media. Service providers today include your local phone company, familiar long-distance companies, and companies that specialize in data transmission.

WAN links are usually composed of one of the following technologies:

- Dial-up telephone connections
- Dedicated digital telephone lines
- Connections over packet-switched networks

Each of the technologies is discussed in detail within this chapter. First, however, it is necessary for you to understand the types of connections available to you.

Types of Connections

If you were to purchase your own cable and physically run it between two buildings, you would have your own private connection. As mentioned in the preceding section, most organizations cannot afford this and opt instead to lease lines from a service provider. The leased connection can take two forms: a dedicated connection or a connection through some type of switched network.

Dedicated Connections

A *dedicated connection* involves having a permanent, full-time open connection between two points. Essentially, the service is the same as if you yourself had run the cable. The difference is that it is owned and maintained by someone else.

With a dedicated connection, you have complete access to the cable and can send as much data down the connection as the cable will handle. No one else can use the lines you have leased.

Cost-wise, you pay the same amount for the connection, regardless of how much data you send (or do not send) down the line. Dedicated lines at high speeds are usually quite expensive.

Switched Networks

In contrast to a dedicated connection, *switched networks* allow multiple users to share the same line. This is accomplished using hardware and software that switch back and forth among all the different sources seeking to use a given connection.

The difference can be seen in Figure 14.1. With a private network, you establish a dedicated connection between each site. You maintain all the equipment to link the sites together and merely lease the actual connections from a service provider.

With a switched network, you connect each site to your service provider's network. The service provider maintains all the equipment and establishes the connections between sites. Switched networks are often represented with the symbol of a cloud because they are, in fact, a mesh network with many paths for data to flow between connections.

One of the strengths of switched networks is that they can provide "any-to-any" connectivity, where multiple sites can be easily connected. If you had to move one of the offices on the private network in Figure 14.1, you would have to terminate and then reinstall all the dedicated connections at great expense. With the switched network, each office has only one connection to the larger switched network. Moving the office would involve moving only one data connection.

CH
14

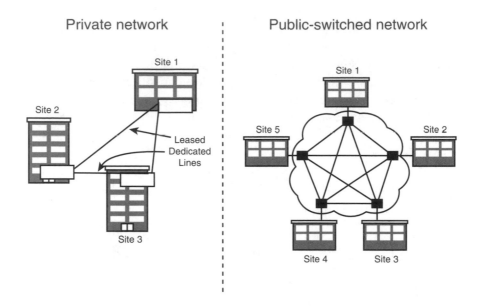

Figure 14.1
A private network uses dedicated connections, and a switched network uses a shared network of connections.

Switched networks also can easily accommodate the growth of an organization. As a company grows and needs more network bandwidth, a switched connection can often be easily expanded. Some switched networks even allow *bandwidth-on-demand,* where a company can use more bandwidth just at peak times and be charged a fee beyond the normal monthly rate. For instance, a company might contract for a network with 128Kbps of network bandwidth. However, it might actually be allowed to use up to 256Kbps, but would be charged for the additional bandwidth only when it used it.

Fees, in general, are different with switched networks than with dedicated lines. With a leased line, you usually pay a flat monthly fee, regardless of how much actual use you make of the connection. Switched networks, on the other hand, can charge fees based on the actual amount of network bandwidth used.

There are two types of switched networks in use today:

- *Circuit switching*—Provides a temporary connection between two points
- *Packet switching*—Provides a connection between multiple points

Circuit Switching

Every time you pick up the telephone, you are using a circuit-switched network. When you call someone, a *circuit* is established between your phone and the other party's phone. For the duration of your phone call, you have exclusive access to those phone lines. Only when you hang up, can anyone else use the phone lines on which your signal traveled.

If you called the same person 10 times in one day, your phone call might be carried across the same exact phone lines all 10 times—or it might be carried across 10 sets of phone lines. You do not know, nor do you have to know, exactly what path your phone call took to reach its destination.

Likewise in the computer world, a circuit-switched connection can be established over a service provider's network between any two PCs. Examples discussed later in the chapter include dial-up telephone connections, ISDN, and Switched-56 services.

Circuit-switching networks can be economical, but are limited in speed.

Packet Switching

To understand packet switching, consider the following situation. You are in charge of shipping cargo for a company in Boston. You must send a large shipment to San Francisco that is too big to travel by plane. Instead, you must evaluate shipping that cargo by train or truck. If you send it by train, it will take some time to load all the cargo into railroad cars, connect all the cars, and send them on their way. You do not know exactly which route the train will take, but all the cargo will go together. If there are any delays enroute, all the cargo will be delayed. However, when it arrives, it will all get there at the same time.

On the other hand, if you use trucks, you can just load up each truck and tell the drivers the address of where the cargo is to be delivered in San Francisco. As each truck is ready to go, it can just head out on the highway. Each truck driver will decide which routes his or her truck should follow and can change the route as the journey is underway. If there are traffic delays ahead, the truck can change its route to go around the slowdown. Some drivers might choose faster routes, so the cargo might arrive at the destination out of order. For this reason, you provide each driver with a packing list that defines where his or her shipment fits in the overall delivery. When all the shipments arrive, they are reassembled into the proper order.

Packet-switching networks are like the trucks, whereas circuit-switching networks resemble the train. Within a packet-switching network, data is broken up into small packets and sent across the network. Each packet flows out onto the network separately and is routed according to the best path at the instant it enters the network. As it travels across

CH
14

the network, the packet may pass through many connection devices, each of which can reroute the packet along a different path.

As shown in Figure 14.2, this can result in packets taking different paths and arriving out of order at the destination. For this reason, each packet is provided with sequencing information in the packet header so that the data stream can be reassembled in the proper order.

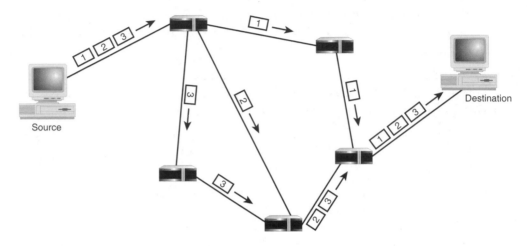

Figure 14.2
In a packet-switched network, each packet may follow a completely different path to the destination.

Because packet-switched networks typically use small packets, the networks can be very fast and very efficient. Users are normally charged only for the amount of data they send onto the actual network versus the flat fee charged for dedicated lines.

 Key Concept

Packet-switching networks break data into small packets that are sent across the network, with each packet potentially following a different route and with the data being reassembled in the proper sequence at the destination.

Some packet-switching networks improve performance by establishing a *virtual circuit* between two points on the network. Essentially, the virtual circuit combines the concepts of circuit-switching and packet-switching networks. When a connection is initiated between two points, a circuit is established across the network between the two points.

All data packets travel across the same route from the source to the destination and yet still share the network with data packets from other users. In the trucking analogy, this would be the same as instructing each truck driver to follow a specific route between Boston and San Francisco. The trucks would all travel the same route, but share the highways with all other drivers.

Virtual circuits allow networks to shave off some of the transmission overhead because connection devices do not have to determine the best route for a packet to travel. The packet usually comes with the circuit in its header, so the connection device merely has to pass it along to the next device in the circuit.

When a virtual circuit is established for a temporary connection between two devices, it is referred to as a *switched virtual circuit (SVC)*. When that connection is permanent—for instance, between two routers that are always online—the connection is called a *permanent virtual circuit (PVC)*. PVCs are used in many of the advanced packet-switching technologies now available.

Key Concept

Virtual circuits establish a path for data to travel across a packet-switched network.

Cell switching is a term used by advocates of Asynchronous Transfer Mode (ATM) technology (discussed later in this chapter in the section "ATM") to describe ATM's variation on packet switching. In cell switching, all data packets are broken into very small, fixed-length *cells* (ATM uses a 53-byte cell) and transmitted across the network. Because traditional packet-switching networks allow the length of the data packet to vary, packet-switching devices must be able to recognize when a data packet begins and ends. The overhead involved with these calculations can affect the speed of network performance.

With fixed-length data packets, cell-switching networks can build the switching into the hardware devices used on the network and allow for more rapid transmission of data.

Key Concept

Cell switching is a variation of packet switching in which the data is broken up into very small, fixed-length cells.

CH
14

WAN Technologies

Several technologies are available to implement a WAN connection. The remainder of this chapter discusses the following WAN technologies:

- Connections through the telephone system
- X.25
- Frame relay
- ATM Asynchronous Transfer Mode (ATM)
- Switched Multimegabit Data Service (SMDS)
- Synchronous Optical Network (SONET)

The Telephone System

One of the basic components of WAN connectivity is the standard telephone system with which we are all familiar. The *Public Switched Telephone Network (PSTN)* has been in existence for more than 100 years and reaches throughout the globe. In many nations, the PSTN is operated by a government agency or other public organization. Within the United States, the PSTN is operated by a complex system involving local telephone companies (for example, the *Regional Bell Operating Companies [RBOCs]*) and various long distance carriers such as AT&T, Sprint, and MCI.

When installing phone lines into your home or office, your local phone company brings in a telephone wire connection to a *demarcation point*, which is often a wall in some closet of your building. As the subscriber to the telephone service, you are responsible for installing and maintaining all internal phone lines that run throughout your office back to the demarcation point. Even though you might contract with your local phone company or another cabling company to install the internal connections, these internal connections are not part of the phone company's responsibility.

However, the phone company is responsible for the connection between the demarcation point and the phone company's nearest *central office (CO)*. This connection, referred to as the *local loop*, is usually UTP or fiber-optic cable. Your local phone company is responsible for all maintenance, signaling (such as the dial tone and busy signal), and noise filtering for this local connection. Over this same connection, the phone company also provides the electrical power necessary for your phones to operate.

Each local CO is connected to other COs through high-speed trunk lines to form the local phone company's larger network. Long-distance carriers then make high-speed connections from their long-distance networks into your local phone company's network.

Your local phone company relies on the long-distance carriers to provide connections to other regions and around the globe.

When connecting telephone calls, the PSTN uses circuit-switching. Your connection between the demarcation point at your office and your local CO is through a dedicated physical cable. Any calls you make will always travel over that single cable to your local CO. However, after calls reach the CO, a circuit is established along whatever route is most appropriate at the time the call is made. All circuits are connected and disconnected at your local CO.

For WAN connections using the PSTN, five types of connections are available:

- Dial-up connections
- Dedicated leased lines
- Switched-56
- T-Carrier System
- Integrated Services Digital Network (ISDN)

Dial-Up Connections

Dial-up connections across the PSTN are very popular today using basic analog telephone lines. With the simple use of a modem, a computer can be connected to another computer over an inexpensive phone line. However, because the PSTN is circuit switched, the quality of the connection can vary each time a connection is made. Additionally, although modem manufacturers are now pushing transmission speeds to approximately 56Kbps, electromagnetic interference generally limits dial-up connections to slow speeds.

Dedicated Leased Lines

As a step up from dial-up connections, telephone companies and other service providers offer *dedicated leased lines* (also referred to simply as *leased lines*). Leased lines provide a dedicated, full-time connection between two points on the PSTN. Because the telephone company is allocating a line for your exclusive use, leased lines can be expensive. However, where they are not circuit-switched, the quality of the line can be tested and equipment properly configured to deliver high-speed data transmission. Dedicated leased lines are available as both analog and digital lines.

Dedicated analog lines using regular modems are available, but are subject to many of the same physical limitations of dial-up connections. Because analog signals are very susceptible to *electromagnetic interference (EMI)*, error-checking mechanisms must be used to ensure successful transmission of data. Such mechanisms render analog connections slow and not terribly useful.

CH
14

Instead, most organizations lease dedicated digital lines. *Digital lines* are conditioned for data use and are not as susceptible to EMI as analog lines because of the digital signal transmission. Digital lines can provide transmission that is essentially 99% error free. Dedicated digital lines are usually called *Digital Data Service (DDS) lines*, in reference to AT&T's original name for the service. DDS lines provide point-to-point connections at speeds of 2.4, 4.8, 9.6, 19.2, or 56Kbps.

Because DDS lines are digital, you do not use a modem to connect to the leased line. Instead, you use a device called a *Channel Service Unit/Data Service Unit (CSU/DSU)*, as shown in Figure 14.3. The CSU portion of the unit connects with the DDS line, and the DSU side is connected to your LAN. The CSU/DSU converts signals from the LAN for transmission over the DDS line, while also providing electronics to protect the signal quality of both networks. (Note that you will also see *DSU* spelled out as *Digital Service Unit* instead of *Data Service Unit*.)

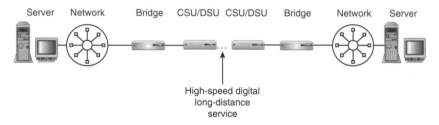

Figure 14.3
CSUs/DSUs are used to link two networks over a leased line.

Although DDS leased lines do provide an alternative to dial-up connections, their expense and limit of 56Kbps have meant a decrease in popularity as new technologies such as frame relay (discussed later in the chapter) have evolved.

Switched-56

Because some companies and organizations wanted the speed of a 56Kbps leased line but did not want to pay for a dedicated line, telephone companies and service providers began offering *Switched-56* service. Switched-56 is really nothing more than a circuit-switched version of the standard 56Kbps DDS leased line. Because users pay only for the time they are connected, the cost involved can be significantly less than that of a dedicated line.

To use Switched-56 connections, both ends of the connections must be equipped with compatible Switched-56 CSUs/DSUs that can dial and connect to each other.

The T-Carrier System

In the early days of the PSTN, each telephone cable could carry only a single telephone conversation. As telephone usage and demand grew, the telephone companies sought a solution to alleviate the overcrowding of the voice lines. In the 1960s, Bell Telephone Laboratories (Bell Labs) developed the *T-carrier system* to address this problem. Although it began as a voice-grade analog system, AT&T began offering digital T-carrier service in 1983.

As shown in Figure 14.4, the T-carrier system uses devices called *multiplexors*, or *muxes*, to combine several data channels for transmission over a communication line. At the receiving end, another multiplexor disassembles (or *demultiplexes*) the transmission and breaks out each data channel.

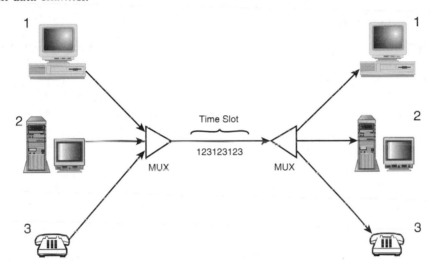

Figure 14.4

Multiplexors combine multiple data channels for transmission over a single communications cable.

The basic unit of the T-carrier system is a *T1 line*. A T1 line consists of 24 64Kbps channels for a total transmission capability of 1.544Mbps. Each of the 24 channels can be used for separate voice or data communication or can be combined with another to attain higher transmission speeds. In telecommunications jargon, the 64Kbps data transmission rate is referred to as *DS-0 (Digital Signal level 0)* and a full T1 line is referred to as *DS-1*. Table 14.1 outlines the capabilities of the types of lines available in the T-Carrier system.

CH
14

Table 14.1 The T-Carrier System				
Signal	Carrier System	Data Rate (Mbps)	Voice Channels	T1 Channels
DS-0	N/A	0.064	1	N/A
DS-1	T1	1.544	24	1
DS-2	T2	6.312	96	2
DS-3	T3	44.736	672	28
DS-4	T4	274.760	4032	168

Note that T1 service is available throughout the United States but might not be available in other countries. In those countries, a similar service, called *E1*, may be available with a base data transmission speed of 2.048Mbps.

Today, the most common type of T-carrier line found in WAN connections is the T1 line. T3 lines may also be found in WAN connections, but are limited because of the extremely high costs associated with leasing T3 lines. T2 lines are not offered to the public and are used only internally by telephone companies. Both T1 and T2 lines can use standard copper wire, whereas T3 and T4 lines require fiber-optic cable or high-speed media such as microwave transmission. Because installation of a T-carrier leased line can be very expensive, service providers offer customers the ability to use part of a T-carrier line through services such as *Fractional T1* and *Fractional T3*. For instance, Fractional T1 allows you to use a certain number of 64Kbps channels (up to 24 channels in a T1 line). As an example, you might decide that you only need a 384Kbps connection between two offices. Rather than pay for the entire T1 line, you could contract with a service provider to use only six channels of a T1 line. An advantage for you is that, should your organization require more bandwidth, you can usually just call your service provider and ask to be allocated more channels.

 Key Concept

A T1 dedicated leased line contains 24 channels of 64Kbps for a maximum data speed of 1.544Mbps. In *Fractional T1*, the customer contracts for a certain number (fewer than 24) of 64Kbps channels.

Connecting your network to a T1 (or other T-carrier) line is quite similar to a connection to a DDS line. You need a T1-compatible CSU/DSU and bridge or router. If you want to share the T1 between voice and data traffic, you need a multiplexor to combine the voice and data signals. T1 lines can be leased from your local telephone company, long-distance carriers, or other service providers and are usually billed on a flat monthly-fee basis. However, because essentially all service providers connect to your local telephone company's network, you will still have to lease a local loop connection from your office to your local telephone company's nearest CO.

ISDN

Integrated Services Digital Network (ISDN) began as a plan to offer combined voice, data, and video over copper telephone lines by converting the telephone signals from analog to digital. ISDN is now being implemented worldwide over both copper and fiber-optic cables using two standards:

- *Basic Rate ISDN (BRI)*—Targeted at the homeowner or small business, this consists of two B-channels operating at 64Kbps and one D-channel operating at 16Kbps. Each of the B-channels can be used for voice or data, and the D-channel is used for call setup and control information. One of the advantages of BRI is that you can use one B-channel for voice and the other for data, or you can combine both B-channels for a connection speed of 128Kbps.
- *Primary Rate ISDN (PRI)*—Targeted at larger organizations, this uses a full T1 line to provide 23 B-channels and 1 D-channel. As in BRI, B-channels can be used for either voice or data, and the D-channel handles control information.

An ISDN connection is a dial up service not intended to be used full-time like a dedicated T1 line. Because users are charged based on their usage instead of a flat monthly fee, ISDN connections can be very cost-effective for situations in which usage of the connection is limited. As line usage increases, an ISDN line can become more expensive than a regular dedicated leased line. You connect to an ISDN line using a device resembling a modem (and now referred to as an *ISDN modem* by many vendors) into which you can plug your computer and regular telephone.

 Key Concept

Basic Rate ISDN provides speeds up to 128Kbps.

X.25

Beginning in the mid-1970s, organizations seeking an alternative to dedicated lines could use X.25 packet-switching networks for communication. The X.25 series of protocols was defined by the CCITT/ITU to specify how devices could connect over an internetwork. Although the X.25 protocols were designed so that they can be generically applied to any public or private network, X.25 came to be synonymous with the packet-switching *Public Data Networks (PDNs)* operated by companies such as AT&T, Tymnet, and General Electric. Originally designed to connect terminals to mainframe computers, these PDNs can provide customers with connections between LANs at a relatively low cost.

As shown in Figure 14.5, X.25 networks are often represented with a cloud, due to the mesh nature of their topology. Packets travel across the network taking the best path available at any given moment.

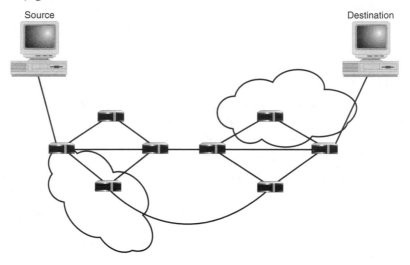

Figure 14.5
X.25 networks use packet switching to route data across their mesh topology.

Because X.25 networks were developed when telephone lines were still somewhat unreliable, the protocols incorporated a large degree of error checking. For that reason, X.25 networks are relatively slow and can attain speeds of only approximately 64Kbps.

Connecting your LAN to an X.25 network usually involves leasing a line between your LAN and one of the PDNs available for commercial use. The actual connection to your LAN may be accomplished through a computer with an X.25 interface or through a device called a *packet assembler/disassembler (PAD)*.

Although X.25 networks provide proven, reliable, and virtually error-free connections, their popularity has been fading because of their slow speed and the evolution of technologies such as frame relay and ATM.

Key Concept

X.25 packet-switching networks can supply low-cost connections up to 64Kbps through worldwide Public Data Networks (PDNs).

Frame Relay

As digital transmission technology evolved, the need for high levels of error checking diminished. *Frame relay* technology evolved from ISDN and X.25 by stripping off the error-checking and accounting functions of X.25 and operating primarily over fiber-optic media. Frame relay connections assume that the network media will provide a high-quality transmission capability and that all error checking will be handled by devices at either end of the connection. Frame relay connections use variable-length frames that operate at the data link layer of the OSI Model.

Additionally, whereas X.25 packet switching uses the best route available for each packet, frame relay establishes a *Permanent Virtual Circuit (PVC)* between two points on the network. The PVC defines a path through the frame relay network; therefore, each node in the frame relay network does not have to spend time determining which path a data frame should take. Because of the elimination of error checking and the use of PVCs, frame relay connections can operate between 56Kbps and 1.544Mbps.

One of the attractions to customers is that frame relay connections can be established for any bandwidth requirement. When you arrange for a frame relay connection with a service provider, you contract for a *Committed Information Rate (CIR)*, which is the guaranteed data transmission capacity of that connection. CIRs are available in increments of 64Kbps. If you contract for a CIR of 384Kbps, you are guaranteed to have that much capacity. Service providers can also provide higher bandwidth on demand, so you pay a flat fee for your CIR and an additional charge for higher usage.

Frame relay connections are quite popular at this time because they provide one of the least expensive high-speed WAN connections. At the time of this writing, a frame relay connection costs significantly less than a dedicated leased line or an ATM connection.

Frame relay connections are accomplished using a frame relay–compatible CSU/DSU and router or bridge.

Key Concept

Frame relay networks provide a high-speed connection up to 1.544Mbps using variable-length packet switching over digital fiber-optic media.

CH
14

ATM

Asynchronous Transfer Mode (ATM) is an advanced packet-switching technology that can provide high-speed data transmission over both LANs or WANs. ATM can be used over a variety of media and can be used with both baseband and broadband transmission systems.

ATM's implementation of packet switching is referred to as *cell switching* because it uses fixed-length data packets. Unlike frame relay, in which the data packet length can vary, ATM packets (called *cells*) have a fixed length of 53 bytes. Of this 53 bytes, 48 bytes contain data, and 5 bytes are used for header information. Because data packets of a uniform length are far easier to move than random-size packets, ATM accomplishes most of its switching and routing through hardware devices. The efficiency gained by using hardware switching with small data cells enables ATM to achieve speeds of up to 622Mbps. (It is theoretically possible for ATM to achieve speeds up to 1.2Gbps; however, fiber-optic cable at this time is limited to around 622Mbps.)

Like frame relay, ATM assumes a noise-free line and leaves error checking to the data link layer devices at either end of a connection. Also, similar to frame relay, ATM establishes a PVC between two points across an ATM network.

The primary hardware device within an ATM network is an *ATM switch*, which acts as a multiplexor to allow multiple devices to simultaneously transmit across the WAN connection, as shown in Figure 14.6. The WAN connection to which the switch is connected can be a coaxial or twisted-pair cable, but neither of those media can truly support ATM's high speeds. Instead, you will usually find ATM operating over T3 lines (45Mbps), FDDI networks (100Mbps), or OC3 SONET connections (155Mbps).

Although the hardware necessary for ATM is still expensive, ATM is widely viewed as the primary transmission method for future computer networks. This view is primarily due to ATM's speed, efficiency, and capability to scale from small to global networks and function over a variety of media.

Key Concept

ATM is an advanced packet-switching technology that transmits data in fixed-length, 53-byte cells at speeds up to 622Mbps.

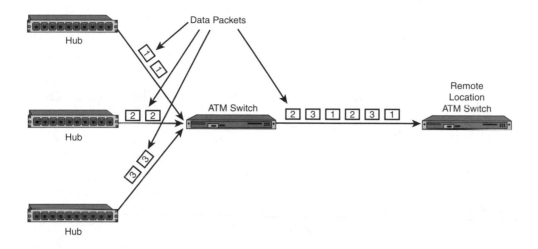

Figure 14.6
ATM switches act as multiplexors and allow the transmission of multiple data channels over a single communication link.

SMDS

Switched Multimegabit Data Service (SMDS) is a WAN technology developed by Bellcore and offered by local telephone companies in some metropolitan areas of the United States. Although SMDS uses cell switching on fixed-length cells like ATM, SMDS operates at speeds of 1.544 to 45Mbps. Like both frame relay and ATM, SMDS does not provide any error checking and leaves that function to devices at the connection points. SMDS is considered a competitor to frame relay, but is in limited use because of lack of availability and the high cost of SMDS equipment.

SONET

Synchronous Optical Network (SONET) defines how fiber-optic technologies can deliver voice, data, and video over a network at speeds over 1Gbps. SONET is actually a physical layer standard that unifies worldwide telecommunication standards for fiber-optic transmission. It uses a mesh or ring topology with multiplexing.

Before SONET, global standards diverged, with some nations (such as the United States) championing standards based on a T1 line (1.544Mbps) and other nations championing standards based on an E1 line (2.048Mbps). SONET has unified all factions behind a new system that defines data rates in terms of *optical carrier (OC)* levels. The base level OC-1 specifies a data transmission rate of 51.8Mbps. Each additional OC level is simply

CH
14

an integer multiple of OC-1. For example, OC-3 specifies a transmission rate of 3 × 51.8 or 155.52Mbps. Today, the highest practical level is OC-12 at 622Mbps, although the specification does define OC-48 at 2.48Gbps. The most common SONET implementation today is OC-3 at 155.52Mbps.

Note that SONET also defines an electrical equivalent to the OC levels used for fiber-optic cables. *Synchronous transport signals (STS)* use the same scale as the OC levels, but are applied to traditional copper media. For example, STS-1 is the electrical equivalent to OC-1 operating at 51.8Mbps. STS-12, like OC-12, defines a rate of 622Mbps.

As SONET has been incorporated by the ITU into the ITU's *Synchronous Digital Hierarchy (SDH)* recommendations, networks using SONET will be able to begin with a local network and ultimately expand to a global scale. Boundaries between telephone companies throughout the world are being removed by SONET.

As mentioned previously, SONET defines the physical layer for a network connection and relies on other technologies, such as ATM and SMDS, to accomplish the actual transmission of data.

xDSL

In the late 1990s, several versions of *Digital Subscriber Loop (DSL)* technology have emerged that allow users to achieve far greater speeds using their normal copper telephone connections. The most popular of these is *Asymmetric Digital Subscriber Loop (ADSL)*, which is now becoming available in many locations throughout the United States. Although this new technology can offer you important connectivity options, at this point it is not covered by the Networking Essentials exam.

Cable Modems

During the past few years, we have also seen a rise in availability of network connections using the broadband cable networks widely deployed for cable TV. These systems offer the advantage of providing a full-time network connection that, on some systems, approaches LAN speeds of 10Mbps. Like xDSL, cable modems are a technology you should be aware of, but you will not be tested on them on the exam.

Summary

A wide area network (WAN) links multiple LANs across a large geographic distance and usually consists of connections leased from service providers, dial-up telephone connections, dedicated telephone lines, and connections over packet-switched networks.

Dedicated connections involve establishing an exclusive, permanent, full-time open connection between two points. Switched networks allow multiple users to share the same connection line and can use either circuit switching or packet switching at a significantly lower cost than dedicated connections.

To implement a WAN connection, several technologies are available, including the telephone system, X.25, frame relay, ATM, SMDS, and SONET.

The basic telephone system can provide dial-up connections, dedicated leased lines, T-carrier lines, or ISDN connections. Dial-up connections are made through a modem over regular analog telephone lines. Dedicated leased lines can be analog or digital, whereas Dedicated Digital Service (DDS) leased lines use a Channel Service Unit/Data Service Unit (CSU/DSU) to connect your network to the digital line.

The T-carrier system uses multiplexors to combine several voice or data channels for transmission and consists of 24 64Kbps channels for a maximum transmission speed of 1.544Mbps.

Integrated Services Digital Network (ISDN) allows users to combine voice and data over a digital line. Primary Rate ISDN provides 23 64Kbps B-channels and one 64Kbps D-channel, using the full bandwidth of a T1 line.

X.25 is a CCITT/ITU series of protocols that define how packet switching can occur across an internetwork. Used primarily in Public Data Networks (PDNs) to which organizations can connect, X.25 provides reliable and virtually error-free communication.

Frame relay provides packet switching like X.25, but assumes that it will be running on top of a more reliable media and leaves error checking to devices at the end connections.

Asynchronous Transfer Mode (ATM) uses an advanced form of packet switching referred to as *cell switching*, in which all data is packaged into 53-byte cells for transmission.

Switched Multimegabit Data Service (SMDS) is a service offered by some local telephone companies using ATM technology to provide connections from 1.544 to 45Mbps. Like both frame relay and ATM, SMDS does not provide any error checking.

Synchronous Optical Network (SONET) is a physical layer standard that defines transmission speeds and other characteristics of fiber-optic cables. Both ATM and SMDS can use SONET as the underlying physical transportation medium.

CH
14

QUESTIONS AND ANSWERS

1. What is the difference between a dedicated leased line and a switched network?

   A: With a dedicated leased line, you essentially own an open line between the two endpoints and pay for it whether or not you use it. Very often, you yourself also have to maintain the equipment. With a switched network, you connect the endpoints to a public data network of some type, and your packets flow across shared data lines.

2. Explain circuit switching versus packet switching.

   A: In circuit switching, a dedicated pathway is established when the connection between two endpoints is opened and remains open for the entire duration of the connection. In packet switching, when the connection is opened, individual data packets travel between the two endpoints, possibly taking different paths.

3. What is a virtual circuit?

   A: A predetermined path through a packet-switched network.

4. With a digital leased line, what device do you connect to the line on your end?

   A: A Channel Service Unit/Data Service Unit (CSU/DSU)

5. At what speed does a T1 line allow you to send data?

   A: 1.544Mbps

6. When calculating fractional-T1 service, what is the interval used?

   A: 64Kbps. A T1 consists of 24 channels, each of which has a bandwidth of 64Kbps. Fractional T1 consists of choosing how many channels you will use.

7. Why is X.25 so slow?

   A: As a packet traverses the X.25 network, a new route for the packet must be calculated at each and every stop on the way.

8. What are the advantages of frame relay?

   A: Comparatively low cost, up to T1 speed, the capability to "burst" above committed rate

9. ATM breaks data packets into cells with a length of _____.

   A: 53 bytes

10. If a line is rated as OC-3, at what speed can data flow through the line?

    A: 155.52Mbps (51.8Mbps×3)

PRACTICE TEST

1. Within a packet-switching network, a dedicated path between two endpoints is referred to as what?

a. Switched Virtual Circuit

b. Dedicated leased line

c. Permanent Virtual Circuit

d. Digital Data Service

Answers a, b, and d are incorrect. **Answer c is correct.**

2. What is cell-switching?

a. A packet-switching implementation using variable-length data packets.

b. A packet-switching implementation using fixed-length data packets.

c. A circuit-switching implementation using fixed-length data packets.

d. A circuit-switching implementation using variable-length data packets.

Answers a, c, and d are incorrect. **Answer b is correct.**

3. Which of the following statements are true about packet-switching networks? (Choose all that apply.)

a. Each packet may follow a completely different path to its destination.

b. Users are often charged only for the amount of data sent across the network.

c. Users have exclusive access to the actual data transmission lines for the duration of the connection.

d. Packet-switching networks are limited to speeds under 56Kbps.

Answer a is correct. Answer b is correct. Answer c is incorrect because packet-switched networks use shared communication lines. Answer d is incorrect. As an example, frame relay networks can go up to 1.544Mbps, and ATM networks can go up to 622Mbps.

4. You want to connect two offices using a WAN that will provide network throughput in excess of 100Mbps. Which of the following technologies can you use? (Choose all that apply.)

a. ISDN

b. T1 line

c. ATM

d. Frame relay

Answer a is incorrect because ISDN can reach only 128Kbps. Answer b is incorrect because a T1 line can reach only 1.544Mbps. **Answer c is correct; ATM can reach speeds over 100Mbps.** Answer d is incorrect because frame relay can reach only 1.544Mbps.

CH
14

5. Your Texas company recently acquired another company in Chicago. You have been charged with designing a WAN to connect the two offices.

REQUIRED RESULT: The network must operate in excess of 1Mbps.

OPTIONAL DESIRED RESULTS: The network should be scalable so that it can be expanded as your organization grows. The connection should also be as inexpensive as possible.

PROPOSED SOLUTION: You propose connecting the two offices with a dedicated T1 line. Which results does the proposed solution produce?

a. The proposed solution produces the required result and produces both the optional desired results.

b. The proposed solution produces the required result and produces only ONE of the optional desired results.

c. The proposed solution produces the required result but does *not* produce any of the optional desired results.

d. The proposed solution does *not* produce the required result.

Answer c is correct. A dedicated T1 does meet the required result of operating above 1Mbps. However, it is not easy to scale (you must remove the line), and it is not an inexpensive solution.

6. You have to connect two offices and need a solution that can provide data transmission speeds of at least 1Mbps. Which type of WAN connections can you consider? (Choose all that apply.)

a. Frame relay
b. Dedicated Digital Service
c. ATM
d. Basic Rate ISDN

Answer a is correct because frame relay can go up to 1.544Mbps. Answer b is incorrect because DDS reaches only 56Kbps. **Answer c is correct because ATM can go well beyond 1Mbps.** Answer d is incorrect because Basic Rate ISDN can go only to 128Kbps.

7. Your West Coast company recently acquired another company on the East Coast. You have been charged with designing a WAN to establish a full-time connection between the two offices.

REQUIRED RESULT: The network must operate in excess of 100Kbps.

OPTIONAL DESIRED RESULTS: The network should be scalable so that it can be expanded as your organization grows. The connection should also be as inexpensive as possible.

PROPOSED SOLUTION: You propose connecting the two offices using a 128Kbps frame-relay connection. Which results does the proposed solution produce?

a. The proposed solution produces the required result and produces both of the optional desired results.

b. The proposed solution produces the required result and produces only *one* of the optional desired results.

c. The proposed solution produces the required result but does *not* produce any of the optional desired results.

d. The proposed solution does *not* produce the required result.

Answer a is correct because the proposed 128Kbps frame-relay link meets the required result of operating in excess of 100Kbps. It also meets both optional results because it is very easy to scale (usually this merely involves calling your service provider and asking for more bandwidth) and is also a very inexpensive solution.

8. Digital Data Service can operate at which of the following speeds? (Choose all that apply.)

a. 1.544Mbps

b. 56Kbps

c. 19.2Kbps

d. 128Kbps

Answers b and c are correct because DDS has a maximum of 56Kbps. Answers a and d are incorrect.

9. Basic Rate ISDN provides what?

a. Twenty-three 64Kbps B-channels and one 64Kbps D-channel

b. Twenty-four 64Kbps B-channels and one 64Kbps D-channel

c. Four 64Kbps B-channels and one 16Kbps D-channel

d. Two 64Kbps B-channels and one 16Kbps D-channel

Answers a, b, and c are incorrect. **Answer d is correct.**

10. What data transmission speed can be achieved through a T1 line?

a. 45Mbps

b. 128Kbps

c. 1.544Mbps

d. 51.8Mbps

Answer a is incorrect because it is the speed of a T3 line. Answer b is incorrect because it is the speed of Basic Rate ISDN. **Answer c is correct; a T1 line can reach 1.544Mbps.** Answer d is incorrect and is the basic unit of measurement in SONET.

CH
14

CHAPTER PREREQUISITE

Before reading this chapter, you should understand network protocols, especially TCP/IP, as discussed in Chapter 9, "Network Protocols." You also should understand issues and terminology involved with larger networks, as discussed in Chapter 13, "Creating Larger Networks," and Chapter 14, "Wide Area Networks (WANs)."

The Internet

⎯ WHILE YOU READ ⎯

1. What are some of the services available on the Internet?

2. What is the protocol used for the Web, and what does it stand for?

3. What is NNTP used for on the Internet?

4. What does the `telnet` command allow you to do?

5. Differentiate between a DNS domain name and a Windows NT Server domain.

6. At its core, what does DNS do?

7. What is a firewall?

8. How does a proxy server protect your organization?

Origins of the Internet

The vast, global Internet of today had rather humble origins. In 1969, the Department of Defense Advanced Research Projects Agency (ARPA) developed an experimental network called *ARPAnet* to link four supercomputing centers for military research. This network's design required that it be fast, reliable, and capable of withstanding the loss of any one computer center on the network. (Significant research was being conducted at the time on making communication networks that could survive a nuclear blast.) From those original four computers, this network evolved into the sprawling network of millions of computers we know today as the *Internet*.

Although the threat of nuclear bombs might be diminished today, this network turned out to be a great asset for communication. Each computer is responsible for delivering its information to another computer. The network itself doesn't have much responsibility at all. If a computer or a link to a computer fails for some reason, communication to that computer will cease, but the rest of the computers will continue to operate and communicate among themselves. The network does not fail because of one computer.

Perhaps ARPAnet's greatest contribution was the development of the *TCP/IP* protocol suite. As this became the standard protocol suite used in networks, it allowed computers of all types to interconnect and share information.

Over time, ARPAnet faded away and was replaced by another government-funded network, the *NSFnet*, operated under the auspices of the National Science Foundation (NSF). The NSFnet, in turn, dissolved and was replaced with the mesh of commercial networks we have today. The U.S. government still funds some government, military, and educational portions of the Internet, but the Internet is primarily a commercial operation at this time.

The Internet itself is really a massive "network of networks." There is no central "Internet, Inc." to which you can connect. Essentially, it is a collection of *Internet service providers (ISPs)* that operate their own networks, with their own clients, and agree to connect with one another and exchange packets. Many of the large ISPs sell connections to their networks to smaller ISPs, some of whom again sell connections to other ISPs.

Ultimately, these ISPs at all levels sell connections to individuals and corporations, which then merge their networks (or individual computers) into this larger network.

Although there is no exact governance of the Internet, communication standards and coordination of ISP actions are overseen by a nonprofit organization called the *Internet Society*. An affiliated organization, the *Internet Engineering Task Force (IETF)* coordinates the work of numerous committees that define Internet communication standards and research methods of expanding and improving Internet communication. The actual communication standards are referred to as *RFCs (Requests for Comments)* and are voluntarily adhered to by all ISPs.

Note that the structure of the Internet is similar to that of the telephone network. If you think about it, when you call someone, your call goes from your local phone company to your long distance carrier. From there, it goes to the local phone company of the person you are calling, where it is actually connected. Conceivably, there could even be another long-distance carrier in between. All the local phone companies and long-distance companies agree to connect their systems. You don't know how the call reaches the recipient—you just know that the call goes through.

If you are interested in learning more about the history and structure of the Internet, visit the home pages of the Internet Society at `http://www.isoc.org/` and the Internet Engineering Task Force at `http://www.ietf.org/`.

Internet Services

When you are connected to the Internet, you have access to a wide variety of information services. The primary services include

- The World Wide Web
- Electronic mail
- File Transfer Protocol (FTP) servers
- Chat
- Newsgroups
- Telnet
- Gopher

New services are created almost daily, and as technology evolves to enable greater use of audio and video, the number of services will only continue to explode. All these services function primarily at the application layer of the OSI Reference Model.

The World Wide Web

The World Wide Web (WWW) began in 1989 as a means of publishing academic research papers so that they could be viewed by scientists around the world. Since the software for both viewing and publishing information was made freely available, users around the world have been creating what are known as *Web sites*. Today, the Web has become the dominant means of accessing information on the Internet. Literally thousands of new Web sites start publishing information *each day*.

The structure of the Web is simple. When you want to publish information for others to view, you make your documents available through a *Web server*. These documents, also referred to as *Web pages*, are primarily written in *Hypertext Markup Language (HTML)* and can include text, graphics, sound, and video. From your Web pages, you can create *hypertext links* to pages written by other people on other Web servers. Other sites, especially directories and search tools, may choose to create a link to your site so that users can find your pages. All this linking among Web sites creates a global mesh that truly resembles a spider's web.

Note that with Windows NT 4.0, Microsoft includes a Web server so that you can begin publishing material to the Internet right away. In Windows NT Server 4.0, the Web server is Microsoft's *Internet Information Server*. In Windows NT Workstation 4.0, the Web server provided is *Peer Web Services*, which is designed for light use. Beyond these two servers from Microsoft, Web servers are currently available for almost every known type of computer.

Because Microsoft is constantly improving its Internet Information Server product, you should visit its Web site at `http://www.microsoft.com/iis/` to make sure that you have the latest version.

Users explore the Web using a piece of software called a *browser*. This program enables users to specify the Web server to which they want to connect. Usually, the browser also provides a series of pointers for users who are unsure of where to start looking.

The two primary browsers in use at this time are Netscape's *Navigator* and Microsoft's *Internet Explorer* (see Figure 15.1). Both enable users to see high-resolution graphics, use sound and video, view Web pages with complicated page layouts, and easily search for new Web sites.

Browsers communicate with the various Web servers using the *Hypertext Transfer Protocol (HTTP)*. The beauty of the system is that the whole browser/server interaction consists of a simple request for a document. When the server sends the document back to the browser, the connection ends. The browser does not have to "log out" of the Web server or indicate in any way that it is finished using the server. There is no further connection (unless the user requests another document from the server).

Key Concept

In the midst of all the acronyms used for network protocols, remember that *HTTP* is used *only* for the World Wide Web. Exam questions have occasionally included HTTP, along with other network protocols, to throw you off.

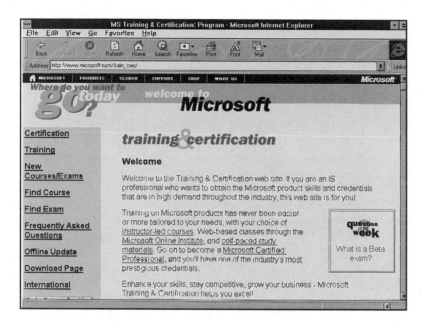

Figure 15.1
Microsoft's Internet Explorer can be used to view Web sites such as Microsoft's Training and Certification Web site.

The success of the Web and the wide availability of browsers have turned Web technologies into a major publishing medium. Many businesses and organizations have developed *intranets*, where Web servers are used to publish information on an internal LAN or WAN. For instance, human resources manuals and company policies can be distributed via a Web server on an intranet rather than printed out and distributed.

Key Concept

When people speak about developing an *intranet*, all they are talking about is the use of Internet technologies on an internal network. Generally, Web servers made available on this internal network are *not* available to users on the Internet.

If you are interested in staying on top of the latest developments of the World Wide Web, visit the home page of the World Wide Web Consortium at http://www.w3.org/.

Electronic Mail

Electronic mail, or *email*, is the primary reason why many people are connected (or connect their organization) to the Internet. Although the Web is the primary means people use to find information—and is certainly more exciting and interesting than electronic mail—email is the workhorse of the Internet that keeps communication flowing.

To use email, a user simply needs an email *client* program. This may be a program geared specifically toward Internet mail or may be a corporate email program (such as Microsoft Exchange, Microsoft Mail, or Lotus cc:Mail) that has a *mail gateway* to the Internet.

Users send a message to someone using Internet-style addresses in the form of `user@domain`, where the `user` is the user's name assigned by the ISP and the `domain` is something like `microsoft.com`. Domain names often include the name of the company or organization, followed by a three-character, top-level domain. (See the later section "The Domain Name System" for more information on domain naming.) For instance, to communicate with Microsoft about the Microsoft Certified Professional program, you would send email to `mcp@msprograms.com`.

Email messages are sent through the Internet through a network of *mail servers* responsible for delivering and receiving email. These servers primarily use *Simple Mail Transfer Protocol (SMTP)* to send and receive email. Email for a user whose computer is not currently online may be stored on a server for that user to retrieve later using *Post Office Protocol 3 (POP3)*. These protocols operate at the application layer of the OSI Model.

Again, don't let the exam fool you when it comes to network protocols. Remember that SMTP and POP3 are protocols used for sending and receiving Internet email and are not network transport protocols.

File Transfer Protocol (FTP) Servers

Although the Web contains vast amounts of information, most of it is text or graphics. If you want to download software, you will usually have to rely on the *File Transfer Protocol*. Because it is so heavily used, FTP is almost always included with any installation of the TCP/IP protocol suite. For that reason, most software vendors make their software available via an *FTP server*. A user connected to the Internet might not necessarily have a Web browser installed, but he will almost definitely have an *FTP client*.

FTP clients are available in two forms: text-based and graphical. *Text-based FTP clients* originated in the world of UNIX and maintain the short commands from that UNIX system. From a text window such as a command prompt (see Figure 15.2), you can simply issue the command `ftp`, begin connecting to a host operating an FTP server, and start retrieving software.

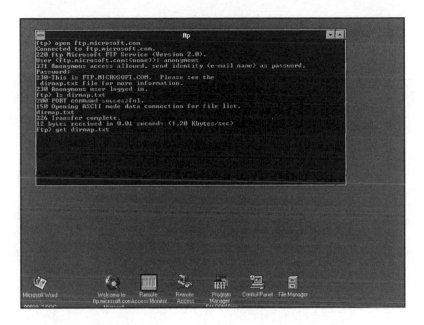

Figure 15.2
A text-based FTP client is provided with many operating systems.

Note that a text-based FTP client is included in Windows 95/98 and Windows NT when you install TCP/IP.

Graphical FTP clients are available in several forms. Specific programs are dedicated to providing FTP access through a graphical interface. However, more commonly, you will see people using Web browsers to retrieve software. Both Microsoft Internet Explorer and Netscape Navigator, as well as most other browsers, support the retrieval of files via FTP, as shown in Figure 15.3.

Because of the ease of file retrieval through Web browsers, many users of the Web go about their business downloading software, completely unaware that at times they are actually using FTP.

For your information, Microsoft's Internet Information Server, bundled with Windows NT 4.0, functions as a Web server but also can function as an FTP server.

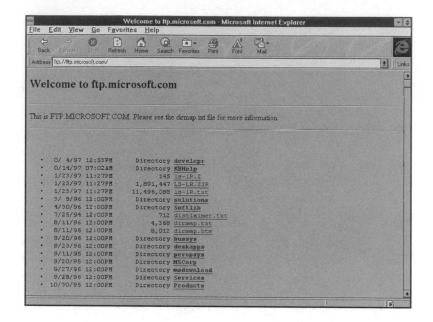

Figure 15.3
Microsoft's Internet Explorer Web browser can be used to retrieve files using FTP.

Key Concept

The *File Transfer Protocol (FTP)* is used to transfer files between computer systems over TCP/IP networks such as the Internet.

Newsgroups

At the time the Internet was just evolving, a parallel effort was underway to develop a network linking computers to share discussion groups. This network, known as *Usenet*, evolved into a series of *newsgroups* that were shared among computers using the *Network News Transport Protocol (NNTP)*. Over time, these newsgroups were transported over the Internet and today are considered part of the Internet's services.

Today, literally tens of thousands of newsgroups discuss virtually every subject imaginable. From operating systems to sports, politics, religion, and entertainment, thousands of articles are posted to newsgroups around the world each minute of the day.

The whole system operates through a series of *news servers* usually operated by Internet service providers, universities, or corporations. Each news server carries some number of newsgroups that are shared among its users. When you *post* an article to a newsgroup, it is soon available through your provider's news server. In a matter of minutes to hours, your article will be propagated to every other news server in the world that carries that particular newsgroup. In this manner, global discussions occur.

People read and participate in newsgroups through a client program usually referred to as a *news reader*. Although some users might use a special news reader program, the capability to read and participate in newsgroups has also been integrated into Web browsers such as Microsoft Internet Explorer and Netscape Navigator, as shown in Figure 15.4.

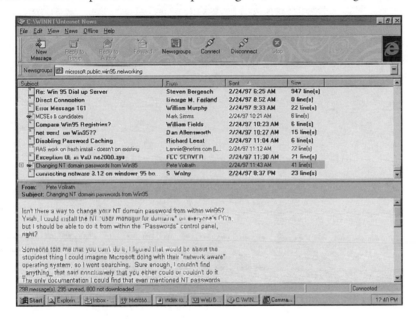

Figure 15.4
Microsoft's Internet News can be used to read newsgroups.

Note that many corporations have installed news servers on their intranet to provide online forums for employees to discuss issues within the company.

Telnet

In the early days of the Internet, high-speed computers were extremely expensive and rare. In fact, the original ARPAnet was created to share supercomputers among many researchers. One of the most common needs was for researchers at one location to log in to these remote supercomputers to perform research calculations. For this purpose, the Telnet program was developed. Using the `telnet` command, you can log in to a remote host, usually a UNIX or Linux system, and communicate with that computer as if you were directly connected (see Figure 15.5). The remote host must be running a *Telnet server* (usually referred to as a *Telnet daemon or Telnetd*) and must allow multiple users to log in simultaneously.

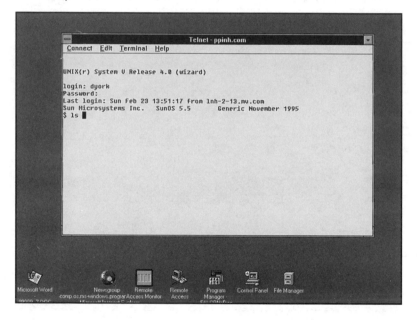

Figure 15.5
The `telnet` command allows you to connect to a remote host.

Windows 95/98 and Windows NT install a *Telnet client* when TCP/IP is installed. At the time of writing, a beta version of a Telnet server for Windows NT Server is available from Microsoft's Web site and as part of the Windows NT 4.0 Server Resource Kit.

Key Concept

Telnet allows you to log in to a remote host and execute commands on that computer system.

Gopher

Before the phenomenal success of the World Wide Web, *Gopher* was the tool of choice for users wanting to access information on the Internet. Developed at the University of Minnesota (home of the Golden Gophers sports team), Gopher presented information as a series of menus. Users would just make choices and travel through menus until they came to the text or graphics that interested them. Unlike the Web, text could not be formatted, nor could a text page contain graphics. A menu choice might display a graphic, but that would be all you would see. The graphic would not be surrounded by any text.

In a fashion very similar to the Web, organizations that wanted to publish information operated *Gopher servers*, and users wanting to access information used *Gopher clients*. Both text-based and graphical Gopher clients were available, and all Web browsers could (and still can) access information from Gopher servers. At the height of its popularity, there were perhaps a few thousand Gopher servers and even a tool called *Veronica* for searching the so-called *Gopherspace*.

What happened to Gopher? It was a great tool that brought some degree of order to the chaotic world of the Internet and was a useful way of organizing information. But its menu-based system with only plain text simply couldn't compete with the page-based world of the Web that allowed formatting and integrated text, graphics, and other media. Many Gopher servers remained active for quite some time, and some are still active today, but most sites have moved their content over to the Web.

Note that Microsoft's Internet Information Server, bundled with Windows NT 4.0, was able to function as a Gopher server up to IIS version 3.0. With IIS version 4.0, the Gopher server functionality was removed, which is to be expected given that Gopher usage has declined to nearly nothing.

Chat

Many of today's Internet users are "chatting" using software packages such as *ICQ* or various *Internet Relay Chat (IRC)* clients. Chat is a real-time direct link between users connected to the Internet. Many chat programs allow for video and audio if sufficient bandwidth is available, although text only is the standard.

The Domain Name System

In Chapter 9, "Network Protocols," you learned about TCP/IP and how computers communicate using IP addresses that take a numeric form, such as 192.168.10.123. Although this works fine for computers, humans have a more difficult time remembering all these numbers. If you were speaking with someone who said, "To learn more about our company, visit our Web site at http://207.22.13.4," you would probably just smile and promptly forget that address.

To cope with this need to remember addresses, the Internet community developed the *domain name system*, commonly known as *DNS*. In this system, every organization is assigned a domain name, such as microsoft.com or propoint.com, that uniquely identifies its organization to the rest of the Internet.

 Key Concept

A *DNS domain name* is very different from the Windows NT concept of a domain. A DNS domain name identifies your organization to other Internet users. If you send and receive email or publish information on the Web, your DNS domain name will be incorporated into your email address or Web server address. This text address will be mapped to an IP address and allow remote systems to communicate with your systems. A *domain* within a Windows NT Server network is a collection of computers utilizing user-level security.

Whenever you connect across the Web to an address such as www.microsoft.com, your computer first queries a local *DNS server* (also called a *name server*) to determine the IP address for www.microsoft.com. When that DNS server returns the appropriate IP address, your computer then sends off its packets to that address. All communication between computers uses IP addresses. If for some reason your DNS server cannot find the IP address for the domain name you typed, no communication can occur.

Note that DNS uses a whole hierarchy of distributed DNS servers to resolve addresses. If your local DNS server knows the IP address of www.microsoft.com, it sends that address back to your computer. If it doesn't, it queries some top-level DNS servers to find out which DNS server has responsibility for microsoft.com. Your local DNS server then communicates with that remote DNS server to find the IP address of www.microsoft.com. It returns this IP address to your computer and *caches* (stores) the address locally in case you, or others on your network, want to visit that site again.

Also, note that when you are working on TCP/IP and the Internet, you might hear people talk about a computer's *fully qualified domain name (FQDN)*. This is the name of the server and the domain name. For instance, if you had a server named `server1` that was in a network using the domain name `propoint.com`, the FQDN would be `server1.propoint.com`.

Domain names are divided into several *top-level domains*, as shown in Table 15.1. Organizations located in countries outside the United States generally use a two-letter country code.

Table 15.1	DNS Top-Level Domains
Domain	**Description**
`.com`	Commercial organizations.
`.edu`	Educational institutions such as four-year colleges and universities.
`.gov`	Government agencies, primarily of the U.S. federal government.
`.mil`	U.S. military organizations and sites.
`.net`	Internet service providers and other network-related organizations (note that some ISPs also use `.com`).
`.org`	Nonprofit organizations and others that do not fit into other categories.
`.int`	International organizations.
`.xx`	Two-letter country codes that indicate the location of the organization. (For example, `.fr` is for France, `.au` is for Australia, and `.jp` is for Japan.)

For your information, although there is the option to use `.us`, most organizations within the United States use one of the *three-letter domains*. The Internet was built primarily by U.S. organizations and agencies, and they developed and used the three-letter domains used today. As the Internet expanded to other nations, the *two-letter country domains* came into being. Some nations have taken to using the U.S. domains inside their country's domain, such as `.com.au` or `.edu.au` for Australian domains.

Allocation of domain names for the United States and much of the world was previously handled by an organization called the *InterNIC* (`http://www.internic.net/`). This organization, which also allocated IP addresses, was operated under contract to the U.S. government by a private company. Today, this whole process is changing with a new organization, the *Internet Corporation for Assigned Names and Numbers (ICANN)*, `http://www.icann.org/`, in charge of IP and domain name allocation and management. ICANN is opening the registration process to multiple registrars and also expanding the list of top-level domains. This process has been controversial and will undoubtedly continue to be so for some time. Visit the ICANN Web page and the Web page for the Internet Society (`http://www.isoc.org/`) for more information.

To obtain a domain name, you determine which top-level domain is appropriate for your organization and then attempt to find a name not already in use by someone else. This is the real struggle of the DNS world and has created no end of legal suits involving trademarks, copyrights, and so on. Because there can be only *one* user of a domain name, organizations in different industries with similar names or initials can't have the same domain name.

For your information, the problem of having a single user for each of the limited number of domain names affected one of the sponsors of this book; Productivity Point International would have liked to use the domain `ppi.com`. However, that domain was already obtained by a pharmaceutical company (whose initials are also *PPI*) when Productivity Point International wanted to connect to the Internet. As a result, Productivity Point International had to obtain the domains `propoint.com` and `productivitypoint.com`.

After you obtain a domain name, you or your ISP must operate a *DNS server* that will answer requests from other Internet sites for information about your domain. You are responsible for establishing names such as `www.yourcompany.domain` and pointing those names to valid IP addresses.

Key Concept

The *domain name service (DNS)* is a system that translates *domain names* to IP addresses and allows people to interact with Internet services such as the Web using text names instead of numbers.

Microsoft Windows NT Server 4.0 now includes a DNS server that you can use on your network.

Connecting to the Internet

The process of connecting your network to the Internet involves several steps:

1. Determine which ISP you will use for your connection.
2. Obtain a valid range of IP addresses from your ISP.
3. Convert your network to use TCP/IP with the new addresses.
4. Install the required hardware and activate the connection.

Choosing an Internet Service Provider

Choosing an ISP can be a difficult decision. ISPs range from huge telecommunication companies to small "mom-and-pop" operations. They vary widely in services offered, support options, and pricing.

Important questions to ask a prospective ISP include

- *Technical support*—No matter what the marketing people might say, no LAN connection to the Internet is as simple as connecting your network to a phone jack in the wall. What type of support will the ISP offer for installation? Will the company send someone out to help? Is there a support center—sometimes called a *Network Information Center (NIC)* or *Network Operations Center (NOC)*—with full-time staff? Is someone available 24 hours a day, seven days a week?

- *Redundancy*—How are they connected to other ISPs? Do they have only one line connecting them to a larger provider? Do they have multiple lines? What are their provisions for outages?

- *Proximity to the backbone*—The largest ISPs operate their own global *backbones*, which consist of extremely high-speed communication lines. Most other ISPs ultimately buy connections from these large ISPs. How close is your ISP to these backbones? Is it leasing lines directly from one of the large ISPs? Or is it several connections removed from the backbones? If you're looking for just an email connection, the difference might not matter much. If you are going to be a heavy user of the Web, either as a reader or publisher, the distance from the backbones can significantly affect the speed at which you can access Internet services. You will, however, normally pay much more as you get closer to the backbone.

- *Security*—What kind of security protection can they offer? Some ISPs will establish firewalls for you. Some will monitor your site. Others are just selling you a connection.

- *Services*—What type of services will they offer? Will they host Web pages for you? Will they operate a mail server? Will they provide newsgroup access?

- *IP addressing*—How many IP addresses can your ISP provide you? Can it allocate enough addresses for all your computers? Or is it only willing to give you a few addresses?

- *Domain names and DNS*—Will the ISP obtain a domain name (described in more detail later) for you? Will the ISP operate a DNS name server to support that domain?

- *Connection equipment*—Will your ISP provide the necessary connection equipment (routers, CSU/DSUs) for you? Will it lease them to you? Will it require you to buy them? If so, can it offer you competitive pricing?

You have to decide what type of connection you need. Is your Internet connection going to be a mission-critical part of your communication infrastructure? Do you require that it be guaranteed operational at all times? Are you going to rely heavily on your connection for sales and marketing? Or is your connection going to be more of an experimental tool for research and development? Is it something only a few people in your organization will be using? Or will it be part of everyone's workplace?

All these questions must be addressed before you can make the right choice of an ISP for your organization.

Obtaining a Valid Range of IP Addresses and a Domain Name

When you are using the TCP/IP protocol suite on your own internal network, you can use any block of IP addresses. However, after you connect your network to the Internet, you must use a range of IP addresses that no one else in the entire Internet is using.

Think about this in terms of the telephone system. Every phone number is unique. When you dial 603-471-0848, you contact a specific location in the United States. If you are outside the United States, you must prefix this phone number with a country code. This combination of country codes and phone numbers provides an individual "address" of every telephone on the planet. It has to work this way, or else calls wouldn't go through.

Likewise, in the world of the Internet, every computer must have a unique IP address. Similar to a telephone number, this address will identify your computer to the rest of the world as you use services on the Internet.

After you have chosen an ISP, you must obtain a range of IP addresses, from the ISP, for the machines on your network. Most ISPs have been assigned a block of addresses by the InterNIC, the organization that currently handles assignment of IP addresses and domain names. When you receive your address range, you must ensure that all computers in your organization that will be accessing the Internet are using TCP/IP with these new addresses. If you do not use valid addresses, your computers cannot communicate with other Internet sites.

If your ISP can provide you with only a few IP addresses (or a single IP address), you can use a proxy server (mentioned later in the chapter) to hide your entire organization essentially behind a single IP address. However, on your internal network, it is extremely important that you use a range of addresses that are unassigned elsewhere on the Internet. For this purpose, the InterNIC has permanently set aside three blocks of IP addresses: the entire class A address 10.0.0.0, the entire class B address 192.168.0.0, and a range of class B addresses from 172.16.0.0 to 172.131.255.255. These are the only IP addresses you should use on your internal network. See RFC 1918 for more information (http://www.isi.edu/in-notes/rfc1918.txt).

Your ISP can also work with you to obtain a valid *domain name* for your organization. This name, such as microsoft.com, will identify you to the outside world for both your email addressing and your Internet publishing efforts (Web sites, FTP servers, and so on). As mentioned in the preceding section, someone—either you or your ISP—will have to provide DNS name service for this domain name. After that is set, you're ready to go.

Activating the Connection

Finally, activating the connection is no different than what was discussed in Chapter 13, "Creating Larger Networks," and Chapter 14, "Wide Area Networks (WANs)." An Internet connection is nothing more than a TCP/IP WAN connection between your network and your ISP's network. You must have the necessary equipment (usually a router and CSU/DSUs), have your local telephone company install the local connection, and have your ISP activate its connection to you.

Again, note that when your ISP activates your connection to the Internet, you *must* be using valid IP addresses, or you will be unable to communicate with other sites on the Internet.

Security and the Internet

Security on the Internet is a topic that could easily occupy several books by itself. There *are* definite issues that must be addressed before you connect to the Internet. After you make the final connection to your ISP, your TCP/IP packets can flow out to sites anywhere on the global Internet. Of course, this means that TCP/IP packets from the rest of the Internet can also flow into *your* network.

With careful preparation and planning, the threat to your network can be reduced, although never completely eliminated. Whether for "fun" or for corporate espionage, some users on the Internet are constantly finding new ways to break into systems. The only network completely secure from Internet intruders is a network that, well, *isn't* connected to the Internet.

Barriers protecting you from intruders are commonly referred to as firewalls. A *firewall* is usually a series of hardware devices and software programs that restrict access to your network. Some firewalls are implemented using only hardware devices. Others are based primarily in software programs. The best firewalls combine elements of both.

Typically, firewalls involve a number of components. A couple of these are so common that they bear mentioning here.

Key Concept

A *firewall* is software and hardware that act as a barrier to protect your network from outside intruders when you are connected to a larger network (such as the Internet).

Packet-Filtering Routers

Most routers today allow you to filter TCP/IP packets as they approach your network. Operating at the network layer of the OSI Model, these routers deny access to your network for packets from specific sites. They allow access to only certain services (such as your Web servers) or certain computers on your network (such as your mail server). All attempts to connect to other computers in your network will be denied. Although not a bullet-proof defense, such routers do provide a strong first line of defense.

Proxy Servers

When you connect on the Internet to a Web server, that Web server records certain information about your visit, such as the IP address of your computer, the type of browser you are using, and the time of your visit. As shown in Figure 15.6, when users in your organization visit Web servers, those servers accumulate addressing data about your organization. It is possible that sophisticated users could then use those addresses to attempt to break into your network.

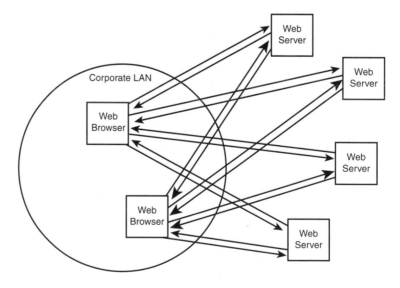

Figure 15.6
Without a proxy server, all users connect directly to Web sites.

A *proxy server* is a software program that reduces this break-in threat. Once installed, when a user seeks to retrieve a page from the Web, his or her browser will first connect to the proxy server, which will then retrieve the actual page and return it to the user. As depicted in Figure 15.7, the result of this is that Web servers on the Internet record only the address of the proxy server. They won't know the addresses of the actual computers requesting the pages. Usually, the proxy server operates on a computer that has been rein-forced with additional firewall software to make it difficult to penetrate.

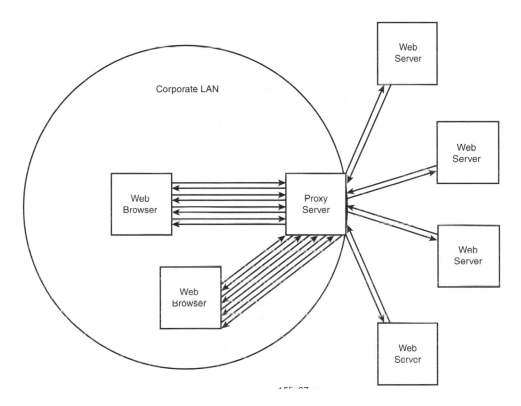

Figure 15.7
When using a proxy server, all users connect to Web sites by first going through the proxy server.

Proxy servers are also used to log information about what Web sites your users are visit-ing, as well as to restrict access to specific sites. These servers can also cache frequently requested pages to a local disk so that future requests will be quickly fulfilled.

Summary

Originating from Cold War military research, the Internet today is a global communication medium. It is essentially a huge TCP/IP wide area network that consists of many interconnected networks of Internet service providers. Once connected to the Internet, you have access to numerous services, including the World Wide Web, electronic mail, FTP, and newsgroups.

All communication on the Internet occurs between computers using IP addresses. However, to aid in remembering addresses, the *domain name system (DNS)* was created. DNS enables us to associate a *domain name* with an IP address and use meaningful names for communication purposes.

To connect to the Internet, you must arrange for a connection with an *Internet service provider (ISP)*. Many types of ISPs exist, and the choice for your organization can be a difficult one. After you have chosen an ISP, you must obtain a range of valid IP addresses and a domain name.

Before you finally activate your Internet connection, you must consider security issues and configure some type of firewall to protect your network from Internet intruders.

QUESTIONS AND ANSWERS

1. What are some of the services available on the Internet?

    A: Multiple possible answers: email, Web, FTP, Gopher, Telnet, Chat, and newsgroups

2. What is the protocol used for the Web, and what does it stand for?

    A: HTTP (Hypertext Transfer Protocol)

3. What is NNTP used for on the Internet?

    A: Newsgroups (also called *USENET*)

4. What does the `telnet` command allow you to do?

    A: `telnet` allows you to log in to a remote host running a Telnet server.

5. Differentiate between a DNS domain name and a Windows NT Server domain.

    A: A DNS domain name identifies you or your organization to others on the Internet and maps your names, such as `www.propoint.com`, to your Web or email servers. A Windows NT Server domain is a collection of computers using centralized user-level security.

...continues

...continued

---

6. At its core, what does DNS do?

A: Essentially, DNS translates human-friendly text names to computer-friendly IP addresses.

7. What is a firewall?

A: A firewall is software and hardware that act as a barrier to protect your network from outside intruders when you are connected to a larger network (such as the Internet).

8. How does a proxy server protect your organization?

A: A proxy server can be part of a firewall solution by being the only point of contact between your network and the Web servers on the Internet. The proxy server retrieves Web pages on behalf of all those computers behind it on your network. The external Web servers learn only the IP address of your proxy server and can try to crack only into that machine (which is usually also hardened against attack by other software and hardware).

PRACTICE TEST

1. FTP operates at what level of the OSI Reference Model?

a. Transport
b. Network
c. Presentation
d. Application

Answers a, b, and c are incorrect. **Answer d is correct; FTP operates at the application layer.**

2. The Internet uses which protocol for communication?

a. IPX/SPX
b. TCP/IP
c. NetBEUI
d. DLC

Answer a is incorrect because IPX/SPX is used in NetWare networks. **Answer b is correct; the Internet uses TCP/IP for communication.** Answer c is incorrect because NetBEUI is used in very small Microsoft networks. Answer d is incorrect because DLC is used to communicate with some network printers and mainframes.

3. A security barrier that prevents intruders on the Internet from penetrating your network is referred to as a what?

 a. Bastion
 b. Proxy server
 c. Firewall
 d. SecureID

Answer a is incorrect. Answer b is incorrect because a proxy server is *part* of a firewall solution. **Answer c is correct.** Answer d is incorrect because SecureID can be part of a firewall.

4. The system for translating alphanumeric names into numerical addresses for use on the Internet is known as what?

 a. DNS
 b. WINS
 c. HTTP
 d. InterNIC

Answer a is correct; the domain name system maps text names into IP addresses. Answer b is incorrect because WINS maps NetBIOS names into IP addresses. Answer c is incorrect because HTTP is used by Web applications. Answer d is incorrect because InterNIC is the organization that previously handled the administration of DNS names.

5. You want to connect your organization to the Internet. You are very concerned about security threats, but your LAN users are clamoring for access to the Web. You decide to install a _____ to provide Web access while reducing security threats.

 a. Firewall server
 b. DNS server
 c. HTTP server
 d. Proxy server

Answer a is incorrect because the term *firewall* is generically used to refer to the entire security solution, but does not specifically address this type of Web access. Answer b is incorrect because a DNS server does nothing with Web pages. Answer c is incorrect because an HTTP server (that is, a Web server) publishes pages, but does nothing about giving external access to internal users. **Answer d is correct.**

6. Which of the following are Internet services? (Choose all that apply.)

  a. Gopher

  b. MHS

  c. FTP

  d. Telnet

Answer a is correct. Answer b is incorrect because MHS is an email protocol used on some Novell NetWare networks. **Answer c is correct. Answer d is correct.**

7. Every computer on the Internet must have a unique IP address.

  a. True

  b. False

Answer a is correct. Answer b is incorrect.

8. Which protocols are used for the sending and receiving of electronic mail on the Internet? (Choose all that apply.)

  a. DNS

  b. SMTP

  c. HTTP

  d. POP3

Answer a is incorrect because DNS is not directly used for transferring email (although mail transfer programs *do* use DNS to look up the IP address of the destination host). **Answer b is correct; SMTP is used for delivery of email.** Answer c is incorrect because HTTP is used for Web applications. **Answer d is correct; POP3 is used for retrieval of email.**

9. Which Internet service provides forum areas where people can discuss different topics?

  a. Gopher

  b. Newsgroups

  c. Telnet

  d. RealAudio

Answer a is incorrect. **Answer b is correct; Usenet newsgroups are discussion groups.** Answer c is incorrect. Answer d is incorrect.

10. Which of the following are protocols functioning at the application layer of the OSI Reference Model? (Choose all that apply.)

    a. SMTP

    b. IP

    c. HTTP

    d. TCP

Answer a is correct; SMTP operates at the application layer. Answer b is incorrect because IP operates at the network layer. **Answer c is correct; HTTP operates at the application layer.** Answer d is incorrect because TCP operates at the transport layer.

Network Administration

WHILE YOU READ

1. What is the difference between a domain and a workgroup?

2. Explain the roles of a PDC and a BDC.

3. Identify the security problem regarding user accounts on a Windows 95/98 computer.

4. True or False. A Windows NT domain implements peer-to-peer networking.

5. What is the name of the user account in Windows NT that gives you privileges to create users and perform system tasks?

6. True or False. In Windows NT 4.0, the guest account is enabled by default.

7. Why do we use group accounts?

8. What is the name of the tool used in Windows NT to administer users and groups?

9. Explain the difference between share-level and user-level security.

10. What role does auditing play in providing security?

Administering a Network

Once you have installed and initially configured the network, your work with the network has only just begun. There will be constant adjustments to the network as new users are added. New printers will need to be configured and shared. Disk drives on file servers will fill up and require reorganization. Computers will fail and data will need to be restored. Network bottlenecks will develop. Users will leave your organization, and their accounts will need to be removed.

Network administrators are responsible for managing the network and resolving these types of problems. As a network administrator, you are responsible for maintaining the successful operations of your network. (And when the network fails for some reason, guess who gets the irate phone calls?)

When you serve as a network administrator, your responsibilities can be broadly defined as

- Creating network resources
- Managing existing network resources
- Securing the network from unauthorized access
- Protecting the network from failures
- Maintaining the network

Earlier in the book, you learned the basics of managing network resources such as shared folders and printers. This chapter discusses creating and managing user accounts. You also learn about network security and how to assign access permissions to network resources.

First, however, you need to understand the context in which you will be performing network administration. Within Microsoft networks, you will be working within either a *domain* or *workgroup*. The tools you use vary slightly depending on the environment in which you work.

Domains and Workgroups

A domain or workgroup provides a mechanism to logically group a collection of computers together. For instance, imagine you have 200 computers on your network, but your sales group consists of only 10 of those 200 computers. If all the computers are in one large group, each time a sales representative wants to access information from another computer within the sales department, he or she must spend time browsing through the list of 200 computers to find the specific computer desired.

Instead, you could organize the 10 computers in the sales department into a workgroup or domain called SALES. Now, when a sales representative wants to access information from another computer, he or she will first see only the other computers in the SALES workgroup or domain. If the sales representative wants to access a computer from outside of the sales group, he or she could do so, but it would involve an extra step of browsing another workgroup or domain.

There can be multiple domains or workgroups on the same physical LAN. For instance, you might have domains or workgroups such as SALES, MARKETING, RESEARCH, IS, ACCOUNTING, and TRAINING. Each domain or workgroup provides a logical grouping of computers, and each can provide its own security and user context. When you connect your computer to a network, you have the choice of having your computer join either a workgroup or a domain, as shown in Figure 16.1. A computer cannot be a member of multiple workgroups or domains, nor can it be a member of a workgroup and also a domain. A computer can only be a member of one logical grouping.

Key Concept

A computer can be a member of either a *domain* or *workgroup*, but cannot be a member of both simultaneously.

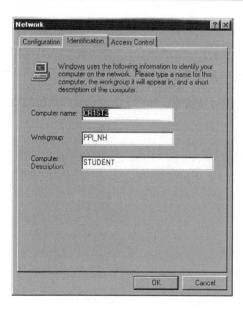

Figure 16.1
Windows 95/98 Network Properties allows a user to join either a domain or a workgroup through entries in the Network dialog box.

As to the difference between workgroups and domains, recall the discussion in Chapter 2 where you learned about peer-to-peer and server-based networks. Within networks using Microsoft operating systems, a workgroup implements peer-to-peer networking, while a domain implements server-based networking.

In a workgroup, each computer is responsible for maintaining its own list of users and security settings. Users are added to the account database on each individual computer on the network. If you work on several different machines, you need to set up your account on each computer.

When you want to access information from another computer in the workgroup, the operator of that computer must give you permission to do so. This permission may come in the form of requiring a password (Windows 95/98, Windows for Workgroups) or setting permissions for your user name (Windows NT). Server computers may be installed into a workgroup, but the servers, too, must handle their own security and access permissions.

Key Concept

A *workgroup* is a collection of computers where each computer maintains its own user list and security settings.

On the other hand, domains are implemented using Windows NT Server and provide a server-based mechanism for central control of user accounts and access permissions. A Windows NT Server computer, called a *primary domain controller (PDC)*, provides a central repository of all user information. When a user wants to log on to a computer, his user name is checked against the PDC's master user list. Once on the network, any requests for network resources are again checked against the central user list.

Realize that while the PDC maintains the master list of users and permissions, it may be supported by one or more *backup domain controllers (BDCs)*. The BDCs provide the same functions as the PDC and can authenticate users when the PDC is either too busy or in case the PDC computer fails.

Within a workgroup, a user is added to each individual computer, whereas within a domain each user is added to the PDC's master user list. Once added, that username is available for use on computers throughout the domain (provided that the user has permission to log on to a specific machine). When domain users share folders or printers, permissions are assigned to domain users and groups, rather than locally created users as they are in workgroups.

When speaking about domains, you will hear mention of establishing *trusts* between domains. A trust is a relationship where one domain allows users from another domain to access network resources within the first domain.

Key Concept

A Windows NT domain is a collection of computers with a central database of user accounts. This account database is maintained by a *Primary Domain Controller (PDC),* which might be assisted by one or more *Backup Domain Controllers (BDCs).*

Note that the workgroup security settings vary according to operating system. In Windows NT, you will create an actual local-user account for each user. However, in Windows 95/98, you do not actually create a user account, but rather a *user profile* that keeps track of the user's preferences and password.

The difference is that Windows NT user accounts can only be created by someone with administrative privileges and provide a strong level of security, while Windows 95/98 user profiles can be created by anyone who sits down at the Windows 95/98 machine. If a user has not logged on previously on a Windows 95/98 computer, he or she can enter a user-name and password in the logon window. At that point, a new user profile will be created. With this arrangement, Windows 95/98 provides essentially no security in that anyone can log on to any Windows 95/98 machine. Note that if the Windows 95/98 computer is part of an NT domain, someone will have to have a valid username to log on, but the person can click Cancel on the Windows 95/98 Logon dialog box and have full access to the local computer (but not to the network).

So which model should you use? Workgroups are fine for small installations (perhaps 10 computers or smaller) where security issues are not a major concern and there is limited support staff. However, because administration increases as more users want to access network resources, a domain is the natural choice for larger networks due to its centralized administration. (Return to the section, "Types of Networks" in Chapter 2, for more details on the advantages and disadvantages of peer-to-peer versus server-based networks.)

Creating Users and Groups

Within a network operating system, users are identified by a user name and, in most instances, need to enter a password to gain access to the network. Additionally, user accounts typically can be assigned to group accounts for purposes of assigning access permissions.

User Accounts

User accounts in a network operating system are typically created by a network administrator. The administrator can establish the following information with a user account:

- *Username.* Often, a short name used for login purposes.
- *Password.* A word with some combination of letters, numbers, and symbols.
- *Full name.* A name that is displayed in listings of users.
- *Description.* A description of the user's role in the organization (for example, Training or Sales).
- *Home directory.* Default location for the user to save files.
- *Login scripts.* Scripts executed whenever the user logs on (for example, to establish connections to network resources).

Exactly how an administrator configures these options and whether all these options are available depends on the network operating system in use. Some operating systems, such as Windows NT, also allow the administrator to specify such items as when the user is allowed to log in and when the account will expire and be unusable (often used for temporary workers).

In most operating systems today, users' accounts are established through some type of graphical interface, with the exception of a few special accounts that are pre-installed on the computer.

Special User Accounts

Within each network operating system, there is usually a user account identified as the *administrator* for a particular computer. This account is referred to as Administrator in Windows NT, Supervisor in Novell NetWare, and root in most UNIX/Linux operating systems. Often, this account and password are established at the time that the operating system is installed on the computer. In many operating systems, this administrator account is the account that must be used to establish the first user accounts on a computer. The administrator account can also assign *administrative privileges* to other user accounts.

Key Concept

Most operating systems have a preinstalled user account that has special administrative privileges such as the capability to create other user accounts. In Windows NT Server, this account is called Administrator.

Another special account created by default is a *guest account*. The guest account, often called Guest, allows users to log on to a computer with no password or a simple password. Guest users are usually restricted to minimal access to computer resources. Note that within Windows NT Server 4.0, the guest account is disabled by default. (In Windows NT 3.51, the guest account is enabled by default.)

Adding User Accounts

In operating systems using Microsoft operating systems, there are two mechanisms for adding users to a computer. Windows for Workgroups and Windows 95/98 provide an insecure method for adding users, whereas Windows NT uses a more secure method.

When using Windows for Workgroups or Windows 95/98, a user's account is established during the first time that the user logs on to the computer. After the user enters a username and password, the user is asked to confirm the password. At this point, the user's account is now established on the computer; no further information about the user, such as a description, can be entered.

If the Windows 95/98 or Windows for Workgroups computer is configured to be part of a domain, the user's account and password will be authenticated by a domain controller. If the user's name and password are verified as correct, the user will then have full access to both local and network resources. If the authentication fails, the user will not be able to access network resources, but *will* be able to access resources on the local computer.

In contrast, a user's account on a Windows NT computer must be established prior to the user attempting to log on. When a user logs on to a Windows NT computer, the account information is authenticated using either the local account database or the domain controller's database (if the computer is part of a domain). The user account must exist in the account database or the user will be unable to use the computer.

How you add users to a Windows NT machine will vary depending on your network configuration. If the computer is part of a workgroup, you will use the standard User Manager window to add users to the local account database. If the computer is part of a domain, the user will need to be added to the domain account database using the User Manager for Domains shown in Figure 16.2. Additionally, the domain account database can only be modified from the PDC, BDC, or another computer with the domain management software installed.

CH
16

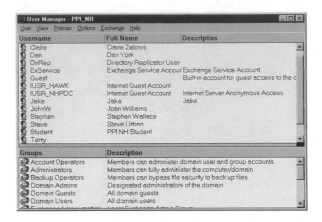

Figure 16.2
The Windows NT User Manager for Domains dialog box allows an administrator to create user accounts.

A username within Windows NT can consist of up to 20 characters using any combination of letters, numbers, or symbols, except for the following:

" / \ : ; ¦ = + * < >

Windows NT also allows the administrator to control additional settings about the user account, as shown in Figure 16.3. Beyond some password control options, the administrator can configure options controlling logon times, dial-in privileges (to access the network remotely), and to what groups the user account belongs (discussed later in the section, "Group Accounts").

Modifying User Accounts

After an account has been created, there may be a need to go back and modify certain settings. For instance, a user's name could change after a marriage or the user might move to a different department and need an updated description field. Most network operating systems allow an administrator to modify user accounts using the same interface used to add user accounts. Within Windows NT, administrators can use the User Manager (or User Manager for Domains) to modify information about user accounts.

As Windows 95/98 and Windows for Workgroups do not really have the concept of a user database, about the only item that can be changed is the user account's password. For that, a user needs to log in with the current password, go to the Control Panel, and use the Passwords Control Panel.

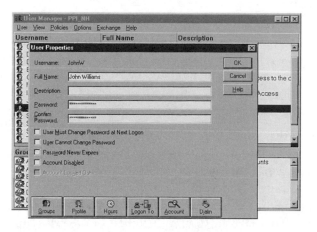

Figure 16.3
Administrators in Windows NT can configure settings for user accounts through the User Properties dialog box.

Deleting User Accounts

Occasionally, user accounts need to be deleted. For instance, full-time employees might leave the organization or contract employees may reach the end of their contract. To delete a user account, you need to return to the interface used to create users. Within Windows NT, an administrator enters into the appropriate User Manager (refer to Figure 16.2), selects the user's account, and presses the Delete key. After a confirmation dialog box appears, that user account is permanently deleted from the account database.

When thinking about deleting a user account in Windows NT, consider that NT user accounts are actually mapped to an underlying unique *security identification number (SID)* created when the user account is established. All file permissions and ownership are in fact assigned to the SID rather than the user name. If you accidentally delete a user account and then attempt to re-create a user account with the same name, the new account will have a different SID and, by default, will not have the same group memberships or access permissions as the original account. For this reason, deleting a user account in Windows NT should be carefully considered.

Some operating systems, such as Windows NT and many UNIX/Linux variants, allow the administrator to disable a user account. The account is not actually deleted, but it can no longer be used to log on to the network. Within Windows NT, an account can be disabled using the User Manager or User Manager for Domains.

Group Accounts

When you want to grant access to a network resource to a number of users, most network operating systems allow you to grant access to each individual user account. However, as the number of users increases, this method of access control becomes cumbersome. Instead, many network operating systems allow you to create group accounts, add users to the group account, and then assign permissions to the group account itself.

For example, imagine that your human resources department needs to restrict access to only HR personnel to a series of folders on a file server. If your HR department had 10 users, you could grant access for each of the folders to each user account. However, if a user left the HR department, you would need to go to each of the folders and remove that user's account name from the access list. With group accounts, you could create a group account called HR, make all 10 users members of the HR group, and then assign access permission for each folder to the HR group. Now when a user leaves, you simply remove the user's name from membership in the HR group, and the user will no longer be able to access the HR folder.

Most operating systems allow you to create groups subject to the same restrictions on naming as groups. Additionally, a user account can typically be included in multiple group accounts.

Within Microsoft operating systems, only Windows NT allows you to create groups for users. If Windows 95/98 and Windows for Workgroups computers are part of a domain, they can assign permissions to groups. However, groups cannot be created on a stand-alone Windows 95/98 or Windows for Workgroups machine.

Inside Windows NT, creating a group account occurs in the same manner as creating a user account. As shown in Figure 16.4, the Windows NT User Manager (or User Manager for Domains) is used to create groups. You simply create a group account and then add the appropriate users to the group.

When operating inside of a domain, Windows NT allows for the creation of local and global groups. *Local groups* are only accessible on the computer on which the group is defined. For instance, if you created a local group called Staff on a computer called ServerA, you could then assign access permissions for the Staff group to any folder or printer connected to ServerA. However, when you go to assign access permissions to folders on another computer called ServerB, the Staff group will not be defined. You would need to create a Staff local group on ServerB and assign the appropriate people to the new group.

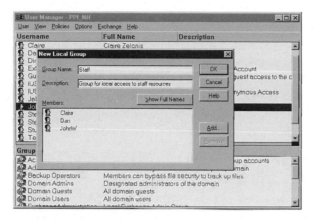

Figure 16.4
In Windows NT, the User Manager can also create groups through the New Local Group dialog box.

On the other hand, *global groups* are visible to all computers within a domain. If you created a Staff global group on a domain controller and added the appropriate users, that group would now be visible to all computers. You could assign access permissions for folders on both ServerA and ServerB to the Staff global group.

Windows NT also includes a number of built-in groups, such as Administrators, Power Users, Users, and Account Operators, that are preconfigured with appropriate levels of access to system resources.

Group accounts can usually be modified in a similar manner to user accounts. Windows NT allows group accounts to be renamed or deleted using the standard User Manager (or User Manager for Domains).

Key Concept

Group accounts provide an easy way for an administrator to simultaneously assign permissions or user rights to a number of users. The permissions are assigned to the group account and as users are added to that group, they gain the group's level of permissions.

Network Security

The issue of protecting network resources can be one of the most crucial roles of the network administrator. Network security involves not only protecting your network from external intruders, but also protecting sensitive data within your network from other network users. Additionally, there are some resources needed for network operations that you need to protect from intentional or unintentional damage. Your role as a network administrator in protecting network resources can be defined as

- Creating a security policy for your organization
- Assigning appropriate access permissions to network resources
- Monitoring (auditing) enforcement of your security policy and permission settings

Security Policies

The first part of protecting your network involves establishing what you will allow your users to do. A well-planned security policy will address such questions as

- Will users be able to change passwords? If not, how will passwords be assigned?
- What type of passwords can users use? Can they use a common word, or does it have to include a number or symbol?
- Will passwords expire, forcing users to change their password? If so, how often?
- When changing passwords, will you let users use a password they have used before? Will they need to provide a different password each time they change their password?
- How long must a password be? Will you permit blank passwords?
- What times will users be able to log on to the network? Will users be able to log on after regular work hours?
- Will the Guest account be enabled on your network?
- If you have dial-in modem lines, who will be able to dial in, and when? Will users be able to connect in from any phone line, or will your system call them back at a specific phone number?
- Will data encryption be used to protect any information?
- Which user accounts will be included in which group accounts? Who will be able to perform administrative tasks and at what level will they be able to work?
- Who will be allowed to log on to special computers such as servers? Who will be able to perform administrative tasks such as backing up data or configuring printers?

- Will users be allowed to copy files from floppy disks onto the server, or will each file need to be scanned for viruses first?

Your security policy will depend largely on the sensitivity of your data, the size of your network, the number of external connections (such as dial-in or Internet connections), and the resources you have available, as well as your personal level of paranoia about security issues. A good security policy should strike a balance between the need for a secure network and the need for users to be productive. Extremely secure networks can add extra steps to the tasks users need to accomplish, while networks allowing users to do anything can wind up with little or no security.

Some network operating systems provide tools to help administrators establish and enforce security policies. For example, Windows NT allows administrators to establish policies regarding password length and expiration. Administrators can also lock out users after repeated logon failures. In Windows NT, open the User Manager (see Figure 16.5) and choose Account from the Policies menu.

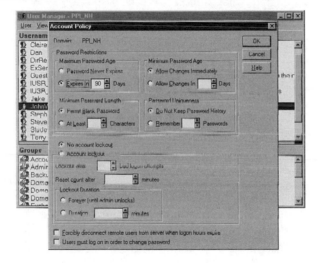

Figure 16.5
The Windows NT Account Policy dialog box permits the administrator to establish a security policy regarding passwords.

Additionally, as shown in Figure 16.6, Windows NT allows an administrator to assign rights to perform system actions to user or group accounts. For instance, domain controllers allow users to access their shared resources across the network. However, by default, local access (physically sitting at the domain controller and logging on locally) is limited to the Administrators group. (To assign user rights in Windows NT, open the User Manager and choose User Rights from the Policies menu.)

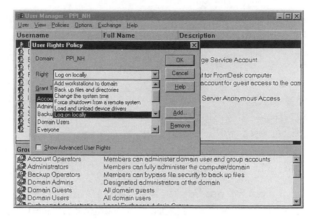

Figure 16.6
The User Manager in Windows NT also allows administrators to assign system rights to users through the User Rights Policy dialog box.

Access Permissions

After you have created users and groups and have established a security policy, you need to assign appropriate permissions to network resources. There are two primary models for assigning access permissions:

- Share-level security
- User-level security

Share-Level Security

In *share-level security* (also referred to as *password-protected shares*), a password is assigned to each individual network resource. If a user knows the password, the user can use the resource. Share-level security is typically found in small (10 users or less) peer-to-peer networks, such as those using only Windows for Workgroups or Windows 95/98. Many networks implement share-level security because it is easy and inexpensive. In environments with Microsoft operating systems such as Windows 95/98, nothing is needed beyond the basic operating system. Additionally, as each user can be in complete control of his resources, a central network administration staff may not be necessary.

However, as more users are added to the network, users may need to remember several different passwords to access shared resources. Additionally, if a user should no longer have access to a network resource, a new password must be created and distributed to all users who should have access to the shared resource.

Some network operating systems provide varying degrees of share-level security. For instance, Windows 95/98 allows users to assign the following types of security to a folder:

- *Read-Only.* Users who know the password may view and copy files in the folder, but may not modify any of the original documents.

- *Full.* Users who know the password have full control over all the files in the folder and can add, delete, or modify any files.

- *Depends on Password.* Two passwords are set for the shared folder. If users know the Full password, they will have full control. If they know the Read-Only password, they will have read-only access.

The dialog box that permits assignment of these different types of share-level security is shown in Figure 16.7. Note that Windows 95/98 allows the password field to be left blank, allowing all users to access the shared folder with the specified type of security. For instance, if the type of permission is set to Full but the password field is left blank, all network users will have full access to the shared folder.

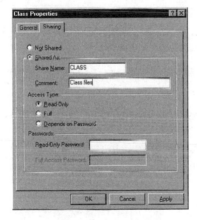

Figure 16.7
The Windows 95/98 Class Properties dialog box allows users to assign different types of share-level security.

Key Concept

In a network using share-level security, there is no central user authentication and control. A resource can be assigned a password at the time it is shared to the network. While users have complete local control, users need to know the password for each individual shared resource they want to access. Windows 95/98 and Windows for Workgroups can use share-level security when not part of a Windows NT Server domain.

User-Level Security

In contrast to share-level security, access permissions in *user-level security* are assigned on a per-user basis. Users log on to the network using one username and password. When users attempt to connect to a network resource, their username and password are checked against a master database. If approved, users are granted the type of access that they have been assigned.

User-level security is usually preferred in large networks because users do not have to remember any passwords beyond their logon password. Users simply log on and start using the network resources to which they have permission. User-level security is also considered more secure because users are less apt to widely distribute their primary logon password and, with only one password to remember, users are less apt to write down their passwords in prominent places.

Additionally, administration of multiple shared resources is much simpler than in share-level security. Network resources are assigned permissions for each user account or for a group account. When a user should no longer have access to a share resource, the user's account is removed from the permission list for the resource.

One major difference from share-level security is that network resource permissions are set by administrators or other users with administrative privileges. Most network users do not have the ability to set permissions or even to share folders or printers with other network users.

Finally, systems using user-level security normally provide more types of access control than share-level security. For instance, while Windows 95/98 provides essentially three types of access control (No Access, Read-Only, Full), Windows NT provides seven types of access controls, as shown in Table 16.1. These permissions may be combined to give specific access control permissions to a user.

Table 16.1   File/Folder Access Permissions in Windows NT

Permission	Description
Read (R)	The user can view and copy files in the folder.
Write (W)	The user can modify files in the folder.
Execute (X)	The user may execute (run) programs in the folder.
Delete (D)	The user may delete files in the folder.
Change Permission (P)	The user may change the permissions on files.
Take Ownership (O)	The user may take ownership of files.
No Access	The user does not have permission to access any files or even to view the folder contents.

When sharing files, Windows NT combines these access permissions to provide four types of user-level security:

- *No Access.* Users have no access to a shared resource.
- *Read (RX).* Users may view or copy files and run applications.
- *Change (RWXD).* Users can view, modify, add, or delete files as well as run applications.
- *Full Control (RWXDOP).* Users have administrator privileges to access files in the folder.

Each type of access control can be applied to a specific user or to a group account, subject to user rights settings. Note that some of these permission settings depend on the type of disk file system used and other system policies within Windows NT. While a full discussion of Windows NT permission settings is beyond the scope of this book, Table 16.1 is provided here as an example.

User-level security does have a few disadvantages. For instance, because user-level security relies (in a domain environment) on domain controllers for user authentication, the failure of all domain controllers can leave users unable to log on to the network or access network resources. Additionally, users migrating to systems using user-level security from share-level security may be upset about their lack of control over sharing of resources and setting permissions.

Still, user-level security with its improved security, easier use of resources, and easier administration is the dominant model found in server-based network environments. Within Microsoft operating systems, user-level security is the prime model used in Windows NT (both for networked and standalone Windows NT computers) and can also be used within Windows 95/98 and Windows for Workgroups when they are part of a domain. Windows 95/98 computers can also implement user-level security by using the user account database on a standalone Windows NT computer that is not part of a domain.

Windows NT is different from Windows 95/98 and Windows for Workgroups in that it will *always* use user-level security on local resources. Even in a workgroup environment, Windows NT still applies user-level security to files, folders, and printers. A Windows NT computer can access resources on a Windows 95/98 computer using share-level security. However, that Windows 95/98 computer must use user-level security when accessing shared resources on the Windows NT computer. The implication of this is that when a Windows NT computer is added to a peer-to-peer network using share-level security, users cannot use a password to access resources on the Windows NT machine. Instead, each individual user must be added to the Windows NT computer's accounts database.

Key Concept

A network using *user-level security* contains a central server maintaining a listing of all user accounts and providing central authentication of users. On these networks, users normally need to only know their one password to log on to the network. After that, they are permitted to use whichever network resources for which they have been granted permission. Windows NT Server networks use user-level security.

Auditing

Another component of properly protecting your network is to audit security events on your computer. *Auditing* refers to the process of tracking activities of user accounts and other network events. An *audit log* can provide information about what users are doing on the system, who is trying to connect to the system, and what resources are being heavily used on the network. Audit logs can help an administrator track down unauthorized activity or determine that intruders are trying to penetrate the network.

Audit logs typically track such events as

- Success and failure of logon and logoff attempts
- Connections to network resources
- System shutdowns or restarts
- Changes to files or folders
- Password changes
- Addition or deletion of user or group accounts
- Permission changes to files or folders
- Opening or closing of files

As shown in Figure 16.8, some operating systems provide a graphical tool to view the data from audit logs. Additionally, the audit log data can be transferred to other applications where it can be filtered or charted.

Within Windows NT, you can enable auditing by choosing Audit from the Policies menu of the User Manager (or User Manager for Domains). As shown in Figure 16.9, you can configure which system events will be monitored. Once Auditing has been enabled, auditing messages and alerts can be viewed in the Security Log of the Windows NT Event Viewer.

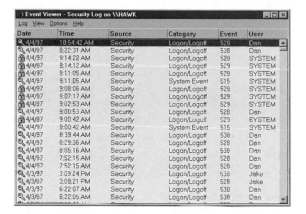

Figure 16.8

The Windows NT Event Viewer allows the administrator to view security audit logs.

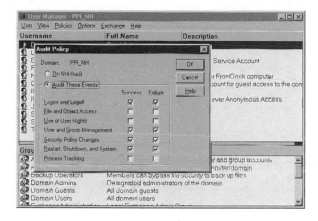

Figure 16.9

In the Audit Policy dialog box of the User Manager, you can specify which system events should be audited.

Key Concept

For the exam, familiarize yourself with the auditing process in Windows NT. Specifically, be familiar with the Audit These Events check box shown in Figure 16.9. Exam questions have been known to include checking this box as part of a procedure. (Questions have also left checking the box out of procedures to try to catch you!)

Summary

Once a network is installed, your role as network administrator is only just beginning. As the network continues to operate, you need to create new network resources, manage existing network resources, and secure the network from unauthorized access.

Much of network administration involves creating user accounts and assigning permissions to network resources. Within Microsoft operating systems, these duties can take place in the context of a workgroup or a domain. A workgroup is a logical collection of computers in a peer-to-peer network. A domain uses a server-based model where user account administration is handled from a central location.

Network administrators may often create user accounts through a graphical interface and include additional information about users in the user listing. Most network operating systems have special user accounts for allowing administrative access to the system and for providing guest access.

In systems using user-level security, you can also create group accounts to which you can assign permissions. Group accounts provide a mechanism for logically grouping users together when assigning permissions.

Another primary responsibility of the network administrator is network security. Network security involves establishing a security policy, assigning appropriate access permissions to network resources, and monitoring network events.

A good security policy balances the need for network security with the users' need to be productive. A security policy will include items such as password aging, login time limits, guest accounts, and administrative privileges. Some operating systems such as Windows NT provide a graphical tool for setting security policies.

When assigning access permission to network resources, there are two security models available. In share-level security, a password is assigned to each shared network resource. If a user knows the password, the user can access the resource. Each computer user is responsible for maintenance and security of his or her own computer. In user-level security, access is permitted on a per-user basis. When a user attempts to connect to a network resource, the user's name and password are checked against a central database.

Finally, part of network security involves using auditing programs to monitor the connections to the computer and the use of shared resources. Audit logs can provide a means of determining if unauthorized access to your network is occurring.

QUESTIONS AND ANSWERS

1. What is the difference between a domain and a workgroup?

   A: A workgroup is a collection of computers with no shared account database. A domain is a collection of computers using a shared central database of user and group accounts.

2. Explain the roles of a PDC and a BDC.

   A: The Primary Domain Controller (PDC) maintains the master copy of all NT domain user account information. The PDC sends this information to the Backup Domain Controller (BDC). The BDC can share the load of authenticating users with the PDC and also serves as a backup should the PDC go down. There can be multiple BDCs on a network but only one PDC.

3. Identify the security problem regarding user accounts on a Windows 95/98 computer.

   A: If a Windows 95/98 computer is part of a workgroup and a user does not have an "account" on the computer, the user can type in a new username and gain access to the local machine. When a Windows 95/98 computer is part of a Windows NT domain, the user must have a valid username to log on, but the user can cancel the logon dialog box and gain complete access to the local computer.

4. True or False. A Windows NT domain implements peer-to-peer networking.

   A: False. A Windows NT domain implements server-based networking.

5. What is the name of the user account in Windows NT that gives you privileges to create users and perform system tasks?

   A: Administrator

6. True or False. In Windows NT 4.0, the guest account is enabled by default.

   A: False. It is *disabled* by default.

7. Why do you use group accounts?

   A: To simplify administration and assign permissions or user rights to multiple user accounts in a single action.

...continues

...continued

---

8. What is the name of the tool used in Windows NT to administer users and groups?

    A: User Manager (on a member server or NT Workstation) or User Manager for Domains (on a PDC or BDC)

9. Explain the difference between share-level and user-level security.

    A: In user-level security permissions are assigned to user accounts. As long as someone connects to the server with the correct username and password, he can access all shares or resources for which he has been assigned permission (without reentering his password). In share-level security, a password is assigned to an individual shared resource. Any user knowing the appropriate password can access that resource. A user must know the password for each distinct shared resource.

10. What role does auditing play in providing security?

    A: Auditing tracks and logs network events and provides a trail that can be followed to see who is doing what on the network. Auditing can track things such as the use of files, printers, the exercise of user rights or who logs on and off the network.

PRACTICE TEST

1. You are a member of a small consulting company with a network of five computers running Windows 95. Because you do not have an extra staff to administer the network, you need each person to be responsible for maintaining his own machine. Which type of security should you use?

    a. Share-level security
    b. User-level security

Answer a is correct; share-level security would leave each person responsible for her own security. Answer b is incorrect.

2. Which operating systems can provide share-level security? (Choose all that apply.)

    a. Windows for Workgroups
    b. Windows 95
    c. Windows NT Workstation
    d. Windows NT Server

Answers a and b are correct; both Windows for Workgroups and Windows 95 support share-level security. Answers c and d are incorrect because all versions of Windows NT can only use user-level security.

3. At the small company where you work, your manager recently upgraded all the computers to Windows 95 and would like you to network them together. He is concerned about security and would like you to propose a solution to him for adequately providing network security.

   REQUIRED RESULT: The solution must be capable of being implemented using existing hardware and software. No additional expenses may be involved.

   OPTIONAL DESIRED RESULTS: Your solution should provide a high degree of security. Your solution should allow users to easily access network resources.

   PROPOSED SOLUTION: You propose implementing user-level security by including all workstations in a domain. Which results does the proposed solution produce?

   a. The proposed solution produces the required result and produces both of the optional desired results.

   b. The proposed solution produces the required result and produces only *one* of the optional desired results.

   c. The proposed solution produces the required result but does *not* produce any of the optional desired results.

   d. The proposed solution does *not* produce the required result.

Answer d is correct because you cannot implement a domain with only Windows 95 and the required result was to use only existing hardware and software. You would need to buy Windows NT Server to implement a domain.

4. The guest account in Windows NT 3.51 is enabled by default?

   a. True

   b. False

Answer a is true; in Windows NT 3.51 the guest account is *enabled*, while in Windows NT 4.0 it is *disabled* by default. Answer b is correct.

5. Within networks using Microsoft operating systems, what is the name for a collection of computers where all user accounts are stored in a centralized database?

   a. Server

   b. Workgroup

   c. Domain

   d. Peer

Answers a, b, and d are incorrect. **Answer c is correct.**

6. A single user account can only be included in one group account.

   a. True

   b. False

Answer a is incorrect. **Answer b is correct because a user account can be included in** *many* **group accounts.**

7. Which of the following is *not* a type of access control provided in share-level security within Windows 95?

   a. Read-Only

   b. Full

   c. Change

   d. Depends on Password

Answers a, b, and d are incorrect because they *are* provided in Windows 95. **Answer c is correct because there is no Change permission that can be assigned.**

8. The process of _____ maintains logs of security events and allows an administrator to find incidents of unauthorized access.

   a. tracking

   b. performance monitoring

   c. analyzing

   d. auditing

Answers a, b, and c are incorrect. **Answer d is correct.**

9. Your Windows 95 computer is connected to a network consisting only of other Windows 95 computers. If you want others to access files on your computer, what kind of security can you use?

   a. Share-level security

   b. User-level security

Answer a is correct because Windows 95 computers alone cannot implement user-level security—there needs to be at least one Windows NT (Server or Workstation) computer on the network in order for user-level security to work. Answer b is incorrect.

10. If you want others to access files on your Windows NT machine, what kind of security can you use?

   a. Share-level security

   b. User-level security

Answer a is incorrect because Windows NT cannot support share-level security. **Answer b is correct because Windows NT only supports user-level security.**

CHAPTER PREREQUISITE

Before reading this chapter, you should understand the fundamentals of computer networks, network operating systems (see Chapter 10, "Network Operating Systems"), network applications (see Chapter 11, "Network Applications"), and network administration (see Chapter 16, "Network Administration").

Network Problem Prevention

— WHILE YOU READ —

1. When doing performance monitoring, how does a baseline help?

2. _____ is a tool in Windows NT that enables you to graphically monitor statistics about your system.

3. What does SNMP do for a network administrator?

4. Explain the difference between an incremental and differential backup.

5. What does a UPS do to help prevent network problems?

6. What is RAID an abbreviation for?

7. Identify the RAID levels supported by Windows NT.

8. Contrast disk mirroring and disk duplexing.

9. With what type of disk drives can Windows NT provide sector sparing?

10. A _____ _____ plan can help you prevent catastrophic data loss.

Protecting Your Network

As a network administrator, one of your primary tasks is to protect the network against data loss and to prevent network problems before they occur. The steps involved with preventing network problems include the following:

- Properly documenting the network configuration.
- Monitoring network performance.
- Backing up data.
- Providing hardware mechanisms to avoid equipment failure.
- Developing a comprehensive disaster recovery plan.

Each of these steps will be discussed in detail in the following sections.

Documentation

The first step to preventing network problems is to document your network installation and configuration. The network documentation should include information about both LAN and WAN connections. If you are in charge of a larger network encompassing several individual LANs, each LAN should have its own documentation. Additionally, you should constantly update your documentation with the latest changes to your network.

Although the elements of a documentation set will vary, the following list includes suggested information that should be documented:

- *Cable installation information.* What type of network cable is installed on your LAN? Do you have network diagrams illustrating the connections between wall jacks and jacks on a patch panel in a wiring closet? Do you have contact numbers for the people responsible for the actual installation? At what speed is the cable rated?

- *Equipment information.* When were the individual pieces of equipment purchased (both regular PCs as well as specialized network equipment)? What are the serial numbers? Who were the vendors? Do you have contact information for the vendors? Do you have warranty information?

- *Software configuration.* What software is installed on each network node? What drivers had to be loaded for the computer to correctly access the network? Which configuration files (such as CONFIG.SYS and AUTOEXEC.BAT) are loaded on each machine and what special instructions are included in them? Are there any unusual applications in use on the network or any unusual configurations?

- *Network resources.* What are the most common network resources used on your network? Are there particular drive mappings that you want to use throughout the network?

- *Network addressing.* How have you allocated network addresses? Can you provide a map or diagram of which computers are using which addresses?

- *Network connections.* Is your network connected to other networks? If so, how? Who are the service providers? Do you have contact information for each provider?

- *Network performance baseline.* What are "normal" traffic levels on your network? Where are the typical bottlenecks to network performance?

- *User administration.* Do you have a set method for creating usernames? Are there specific groups to which you want all users to be added?

- *Policies and procedures.* Have you or any other member of the organization defined and distributed specific procedures for network operation? Has your upper management issued any guidelines for network use?

- *Hardware/software changes.* What changes have been made since the network was installed? When did those changes take place?

- *Software licenses.* Do you have valid licenses for all software installed at your location? Are all serial numbers recorded and tracked for expiration dates?

- *Troubleshooting history.* What problems have you faced on the network, and how did you solve them?

A documentation set outlining items such as those listed here can be of tremendous benefit when you are trying to diagnose network problems. Additionally, as you plan for network growth or upgrading equipment, your documentation can assist you in moving forward with planned changes.

Note that your documentation should be available in hard copy as well as electronic form for those times when the network is not accessible.

Note that due to the increasing complexity of networks, many vendors have responded with tools that will manage your overall system and help you provide documentation for your network configuration. Microsoft's entry into this field is the *Systems Management Server (SMS)* included as part of Microsoft BackOffice. SMS can build an inventory database by collecting information about what is stored on each computer in your organization. After collecting the data, SMS can install and configure new software directly on the network client computers. SMS also provides advanced network monitoring capabilities that enable you to analyze network traffic.

CH
17

Network Performance Monitoring

As you document your system, it is important to understand how the system is functioning on a regular basis. To gain this understanding, you will need to use any number of performance monitoring tools. Network administrators have a number of reasons for monitoring network performance, including the following:

- Identifying devices that are network bottlenecks.
- Providing data for forecasting future growth needs and capacity planning.
- Developing plans to increase network performance.
- Monitoring the effects of any changes made to hardware or software configurations.
- Identifying trends in network traffic patterns.

Of this list, network administrators probably spend the most time trying to find bottlenecks. *Bottlenecks* are simply situations that for some reason introduce delays into the flow of network traffic. Although bottlenecks often develop inside server computers such as CPUs, memory (RAM), network interface cards (NICs), and disk controllers, bottlenecks can also occur in network media or connectivity devices such as routers and gateways. Typically, a bottleneck occurs because the device does not have the capacity to handle the volume of network traffic that it is encountering.

Although performance monitoring can help you see current network conditions, it won't help you identify potential network problems unless you first establish a *baseline* that defines "normal" network operations. If you monitor your network for a period of time when there are no problems, you can use this period as a baseline for comparison when you later try to identify problems. How could you know that network traffic is excessive if you do not know what the traffic levels were before? How could you know that the CPU is overworked if you do not know its normal levels of operation? Establishing a baseline will help you address these concerns.

Windows NT Performance Monitor

Most network operating systems include some type of graphical tool to monitor network performance. Such tools generally provide a mechanism to view data in both a log listing as well as a graphical chart.

Within Windows NT, the Performance Monitor enables you to graphically monitor statistics about virtually every aspect of your computer's operations, as shown in Figure 17.1. You can view data either in real time, or you can collect it into log files for later analysis. In addition to graphical charts, the Performance Monitor can also provide listings of log files and text reports.

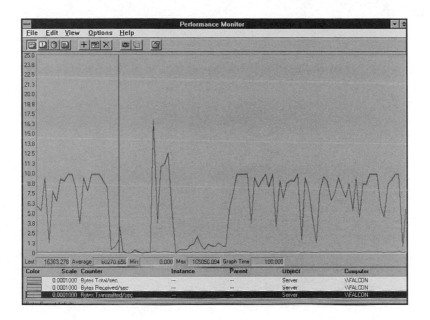

Figure 17.1
The Windows NT Performance Monitor enables you to monitor network statistics on
your server computers.

When certain conditions are met, the Performance Monitor has the capability to send an
alert to a network administrator or to trigger another program.

Key Concept

As exam questions sometimes tend to focus on the Performance Monitor, you
should get as much hands-on experience as possible using it before you take the
exam.

SNMP

One of the tools you have for monitoring network conditions is the *Simple Network
Management Protocol (SNMP)*. SNMP is a standard supported by most manufacturers of
network equipment, including manufacturers of hubs, NICs, routers, servers, bridges, and
other network equipment.

When SNMP is used in an environment such as that depicted in Figure 17.2, *software agents* are loaded onto each network device that will be managed. Each agent monitors both the network traffic and the device status and stores that information in a *management information base (MIB)*.

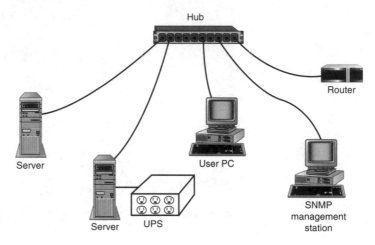

Figure 17.2
SNMP enables network devices to be managed from a central management station.

To collect and make sense of this data, special network management software periodically polls each device and gathers the information collected in each MIB. The management program can then combine the information from all the devices and generate statistics or charts detailing current network conditions. Thresholds can be set so that alerts will be sent to network administrators when certain levels are exceeded. Some network components using SNMP also can be remotely administered from the network management software.

Key Concept

Simple Network Management Protocol (SNMP) provides a mechanism that enables network administrators to collect data from network components and develop an overall picture of network conditions.

Backup Systems

As you consider methods to avoid data loss, the easiest mechanism to prevent problems is to use some type of *backup system*. The steps you need to develop a reliable backup plan include the following:

1. Determine what data on your network is critical and should be backed up.

2. Develop a schedule for backing up data. Data that does not change often can be backed up on a periodic schedule, whereas critical data that is constantly changing should be backed up daily. Also, because backup systems often affect network performance, backups should be scheduled for hours when the network is least used.

3. Identify the person (or persons) who will be responsible for maintaining backups and ensure that he understands his responsibilities.

4. Select a magnetic tape drive. Most backup systems use tape drives with removable cartridge tapes to back up data. The type of tape drive you choose will depend on the volume of data to be backed up, the speed at which you need the drive to operate, and the costs associated with both the drive and media. Ideally, you want to put all the backup data onto a single tape or as few tapes as possible. Another concern to address is the interchangeability of the media with other systems. If your building is destroyed, is your tape media format common enough that you can bring the backup tapes to another office and quickly restore the data?

5. Determine what methods will be used to back up the data. As shown in Table 17.1, there are several different methods of performing data backups. A reliable backup system will use a combination of methods, perhaps performing a full backup weekly with differential or incremental backups performed daily.

6. Test the backup system. Run through several cycles of backing up the data. Pretend that some data has been deleted (move the data to a different directory) and test your capability to quickly restore data. Additionally, when the backup system is in operation, it should be tested periodically to ensure that data is being backed up reliably.

7. Identify storage locations both onsite and offsite. At your location, data backups should be stored somewhere that is easily accessible. You should also store backup tapes somewhere offsite where the tapes can be retrieved after a catastrophe. In both onsite and offsite locations, you should ensure that only authorized personnel will have access to the backup tapes.

8. Maintain a comprehensive backup log indicating what data was backed up, when the backup occurred, and who performed the backup. You should also include identification numbers that clearly indicate which tape was used for the backup.

CH

17

If you develop a backup system encompassing these steps, you will be prepared to avoid data loss in most situations.

Finally, you should note that the location of the backup tape drive is very important for the backup speed as well as the impact of the backup system on your network. Ideally, the tape drive will be installed locally on a server. If it is used across a network, it will generate a large amount of network traffic because you are essentially copying your server's entire hard drive across the network. If there is a need to back up several servers using one tape drive, many organizations will actually install a separate network segment using a second NIC in each server. With a separate network segment, all network backup traffic will not affect the main flow of the network.

Table 17.1   Backup Methods

Method	Description
Full Backup	Backs up all selected files, regardless of whether they have changed since the last backup, and marks them as being backed up.
Copy	Backs up selected files without marking them as backed up.
Incremental	Backs up and marks selected files only if they have changed since the last backup.
Daily Copy	Backs up all files modified on a given day, without marking the files as backed up.
Differential	Backs up selected files only if they have changed since the last backup, but does not mark files as backed up.

As a clarification of the differences in backup methods described in Table 17.1, consider a typical backup schedule: Tape 1 is used for a full backup each Sunday night, and Tapes 2–7 are used for incremental backups on the other nights of the week. On Monday, Tape 2 backs up all the files that were modified since the full backup Sunday night. On Tuesday, Tape 3 backs up all the files modified since the incremental backup on Monday night, and so on. If there is a failure of the file server on Friday, it would be necessary to first restore data from the full backup on Tape 1. You would then need to restore data from each of Tapes 2–5 (Monday through Thursday nights) to return to the file status before the network failure.

Although this backup system provides a high level of data security, it requires that someone change the tape before each nightly backup. If someone does not change the tape, some backup data will be lost. For instance, in the previous scenario, if Tape 2 is left in the tape drive on Tuesday, Tuesday's modified data will be written to the tape, overwriting the data previously recorded from Monday. For this reason, the tapes must always be changed.

In a smaller office environment, that might not be practical. Instead, a smaller system would use Tape 1 for a full backup on Sunday nights, but it would use Tape 2 for differential backups throughout the week. On Monday night, Tape 2 would back up all the files modified since the full backup on Sunday. On Tuesday night, Tape 2 would again back up all files modified since the full backup on Sunday. If a failure occurred on Friday, data would be first restored from the Sunday full backup on Tape 1 and then restored from Tape 2. Although this system is simpler than the incremental system described earlier, it is not as reliable. If something were to happen on Thursday night where the backup tape did not function properly, all data from the time of the Sunday night full backup would be lost.

Key Concept

For the exam, make sure you understand the different types of backups, especially the difference between an incremental and differential backup.

Uninterruptible Power Supply

Because even the slightest fluctuation in electrical power can wreak havoc on a network, an *Uninterruptible Power Supply (UPS)* provides a level of support for network systems. Essentially, a UPS is nothing more than a series of batteries (in some cases, not terribly different from car batteries) that provide a backup for network equipment in the event of a power failure. As shown in Figure 17.3, a UPS is plugged into your electrical wall outlet with your server and other equipment plugged into the UPS. When the power fails, your UPS instantaneously takes over, providing power to the computer equipment. Most UPS systems are designed to provide power for somewhere between 5 and 20 minutes, although more expensive systems can provide several hours of power.

UPS systems are categorized as either *online* or *standby* systems. Standby UPS systems pass the electrical power from the wall outlet directly to the computer equipment plugged into the UPS while at the same time keeping the UPS batteries fully charged. When the power fails, a standby UPS system activates and begins providing power to the computer equipment. However, there can be a momentary power drop while the UPS system activates, and this power drop can in some circumstances cause data loss. The primary advantage to standby UPS systems is that they are usually inexpensive.

Online UPS systems use the electrical wall outlet to constantly charge their batteries and provide all power to computer equipment directly from those batteries. When a power failure occurs, the computer equipment will not register an interruption because all along the equipment has been receiving power from the UPS system's batteries. Online UPS systems provide "cleaner" power but are more expensive than standby UPS systems.

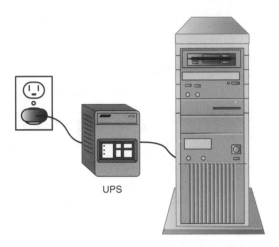

Figure 17.3
A UPS system is connected between the power outlet and the server computer.

All good UPS systems should have some mechanism to alert the systems to which they are connected that there has been a power failure. Typically, a serial cable is attached from a port on the UPS to a serial port on the server. As shown in Figure 17.4, server computers usually have software that can receive an alert from a UPS system, warn network users of the power failure, provide a time period for users to close their files, and initiate an orderly system shutdown. If power is restored before the shutdown has been initiated, the UPS will alert the server that power has returned.

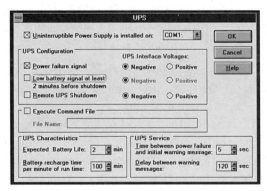

Figure 17.4
Windows NT includes a Control Panel facility for handling alerts from UPS systems.

Key Concept

It is a good idea to use a UPS to protect not only your network servers, but also your network connectivity equipment such as routers, bridges, and hubs. If servers are maintaining open network connections, connectivity devices can be crucial for the server to shut down properly.

Key Concept

After connecting your servers and other network devices to an *Uninterruptible Power Supply (UPS)*, the UPS will protect those devices from power failures and surges.

Fault-Tolerant Disk Storage

One way to prevent network problems is to use fault-tolerant disk storage for your critical data. A *fault-tolerant system* is one in which the system can continue to function even with the failure of one component. Fault-tolerant disk storage systems might be based entirely in hardware, or they might also include a software component. Most network operating systems include some capability to use fault-tolerant disk storage.

The primary method of categorizing fault-tolerant disk storage systems is through a RAID level. *Redundant Arrays of Inexpensive Disks (RAID)* defines several levels of disk storage systems, as shown in Table 17.2.

CH 17

Table 17.2   RAID levels

RAID Level	Description
0	Disk striping by block
1	Disk mirroring or duplexing
2	Disk striping by bit with error correction codes
3	Disk striping by byte with parity information stored on a single drive
4	Disk striping by block with parity information stored on a single drive
5	Disk striping by block with parity information stored across multiple drives

RAID systems primarily use the process of *disk striping* where data is written across multiple disk drives. The data can be transferred by a single disk controller to each disk drive by individual bytes of data or by larger blocks of data. The only condition for disk striping is that most network operating systems cannot have their system or boot partition stored on a set of striped disks.

Within Microsoft environments, Windows NT supports RAID levels 0 (disk striping), 1 (disk mirroring), and 5 (disk striping with parity) through a utility called the *Disk Administrator*. Because RAID level 5 derived from work on RAID levels 2, 3, and 4, RAID level 5 represents the latest capabilities in fault-tolerant disk storage. For that reason, Microsoft chose to support RAID level 5 and not RAID levels 2–4. Windows NT also supports an advanced mechanism for fault-tolerant disk storage referred to as *sector sparing.*

RAID 0—Disk Striping

In RAID level 0, blocks of data (64KB blocks in Windows NT) are written across multiple disk drives, as shown in Figure 17.5. Through this process of spreading data across several drives, read and write performance can be greatly increased due to the fact that data can be written simultaneously to multiple drives. Additionally, space on disk drives can be effectively used because *striped sets* of data can make use of extra unused partition space on multiple drives. (This can be accomplished subject to the restriction that all partitions used in a striped set must be of equal size.)

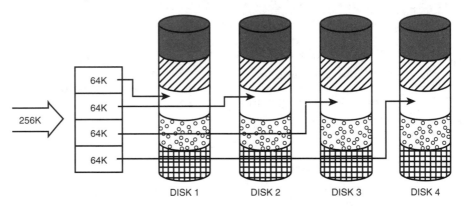

Figure 17.5
RAID 0 systems write blocks of data across multiple drives.

However, despite being categorized as part of the RAID system, RAID level 0 does not provide any actual fault tolerance. If one of the disk drives fails, the data on the other drives will not be of any use. There is no way to recover the data on the failed drive. Windows NT provides support for RAID level 0, but you should consider it as a performance enhancement rather than a choice for fault tolerance.

Key Concept

RAID level 0 uses disk striping to enhance disk performance by spreading data across multiple drives. RAID level 0 does not provide any degree of fault tolerance.

RAID 1—Disk Mirroring/Duplexing

RAID level 1 uses a technique called *disk mirroring* to make a duplicate copy of one disk drive. Essentially, two disk drives are connected to a single disk controller card, as shown in Figure 17.6. Just as applications send data to the disk controller to be written to disk, the disk controller sends the data to both disk drives. In this manner, one disk drive is the mirror image of the other. If one disk drive fails, data can be retrieved from the other disk drive as if nothing had happened.

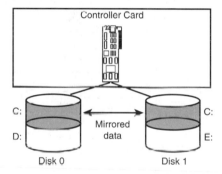

Figure 17.6
RAID level 1 provides fault tolerance through disk mirroring.

Disk mirroring requires two disk partitions of identical size located on two different disk drives. You do not need to allocate all the space on a disk drive for mirroring use, but whatever amount of space used must be identical on both drives. For ideal performance, the two disk drives should be from the same manufacturer and/or have identical performance characteristics. Disk mirroring is popular if you only have one drive to protect or if you want to protect the system or boot partition.

The primary drawback to RAID level 1 is that it can be expensive to maintain duplicate sets of hardware. If you have two disk drives with 1GB of storage on each, you can still only store 1GB of information because you are duplicating all information.

Key Concept

RAID level 1 uses *disk mirroring* to write the identical data to two separate disk drives. In the event of the failure of one drive, users can just continue using the second drive.

Although disk mirroring provides a high level of fault tolerance, there still is a single point of failure in the form of the single disk controller card. If the card should fail for some reason, users will not be able to access any of the information on either of the disk drives until the controller card is replaced. To avoid this problem, *disk duplexing* (see Figure 17.7) implements disk mirroring using a separate disk controller card for each disk drive. Not only is the data duplicated, but now if a disk controller card fails, users will not notice the failure.

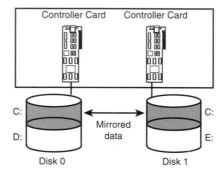

Figure 17.7
By using two disk controller cards, disk duplexing ensures that data will still be available if one disk controller card fails.

Key Concept

Disk duplexing is a variation on disk mirroring where each disk drive uses a separate disk drive controller card.

RAID 5—Disk Striping with Parity

Whereas disk mirroring (Raid level 1) can be expensive, RAID level 5 maximizes the use of space on multiple disk drives while providing a high level of fault tolerance. As shown in Figure 17.8, data is striped across multiple disks with the addition of error-checking (parity) information. As each stripe of data is written to disk, parity information is included in one of the blocks written to disk. If one disk fails, the information on that disk can be completely reconstructed from the other disks using the data and the parity information. Windows NT supports RAID level 5 using 3–32 disk drives.

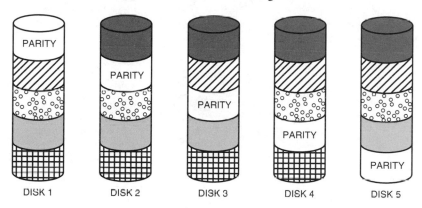

DISK 1   DISK 2   DISK 3   DISK 4   DISK 5

Figure 17.8
RAID level 5 stripes data across multiple disks and includes parity information.

Implementing disk striping with parity can be more cost-effective than disk-mirroring because disk space is better used when disk striping with parity is present. Whereas disk mirroring only allows use of 50 percent of the total available disk capacity, disk striping with parity makes available almost all of the space on the disk drives. Parity information occupies some space ($1/n$ of the available space, where n is the number of drives used), but the rest remains available for data storage.

Key Concept

RAID level 5, known as *disk striping with parity*, writes data and parity information across multiple disks. If any disk fails, data can be reconstructed from the data and parity information stored on all other disks.

Sector-Sparing

Whereas RAID levels address failure of disk drives, another fault-tolerant mechanism addresses failures of individual sectors on a disk drive. Through a technique called *sector-sparing*, or hot-fixing, the disk controller and fault-tolerant software driver can detect when data is being read from or is about to be written to a bad sector on the disk drive. As shown in Figure 17.9, when data is found in a bad sector, the data is moved to a good sector, and the.bad sector is mapped out as no longer available for data.

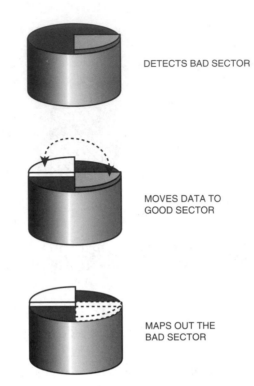

DETECTS BAD SECTOR

MOVES DATA TO
GOOD SECTOR

MAPS OUT THE
BAD SECTOR

Figure 17.9
Risk sectors to good sectors.

Windows NT includes a fault-tolerant driver that can support sector sparing on SCSI disk drives. Windows NT also includes a utility to alert administrators when bad sectors have been found.

Key Concept

Sector-sparing is a fault-tolerant mechanism where data is moved from a bad sector to a good sector, and the bad sector is removed from use. Windows NT supports sector sparing on SCSI disk drives.

Disaster Recovery Plan

Even with all the best network problem prevention plans, there can still be catastrophic failures. Buildings can burn down. Natural disasters such as floods and earthquakes can demolish your office building. Thieves can clean out your computer center. Extended power failures can leave you without network capabilities.

Although you might not be able to prepare for every catastrophic event, a well thought-out disaster recovery plan can prevent prolonged loss of network capability. A disaster recovery plan should be a written document that should be distributed to staff and stored both onsite and offsite. Your disaster recovery plan should address such issues as the following:

- Where is documentation stored about network configuration?
- What data is backed up and how often? What about system configuration information that is not regularly backed up?
- How and where are backups stored onsite? How easily can they be retrieved? How easily can they be restored?
- How and where are backups stored offsite? How easily can they be retrieved?
- Are all servers connected with UPS systems to automatically power down?
- What type of fire-suppression systems are installed in your computer areas?
- If you are connected to the Internet, what provisions have been made to reroute inbound email or other Internet traffic to an alternative site?
- What are the telephone numbers of your network and telecommunications providers? Who within your organization (information systems staff, management, and so on) should be notified in case of a disaster?
- What type of business insurance do you have? Will it cover loss of data?
- What level of training does your staff require to be able to quickly and effectively respond to network failures?
- Is data replicated between sites so that operations can continue at other sites in the event of failure?
- Do you have the capability to transfer network operations to another location?

Your answers to these questions will vary depending on the size of your organization, the amount of data, the intensity of network operations, and the importance that network data plays within your daily operations. Having given careful thought to developing a comprehensive disaster recovery plan can aid you in avoiding catastrophic data loss that will impact the bottom line of your business.

CH
17

Summary

As a network administrator, part of your responsibilities will be to prevent network problems before they occur. Doing this involves properly documenting your network, monitoring network performance, backing up data, providing mechanisms to avoid equipment failure, and developing a comprehensive disaster recovery plan.

In documenting your network, you should develop documents that outline the hardware and software components and configuration of your network. Including such information as key contact phone numbers, vendor relationships, and any successful problem resolutions will greatly increase the value of your documentation when you are trying to diagnose problems.

When monitoring network performance, you will spend most of your time searching for performance bottlenecks. Bottlenecks include network devices that are too slow or are stretched beyond their capabilities due to the level of network traffic. A tool that can assist you is the Performance Monitor included with Windows NT. Devices that use Simple Network Management Protocol (SNMP) can also be of great assistance. In SNMP, each monitored device contains an agent that records traffic and statistics about the device. That data is then collected by a central monitoring program that can analyze the data and present graphs and reports on current network conditions.

Perhaps the most crucial mechanism to prevent network problems is a reliable backup system. A good backup system involves determining what data you need to back up, how you will back it up, what type of schedule you will use, and who will perform the actual backup procedure.

To prevent equipment failures, you can use an Uninterruptible Power Supply (UPS) to avoid damage from power fluctuations. After a UPS is plugged into an electrical wall socket, you connect computer equipment to the UPS. When the power fails, the UPS will continue to power the equipment for a period of time. Good UPS systems can alert servers of the power failure so that the server can shut down in an orderly fashion.

Another means to protect against equipment failure is to use fault-tolerant disk storage. Fault-tolerant disk storage systems use either disk striping, where data is spread across several disk drives, or disk mirroring, where data is written identically to two separate disk drives. Fault-tolerant systems are categorized by RAID (Redundant Arrays of Inexpensive Disks) levels. Within Microsoft environments, Windows NT supports RAID levels 0 (disk striping), 1 (disk mirroring), and 5 (disk striping with parity).

Lastly, as a network administrator, you should develop a comprehensive disaster recovery plan to address what happens when you experience a catastrophic failure such as a fire, extended power outage, flood, or other natural disaster.

QUESTIONS AND ANSWERS

1. When doing performance monitoring, how does a baseline help?

    A: It provides a view of "normal" network performance that can help you identify performance problems.

2. _____ is a tool in Windows NT that enables you to graphically monitor statistics about your system.

    A: Performance Monitor.

3. What does SNMP do for a network administrator?

    A: Simple Network Management Protocol enables administrators to remotely monitor network devices such as hubs, routers, and servers.

4. Explain the difference between an incremental and differential backup.

    A: After an incremental backup, files are marked as having been backed up, so the next backup will *not* back up these files. After a differential backup, files are *not* marked as having been backed up, so the next backup *will* back up these files.

5. What does a UPS do to help prevent network problems?

    A: It reduces the potential for damage to servers and network devices caused by power outages or surges.

6. What is RAID an abbreviation for?

    A: Redundant Arrays of Inexpensive Disks.

7. Identify the RAID levels supported by Windows NT.

    A: RAID 0, 1, 5.

8. Contrast disk mirroring and disk duplexing.

    A: Although both involve writing the same data to two separate disk drives, disk mirroring uses only one disk controller card. Disk duplexing uses two disk controller cards, thereby eliminating another potential failure point (the single controller).

9. With what type of disk drives can Windows NT provide sector sparing?

    A: SCSI.

10. A _____ _____ plan can help you prevent catastrophic data loss.

    A: Disaster recovery.

CH
17

PRACTICE TEST

1. RAID level 1 provides what type of fault-tolerant disk storage?

a. Disk mirroring

b. Disk striping

c. Sector sparing

d. Disk striping with parity

Answer a is correct; disk mirroring is RAID 1. Answer b is incorrect because disk striping is RAID 0. Answer c is incorrect because sector sparing is not a RAID feature. Answer d is incorrect because disk striping with parity is RAID 5.

2. Your small company has recently installed Windows NT Server on your network file server. The file server is a Pentium PC with three hard disk drives currently installed. Your management has asked you to develop a plan for providing continual access to data regardless of disk storage failures.

REQUIRED RESULT: In the event of the failure of one disk drive, users must be able to continue accessing data.

OPTIONAL DESIRED RESULTS: Your solution should make use only of available hardware and software. Your solution should also make use of the maximum amount of disk space available on the three disk drives.

PROPOSED SOLUTION: You propose utilizing a RAID level 0 disk-striping storage system across the three disk drives in the server. Which results does the proposed solution produce?

a. The proposed solution produces the required result and both of the optional desired results.

b. The proposed solution produces the required result and only *one* of the optional desired results.

c. The proposed solution produces the required result but does *not* produce any of the optional desired results.

d. The proposed solution does *not* produce the required result.

Answer d is correct because RAID 0 provides *no* fault tolerance and therefore fails to meet the required result.

3. What does SNMP stand for?

a. Simple Network Monitoring Protocol

b. Secure Network Monitoring Protocol

c. Simple Network Management Protocol

d. Standard Network Monitoring Protocol

Answer a is incorrect. Answer b is incorrect. **Answer c is correct.** Answer d is correct.

4. Which of the following statements describes sector-sparing?

  a. Data is written across multiple disk sectors on several different disk drives.

  b. Bad sectors are identified, data is moved to a good sector, and the bad sector is removed from use.

  c. Disk sectors are examined on each disk read/write operation. When good sectors are found, the data is retrieved. When bad sectors are found, parity information is used to reconstruct the missing data.

  d. Bad sectors are identified, data is moved to a good sector, and the bad sector is repaired and reactivated for use.

Answer a is incorrect because it describes disk striping. **Answer b is correct and defines sector sparing.** Answer c is incorrect because it describes disk striping with parity. Answer d is incorrect because sector sparing does not repair the bad sector.

5. Your small company has recently installed Windows NT Server on your network file server. The file server is a Pentium PC with three hard disk drives currently installed. Your management has asked you to develop a plan for providing continual access to data regardless of disk storage failures.

REQUIRED RESULT: In the event of the failure of one disk drive, users must be able to continue accessing data.

OPTIONAL DESIRED RESULTS: Your solution should make use only of available hardware and software. Your solution should provide the most disk space available while still maintaining fault-tolerance on the three disk drives.

PROPOSED SOLUTION: You propose utilizing a RAID level 5 disk-striping storage system across the three disk drives in the server. Which results does the proposed solution produce?

  a. The proposed solution produces the required result and both of the optional desired results.

  b. The proposed solution produces the required result and only *one* of the optional desired results.

  c. The proposed solution produces the required result but does *not* produce any of the optional desired results.

  d. The proposed solution does *not* produce the required result.

Answer a is correct. A RAID 5 solution will provide the required fault tolerance while also making use of existing hardware and maximizing available disk space.

CH
17

6. Your management wants the network to be able to withstand power outages for as long as five minutes. To what device should you connect your server and network devices?

   a. Generator

   b. UPS

   c. RAID 5 disk storage system

   d. Time-domain reflectometer

Answer a is incorrect, although not a bad idea. **Answer b is correct because a UPS should provide at least five minutes of power.** Answer c is incorrect—no power, no disks! Answer d is incorrect because a TDR is used for troubleshooting and does nothing to help with power problems.

7. You want to provide a fault-tolerant means of completely protecting the boot partition of your Windows NT Server. Which of the following disk storage systems can you use? (Choose all that apply.)

   a. RAID level 5

   b. RAID level 1

   c. RAID level 0

   d. Disk duplexing

Answer a is incorrect because you can't use Windows NT's disk striping with parity on the boot partition of Windows NT Server. **Answer b is correct because disk mirroring (RAID 1) *can* protect the boot partition.** Answer c is incorrect because RAID 0 provides no fault tolerance whatsoever. **Answer d is correct because disk duplexing is merely a variation on disk mirroring.**

8. The consulting organization for which you work has recently installed Windows NT Server on your network file server. The file server is a Pentium PC with two hard disk drives currently installed. You have been asked to develop a plan for providing continual access to data, regardless of disk storage failures.

   REQUIRED RESULT: In the event of the failure of one disk drive, users must be able to continue accessing data.

   OPTIONAL DESIRED RESULTS: Your solution should make use only of available hardware and software. Your solution must be able to continue functioning in the case of failure of any single component in the disk storage system.

   PROPOSED SOLUTION: You propose utilizing a RAID level 1 disk-mirroring storage system by using the two disk drives in the server. Which results does the proposed solution produce?

a. The proposed solution produces the required result and both of the optional desired results.

b. The proposed solution produces the required result and only *one* of the optional desired results.

c. The proposed solution produces the required result but does *not* produce any of the optional desired results.

d. The proposed solution does *not* produce the required result.

Answer b is correct because RAID 1, disk mirroring, meets the required result and the optional result for using existing equipment. However, it fails the optional result about protecting against a single point of failure because it uses only one disk controller. *Disk duplexing* **would solve this problem with a second disk controller.**

9. You would like to gather statistics about the utilization of the CPU and RAM within your Windows NT computer. Which tool should you use?

a. SNMP

b. SMS

c. Performance Monitor

d. Protocol analyzer

Answer a is incorrect because SNMP is a protocol used by other tools. Answer b is incorrect because SMS won't do direct monitoring. **Answer c is correct; Performance Monitor would let you measure this information.** Answer d is incorrect because a protocol analyzer will measure network statistics.

10. When backing up data onto a tape, you back up only the data that has been changed since the last backup and mark the data as backed up. What backup method have you just used?

a. Full backup

b. Incremental

c. Differential

d. Daily copy

Answer a is incorrect because a full backup would back up *all* data. **Answer b is correct; an incremental backup backs up the data and marks it as backed up.** Answer c is incorrect because a differential backup would not mark the data as backed up. Answer d is incorrect because it would not mark the data as backed up.

CHAPTER PREREQUISITE

This chapter discusses aspects of diagnosing all components of a computer network. Therefore, you should be familiar with the material in all the previous chapters.

Troubleshooting

WHILE YOU READ

1. What are a couple of basic troubleshooting techniques you can use before going too far investigating a problem?

2. Name three troubleshooting tools you can use.

3. What is the difference between a DVM and a TDR?

4. At what layer of the OSI model do a DVM and TDR operate?

5. Where in the OSI model does a protocol analyzer fit?

6. How does a cable tester differ from a DVM or TDR?

7. How can a terminator be used in troubleshooting coaxial cable?

8. If you are trying to figure out the source of a broadcast storm, which tool would you use?

9. You have a coaxial network and suspect a break somewhere in the cable. Which tool will help you locate the break?

10. Identify four common network problems.

Troubleshooting Overview

Network troubleshooting is not so much a science as it is an art that you develop over the years as you work with computer networks. If you have worked with personal computers for a while, you have already developed some troubleshooting tips regarding PCs. For instance, most Windows users know that when an application freezes, you can press Ctrl+Alt+Delete to terminate the application and reboot the computer. Most Windows-based PC users know that, when in doubt, completely restarting the computer often solves problems!

Just as you have developed tips for troubleshooting PC applications, you will develop network troubleshooting tips as you become more familiar with network problems. The following are some basic techniques for troubleshooting network problems involving one computer:

- *Make sure that the problem is not a mistake by the user.* Before getting too far into troubleshooting, gently question the user reporting the problem. Make sure that what the user was trying to do is something that can, in fact, be done on your network.

- *Check the physical connection.* Perhaps the largest cause of network problems is simply the physical media. Check that the network cable is correctly connected to the computer, to the hub, or to the other computers (depending on topology). Check that coaxial cables are properly terminated and that all connectivity devices, such as hubs, are functioning properly.

- *Check the network interface card (NIC).* Most NICs have two LEDs on the back of the card. One light indicates that the card is working, and the other (commonly referred to as the *link light*) indicates that the computer has an operating link to the network.

- *Restart the computer.* Shutting down and restarting the user's Windows-based computer can often solve networking issues.

If these techniques do not solve the problem, or if the network problem involves multiple computers, you must take a more structured approach to solving the problem.

A Structured Approach

When addressing complex network problems, Microsoft recommends a structured approach that involves these five steps:

1. Set the problem's priority.
2. Collect information to identify the symptoms.

3. Develop a list of possible causes.

4. Test to isolate the cause.

5. Study the results of the test to identify a solution.

Setting Priorities

The first step in the process is to identify the severity of the problem. Is the entire sales department unable to work because the database server is down? Are several users unable to play Hearts across the network? Is the company president unable to access the file server? Your first task is to assign a priority to the problem.

Collecting Information

The next stage is to collect information from both users and network monitoring reports. Questions to ask network users include the following:

- What exactly is the problem they are experiencing? Is the network too slow? Is an application not functioning? Can the user not see a specific network resource?

- When did the problem start? Did the network just start malfunctioning, or has it been this way for some time? Is the problem constant or only occasional?

- What has changed on the user's computer since the problem began? Did the user recently install an application or upgrade the operating system? Has the user attempted to fix the problem (and what has he or she done)?

After collecting data from the users reporting the problem, you must assess your network and ask other questions, including the following:

- Is the problem affecting the entire network or only isolated segments?

- What has changed on the network since the time the problem began? Were any of the servers reconfigured? Has new equipment been added, or old equipment removed? Have new applications been installed on the servers?

- Does your network monitoring software or hardware show you any trends in network traffic? Does a particular segment show excessive traffic? Can you identify any network bottlenecks?

- Does anyone else in your organization know of similar problems occurring on your network in the past?

After you have developed a comprehensive list of symptoms, you are ready to proceed and determine what could be causing the problem.

CH
18

Determine Possible Causes

The next step is to assemble all the information you have gathered and try to determine the cause of the problem. Based on your own experience with your network, develop a list of possible causes. What do you think could be wrong? Use resources like Microsoft TechNet to identify potential problems to add to your list. When you have a list of possible causes, rank them in order of the most probable to the least probable causes.

Isolate the Problem

After you have determined the possible causes, begin testing with the most likely cause. If you suspect the physical connection between a computer and the hub to be the issue, try replacing the cable. If you believe that the NIC might be malfunctioning, replace it with a new NIC. If you think that the TCP/IP settings are to blame, reconfigure those settings.

During this stage, it is best to make only one modification at a time. Make sure that any changes you make are reliable and do not introduce any other problems. For instance, when replacing a NIC, make sure that your replacement is a properly functioning card before replacing the faulty card.

It is also important to keep a record of any changes made to the system hardware, software, and configurations. Each time you make a change, you can potentially cause another problem. Keeping a record enables you to back out of all changes, if necessary, returning to the point where you started.

Study the Results

After each test, study what happened to see whether it fixed the problem. If so, document the problem and how you solved the issue. If not, return to your list of possible causes, and continue testing each possibility.

Troubleshooting Tools

As you work with networks, you will soon find that most network problems are the result of physical layer problems. Breaks or shorts in cables, faulty NIC cards, bad connections, and improperly terminated networks all can wreak havoc on your network. Physical problems can sometimes be the most difficult to track down. However, several tools are available to assist you, including

- Digital volt meters (DVMs)
- Time-domain reflectometers (TDRs)

- Protocol analyzers
- Advanced cable testers
- Network monitors
- Terminators

Key Concept

For the exam, make sure that you understand all the troubleshooting tools, but especially the differences among DVMs, TDRs, and protocol analyzers.

Digital Volt Meter (DVM)

One of the basic electronic measuring tools available today is the *digital volt meter (DVM)*, shown in Figure 18.1. Whereas a DVM can be used to measure the voltage of batteries or household electrical currents, its use within networking is for continuity testing. The test leads for a DVM can be connected to either end of a cable, and a small current sent through the cable. If the DVM shows no resistance, the current is flowing freely and there is no break in the cable. If the DVM shows resistance, a break in the cable is not letting the current flow through.

CH 18

Figure 18.1
A digital volt meter can be used to check continuity.

Alternatively, you can use the DVM to test for a short by connecting one lead to the central core and the other to the layer of shielding. In this arrangement, the existence of a current means that somehow the central core and the shielding are touching and shorting out the connection.

Key Concept

A *digital volt meter (DVM)* can be used to test for the existence of a break or short in a cable. A DVM operates at the physical layer of the OSI Reference Model.

Time-Domain Reflectometer (TDR)

Like a DVM, a *time-domain reflectometer (TDR)*, depicted in Figure 18.2, can be used to determine whether a break or short exists in a cable. Whereas a DVM merely indicates the existence of a break, a TDR sends an electric pulse down a cable to determine where a break or short occurs. When the pulse encounters a break or short, the pulse is reflected back towards where it originated. The TDR measures the time the pulse takes to reflect back and, based on the type of cable being tested, estimates how far away from the TDR the break or short is located. Good TDRs can estimate the distance to within a few feet of the break. TDRs are available to test both electrical and fiber-optic cables.

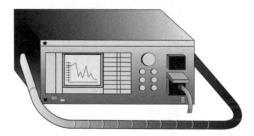

Figure 18.2
A time-domain reflectometer can estimate where a break occurs in a cable.

Key Concept

A *time-domain reflectometer (TDR)* uses a sonar-like pulse to determine where a break or short has occurred within a cable. A TDR operates at the physical layer of the OSI Reference Model.

Protocol Analyzer

Whereas DVMs and TDRs test only the physical integrity of cable, *protocol analyzers* examine the total health of the network by monitoring network traffic and examining packets. Protocol analyzers, also referred to as *network analyzers*, are hardware products or combinations of hardware and software. Protocol analyzers collect data by examining the contents of packets and developing a picture of the overall network.

As a result, protocol analyzers can be used to find problems such as

- Network bottlenecks
- Malfunctioning NICs
- Conflicting applications
- Abnormal network traffic from a particular computer
- Connection errors
- Faulty network components

Hardware protocol analyzers usually include a time-domain reflectometer to identify cable breaks at the physical layer, but their strength lies in their capability to analyze packets at the data link, network, and other upper OSI Reference Model layers. This capability enables protocol analyzers to zoom in on a particular network segment or protocol and determine how that segment or protocol is affecting overall network traffic.

Protocol analyzers can also be used to track network performance and usually include the capability to trigger alerts if certain network conditions are met. For instance, an administrator might want to be notified when network traffic reaches a certain level or when excessive levels of broadcast packets flood the system (a *broadcast storm*).

Many protocol analyzers (sometimes called *network analyzers*) are available on the market from companies such as Hewlett-Packard, Novell, and Fluke Corporation. Windows NT Server 4.0 also includes (free) Network Monitor, a software-based protocol analyzer.

Key Concept

A *protocol analyzer* is a powerful tool that can monitor network traffic, find faulty network components, and analyze the overall network performance. A protocol analyzer operates at many layers of the OSI model, although primarily the physical-through-network layers.

CH
18

Advanced Cable Testers

Like DVMs and TDRs, *cable testers* can test a cable for breaks and shorts. However, cable testers can also determine other information about a cable, such as its impedance, resistance, and attenuation, and other physical characteristics. Advanced cable testers can go beyond the physical layer and collect information about message frame counts, excess collisions, and congestion errors.

For instance, if you connected a cable tester to a Thinnet (RG-58A/U) cable, the cable tester would show an impedance of 50 ohms. If you connected a cable tester to an ARCnet (RG-62) cable, the cable tester would show an impedance of 93 ohms. With some knowledge of impedance values like these, a technician can use a cable tester to diagnose problems.

Network Monitor

Network monitors are software programs that can be used to monitor network traffic. By examining packets to determine packet types, network monitors can generate reports and charts about packet traffic, errors, and overall network traffic. Although network monitoring capabilities are provided by the protocol analyzers mentioned earlier, basic network monitoring software is provided with most Microsoft operating systems (see Figure 18.3). The *Performance Monitor* provided with Windows NT is one such example. Another is the *Network Monitor* provided with Windows NT Server 4.0, which is a free version of a tool provided with *Microsoft System Management Server (SMS)*. The free version allows you to monitor statistics about your own machine, whereas the SMS version allows you to monitor statistics about machines all across your network.

As mentioned in Chapter 17, "Network Problem Prevention," monitoring network performance to establish a baseline for your network can aid your troubleshooting. Network monitors work primarily from the OSI Reference Model data link layer up through the upper OSI layers.

Key Concept

Exam questions might ask about using *Performance Monitor* to monitor network traffic. If at all possible, you should try to get some hands-on experience using Performance Monitor before taking the exam.

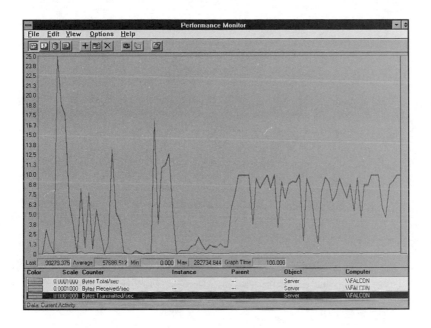

Figure 18.3
Windows NT Performance Monitor gives a visual representation of the network traffic it measures.

Terminator

When you are diagnosing cable problems in a network using coaxial cable, a TDR can estimate where the break occurs and assist you in locating the problem. However, if you do not have a TDR, a simple *terminator* can provide a degree of assistance. As mentioned in the earlier discussion of DVMs, a terminator can be placed on one end of a cable while a DVM measures the cable continuity.

You can also manually attempt to find the cable break by using terminators. In a coaxial bus network, find a network connection roughly in the middle of the network. Break the connection and place a terminator on either end, splitting your network into two separate halves. If there is only one break, one half of your network should now be functioning; the other half should not. Repeat this procedure on the half that is not functioning and continue breaking the network in half until you have isolated the cable segment with the break. This procedure is not as easy as using a TDR, but it accomplishes the task.

Note that this procedure can be difficult also if all your servers are located on one network segment when the network is divided. If this occurs, communication may still not occur on the other segment because of the lack of servers. You might have to divide the network so that at least one server is on each network segment.

Operating System Tools

Keep in mind, too, that many tools available within your operating system can help with troubleshooting problems, especially those related to your computer's hardware and software configuration. For instance, in Microsoft operating systems, the *Network* portion of the Control Panel provides access to network configuration settings. In Windows NT, the *Windows NT Diagnostics* tool can provide information about various system settings.

Resources for Troubleshooting

As you troubleshoot your network, you will find several resources helpful in your search for answers to your network problems, including

- Microsoft TechNet
- Microsoft Knowledge Base
- Vendor support sites
- Newsgroups
- Periodicals

Microsoft TechNet

If you are working within networks using Microsoft operating systems, one of the greatest resources available to you is Microsoft's *Technical Information Network (TechNet)*. As a TechNet subscriber, each month you receive a set of CDs containing an enormous wealth of product information, technical support updates, software drivers, and online tutorials. The easy-to-use interface (see Figure 18.4) allows you to query the CD database of technical support to find answers to networking problems.

TechNet is an extremely worthwhile resource to have available when diagnosing network problems. You can subscribe to TechNet through the TechNet Web site or by calling 1-800-344-2121. Depending on your level of Microsoft certification, you might be eligible for a free subscription. (Currently, this applies only to MCPs who have attained full MCSE status.)

You can obtain more information about Microsoft TechNet on the Web at `http://www.microsoft.com/technet/`.

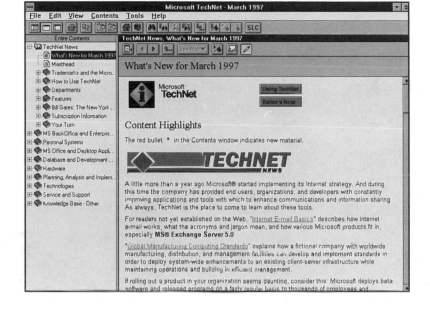

Figure 18.4
Microsoft TechNet provides an easy way to search for solutions to networking problems.

CH
18

Microsoft Knowledge Base

If you do not have access to TechNet, you can obtain many of the same support tips
through Microsoft's online Knowledge Base on the Web. As shown in Figure 18.5, the
Knowledge Base provides an interface that allows you to perform a keyword search.

You can retrieve information from Microsoft's online Knowledge Base at
http://support.microsoft.com/search/.

Vendor Support Sites

At this point in time, most vendors of networking products provide some type of technical support for their products. Appendix G, "Internet Resources," lists several vendor sites
of interest.

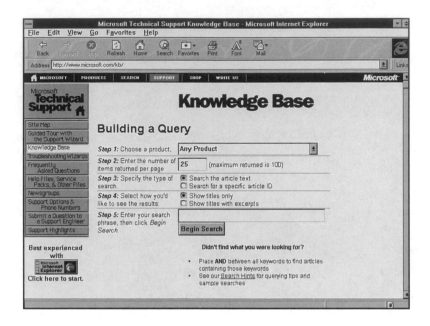

Figure 18.5
Microsoft's online Knowledge Base provides another method of finding technical support tips.

Newsgroups

Do not overlook the power of newsgroups when trying to find the answer to a problem. Appendix G lists a number of newsgroups that address networking issues. Frequently, a question posted to the appropriate newsgroup can quickly yield a solution from other network professionals. Additionally, because most of the popular Web search tools now give you the ability to search through newsgroups, you can search to see whether someone has already asked (and answered) your question.

There are now Web sites like DejaNews (http://www.deja.com/) specializing *only* in searching newsgroups. Many of the popular search engines, such as AltaVista (http://www.altavista.com/), also provide a means for you to search the newsgroups. Note that in some cases they refer to newsgroups by their original name of *USENET*.

Periodicals

With the extremely fast pace of change in the networking industry, periodicals can be an effective way to keep informed about the newest trends and technologies within computer networking. Many excellent weekly and monthly magazines address networking issues, including *LAN Magazine, LAN Times, Communications Week, InfoWorld,* and *PC Week.* Many magazines offer free subscriptions if you fill out a survey and meet their qualifications. Most networking-related magazines also have Web sites where they offer online editions, subscription information, and often forums and technical support areas. A listing of several online periodicals appears in Appendix G.

Common Problems

As mentioned earlier, the structured approach to solving problems can help you find solutions to complex problems. The following are a few of the more common problems plaguing computer networks:

- Cable problems
- Faulty network interface cards
- NIC configuration issues (IRQ and Base I/O port)
- Network driver problems
- Incorrect network protocol settings
- Network protocol mismatch
- Connectivity device failure
- Network traffic congestion
- Broadcast storms
- Network applications
- Power fluctuations

Cable Problems

As mentioned previously, many network problems can be attributed to faulty cables. Check that the cable is connected correctly. Make sure that the proper type of cable is being used. For instance, make sure that you are not using Cable TV coaxial wire (RG-59) within a Thinnet (RG-58A/U or C/U) network. Check that you are using the same type of UTP throughout your network. Ensure that you are not exceeding recommended cable lengths. DVMs and TDRs can assist in identifying cable problems.

Faulty Network Interface Cards

As mentioned earlier in the section "Troubleshooting Overview," you can often determine whether an NIC is functioning correctly by examining the lights on the back of the NIC. But is there an IRQ conflict with another device in the computer? Was the user no longer able to access the network after he installed a sound card in his computer? If everything looks okay and you are using TCP/IP, you can use the PING command to determine

CH
18

whether you can see other nearby computers. You might also consider using a protocol analyzer to determine whether any packets from the computer are making it onto the network.

NIC Configuration Problems (IRQ, Base I/O Port)

Examine the network interface card configuration settings to ensure that no IRQ or base I/O port address conflict exists with other hardware devices. Refer to Chapter 7, "Data Transmission," for a list of configuration settings and possible conflicts. If a conflict exists, the processor will be unable to communicate with the NIC. Try using alternative settings.

Network Driver Problems

Make sure that the appropriate driver for your network interface card is being used. Through your Network Control Panel, you may try removing the adapter and then reinstalling the adapter. This process should force your operating system to reinstall the NIC driver from the original media. (Note that this does *not* involve physically removing the NIC. You are removing it only from the Network Control Panel.)

Incorrect Network Protocol Settings

Make sure that the settings for the network protocol are correct. If using TCP/IP, is the subnet mask set correctly? Is the computer configured with the correct default gateway? If using IPX/SPX, is the correct frame type chosen?

Network Protocol Mismatch

If a computer is functioning properly but cannot see certain network resources, check that both the computer and the network resource are using the same network protocol. For instance, if a computer using only IPX/SPX tries to access shared resources on a server running only TCP/IP, no communication will occur. Add the appropriate protocols to one of the machines to resolve the problem.

Connectivity Device Failure

If one segment of a network functions properly, but another segment does not, immediately suspect whatever device connects the faulty segment. Check that hubs are working properly. It sounds stupid, but make sure that someone did not inadvertently disconnect an active hub from a power source. If two segments both work but cannot see each other, examine the bridge or router connecting the two network segments.

Network Traffic Congestion

A protocol analyzer or network monitor can tell you whether your levels of network traffic are too high. A good protocol analyzer can help you isolate which segments of your network are generating high levels of network traffic. From this information, you can make decisions about segmenting your network using bridges or routers to reduce overall traffic. Protocol analyzers can also point out network bottlenecks.

Broadcast Storms

It is possible that network devices such as NICs and hubs can malfunction and start generating excessive numbers of broadcast packets. A *broadcast storm* of this nature can saturate a network and slow regular network traffic to a crawl. You can use a protocol analyzer to determine which network component is malfunctioning and then replace that component. Assuming that you use routable network protocols, routers can provide a degree of protection against broadcast storms because they drop broadcast packets.

Network Applications

If the network is very slow, examine which applications your users are using. Popular network games such as Doom and Quake can bring a network to its knees. Some Internet applications, such as a news service called *PointCast*, can place a burden on network resources with constant updates. Some new technologies—as streaming audio and video, instant messaging, and chat applications—also consume network bandwidth. As the Web becomes more popular and new applications are developed for Web use, Internet applications will require more network bandwidth.

Power Fluctuations

Have there been any power fluctuations recently? A power failure for even a few seconds can cause failure of network servers and potentially prolonged network failure if a server does not return to proper functioning. An uninterruptible power supply (UPS) is the best protection against this type of problem. Note that even minor power fluctuations that occur frequently (but do not last long enough to bring down a server) can also damage sensitive networking equipment. A good UPS should also provide protection against problems with minor power fluctuations.

Summary

Network troubleshooting involves the process of collecting information about what is wrong, isolating the problem, and correcting the situation. Microsoft outlines a five-step approach to network troubleshooting:

CH
18

1. Set the problem's priority.
2. Collect information to identify the symptoms.
3. Develop a list of possible causes.
4. Test to isolate the cause.
5. Study the results of the test to identify a solution.

By using a structured approach like this, you can methodically identify and solve network problems.

To assist you in gathering information, a number of diagnostic tools are available. Working at the OSI Reference Model physical layer, both *digital volt meters (DVMs)* and *time-domain reflectometers (TDRs)* can determine that a cable has a break or a short. Further, by using a sonar-like electrical or optical pulse, TDRs can estimate where the actual break or short occurs. *Protocol analyzers* are more complex tools that, like DVMs and TDRs, can diagnose physical layer problems, but they can also examine packets and solve issues occurring at the data link and network layers. Protocol analyzers can identify more complex problems like network traffic bottlenecks or conflicting applications.

In your search for solutions, many resources are at your disposal. Microsoft TechNet is a CD-ROM–based resource to which you can subscribe that provides a monthly set of CDs with a searchable database of technical support problems and product information. Microsoft also maintains a Knowledge Base on the Web that provides another searchable database. Most vendors are now making information available through the Web, as are numerous networking periodicals.

Finally, the most common problems plaguing network users usually involve cabling issues. Additional common problems include faulty network interface cards, protocol mismatches, and incorrect network drivers.

QUESTIONS AND ANSWERS

1. What are a couple of basic troubleshooting techniques one can use before going too far investigating the problem?

   A: Several answers: Question the user, check the physical connection, check the NIC, restart the computer

2. Name three troubleshooting tools you can use.

   A: Several possible answers: digital volt meter, time-domain reflectometer, protocol analyzer, cable tester, network monitor, terminator

…continues

…continued

3. What is the difference between a DVM and a TDR?

   A: A digital volt meter measures continuity and can detect a break or a short. A time-domain reflectometer can do this and can also locate the break by sending an electrical signal down the wire and measuring the time it takes for the reflected signal to come back.

4. At what layer of the OSI model do a DVM and TDR operate?

   A: The physical layer

5. Where in the OSI model does a protocol analyzer fit?

   A: Primarily between the physical and network layers, although some tools also can utilize the upper OSI layers as well

6. How does a cable tester differ from a DVM or TDR?

   A: A cable tester can examine other properties of a cable beyond simply the fact that a signal gets through. Cable testers can also test the cable impedance, whether the cable meets specifications, and other various factors. Cable testers also often include some data link capabilities to monitor Ethernet activity over the cable.

7. How can a terminator be used in troubleshooting coaxial cable?

   A: By going to a midpoint on the cable and terminating one half of the cable, you can determine whether that half is operational. If so, the problem must be in the other half of the cable. Repeating the procedure on that half of the cable will eventually help you locate the cable break.

8. If you are trying to figure out the source of a broadcast storm, which tool would you use?

   A: A protocol analyzer

9. You have a coaxial network and suspect a break somewhere in the cable. Which tool will help you locate the break?

   A: A time-domain reflectometer

10. Identify four common network problems.

    A: Many possible answers, including cable problems, faulty NICs, NIC configuration problems, NIC driver problems, network protocol mismatch, incorrect protocol settings, connectivity device failure, traffic congestion, broadcast storms, power fluctuations

**CH
18**

PRACTICE TEST

1. Which device can be used to assist in resolving broadcast storms?

    a. Protocol analyzer

    b. Time-domain reflectometer

    c. Oscilloscope

    d. Digital volt meter

Answer a is correct; a protocol analyzer can resolve broadcast storms. Answers b, c, and d are incorrect because these tools operate only at the physical layer and do not understand data packets.

2. What is the primary function of a time-domain reflectometer?

    a. To perform continuity tests to determine the existence of a break or short in a cable

    b. To analyze packets, detect faulty network components, and monitor overall network performance

    c. To estimate where a cable break or short has occurred by using a pulse of electricity

    d. To monitor network packets and show trends in network traffic over time

Answer a is incorrect because it defines a DVM. Answer b is incorrect because it defines a protocol analyzer. **Answer c is correct.** Answer d is incorrect because it defines a network monitor.

3. How does a digital volt meter assist in network troubleshooting?

    a. It analyzes packets, detects faulty network components, and monitors overall network performance.

    b. It performs continuity tests to determine the existence of a break or short in a cable.

    c. It monitors network packets and shows trends in network traffic over time.

    d. It estimates where a cable break or short has occurred by using a pulse of electricity.

Answer a is incorrect because it defines a protocol analyzer. **Answer b is correct.** Answer c is incorrect because it defines a network monitor. Answer d is incorrect because it defines a TDR.

4. Which of the following troubleshooting tools do *not* function *only* at the OSI physical layer? (Choose all that apply.)

    a. Time-domain reflectometer

    b. Protocol analyzer

    c. Digital volt meter

    d. Network monitor

Answers a and c are incorrect because they work only at the physical layer. **Answer b is correct because protocol analyzers can work from the physical layer on up through the rest of the OSI model. Answer d is correct because network monitors typically start at the data link and work through the upper layers of the OSI model.**

5. A user on your 10BASE2 Ethernet network suddenly complains that she is unable to access any network resources. Everything was working fine, and nothing has changed on her computer. All other computer users are experiencing no difficulties. Which of the following could *not* be a cause of the problem with her computer? (Choose all that apply.)

   a. The IRQ of her computer's NIC conflicts with that of another device in her computer.
   b. Her computer's NIC has stopped functioning.
   c. There is a break in the cable media.
   d. The connection of the cable to her computer's NIC has come loose.

Answer a is correct because nothing has changed in her computer; an IRQ conflict would be probable only if new cards or devices had been added to her system. Answer b is incorrect because it *is* a possible cause. **Answer c is correct because if there was a cable break on a 10BASE2 network, all other users would be unable to use the network as well.** Answer d is incorrect because it *is* a possible cause.

6. Two computers (A and B) in your office can access network resources on various file servers without any problems. However, when a user on computer A wants to access a shared folder on computer B, the user finds that she cannot see computer B in her browse window. Other users within the network have no problem accessing the folder on computer B. Which of the following is the most likely cause of the problem?

   a. Both computers are using the same IRQ for their network interface cards.
   b. Both computers are using the same IP address.
   c. There is a protocol mismatch between the two computers.
   d. There is a problem with the cable connection to computer B.

Answer a is incorrect because IRQs matter only inside a single machine; it makes no difference in computer-to-computer communication. Answer b is incorrect because if it was true, both computers would be having problems accessing all network servers, and one of the computers probably would have deactivated its NIC when the IP address conflict was detected. **Answer c is correct; for instance, the two computers could be using different NetWare frame types. Whereas the servers can automatically adjust to the different frame types, the individual computers must use the same type to communicate.** Answer d is incorrect because if it was true, computer B could not use the network.

CH 18

   7. Your users are complaining that the network is exceptionally slow. Which troubleshooting tools can you use to determine the flow of network traffic? (Choose all that apply.)

     a. Digital volt meter

     b. Network monitor

     c. Time-domain reflectometer

     d. Protocol analyzer

Answers a and c are incorrect because both operate at the physical layer and have no concept of data packets. **Answers b and d are correct; both tools can monitor network traffic.**

   8. The function of a digital volt meter is to use continuity testing to determine the existence of cable breaks or shorts.

     a. True

     b. False

Answer a is correct. Answer b is incorrect.

   9. A computer in your office cannot access the network. You have checked the cable connection. The NIC appears to be functioning properly. No IRQ conflicts exist. All network protocols appear to be correct. What device can you use to determine whether packets from that computer are being sent onto the network?

     a. Protocol analyzer

     b. Digital volt meter

     c. Cable tester

     d. Time-domain reflectometer

Answer a is correct; a protocol analyzer can determine whether packets are being sent from the computer. Answers b, c, and d are incorrect because all three function at the physical layer.

   10. A user had no problem accessing the network until he recently installed a sound card. What should you immediately suspect as the problem?

     a. Invalid network driver

     b. Incorrect network protocol settings

     c. Protocol mismatch

     d. IRQ conflict

Answers a, b, and c are incorrect because nothing has changed (that we are told) with the network interface card or the network settings. **Answer d is correct; the NIC was most likely using IRQ5, and now the sound card wants to use the same IRQ.**

Glossary

10BASE-2   An Ethernet network using thinnet (50 ohm, 0.2 inch diameter) RG-58 A/U, or RG-58 C/U coaxial cable.

10BASE-5   An Ethernet network on thicknet (50 ohm, 0.4 inch diameter) coaxial cable.

10BASE-F   An Ethernet network using fiber-optic cable.

10BASE-T   An Ethernet network over Unshielded Twisted-Pair (UTP) cable using RJ-45 connectors.

100BASE-T   Also referred to as Fast Ethernet or 100BASE-X, a 100Mbps Ethernet network that can be subdivided into three categories: 100BASE-TX, 100BASE-T4, and 100BASE-FX.

100VG-AnyLAN   Originally developed by Hewlett-Packard and AT&T, provides speeds up to 100Mbps and uses the demand priority media access method rather than CSMA/CD.

A

ACK   An acknowledgement signal.

acknowledgement   In connection-oriented communication, the process used to guarantee reliable message delivery.

active monitor   A node on a Token-Ring network that periodically sends out a signal to check that the network is free of errors. Usually the first computer to come online on a network.

active transmitter   Transceiver unit that amplifies the signal before retransmitting the signal.

Advanced Program-to-Program Communications (APPC)   A Session Layer protocol used with IBM SNA-based networks.

Advanced Research Projects Agency (ARPA)   The agency responsible for the formation of the forerunner of the Internet. See *Defense Advanced Research Projects Agency.*

AFP   See *AppleTalk Filing Protocol.*

American National Standards Institute (ANSI)   A standards-making organization based in the United States of America.

American Standard Code for Information Interchange (ASCII)   A scheme that assigns letters, punctuation marks, and so on to specific numeric values. The standardization of ASCII-enabled computers and computer programs to exchange data.

American Wire Gauge (AWG)   The standards by which cables are defined based on specified wire diameters. AWG numbers are inversely assigned to diameters, meaning that larger AWG numbers indicate smaller diameters.

analog   A signal with an infinite number of states, rather than just 1s and 0s. Voice, telephone, and television are examples of analog signals.

ANSI   See *American National Standards Institute.*

ANSI character set   An eight-bit character set used by Microsoft Windows that enables you to represent up to 256 characters (0–255) using your keyboard. The ASCII character set is a subset of the ANSI set. See *American National Standards Institute.*

API   See *application programming interface.*

APPC   See *Advanced Program-to-Program Communications.*

AppleTalk   A simple, easy-to-use network architecture used by Apple Macintosh computers and included as part of the Macintosh operating system.

AppleTalk Filing Protocol (AFP)   The AppleTalk protocol describing how files are stored and shared within an AppleTalk network. Operates in Presentation and Application Layers of the OSI model.

AppleTalk Phase 1   The original AppleTalk implementation where up to 32 computers could be connected on a network and only LocalTalk cabling was supported. With the use of hubs, the overall network could increase to 254 computers.

AppleTalk Phase 2   Introduced in 1989, allows the use of AppleTalk network protocols on top of Ethernet (EtherTalk) and Token-Ring (TokenTalk) architectures. Supports up to 16 million network nodes.

application   A computer program that is designed to do some specific type of work—for example, a word processor, spreadsheet, database, game, or other application. An application is different from a utility, which performs some type of maintenance (such as formatting a disk).

Application Layer   The top layer of the OSI Reference Model that is primarily concerned with the interaction of the user with the computer. Services at this level support user applications such as electronic mail, database queries, network printing, and file transfer.

application programming interface (API)
A list of supported functions that allow the programmers to interact with the network. Windows 95 supports the MS-DOS API, Windows API, and Win32 API. If a function is a member of the API, it is said to be a *supported,* or *documented,* function. Functions that make up Windows but are not part of the API are referred to as undocumented functions.

application server   A file server on a network dedicated to providing access to applications.

archiving   See *backup.*

ARCnet   See *Attached Resource Computer Network.*

ARCnet Plus   A successor to ARCnet that supports communication up to 20Mbps.

ARPA   See *Advanced Research Projects Agency.*

ASCII   See *American Standard Code for Information Interchange.*

ASCII character set   A 7-bit character set widely used to represent letters and symbols found on a standard U.S. keyboard. The ASCII character set is identical to the first 128 characters in the ANSI character set.

asynchronous communication   A communication method where data is sent as a serial stream of information with start and stop bits indicating where the data begins and ends.

Asynchronous Transfer Mode (ATM)   A packet-switched WAN technology that breaks up data into 53-byte cells. ATM can reach speeds up to 622Mbps using current technology.

ATM   See *Asynchronous Transfer Mode.*

Attached Resource Computer Network (ARCnet)   Created by Datapoint Corporation in 1977, a very flexible and inexpensive network architecture. ARCnet uses a token-passing scheme to connect up to 255 nodes over twisted-pair, coaxial, or fiber-optic cable. ARCnet is limited to speeds of 2.5Mbps.

Attachment Unit Interface (AUI)   The connector used with 10BASE-5 Ethernet (thicknet). It is often found as one of the ports on the back of a network interface card (NIC) and is also referred to as a *DIX connector.*

attenuation   The degeneration of a signal over distance on a network cable. As an electrical signal travels farther along a cable, part of the signal is absorbed by the network media, eventually rendering the signal unreadable by receiving network nodes. Attenuation is measured in decibels.

auditing   The process of monitoring user activity on a network to track unauthorized or unintentional network usage. Auditing can be enabled to track such items as logon attempts, directory creation, file modification, and password changes. Auditing normally involves the creation of log files that track these system events.

AUI   See *Attachment Unit Interface.*

AWG   See *American Wire Gauge.*

B

back end   In client/server applications, the software component running on the server that communicates with the front end or client software.

backbone   The main cable segment to which other network devices are connected. While in 10BASE-5 networks, transceivers are connected directly to a thicknet backbone; in other networks, the term is used to refer to whatever cable is connecting different network segments together.

backup   A duplicate copy of an item made for the purpose of protecting the item. The term is also used to refer to the process of duplicating data. Backing up data is also referred to as *archiving.*

backup domain controller (BDC)
Within a Windows NT Server domain, maintains a duplicate read-only copy of the domain security database and provides security validation in the event of the failure of the primary domain controller (PDC). See *primary domain controller.*

bad-sector remapping   See *sector-sparing.*

bandwidth   In network media, refers to the number of bits that can be sent across the cable at any given time.

barrel connector   A hardware device used to connect two coaxial cables.

base input/output (I/O) port   The address the processor uses when communicating with the motherboard. Like the IRQ, the base I/O port of a device must be unique.

base memory address   Also referred to as the upper memory address (UMA), the starting address in the buffer area of the computer's memory (RAM) for the network interface card.

baseband transmission   Uses digital technology where the 1s and 0s of the data bits are defined as discrete changes in the flow of electricity or light. The entire communication channel is used to transmit a single data signal.

baud rate   A measurement of modem speed named for a French scientist named Baudot who developed an encoding scheme for the French telegraph system in 1877. Often confused with bps (bits per second), the baud rate actually refers to the number of state transitions (from 0 to 1 and 1 to 0) that occur within a single second. Newer compression technologies allow more than 1 bit to be transmitted within a single state transition, so the two measurements are no longer equivalent. A modem transmitting at 9,600bps might in fact transmit at 2,400 baud.

BDC   See *backup domain controller.*

beaconing   The process that allows networks to self-repair network problems. The stations on the network notify the other stations on the ring when they are not receiving transmissions. Used primarily in Token-Ring and FDDI networks. See *Token Ring* and *Fiber Distributed Data Interface*.

binding   The process that links a protocol driver and a network adapter driver.

bit   Short for BInary digiT, the smallest unit of data a computer can store. Bits are expressed as 1 or 0.

BNC (British Naval Connector)   A connector used for coaxial cable.

bottleneck   A component or device that causes network traffic to be significantly slowed.

bps   A measurement within communications of the number of bits per second transmitted.

bridge   A device used to combine different segments of a network into one large network. Bridges can work as repeaters to extend a network and connect network segments, and they can also filter network traffic to reduce congestion. The bridge connects networks at the Data Link Layer of the OSI Model.

bridging table   A comprehensive list of hardware (MAC) addresses for the network. This table is used by a bridge to determine which packets should be delivered to which ports.

broadband transmission   Uses analog communication to divide the network cable into a series of channels. Each channel has its own frequency, and all devices listening at that frequency can obtain the data.

broadcast infrared   Disperses the infrared signal so that multiple units can receive the transmission. See also *infrared*.

broadcast packets   Data packets that are sent to all the computers on the network.

broadcast storm   Occurs when a network device (network interface card or network application) malfunctions and starts to deluge the network with broadcast packets. Routers can be used to limit the effects of broadcast storms.

brouters   Hybrid devices that combine features of both bridges and routers and are only found in networks using multiple protocols. A brouter routes routable protocols and bridges nonroutable protocols.

browse   To look through a list on a computer system. Lists include directories, files, domains, or computers.

browser   On the Internet, a software program used to view documents on the World Wide Web. Also used within the world of Microsoft networks to refer to the computer maintaining a list of NetBIOS names currently in use on the network.

buffer   A temporary holding place reserved in memory, where data is held while in transit to or from a storage device or another location in memory.

buffering   The process of using buffers, particularly to or from I/O devices such as disk drives and serial ports.

bus   A network topology where all the computers are connected together in a line. Messages are passed between the computers along a single backbone with a terminator located at the end to stop the network signal. The term can also refer to the data bus used within a computer to communicate between the CPU and hardware components.

bus mastering   Similar to direct memory access (DMA), a technique where your network interface card (NIC) takes control of the computer's data bus and transfers data directly into the system memory without involving the microprocessor. See *Direct Memory Access.*

byte   Eight bits.

C

Carrier-Sense Multiple Access with Collision Avoidance (CSMA/CA) Similar to CSMA/CD, computers will first check the network media to see whether it is in use. Before transmitting the data, the computer will send out a signal indicating that it is about to transmit. After the signal has gone out, the computer will actually transmit. Used in AppleTalk networks with LocalTalk media.

Carrier-Sense Multiple Access with Collision Detection (CSMA/CD)   The basis for the Ethernet network architecture, where multiple computers have access to the network media. The computers will check the network media before transmitting to see whether it is being used. If two or more computers transmit at the same time, a collision is detected and each computer will wait a random period of time before retransmission.

CCITT (Comité Consultatif Internationale de Télégraphie et Téléphonie)   The Geneva-based international organization that specifies communications standards used throughout the world, also referred to as the International Telegraph and Telephone Consultative Committee. The CCITT is part of the *International Telecommunications Union (ITU)*, a United Nations body. Many CCITT standards are now being referred to as ITU standards.

cell   The 53-byte data packets used by ATM.

cell-switching   The process in which data packets are broken into very small, fixed-length cells that are transmitted across the network.

central office (CO)   The office of a local telephone company to which all local phone lines within a region are connected. WAN connections typically involve a link (the "local loop") from your office to the nearest CO where connections are then made to long-distance carriers. See *local loop.*

central processing unit (CPU) The computational and control unit of a computer; the device that interprets and executes instructions. The CPU or microprocessor, in the case of a microcomputer, has the ability to fetch, decode, and execute instructions and to transfer information to and from other resources over the computer's main data-transfer path, the *bus*. The CPU is the chip that functions as the "brain" of a computer.

Channel Service Unit/Data Service Unit (CSU/DSU) A hardware device used to connect a computer network to a digital line used in WAN communication.

character A letter, number, punctuation mark, or control code. Usually expressed in either the ANSI or ASCII character set.

checkpoints Bits of data placed in the data stream at the Session Layer of the OSI model to facilitate recovery from network transmission problems. If a network failure occurs, only data transmitted since the last checkpoint will need to be retransmitted.

circuit In network communications, a communication path between two network endpoints.

circuit-switched network A switched network in which a communication channel is established between two endpoints for the duration of a communication session. The telephone system is an example of a circuit-switched network.

cladding A layer of glass surrounding the central fiber of glass inside a fiber-optic cable. The purpose of the cladding is to reflect the light that is being transmitted down the fiber, back into the central fiber. This prevents the light from traveling in all directions.

client A computer that accesses shared network resources provided by another computer, called a *server*. See also *server*.

client software Software that allows users to access and use network resources such as file servers and printers.

client-access licenses Licenses for network applications specifying how many users can use the application.

client/server architecture A network architecture that divides processing between client software located usually on desktop PCs and server software located on servers. The client programs handle user interaction and make requests for data. Server programs process data and fulfill requests from clients.

coaxial cable Also referred to as *coax*, consists of an inner wire core that transmits the data and an outer layer of electrically conductive shielding to reduce interference. Within Ethernet networks, thinnet and thicknet are common coaxial cables.

collision A situation where two or more network devices transmit simultaneously.

communications protocol The rules that govern a conversation between two computers that are communicating via an asynchronous connection.

computer name   A unique name that identifies a particular computer on the network. Microsoft networking uses NetBIOS names, which can have up to 15 characters and cannot contain spaces.

concentrators   A generic term for a device that provides a central connection point for the connection of terminal, computer, or communications devices. Also, a specific term used to refer to an FDDI hub.

contention   The situation when multiple devices compete for the use of the network media. Contention-based access methods, such as CSMA/CD, provide rules for governing contention and limiting collisions. See also *Carrier-Sense Multiple Access with Collision Detection (CSMA/CD)*.

controller   See *domain controller*.

CPU   See *central processing unit*.

CRC   See *Cyclical Redundancy Check*.

crosstalk   Occurs when two wires are placed next to each other inside a cable. The noise from each line can interfere with the signal in the other line.

CSMA/CA   See *Carrier-Sense Multiple Access with Collision Avoidance*.

CSMA/CD   See *Carrier-Sense Multiple Access with Collision Detection*.

CSU/DSU   See *Channel Service Unit/Data Service Unit*.

Cyclical Redundancy Check (CRC)   A number produced by a mathematical calculation and added at the end of a data packet before transmission. On receipt, the CRC is recalculated and compared against the transmitted number to ensure that the data was not corrupted during transmission.

D

DARPA   See *Defense Advanced Research Projects Agency*.

DAS   See *Dual Attachment Stations*.

data frame   The structured packets into which data is placed by the Data Link Layer. A more specific definition would be a transmission unit of fixed maximum size that consists of binary information representing data, addressing information, and error-correction information, created by the Data Link Layer.

Data Link Layer   The layer of the OSI Reference Model that is responsible for packaging data into frames and providing an error-free link between two computers. The Data Link Layer was further subdivided by the IEEE 802 Project into the logical link control and media access control sublayers.

database access language   A language such as SQL used to extract information from a database. See *Structured Query Language (SQL)*.

Database Management Systems (DBMS) A sophisticated software system that manages communications between users and the database program.

database servers Servers on a network dedicated to the task of fulfilling database requests.

datagram A packet of information and delivery data that is routed on a network.

DBMS See *Database Management Systems.*

DECnet A protocol suite developed by Digital Equipment Corporation.

dedicated server A computer that is used only as a server and not as a client workstation.

Defense Advanced Research Projects Agency (DARPA) An agency of the U.S. Department of Defense that sponsored the development of the protocols which became the TCP/IP suite. DARPA was previously known as *ARPA, the Advanced Research Projects Agency*, when ARPAnet was built.

demarcation point The place at your home or office building to which your local telephone company brings in all phone lines. The telephone company is responsible for all line and equipment maintenance from the local phone network up to the demarcation point. As the customer, you are responsible for all interior wiring from the demarcation point to your telephones or telephone system. Also referred to as the demarc.

device A generic term for a computer component, such as a printer, serial port, or disk drive. A device frequently requires its own controlling software called a *device driver.*

device driver A piece of software that translates requests from one form into another. Most commonly, drivers are used to provide a device-independent way to access hardware.

DHCP See *Dynamic Host Configuration Protocol.*

Dial-Up Networking (DUN) Formerly known as *remote access service (RAS)*, provides remote access to networks. DUN allows a remote user to access his network. When connected, it can be as if the remote computer is logically on the network; the user can do anything that he could do when physically connected to the network, depending on security.

digital A signal with only two states, such as 1s and 0s. Computers and most electronic networking devices use digital communication. For an opposite, see *analog.*

digital volt meter (DVM) A basic electronic tool that measures the amount of voltage passing through a given electrical circuit. In network communications, a DVM can be used to test continuity to determine if a cable has any breaks.

DIP switch Short for Dual Inline Package switch. Used to configure hardware options, especially on adapter cards.

Direct Memory Access (DMA) A technique used by hardware adapters to store and retrieve information from the computer's RAM memory without involving the computer's CPU.

direct-sequence modulation A form of spread-spectrum transmission that breaks data into chips and then transmits that data on several frequencies.

Directory Services A means of locating users on a network or messaging system. Some email examples include Microsoft's Personal Address Book and Global Address List. Also, X.500 is an international standard for directory services.

disk duplexing A data protection technique similar to disk mirroring, but involving the use of multiple disk drive controller cards to provide extra protection from failures.

disk mirroring A data protection technique where data is simultaneously written in the identical manner on multiple disk drives. If one drive fails, the data will still be available on the second drive. Disk mirroring usually uses two or more disk drives with a single disk drive controller card.

distance-vector algorithm A method used in building routing tables where a cost is calculated for each route based on the number of routers (or hops) in between two networks.

DIX connector Another name for the AUI connector. The name is derived from the creators of the connector: Digital Equipment Corporation, Intel, and Xerox. See *Attachment User Interface (AUI)*.

DMA See *Direct Memory Access*.

DMA channel A channel for DMA transfers, those that occur between a device and memory directly, without involving the CPU.

DNS See *domain name service*.

DNS name servers The servers that hold the DNS name database, and supply the IP address that matches a DNS name in response to a request from a DNS client. See also *domain name service*.

domain For DNS, a group of workstations and servers that share a single group name. For Microsoft networking, a collection of computers that share a security context and account database stored on a Windows NT Server domain controller. Each domain has a unique name. See also *domain name service*.

domain controller The Windows NT Server computer that authenticates domain logons and maintains a copy of the security database for the domain. See *primary domain controller* and *backup domain controller*.

domain name service (DNS) A static, hierarchical name service for TCP/IP hosts. Do not confuse DNS domains with Windows NT domains.

drive designators   The disk drive letters used by a client redirector to make network resources appear as if they are local.

driver   A small piece of software that is installed into the operating system to allow it to use a specific device—for example, the printer or network interface card (NIC).

dual attachment concentrators   In FDDI, these are connected to both rings and have ports allowing the connection of workstations. Similar to hubs in other architectures.

Dual Attachment Stations (DAS)   FDDI network interface cards that are attached to both rings and are intended primarily for servers, concentrators, and other devices that need the reliability afforded by the dual-ring structure.

DVM   See *digital volt meter.*

Dynamic Host Configuration Protocol (DHCP)   A protocol for automatic TCP/IP configuration that provides static and dynamic address allocation and management.

dynamic routers   Choose the best route for the data packet to travel. In order to calculate which route is better, the dynamic routers use two methods: *distance-vector algorithm* and *link-state algorithm.*

E

EISA   See *Extended Industry Standard Architecture.*

electromagnetic frequency   The number of wave cycles per second, measured primarily in terms of hertz (Hz).

electromagnetic interference (EMI)   A type of signal that interferes with the correct transmission of signals through a network medium. For instance, electrical motors placed in close proximity to network cables could generate enough EMI to interfere with the network signal passing through the cables.

electromagnetic spectrum   The range of the transmission of energy waves from electrical power and telephones at the low end to X-rays and gamma rays at the high end.

electronic mail (email)   An electronic message sent from one user to another.

electronic messaging system (EMS)   A system that allows users or applications to correspond using electronic mail.

email   See *electronic mail.*

email client   In an email system, the program responsible for all the user interaction, such as reading and composing messages. Also called a *User Agent (UA).*

EMI   See *electromagnetic interference.*

encryption   The process of encoding messages so they cannot be read during transmission.

enterprise (or enterprise-wide) network
See *wide area network.*

Ethernet   A LAN network architecture originally developed by Xerox in 1976 and later standardized as IEEE 802.3. Designed to use a bus architecture and the CSMA/CD access method, and to transmit data at 10Mbps. Uses coaxial, twisted-pair, or fiber-optic cable.

Ethernet 802.2   The default Ethernet frame type used in Novell NetWare 4.x networks.

Ethernet 802.3   Also referred to as raw Ethernet, the Ethernet frame type used primarily in Novell NetWare 2.x and 3.x networks.

Ethernet SNAP (SubNetwork Address Protocol)   The Ethernet frame type used in *AppleTalk Phase II* networks.

Ethernet II   Ethernet frame type used in TCP/IP networks and networks using multiple network protocols.

EtherTalk   Allows a network to use AppleTalk network protocols over 10Mbps IEEE 802.3 Ethernet network.

ev   See *hertz volt.*

Extended Industry Standard Architecture (EISA)   An enhancement to the bus architecture used on the IBM PC/AT, which allows the use of 32-bit devices in the same type of expansion slot used by an ISA adapter card. EISA slots and adapters were common in server computers, but have been mostly replaced with PCI slots.

F

fault tolerance   A generic computing term for the condition of being able to provide some protection against failure. The fault tolerance of a network is the degree of network problems that can occur before the network fails.

FDDI   See *Fiber Distributed Data Interface.*

Fiber Distributed Data Interface (FDDI) Uses fiber-optic cable and token-passing to create a very fast and reliable network operating at speeds up to 100Mbps. FDDI networks are implemented as a true physical ring.

fiber-optic cable   Cable in which the data is transmitted in the form of light rather than electrical signals. Fiber-optic cables are not susceptible to electromagnetic interference which degrades copper wires.

file   A collection of information stored on a disk, and accessible using a name.

file sharing   The ability of a network computer to share files or directories on its local disks with remote computers. Windows 95 and Windows NT enable you to share your files if the File and Print Sharing services are enabled on your computer.

file system   In an operating system, the overall structure in which files are named, stored, and organized.

file transfer protocol (FTP) The standard method of transferring files using TCP/IP. FTP allows you to transfer files between dissimilar computers, with preservation of binary data and optional translation of text file formats.

firewall A security barrier constructed of hardware and software to keep intruders out of a network.

folder In Windows Explorer, a container object—that is, an object that can contain other objects. Examples include disk folders, the Fonts folder, and the Printers folder. A replacement for the term *directory*.

frame See *data frame*.

frame relay A packet-switching technology that uses variable-length packets and establishes permanent virtual circuits between endpoints. One reason frame relay networks are popular is that customers can specify the amount of bandwidth they want to use.

frequency-hopping A type of spread-spectrum transmission that switches data between multiple frequencies. Both the transmitter and the receiver are synchronized to use the same predetermined frequencies and time slots.

FTP See *file transfer protocol*.

G

gateway A computer connected to multiple networks and capable of moving data between networks using different transport protocols. Unlike routers and brouters, gateways can actually change the format of the data itself. Gateways function at the Application and other upper layers of the OSI Model.

Gbps Gigabits per second. Essentially one billion bits per second.

geosynchronous satellite A satellite located in a fixed location above one location on the ground.

GHz A frequency measurement representing one billion bits per second.

gigabyte Roughly one billion bytes.

Gopher A distributed information system on the Internet developed by the University of Minnesota. Information is presented as a series of menus.

graphical user interface (GUI) A computer system design in which the user interacts with the system using graphical symbols, tools, and events, rather than text-based displays and commands such as the normal Windows user interface.

group Within a network operating system, user accounts can be placed into group accounts, and permissions can be given to the entire group.

groupware applications Also referred to as *workgroup applications*, similar to email systems but provide added functionality to enable a group of people to work better together. Groupware systems include Microsoft Exchange, Lotus Notes, and Novell GroupWise, which provide both email and workgroup functions.

GUI See *graphical user interface*.

H

hertz (Hz) The unit of frequency measurement equal to one cycle per second.

hertz volt (ev) The unit of measurement used when electromagnetic frequencies enter the range of light.

hop When calculating the routing table and determining the best path between two endpoints, each router in the path counts as one hop.

host Another name for any server that is attached to an internetwork.

host ID The portion of the IP address that identifies a computer within a particular network ID.

host name The name of an Internet host. It might or might not be the same as the computer name. In order for a client to access resources by host name, it must appear in the client's HOSTS file, or be resolvable by a DNS server.

HOSTS file A local text file in the same format as the UNIX/Linux /etc/hosts file. This file maps host names to IP addresses. In Windows 95, this file is stored in the \WINDOWS directory. In Windows NT, this file is stored in \WINNT\system32\drivers\ etc, assuming that \WINNT is where you have installed Windows NT. The HOSTS file is used for TCP/IP host name resolution as compared with the LMHOSTS file which is used for NetBIOS name resolution. See also *LMHOSTS file*.

hot-fixing See *sector-sparing*.

HTML See *Hypertext Markup Language*.

hub A connectivity device used in a star network to provide a central connection point for all cable segments. An active hub, sometimes referred to as a *multiport repeater*, requires electrical power and regenerates the signal from each cable segment. A passive hub requires no power and merely serves as a central location to organize wiring. A hub, like a repeater, operates at the Physical Layer of the OSI Model.

Hypertext Markup Language (HTML) A text file format used to create pages for use in the World Wide Web.

Hz See *hertz*.

I

ICMP See *Internet control message protocol*.

IEEE See *Institute of Electrical and Electronic Engineers*.

IEEE 802   Specifications which define the way in which data is actually placed on the physical network media by network interface cards. The IEEE 802 specification divides the OSI Data Link Layer into two sublayers: *logical link control* and *media access control.*

IETF   See *Internet Engineering Task Force.*

IMAP4   See *Internet Mail Access Protocol version 4.*

impedance   The resistance of a wire to the transmission of an electrical signal, measured in *ohms.*

Industry Standard Architecture (ISA) The designation for the data bus and expansion slots used in the original IBM PC/XT. ISA expansion slots will accommodate an 8-bit or 16-bit card.

infrared (IR)   In the electromagnetic spectrum, infrared frequencies occupy the range from 100Ghz through 1,000 terahertz (THz), just below the range of visible light. Infrared communication technology takes two forms: *point-to-point* and *broadcast.*

infrared networks   Networks that use infrared signals instead of physical cables to connect the computers on a network. Infrared networks are generally limited to line of sight, where the network adapter on the computer must be able to "see" its companion network port.

Institute of Electrical and Electronic Engineers (IEEE)   An organization that issues standards for electrical and electronic devices.

Integrated Services Digital Network (ISDN)   A digital communications method that permits connections of up to 128Kbps, using two 64Kbps channels. ISDN is designed as a replacement for the traditional telephone system and requires the installation of a digital line.

International Organization for Standardization (ISO)   The organization that produces many of the world's standards. *Open Systems Interconnect (OSI)* is only one of many areas standardized by the ISO.

International Telecommunications Union (ITU)   A body of the United Nations that develops standards for global telecommunications. The CCITT is a committee of the *ITU.* See *CCITT.*

Internet   The worldwide interconnected WAN, based on the TCP/IP protocol suite.

Internet control message protocol (ICMP)   A required protocol in the TCP/IP protocol suite. It allows two nodes on an IP network to share IP status and error information. ICMP is used by the ping utility.

Internet Engineering Task Force (IETF) A consortium that introduces procedures for new technology on the Internet. IETF specifications are released in documents called *Requests for Comments (RFCs).*

Internet Mail Access Protocol version 4 (IMAP4)   An Internet protocol for retrieving mail from a mail server. Designed as the successor to *POP3.*

Internet protocol (IP) The Network Layer protocol of TCP/IP responsible for addressing and sending TCP packets over the network.

internetwork Two or more networks connected together in such a manner that data can be exchanged between networks while both (or all) networks continue to function independently.

interprocess communications (IPC) A set of mechanisms used by applications to communicate and share data.

interrupt An event that disrupts normal processing by the CPU, and results in the transfer of control to an interrupt handler. Both hardware devices and software can issue interrupts; software executes an INT instruction, while hardware devices signal the CPU by using one of the interrupt request (IRQ) lines to the processor.

interrupt request lines (IRQ) Hardware lines on the CPU that devices use to send signals to cause an interrupt. Normally, only one device is attached to any particular IRQ line.

I/O address One of the critical resources used in configuring devices. I/O addresses are used to communicate with devices. Also known as a *port*.

I/O bus The electrical connection between the CPU and the I/O devices. There are several types of I/O buses: ISA, EISA, SCSI, VLB, and PCI.

I/O device Any device in or attached to a computer that is designed to receive information from, or provide information to, the computer. For example, a printer is an output-only device, whereas a mouse is an input-only device. Other devices, such as *modems*, are both input and output devices, transferring data in both directions. Windows 95 must have a device driver installed in order to be able to use an I/O device.

IP See *Internet protocol.*

IP address Used to identify a node on a TCP/IP network and to specify routing information on an internetwork. Each node on the internetwork must be assigned a unique 32-bit IP address, which is made up of the network ID plus a unique host ID assigned by the network administrator. The *subnet mask* is used to separate an IP address into the host ID and network ID. In Microsoft networks, you can either assign an IP address manually or automatically using a DHCP server.

IP router A system connected to multiple physical TCP/IP networks that can route or deliver IP packets between the networks.

IPC See *interprocess communications.*

IPX/SPX Internetwork packet exchange/sequenced packet exchange. Transport protocols used in Novell NetWare networks.

IR See *infrared.*

IRQ See *interrupt request lines.*

ISA   See *Industry Standard Architecture.*

ISDN   See *Integrated Services Digital Network.*

ISO   See *International Organization for Standardization.*

ITU   See *International Telecommunications Union.*

J

jumper   A small hardware connector that connects two pins together and completes a circuit.

K

K (or KB)   Standard abbreviation for kilobyte; equals 1,024 bytes.

Kbps   Kilobits per second; 1Kbps equals 1,024 bps.

KHz   An abbreviation for kilohertz, measuring frequency in terms of thousands of cycles per second.

L

LAN   See *local area network.*

LAT   See *Local Area Transport.*

LDAP   See *Lightweight Directory Access Protocol.*

learning bridge   See *transparent bridge.*

leased line   A permanently open communication circuit, typically a telephone line, that connects two endpoints forming a private network. Lines are usually leased from local telephone and long-distance carriers.

Lightweight Directory Access Protocol (LDAP)   An emerging Internet standard for providing directory services for electronic messaging systems.

link   A connection at the LLC Layer that is uniquely defined by the adapter's address and the destination service access point. Also, a connection between two objects, or a reference to an object that is linked to another.

link-state algorithm   A method for building routing tables that takes into account factors such as network traffic, connection speed, and assigned costs when calculating the best route for sending data packets.

Linux   A UNIX-like operating system developed in the early 1990s for PCs. See also *UNIX.*

LLC   See *logical link control.*

LMHOSTS file   A local text file that maps IP addresses to the NetBIOS computer names of Windows networking computers. In Windows 95, LMHOSTS is stored in the WINDOWS directory. In Windows NT, LMHOSTS is stored in \WINNT\system32\ drivers\etc, assuming \WINNT is where you installed Windows NT. See also *HOSTS file.*

local area network (LAN)   A computer network confined to a restricted area such as a single building.

Local Area Transport (LAT)   A nonroutable protocol used on some networks from Digital Equipment Corporation.

local bus   Inside a PC, a bus where the same high-speed connection used by the CPU to communicate with onboard devices is extended to communicate with peripherals. PCI is an example of a bus implementation using the local bus concept.

local loop   A term used in telecommunications to refer to the connection between your network and your phone company's nearest central office. Even when using switched networks, a local connection is required.

local printer   A printer that is directly connected to one of the ports on your computer, as opposed to a network printer.

LocalTalk   Refers to the cabling system for AppleTalk networks. The ability to use LocalTalk cabling is built into every Macintosh computer. LocalTalk uses STP cable in a bus topology. See *AppleTalk*.

logical link control (LLC)   One of the two sublayers of the Data Link Layer of the OSI Reference Model, as defined by the IEEE 802 standards. This sublayer is responsible for maintaining the link between two computers when they are sending data across the physical network connection.

logical ring   A network where the signal travels from computer to computer in a ring, even if the physical wiring is not a ring. For instance, the hub in most Token Ring implementations is wired so that the signal travels in a ring but yet the client computers are connected as if it is a star.

login (or logon)   The process by which a user is identified to the computer in a network.

logon script   In Microsoft networking, a batch file that runs automatically when a user logs in to a Windows NT Server. Novell networking also uses logon scripts, but they are not batch files.

M

M (or MB)   Standard abbreviation for megabyte; 1,024 kilobytes; or 1,048,576 bytes.

MAC   See *media access control*.

MAC address   The address for a device as it is identified at the media access control (MAC) layer in the network architecture. MAC addresses (also referred to as hardware addresses) are usually stored in ROM on the network adapter card, and are unique.

mail server   A server dedicated to an electronic messaging system.

mail user agent (MUA)   Another generic term for an email client. See *user agent*.

management information base (MIB)   A set of objects used by SNMP to manage devices. MIB objects represent various types of information about a device. See *Simple Network Management Protocol*.

map   The process of designating a disk drive letter to refer to a directory on a file server.

MAPI   See *Messaging Application Programming Interface.*

MAU   See *Multistation Access Unit.*

Mbps   Megabits per second; 1Mbps equals 1,024Kbps or approximately one million bits per second.

medium   The mechanism that physically carries a message from computer to computer. Some examples of media include copper cable, fiber-optic (glass) cable, and wireless or radio-based technologies.

media access control (MAC)   The lower of the two sublayers of the Data Link Layer in the IEEE 802 network model. This sublayer allows the computers on a network to take turns sending data on the physical network medium. The MAC sublayer is also responsible for ensuring that the data reaches the other computer without any errors.

memory   A temporary storage area for information and applications.

message   A structure or set of parameters used for communicating information or a request. Every event that happens in the system causes a message to be sent. Messages can be passed between the operating system and an application, different applications, threads within an application, and windows within an application.

Message Handling Service (MHS)   The *de facto* standard for transporting email within Novell NetWare environments. MHS is similar to SMTP and X.400 in that it is not used directly, but rather provides a transport mechanism between email clients and servers.

Message Transfer Agent (MTA)   In many electronic mail systems, it is responsible for transporting messages from one user's mailbox to another, or to other MTAs for delivery.

Messaging Application Programming Interface (MAPI)   An application programming interface that allows a desktop application to work with any underlying electronic mail system.

MHS   See *Message Handling Service.*

MIB   See *management information base.*

Micro Channel Architecture   IBM's bus architecture introduced in 1988 that was capable of operating as either a 16- or 32-bit bus.

microwave   Electromagnetic waves operating in the GHz frequency range between radio and infrared. Often used for communication between sites where cable is not an option.

MIME   See *multipurpose Internet mail extension.*

modem   A communications device that allows two computers to communicate over a telephone line by converting the digital signals from the computers into analog signals to travel over the phone line.

MTA   See *Message Transfer Agent.*

MUA   See *mail user agent.*

multiplexor (mux)   A device that allows several communication channels to share the same physical medium. A multiplexor combines the signals at the transmitting end, and a second multiplexor separates the signals on the receiving end.

multiport repeaters   Also referred to as active hubs, use electrical power to amplify the data signal, allowing the signal to travel farther and with better clarity along the network.

multipurpose Internet mail extensions (MIME)   An Internet standard that defines the method in which files are attached to SMTP messages.

Multistation Access Unit (MAU)   A Token-Ring hub which is wired as a logical ring.

mux   See *multiplexor.*

N

NADN   See *nearest active downstream neighbor.*

name registration   The way a computer registers its unique name with a name server on the network, such as a WINS server.

name resolution   The process used on the network to determine the address of a computer by using its name.

named pipe   A one-way or two-way channel used for communications between a server process and one or more client processes. A server process specifies a name when it creates one or more instances of a named pipe. Each instance of the pipe can be connected to a client. Microsoft SQL Server clients use named pipes to communicate with the SQL Server. Also, backup domain controllers use named pipes to communicate with the primary domain controller.

NAUN   See *nearest active upstream neighbor.*

NBF transport protocol   NetBEUI frame protocol. A descendant of the NetBEUI protocol, which is a Transport Layer protocol, not the programming interface NetBIOS.

NBNS   See *NetBIOS Name Server.*

NBT   See *NetBIOS Over TCP/IP.*

NCB   See *network control block.*

NDIS   See *network device interface specification.*

nearest active downstream neighbor (NADN)   In Token-Ring networks, the NADN for a specific computer is the next computer in line to receive the token.

nearest active upstream neighbor (NAUN)   In Token-Ring networks, the NAUN for a computer is the computer from which it receives the network token.

NetBEUI transport NetBIOS (Network Basic Input/Output System) Extended User Interface. A transport protocol designed by Microsoft and IBM for use on small subnets. It is not routable, but it is fast.

NetBIOS interface A programming interface that allows I/O requests to be sent to and received from a remote computer. It hides networking hardware from applications.

NetBIOS Name Server (NBNS) The generic term for a server that provides the resolution of NetBIOS names to IP addresses. The most widely known implementation of an NBNS is Microsoft's WINS server. Another implementation is by the Samba program in Linux/UNIX. See also *Windows Internet Naming Service.*

NetBIOS Over TCP/IP (NBT) The networking module that provides the functionality to support NetBIOS name registration and resolution across a TCP/IP network.

network A group of computers and other devices that can interact by means of a shared communications link.

network adapter Another name for a network interface card (NIC).

network analyzer See *protocol analyzer.*

network applications The applications or programs that run on top of the operating systems and communicate over the network. Some examples of network applications include email programs, File Manager, and the printing systems.

network architecture A term often used to refer to the overall structure of the network, including topology, physical media, and data transmission method. Examples include Ethernet and Token Ring.

Network Basic Input/Output System (NetBIOS) A software interface for network communication. See *NetBIOS interface.*

network control block (NCB) A memory structure used to communicate with the NetBIOS interface.

network device driver Software that coordinates communication between the network adapter card and the computer's hardware and other software, controlling the physical function of the network adapter cards.

network device interface specification (NDIS) In Windows networking, the interface for network adapter drivers. All transport drivers call the NDIS interface to access network adapter cards. An advantage of NDIS is that multiple protocol stacks can use the same network interface card. NDIS was developed by Microsoft and IBM.

network directory See *shared directory*

network file system (NFS) A service for distributed computing systems that provides a distributed file system, eliminating the need for keeping multiple copies of files on separate computers. Usually used in connection with UNIX/Linux computers. NFS was developed by Sun Microsystems.

network ID The portion of the IP address that identifies a group of computers and devices located on the same logical network. Separated from the host ID using the *subnet mask*.

Network Information Service (NIS) A service for distributed computing systems that provides a distributed database system for common configuration files. Used primarily in UNIX/Linux systems. Also has a newer version called NIS+.

network interface card (NIC) An adapter card that connects a computer to a network.

Network Layer The layer of the OSI Model responsible for addressing a message and routing that message across a network.

network media The physical connection method that runs between the network systems. In most networks, the network media is simply a copper cable; however, network media can also include fiber-optic (glass) cable, and microwave or radio-based media.

network operating system (NOS) The operating system, such as Windows NT Server or Novell NetWare, that is used on network servers. A NOS typically provides file and printer sharing, user administration, and network security.

network protocol The language used in order for computers to be able to communicate. This language is usually described in the cryptic form of TCP/IP, IPX, DLC, and more.

network transport Either a particular layer of the OSI Reference Model between the Network Layer and the Session Layer, or the protocol used between this layer on two different computers on a network.

network-interface printers Printers with built-in network cards, such as Hewlett-Packard laser printers equipped with Jet Direct cards. The advantage of network-interface printers is that they can be located anywhere on the network.

next station identifier (NID) In an ARCnet network, the NID for a specific computer is the numerical ID of the next computer that should receive the token. It is similar to the NADN in Token Ring networks.

NIC See *network interface card*.

NID See *next station identifier*.

NIS See *Network Information Service*.

node A generic term for any device such as a server or workstation that can communicate on a network.

noise Essentially another term for electromagnetic interference. Generally thought of as the random electrical signals which can distort the signal on a network cable.

NOS See *network operating system*.

O

ODBC See *Open Database Connectivity*.

ODI See *open data-link interface*.

ohm The unit of measurement for electrical resistance.

onboard microprocessor A separate microprocessor on the NIC to handle data transfer. This will speed up data throughput by removing the need for the computer's central processor to process the actual data.

Open Database Connectivity An application programming interface by Microsoft that allows Windows application developers to integrate database connections into their applications.

open data-link interface (ODI) Similar to NDIS, allows NIC device drivers to be written without concern for which protocols will be using the NIC. As Novell developed ODI, you will find it widely used within NetWare networks.

open shortest path first (OSPF) An algorithm used in link-state routers. See *link-state algorithm.*

Open Systems Interconnect (OSI) The networking architecture reference model created by the ISO. The OSI Reference Model breaks down the communication into the following seven layers: Application, Presentation, Session, Transport, Network, Data Link, and Physical.

operating system (OS) The software that provides an interface between a user or application and the computer hardware. Operating system services usually include memory and resource management, I/O services, and file handling. Examples include Windows 95, Windows NT, and UNIX.

optical fiber See *fiber-optic cable.*

OS See *operating system.*

OSI See *Open Systems Interconnect.*

OSPF See *open shortest path first.*

P

packet A generic term for a block of data transmitted across a network between two network nodes.

packet-switched network A switched network where data is broken into small packets and sent across the network. Each packet can follow a completely different path to the destination according to the best route available.

parity Refers to an error-checking procedure in which the number of 1s must always be the same (either even or odd) for each group of bits transmitted without error.

passive topology When the computers on the network simply listen and receive the signal, they are referred to as passive because they do not amplify or manipulate the signal in any way. An example of a passive topology would be the linear bus or bus topology.

password   A security measure used to restrict access to computer systems. A password is a unique string of characters that must be provided before a logon or an access is authorized.

path   The location of a file or directory. The path describes the location in relation to either the root directory, or the current directory—for example, `C:\Windows\System`. Also, a graphic object that represents one or more shapes.

PC Card   The specification for credit-card size adapter cards used primarily in laptop computers. Previously called *PCM-CIA* cards.

PCI   See *Peripheral Component Interconnect*.

PDC   See *primary domain controller*.

PDN   See *public data network*.

peer-to-peer networks   Networks that allow computers to act as both a client using resources and a server sharing resources. In a peer-to-peer network, there is no centralized control over resources such as files or printers.

peers   Computers in a network acting as both a client and a server. These computers are capable of using network resources while simultaneously sharing their own resources with others.

performance monitoring   The process of determining the system resources an application uses, such as processor time and memory. Most Microsoft operating systems include performance monitoring tools.

Peripheral Component Interconnect (PCI)   The local bus being promoted as the successor to VL. This type of device is used in most Intel Pentium computers and in the Apple PowerPC Macintosh. See *VL*.

permanent virtual circuit (PVC)   A virtual circuit that is established across a packet-switched network for a permanent connection—for instance, between two routers that are always online.

persistent connection   A network connection that is restored automatically when the user logs on.

Personal Computer Memory Card International Association (PCMCIA)   See *PC Card*.

Physical Layer   The lowest layer of the OSI Model responsible for the actual generation of a signal across the network media.

piercing tap   See *vampire tap*.

pixel   Short for picture element, a dot that represents the smallest graphic unit of measurement on a screen. The actual size of a pixel is screen-dependent, and varies according to the size of the screen and the resolution being used. Also known as *pel*.

platform   The hardware and software required for an application to run.

plenum   Within an office building, the space between the false ceiling and the office floor above. Often used to circulate air and provide conduits for wiring.

plenum cabling   Cables that are more resistant to fire and do not produce as many fumes. Plenum cabling is required by fire safety codes when installing network cabling in false ceilings or other spaces with limited air circulation.

Plug and Play (PnP)   A computer industry specification, intended to ease the process of configuring hardware.

Plug and Play BIOS   A BIOS with responsibility for configuring Plug and Play cards and system board devices during system power-up, and providing runtime configuration services for system board devices after startup.

point-to-point   A generic term for a dedicated connection between any two points on a network. Frequently used to refer to leased lines connecting two networks together.

point-to-point infrared   Uses a highly focused narrow beam of energy to connect two sites at high data transmission speeds. See also *infrared*.

Point-to-Point Protocol (PPP)   A communications protocol used to connect computers to remote networking services, including Internet service providers (ISPs). Prior to the introduction of PPP, another communications protocol, SLIP, was used. The Windows 95/98 and Windows NT 4.0 implementation of PPP is Dial-Up Networking.

polling   The process of continually checking others systems to see if action needs to be taken. Within an electronic mail system, the process of constantly checking for mail. Within a host-based network, the process of constantly checking terminals to see if they have data/commands to be processed.

POP3   See *Post Office Protocol version 3*.

port   The socket to which you connect the cable for a peripheral device. See *I/O address*.

port ID   The method TCP and UDP use to specify which application running on the system is sending or receiving the data.

Post Office   The message store used by electronic mail systems such as Microsoft Mail to hold the mail messages. It often exists only as a structure of directories on disk, and does not contain any active components.

Post Office Protocol version 3 (POP3)   An Internet protocol for the retrieval of electronic mail from a mail server.

POTS   Plain Old Telephone Service. Another name for the regular telephone system. See *Public Switched Telephone Network*.

PPI   See *Productivity Point International*.

PPP   See *Point-to-Point Protocol*.

Presentation Layer   The layer of the OSI Reference Model which prepares the data to be presented to either the network (if inbound) or the applications (if outbound). This level is responsible for translating, formatting, and encrypting the data as well as the compression of the data when necessary.

primary domain controller (PDC) Within a Windows NT Server network, the PDC is a server that, among other duties, maintains the master list of domain information. There can be only one PDC within a single Windows NT domain.

process   The virtual address space, code, data, and other operating system resources—such as files, pipes, and synchronization objects—that make up an executing application. In addition to resources, a process contains at least one thread that executes the process' code.

Productivity Point International (PPI) An international computer training provider offering Microsoft certification courses and testing centers.

propagation delay   The delay caused by the time needed to regenerate the data transmission signal as the signal passes through repeaters on the network.

protocol   A set of rules and conventions by which two computers pass messages across a network. There are different protocols that operate at different layers of the OSI Reference Model. As an example, Windows 95 and Windows NT include NetBEUI, TCP/IP, and IPX/SPX-compatible protocols. See also *communications protocol*.

protocol analyzer   A troubleshooting device that monitors network activity and can produce statistics about network performance.

protocol stack   A group of protocols, sometimes referred to as protocol suites.

PSTN   See *Public Switched Telephone Network*.

public data network (PDN)   A commercial packet-switching service offered by a service provider, typically using X.25 technology.

Public Switched Telephone Network (PSTN)   A technical term for the common telephone system.

PVC   A term used for a permanent virtual circuit (see *permanent virtual circuit*) or for the plastic (polyvinyl chloride) outer casing of most network cables.

R

RAID   See *redundant array of inexpensive disks*.

radio network   A network that uses radio waves instead of physical cables to connect computers together on a network.

RAM   See *random-access memory*.

RAM buffering   As data flows at a high speed from the computer's data bus, the information can be temporarily held in a RAM buffer while awaiting transmission out onto the network media. This process can greatly increase the speed of the network adapter.

random-access memory (RAM) The computer's main memory where programs and data are stored while the program is running. Information stored in RAM is lost when the computer is turned off.

redirector The networking component that intercepts file or print I/O requests and translates them into network requests. The redirector is what allows a client computer to access the network. It operates primarily at the OSI Presentation Layer but also at the Application Layer.

redundant array of inexpensive disks (RAID) A method for providing fault tolerance by using multiple hard disk drives. Broken into six levels (RAID 0 through RAID 5), RAID technologies vary in cost, performance, and protection.

relay towers Towers with mounted repeaters used to extend radio or microwave signals across great distances.

remote access service (RAS) See *Dial-Up Networking*.

remote administration The process of administrating one computer from another computer across a network.

remote procedure call (RPC) An industry-standard method of interprocess communication across a network. Used by many administration tools.

repeater A hardware device used to extend the transmission distance of a signal by amplifying or regenerating the signal before passing it along. Repeaters operate at the OSI Physical Layer and have no knowledge of the actual data being transmitted.

requestor See *redirector*.

Requests for Comments (RFCs) The official documents of the Internet Engineering Task Force that specify the details for protocols included in the TCP/IP family.

RFC See *Requests for Comments*.

ring A network topology that connects all the computers in a single loop. Information is passed along in a continual circle. Each computer acts as a repeater, and token passing is usually used for network access.

RIP See *routing information protocol*.

routable protocol A protocol such as TCP/IP or IPX/SPX that can be used with a router.

router A connectivity device that connects two or more networks at the OSI Network Layer. A router uses a routing table of network addresses to determine where a data packet should be sent. As routers work at the Network Layer, they can be used to transmit information between different network architectures. Although the term *router* often refers to an actual hardware device, a router can also be a computer with two or more network adapters, each attached to a different subnet.

routing   The process of forwarding packets until they reach their destination.

routing information protocol (RIP)   A protocol that supports dynamic routing. Used between some routers.

routing table   A table used by a router consisting of network addresses.

RPC   See *remote procedure call.*

RPC server   The program or computer that processes remote procedure calls from a client.

S

Samba   A program available for Linux/UNIX computers that allows them to use the SMB protocol to participate in file and printer sharing. It also allows a Linux/UNIX computer to participate as a WINS client or operate as a WINS server.

SAP   See *service access points.*

SAS   See *Single Attachment Stations.*

satellite microwave   A form of microwave communication which uses the higher frequencies of the low gigahertz range to offer higher transmission rates. Signals will be transmitted between antennas located on the ground and satellites orbiting above the earth.

SCSI   See *small computer system interface.*

sector-sparing   A method of providing fault tolerance where the hard disk is checked before data is read or written. If a bad sector is found, the data is moved to a good sector, and the bad sector is marked as unusable. Also referred to as *hot-fixing* or *bad-sector remapping.*

segment   One portion of a network.

sequence number   Sequence numbers are used by a receiving node to properly order packets.

Serial Line Internet Protocol (SLIP)   The predecessor to PPP, a line protocol supporting TCP/IP over a modem connection. See also *Point-to-Point Protocol.*

server   A computer or application that provides shared resources to clients across a network. Resources include files and directories, printers, fax modems, and network database services. See also *client.*

server message block (SMB)   A block of data that contains a work request from a workstation to a server, or that contains the response from the server to the workstation. SMB is used for file and printer sharing in a Microsoft network.

server software   Software which allows the computer to make network resources available for others to share in addition to performing other administrative functions.

server-based network   A network with a centralized control of resources which depends on server computers to provide security and system administration. Server-based networks are sometimes referred to as client/server networks.

service   A process that performs a specific system function and often provides an application programming interface (API) for other processes to call. Windows 95/98 services include File and Print Sharing and the various backup agents.

service access points (SAP)   Series of interface points that allow other computers to communicate with the other layers of the network protocol stack. Note that there is also a protocol used in Novell NetWare networks, Service Advertising Protocol, that also uses the acronym SAP.

Session Layer   The layer of the OSI Reference Model that performs name recognition and the functions needed to allow two applications to communicate over the network. This layer handles the opening, using, and closing of a session between two computers.

SFD   See *Start Frame Delimiter*.

share   In Microsoft networking, the process of making resources, such as directories and printers, available for network users.

share name   The name that a shared resource is accessed by on the network.

share-level security   A network in which there is no central user authentication and control. A resource can be assigned a password at the time at which it is shared to the network. Users need to know the password for each individual shared resource they want to access. Windows 95/98 and Windows for Workgroups can use share-level security when not part of a Windows NT Server domain.

shared directory   A directory that has been shared so that network users can connect to it.

shared memory   Memory that two or more processes can read from and write to.

shared network directory   See *shared directory*.

shared resource   Any device, data, or program that is used by more than one other device or program. Windows 95 can share directories and printers.

sharepoint   The network name for a folder, directory, or resource that has been shared by a server or peer computer. The sharepoint can be used to access shared data or services.

shielded twisted pair (STP)   Cable that contains a layer of woven mesh shielding inside the cable that reduces interference and allows a slightly higher transmission speed than UTP. See *unshielded twisted pair*.

shielding   Foil or woven steel mesh that is wrapped around cable to reduce the interference to an electrical signal in a cable.

SID   See *station identifier*.

Simple Mail Transfer Protocol (SMTP)   The Application Layer protocol that supports messaging functions over the Internet. SMTP describes how email servers should send and receive messages.

Simple Network Management Protocol (SNMP)   A standard protocol for the management of network components. Windows 95/98 and Windows NT include an SNMP agent.

single attachment concentrators   An FDDI term equivalent to the hub in other network architectures. Can be attached to dual attachment concentrators as a method of allowing more workstations to be connected to the network.

Single Attachment Stations (SAS) FDDI network interface cards that are intended for individual workstations and are attached to a concentrator.

SLIP   See *Serial Line Internet Protocol.*

small computer system interface (SCSI) Pronounced *scuzzy,* a standard for connecting multiple devices to a computer system. SCSI devices are connected together in a daisy chain, which can have up to seven devices (plus a controller) on it.

SMB   See *server message block.*

SMDS   See *Switched Multimegabit Data Services.*

SMTP   See *Simple Mail Transfer Protocol.*

SNA   See *Systems Network Architecture.*

SNMP   See *Simple Network Management Protocol.*

socket   A channel used for incoming and outgoing data that originated in UNIX and is usually used with TCP/IP. In Microsoft operating systems, sockets are defined by the Windows Sockets API and usually use a file called `WINSOCK.DLL`.

source-routing bridges   Used primarily in IBM Token-Ring environments, rely on the source computer to provide path information within the packet. This type of bridge does not require a lot of processing power because most of the work is being done by the source computer.

SONET   See *Synchronous Optical Network.*

spooler   A scheduler for the printing process. It coordinates activity among other components of the print model and schedules all print jobs arriving at the print server.

spread-spectrum   Radio communication transmissions that use several frequencies simultaneously. There are two types of spread-spectrum transmissions: *direct-sequence modulation* and *frequency-hopping.*

SQL   See *Structured Query Language.*

standalone application   Applications designed to be operated on a single computer without requiring a network. Examples would be traditional word processors such as Microsoft Word and WordPerfect or spreadsheets such as Microsoft Excel or Lotus 1-2-3.

standalone computer   A computer that is not connected to a network.

standby monitor   A node on a Token-Ring network that monitors the network status and awaits the signal from the active monitor.

star   A network topology where all the computers are connected in a central *hub.*

Start Frame Delimiter (SFD)   A 1-byte field that indicates the beginning of the frame.

static routers   Require a network administrator to manually configure the routing table. The router will always use the same route to send the packets even though it might not be the shortest route. If there is no route address, the packet cannot be delivered.

station identifier (SID)   The address of an ARCnet computer. Usually configured on the network interface card.

STP   See *shielded twisted pair*.

Structured Query Language (SQL)   A data access language that is used by almost all client/server database applications.

subnet   A generic term for a section of a larger network, usually separated by a router or bridge. On the Internet or any TCP/IP network, any lower network that is part of the logical network identified by the network ID.

subnet mask   A 32-bit value that is used to distinguish the network ID portion of the IP address from the host ID.

SVC   See *switched virtual circuit*.

Switched Multimegabit Data Services (SMDS)   A high-speed packet-switched network server offered in some areas with speeds up to 45Mbps. SMDS is viewed as a competitor to frame relay.

switched virtual circuit (SVC)   A virtual circuit that is established across a packet-switched network for a temporary connection between two devices.

synchronous communication   A transmission method that relies on exact timing coordination between both the sending and receiving units.

Synchronous Optical Network (SONET)   A fiber-optic WAN technology allowing theoretical speeds up to 2.48Gbps and allowing simultaneous transmission of voice, data, and video. Current practical speeds are usually between 155Mbps to 622Mbps.

Systems Network Architecture (SNA)   A network architecture developed by IBM and widely used within mainframe networks.

T

T connector   A piece of hardware used to connect two coaxial cables.

T1 line   The primary type of digital line in use today, providing 24 voice or data channels that can together provide transmission speeds of up to 1.544Mbps. See also *T-carrier system*.

T-carrier system   A telecommunications system developed by Bell Telephone to combine multiple 64Kbps voice or data channels into a single line using multiplexing. A T1 line can support 1.544Mbps, whereas a T3 line can support 45Mbps.

TCP   See *Transmission Control Protocol*.

TCP/IP See *Transmission Control Protocol/Internet Protocol.*

TDI See *transport driver interface.*

TDR See *Time-Domain Reflectometer.*

Telnet The Application Layer protocol that provides virtual terminal service on TCP/IP networks.

terminal A device used by users to communicate with a host computer, primarily comprised of a monitor (referred to as a CRT, for cathode ray tube) a keyboard, and a network connector (often an RS-232 serial cable).

terminal session Users on a desktop PC can use software to open a terminal session with a mainframe. A window on their PC will behave as if it were a regular terminal.

terminator A hardware device used on a bus network to absorb the signal and to prevent it from bouncing back.

terrestrial microwave Microwave communication system that uses higher frequencies of the low gigahertz range to link two sites. Typically used to link networks together over long distances where using cable is not practical or is cost-prohibitive.

thicknet The original coaxial cable used in Ethernet networks. thicknet cable has a thicker core that allows it to transmit data up to 500 meters.

thinnet A coaxial cable that is easy to install and relatively inexpensive. It transmits data at 10Mbps and has a maximum length of 185 meters.

throughput The amount of data passing through a point on the network in a fixed amount of time. For instance, the throughput of a 10BASE-T Ethernet network is theoretically 10Mbps. The term can be used to refer to the overall system or to a specific device such as an NIC or router.

Time-Domain Reflectometer (TDR) A troubleshooting device that sends a pulse down a network cable seeking to find any type of break or problem in the cable.

token A small data frame used in a token-passing network to indicate which computer is allowed to transmit data.

token passing A media access method that eliminates collisions and ensures that every computer gets an equal opportunity to communicate on the network. The token is continually passed around the network, and each computer can only transmit a message when it has the token.

Token Ring A network architecture, developed by IBM in the mid-1980s, that is physically wired using a star topology but is implemented as a logical ring. Token-Ring networks use *token passing* to ensure that each computer on the network gets a chance to transmit data.

TokenTalk Allows AppleTalk network protocols to be transmitted over a 4- or 16Mbps IEEE 802.5 Token-Ring network.

topology The layout of how computers are physically connected. The three major types of network topologies are the bus, star, and ring topologies.

transceiver (transmitter/receiver) A device that converts the parallel data stream from the computer's data bus to the serial stream necessary for the network media. Usually included as part of the network interface card, although in 10BASE-5 networks the transceiver is actually physically connected to the thicknet backbone.

translation bridge A bridge that allows packets to be translated between network architectures. Primarily used to interconnect a Token Ring and Ethernet network. Also referred to as a transparent source-routing bridge.

Transmission Control Protocol (TCP) A connection-based protocol responsible for breaking data into packets which the IP protocol sends over the network. This protocol provides a reliable, sequenced communication stream for internetwork communication.

Transmission Control Protocol/Internet Protocol (TCP/IP) The primary wide area network used on the worldwide Internet. TCP/IP includes standards for how computers communicate and conventions for connecting networks and routing traffic, as well as specifications for utilities.

transparent bridges Used throughout the Ethernet network, these bridges build a bridging table as they receive packets. Also referred to as *learning bridges*.

transport driver interface (TDI) The interface between the Session Layer and the Network Layer, used by network redirectors and servers to send network-bound requests to network transport drivers.

Transport Layer The level of the OSI Reference Model focused on delivering the data without any errors and in the proper sequence.

transport protocol A generic term for protocols that operate at the OSI Transport and Network Layers and provide for the movement of data between computers. Examples include TCP/IP, IPX/SPX, and NetBEUI. In this context, a transport protocol passes data to the network adapter card driver through the NDIS interface, and to the redirector through the transport driver interface.

twisted-pair Multiple pairs of wire that are twisted around each other inside the cable to prevent crosstalk interference between the wires. Twisted-pair cables come in two variations: *shielded* and *unshielded*.

U

UA See *User Agent*.

UDP See *user datagram protocol*.

UNC See *universal naming convention*.

uniform resource locator (URL) An Internet addressing convention that originated with the World Wide Web. The basic format is `protocol://servername/pathname`.

uninterruptible power supply (UPS) A battery-operated power supply connected to a computer to keep the system running during a power failure.

universal naming convention (UNC)
Naming convention, including a server name and share name, used to give a unique name to files on a network. The format is
`\\servername\sharename\path\filename.`

UNIX   A multiuser operating system found primarily on workstations and mini-computers. Tightly linked with TCP/IP, many networking commands and utilities originated in the UNIX environment.

unshielded twisted pair (UTP)   A type of cable consisting of several pairs of wire, with each pair twisted around each other for a specified number of twists per foot. UTP is the most widespread and easiest cable medium to use. It is also used for telephone systems. UTP is highly susceptible to interference and attenuation and has a maximum cable length of 100 meters.

UPS   See *uninterruptible power supply.*

UPS service   A software component that monitors an uninterruptible power supply (UPS) and shuts the computer down gracefully when line power has failed and the UPS battery is running low.

URL   See *uniform resource locator.*

user account   Refers to all the information that identifies a user to an operating system, including username and password, group membership, and rights and permissions.

User Agent (UA)   Also called *email client,* responsible for all the user interaction such as reading and composing messages.

user datagram protocol (UDP)
The transport protocol offering a connectionless-mode transport service in the Internet suite of protocols. See *transmission control protocol.*

user-level security   A network where a central server maintains a listing of all user accounts and provides central authentication of users. On these networks, users normally need to know only their one password to log on to the network. After that, they are permitted to use network resources for which they have been granted permission. Windows NT Server networks use user-level security.

username   A unique name identifying a user account in Windows 95/98. Usernames must be unique, and cannot be the same as another username, workgroup, or domain name.

UTP   See *unshielded twisted pair.*

V

vampire tap   Also referred to as a *piercing tap,* a hardware device used to connect a transceiver to a thicknet cable. The vampire tap actually pierces the cable insulation and makes direct contact with the central core.

virtual circuit   A logical connection between two endpoints across a packet-switched network. The connection can be either temporary or permanent.

VL   Local bus standard for a bus that allows high-speed connections to peripherals, which preceded the PCI specification. Due to limitations in the specification, usually only used to connect video adapters into the system. Also known as *VESA bus.*

volt meter   See *digital volt meter.*

W

WAN   See *wide area network.*

wide area network (WAN)   Two or more networks connected, usually over a large geographic distance, through the use of a long-distance network medium such as the telephone system, microwave towers, or satellites. Also referred to as "enterprise" or "enterprise-wide" networks.

Windows Internet Naming Service (WINS)   A name resolution service that resolves NetBIOS computer names to IP addresses in a routed environment. A WINS server handles name registrations, queries, and releases.

Windows NT   The portable, secure, 32-bit, preemptive-multitasking member of the Microsoft Windows operating system family. Windows NT server provides centralized management and security, advanced fault tolerance, and additional connectivity. Windows NT Workstation provides operating system and networking functionality for computers without centralized management.

WINS   See *Windows Internet Naming Service.*

wireless bridge   A network connection between two LANs using a wireless link, typically in a situation where a cable connection is impossible. Usually implemented with microwave or infrared technology.

workgroup   A collection of computers that are grouped for viewing purposes, but which do not share security information. Each workgroup is identified by a unique name. See also *domain.*

workgroup applications   Also referred to as *groupware applications*, are similar to email systems but provide added functionality to enable a group of people to work better together.

World Wide Web (WWW or Web)   The Internet service providing information as a series of pages connected together by hypertext links and incorporating both text and graphics.

X

X.121   The addressing format used by X.25 base networks.

X.25   An international standard for packet-switched networks. Used by some service providers to create public data networks. Because X.25 was created at the time when standard telephone lines were the best communication medium available, it incorporates a high level of error checking and flow control that limits its speed to around 64Kbps.

X.400   An international messaging standard, used in electronic mail systems.

X.500 An international standard for organization information, used as a basis for directories in some electronic mail systems.

Z

zone file Another name for the file used to provide information about a domain to a DNS server. See *domain name service*.

zones Groups of computers within an AppleTalk network.

Certification Checklist

In addition to using a resource such as this book, the following list of tasks explains what you need to do to proceed with the certification process.

Get Started

When you have decided to start the certification process, you should use the following list as a guideline to get started:

1. Visit Microsoft's Certification Web site
   (http://www.microsoft.com/mcp/).

2. Choose the certification you want to pursue and note the exams required to attain the certification.

3. Take the Networking Essentials Self Assessment Test located on the CD-ROM that accompanies this book to determine your competency level. For exams other than Networking Essentials, you can use the Assessment Exams located at http://www.microsoft.com/mcp/ to get a feel for the type of questions that appear on the exam. (See "Assessment Exams" in Appendix C.)

Get Prepared

Getting started is one thing, but the actual preparation for taking the certification exam is a rather difficult process. The following guidelines will help you prepare for the exam:

1. Use the training materials listed in Appendix C:
   - Self-Paced Training
   - Authorized Technical Education Center (ATEC)
2. Review the Exam Study Guide in Appendix C.
3. Review the Exam Preparation Guide found on Microsoft's Web site at http://www.microsoft.com/mcp/.
4. Gain hands-on experience working with computer networks.

Get Certified

Call Sylvan Prometric at 1-800-755-EXAM or VUE at 1-800-TEST-REG to schedule your exam at a location near you.

Get Benefits

Microsoft will send your certification kit approximately two to four weeks after passing the exam. This kit qualifies you to become a Microsoft Certified Professional.

How Do I Get There from Here?

Becoming certified requires a certain level of commitment. The information in this appendix answers some of the questions you might have about the certification process.

On What Will I Be Tested?

You should be able to apply your knowledge and experience with computer networking to perform the following tasks:

- Use and understand common networking terminology.
- Compare different types of networks.
- Select the appropriate media, topology, and protocols for a network.
- Describe differences among different network media.
- Implement the appropriate security policy for different networks.
- Troubleshoot networks and solve communication problems.

To successfully complete the MCSE Networking Essentials Exam, you must be able to describe, plan, implement, and troubleshoot a computer network.

Analysis Is Good, But Synthesis Is Harder

Microsoft Certified Professional exams test for specific cognitive skills necessary for the job functions being tested. Educational theorists postulate a hierarchy of cognitive levels, ranging from the most basic (knowledge) up to the most difficult (evaluation) and associate a set of skills with each level. These levels are

- *Knowledge*—The lowest cognitive level at which you can identify, define, locate, recall, state, match, arrange, label, outline, and recognize items, situations, and concepts. Questions that ask for definitions or recitation of lists of characteristics test at this level.

- *Comprehension*—The level built immediately on knowledge, requiring that you translate, distinguish, give examples, discuss, draw conclusions, estimate, explain, indicate, and paraphrase, rather than simply play back answers learned by rote.

- *Application*—The level at which hands-on activities come into play. Questions at this level ask you to apply, calculate, solve, plot, choose, demonstrate, design a procedure, change, interpret, or operate.

- *Analysis*—One of the top three levels, requiring a thorough understanding of the skills required at lower levels. You operate at this level when you analyze, state conclusions, detect logic errors, compare and contrast, break down, make an inference, map one situation or problem to another, diagnose, diagram, or discriminate.

- *Synthesis*—A level that is harder than analysis, requiring some creativity and the ability to rebuild and reintegrate what could have been disassembled during analysis. This level requires you to construct a table or graph, design, formulate, integrate, generalize, predict, arrange, propose, tell in your own words, or show the relationship.

- *Evaluation*—The highest cognitive level, based on all the skills accumulated at lower levels. At this level, you assess, apply standards, decide, indicate fallacies, weigh, show the relationship, summarize, decide, look at a situation and tell what is likely to occur, or make a judgment.

Exam Objectives

The following section defines the specific skills Microsoft expects the exam to measure. As you review the list, you can see the level at which the MCSE Networking Essentials Exam tests your knowledge and ability to implement, administer, and troubleshoot networks that incorporate Microsoft operating systems. When an objective or item on the exam includes a verb or verb phrase associated with a given cognitive level (see the preceding section, "Analysis Is Good, But Synthesis Is Harder"), it is asking you to perform at that cognitive level.

For example, the exam objective "Discriminate between a peer-to-peer network and a server-based network" asks you to perform at the Analysis level because it asks you to "discriminate" between items. It's a good idea to be prepared to be tested at the Analysis level or higher for each objective.

You should review the following objectives and be able to apply the listed skills to the tasks described earlier in the section "On What Will I Be Tested?"

Standards and Terminology

You will be tested on your understanding of the following standards and common networking terminology:

- Define common networking terms for LANs and WANs.
- Compare a file-and-print server with an application server.
- Compare user-level security with access permission assigned to a shared directory on a server.
- Compare a client/server network with a peer-to-peer network.
- Compare the implications of using connection-oriented communications with connectionless communications.
- Distinguish whether SLIP or PPP is used as the communications protocol for various situations.
- Define the communication devices that communicate at each level of the OSI model.
- Describe the characteristics and purpose of the media used in IEEE 802.3 and IEEE 802.5 standards.
- Explain the purpose of NDIS and Novell ODI network standards.

Planning

The exam will test your ability to design a network and make choices appropriate to your conditions. You should be able to

- Select the appropriate media for various situations. Media choices include twisted-pair cable, coaxial cable, fiber-optic cable, and wireless media. Situational elements include cost, distance limitations, and number of nodes.

APP
C

- Select the appropriate topology for various Token-Ring and Ethernet networks.
- Select the appropriate network and transport protocol or protocols for various token-ring and ethernet networks. Protocol choices include DLC, AppleTalk, IPX, TCP/IP, NFS, and SMB.
- Select the appropriate connectivity devices for various token-ring and ethernet networks. Connectivity devices include repeaters, bridges, routers, and gateways.
- List the characteristics, requirements, and appropriate situations for WAN connection services. WAN connection services include X.25, ISDN, frame relay, and ATM.

Implementation

You will be tested on your understanding of skills necessary for administering and using an actual network. You must be able to

- Choose an administrative plan to meet specified needs, including performance management, account management, and security.
- Choose a disaster recovery plan for various situations.
- Given the manufacturer's documentation for the network adapter, install, configure, and resolve hardware conflicts for multiple network adapters in a token-ring or ethernet network.
- Implement a NetBIOS naming scheme for all computers on a given network.
- Select the appropriate hardware and software tools to monitor trends in the network.

Troubleshooting

You will be tested on your ability to monitor and resolve problems with computer networks, including how to

- Identify common errors associated with components required for communications.
- Diagnose and resolve common connectivity problems with cards, cables, and related hardware.
- Resolve broadcast storms.
- Identify and resolve network performance problems.

What Kinds of Questions Can I Expect?

Certification exams include three types of items: multiple-choice, multiple-rating, and enhanced. The way you indicate your answer and the number of points you can score depend on the item type.

Multiple-Choice Items

A multiple-choice item presents a problem and a list of possible answers. From the list, you must select the best answer (single response) or the best set of answers (multiple response) to the given question. The following is an example:

> Your company recently moved into an older building. You have been given the task of installing the network cables. There is very little space to work with, and the cables must share the existing conduits with electrical and phone cables. The longest distance you have to cover is 150 meters. What type of cable should you use?
>
> **a.** Fiber-optic
> **b.** Category 5 UTP
> **c.** Thinnet
> **d.** Thicknet

Answer d is correct.

Your response to a multiple-choice item is scored as either correct (1 point) or incorrect (0 points). If the item is a multiple-choice, multiple-response item (for which the correct response consists of more than one answer), your response is scored as being correct only if all the correct answers are selected. No partial credit is given for a response that does not include all the correct answers.

Multiple-Rating Items

In a multiple-choice item, you are asked to select the best answer or answers from a selection of several answers. A multiple-rating item presents you with a list of proposed solutions to a task and asks you to rate how well each proposed solution would produce the specified results. The following is an example:

> Your organization is moving to a new location where offices will be spread throughout a campus consisting of four office buildings. You are in charge of installing the computer network linking all four buildings. The maximum distance between the buildings is 50 meters. Because your company is remodeling the entire interior, you will have plenty of space for cable.

APP
C

REQUIRED RESULT: The network must be capable of operating at speeds up to 100Mbps.

OPTIONAL DESIRED RESULTS: You would like the network to be as secure as possible from electronic eavesdropping. You would like the network to be as inexpensive as possible.

PROPOSED SOLUTION: Your IS department has suggested using fiber-optic cable to link all four buildings.

Which results does the proposed solution produce?

  a. The proposed solution produces the required result and produces both of the optional desired results.

  b. The proposed solution produces the required result and produces only one of the optional desired results.

  c. The proposed solution produces the required result but does *not* produce any of the optional desired results.

  d. The proposed solution does *not* produce the required result.

Answer b is correct because the proposed solution produces the required result and produces one of the optional desired results. Fiber-optic cable can operate at speeds up to 100Mbps and is resistant to eavesdropping, but it is not the least expensive alternative.

Your response to a multiple-rating item is scored as either correct (1 point) or incorrect (0 points).

Enhanced Items

An enhanced item asks you to select a response from a number of possible responses and indicate your answer in one of three ways:

  ■ Type the correct response, such as a command name.

  ■ Review an exhibit (such as a screen shot, network configuration drawing, or code sample), and then use the mouse to select the area of the exhibit that represents the correct response.

  ■ Review an exhibit, and then select the correct response from the list of possible responses.

Your response to an enhanced item is scored as either correct (1 point) or incorrect (0 points).

Be aware that Microsoft is always trying to find new ways to test a candidate's knowledge and from time to time will be deploying new question types. For instance, some of the newer exams (but not MCSE Networking Essentials) have simulation questions. Please continue to visit http://www.microsoft.com/train_cert/ to stay up-to-date on Microsoft's testing technology.

How Should I Prepare for the Exam?

It's simple. The best way to prepare for the MCSE Networking Essentials Exam is to study, learn, and master computer networking. If you'd like a little more guidance, Microsoft recommends these specific steps:

1. Identify the objectives on which you will be tested. (See "Exam Objectives" earlier in this appendix.)

2. Assess your current mastery of those objectives.

3. Practice tasks and study the areas you haven't mastered.

In addition to what's contained in this book, the following are some tools and techniques that might offer a little more help.

Assessment Exams

Microsoft provides self-paced practice, or *assessment,* exams that you can take at your own computer. These assessment exams contain questions very similar to those you will find in the certification exams. Your assessment exam scores do not necessarily predict what your score will be on the actual exam, but the immediate feedback helps you determine the areas where you require extra study. The assessment exams offer an additional advantage—they use the same computer-based testing system as the certification exams, so you don't have to learn to use the testing system on exam day.

An assessment exam exists for almost every certification exam. You can find a complete list of available assessment exams on Microsoft's Web site.

Microsoft Resources

A number of useful resources available from Microsoft are the following:

- *Microsoft networking products, such as Windows 95/98, Windows NT, and Windows 2000*—A key component of your exam preparation is your use of the product. Gain as much real-world experience as possible by exploring the networking capabilities of Microsoft operating systems.

APP
C

- *Microsoft TechNet*—An information service for support professionals and system administrators. If you're a TechNet member, you receive a monthly CD full of technical information. To join TechNet, visit http://www.microsoft.com/technet/.

- *The Microsoft Developer Network*—A technical resource for Microsoft developers. If you're a member of the Developer Network, you can receive information on a regular basis through the Microsoft Developer Network CD, *Microsoft Developer Network News*, or the Developer Network Forum on CompuServe. To join MSDN, visit http://msdn.microsoft.com/.

- *The* Networking Essentials Exam Preparation Guide—A Microsoft publication that provides important specific information about the MCSE Networking Essentials Exam. The *Exam Preparation Guide* is updated regularly to reflect changes and is the source for the most up-to-date information about Exam 70-58.

Note that the *Exam Preparation Guide* can change at any time without notice, solely at Microsoft's discretion. Before you register for an exam, make sure that you have the current exam preparation guide by contacting one of the following sources:

- *Microsoft Sales Fax Service*—Call 800-727-3351 in the United States and Canada. Outside the United States and Canada, contact your local Microsoft office.

- *Internet*—On the Web at http://www.microsoft.com/train_cert/.

- *Sylvan Prometric*—Call 800-755-EXAM in the United States and Canada. Outside the United States and Canada, contact your local Sylvan office. On the Web at http://www.prometric.com/.

- *Virtual University Enterprises*—Call 800-TEST-REG in the United States and Canada. Outside the United States and Canada, contact your local VUE office. On the Web at http://www.vue.com/.

Self-Paced Training

If you prefer to learn on your own, you can obtain Microsoft Official Curriculum training (as well as non-Microsoft Official Curriculum courses) in self-paced formats. Self-paced training kits are available through courses offered on the Microsoft Online Institute. Materials are also available in book, computer-based training (CBT), and mixed-media (book and video) formats.

Microsoft Approved Study Guides, such as this book, are self-paced training materials developed by Independent Courseware Vendors (ICVs) to help you prepare for Microsoft Certified Professional exams. The Study Guides include both single self-paced training courses and a series of training courses that map to one or more MCP exams.

Self-training kits and study guides are often available through Microsoft-authorized training centers or can be purchased where books from Microsoft Press are sold.

Networking Essentials, Course 578, is a self-paced training course offered by Microsoft and available at local bookstores. This course serves as an introduction to networking technology and includes study material, lab exercises, and demonstrations.

Other Online Resources

Both The Microsoft Network (MSN) and CompuServe (GO MECFORUM) provide access to technical forums for open discussions and questions about Microsoft products. Microsoft's World Wide Web site (http://www.microsoft.com) also allows you to access information about certification and education programs.

Training Resources

Microsoft product groups have designed training courses to support the certification process. The *Microsoft Official Curriculum (MOC)* is developed by Microsoft course designers, product developers, and support engineers. MOC courses are instructed by Microsoft Certified Trainers who have achieved a high level of technical and instructional expertise in the products they teach.

Authorized Technical Education Centers (ATECs) are approved by Microsoft to provide training on Microsoft products and related technologies. By enrolling in a course taught by a Microsoft Solution Provider ATEC, you will get high-end technical training on the design, development, implementation, and support of enterprisewide solutions using Microsoft operating systems, tools, and technologies.

You also might take MOC courses via instructor-led training offered by *Microsoft Authorized Academic Training Program (AATP)* institutions. AATP schools use authorized materials and curriculum designed for the Microsoft Certified Professional program and deliver Microsoft-authorized materials, including the Microsoft Official Curriculum, over an academic term.

For a referral to an AATP or ATEC in your area, call 800-SOLPROV.

Suggested Reading

When you're looking for additional study aids, check out the books listed in Appendix F, "Suggested Reading."

How Do I Register for the Exam?

Registering for the MCSE Networking Essentials Certification Exam is simple:

1. Decide whether you are going to take your exam at either a Sylvan Prometric or Virtual University Enterprises (VUE) testing center. Because the exam is identical between both test delivery companies, it really is your choice, based on how close a testing center is to you, as well as scheduling availability.

2. Contact Sylvan Prometric at 800-755-EXAM or VUE at 800-TEST-REG, with the examination number (70-58), your Social Security Number (SSN), and a valid credit card to pay for the class. You can also register through http://prometric.com or http://www.vue.com.

3. Complete the registration procedure by phone. (Your SSN becomes the ID attached to your private file; the credit card takes care of the $100 test fee.) Request contact information for the testing center closest to you.

4. After you receive the registration and payment confirmation letter from Sylvan Prometric, call the testing center to schedule your exam. When you call to schedule, you will be provided with instructions regarding the appointment, cancellation procedures, ID requirements, and information about the testing center location.

At the time of registration, you can verify the number of questions and time allotted for your exam. You can schedule exams up to six weeks in advance or as late as one working day ahead, provided that you take the exam within one year of your payment. To cancel or reschedule your exam, contact Sylvan Prometric or VUE at least one working day before your scheduled exam date. At some locations, same-day registration (at least two hours before test time) is available, subject to space availability.

Testing Tips

You've mastered the required tasks to take the exam. When you have reviewed the exam objectives and are confident that you have the skills specified in the exam objectives, you are ready to perform at the highest cognitive level. It's time to head for the testing center. This appendix covers some tips and tricks to remember.

Before the Test

- Wear comfortable clothing. You want to focus on the exam, not on a tight shirt collar or pinching pair of shoes.

- Leave cellular phones and pagers in your car; they are not allowed during tests.

- Allow plenty of travel time. Get to the testing center 10 or 15 minutes early. Many testing centers are quite busy and expect you to start your exam promptly. Allow yourself time to relax.

- If you've never been to the testing center before, make a trial run a few days before to make sure that you know the route to the center.

- Carry with you at least two forms of identification, including one photo ID (such as a driver's license or company security ID). You will have to show proper identification before you can take the exam.

Remember that the exams are closed-book. The use of laptop computers, notes, or other printed materials is not permitted during the exam session.

At the test center, you'll be asked to sign in. The test administrator will give you a Testing Center Regulations form that explains the rules that govern the examination. You will be asked to sign the form to indicate that you understand and will comply with the stipulations.

If you have any special needs, such as reconfiguring the mouse buttons for a left-handed user, you should inquire about them when you register for the exam with Sylvan Prometric. Special configurations are not possible at all sites, so you should not assume that you will be permitted to make any modifications to the equipment setup and configuration. Site administrators are *not* permitted to make modifications without prior instructions from Sylvan Prometric.

When the administrator shows you to your test computer, make sure of the following:

- The testing tool starts up and displays the correct exam. If a tutorial for using the instrument is available, you should be allowed time to take it.

- You have a supply of scratch paper for use during the exam. Some centers are now providing you with a wipe-off board and magic marker to use instead of paper. After the exam, the administrator will collect all scratch paper and notes made during the exam in order to ensure exam security.

- Some exams might include additional materials or exhibits. If any exhibits are required for your exam, the test administrator will provide you with them before you begin the exam and collect them at the completion of the exam.

- The administrator explains what to do when you complete the exam.

- You get answers to any and all of your questions or concerns before the exam begins.

As a Microsoft Certification examination candidate, you are entitled to the best support and environment possible for your exam. If you experience any problems on the day of the exam, inform the Sylvan Prometric test administrator immediately.

During the Test

On many of the Microsoft certification exams, the testing software enables you to move forward and backward through the items so that you can implement a strategic approach to the test.

1. Go through all the items, answering the easy questions first. Then go back and spend time on the harder ones. Microsoft guarantees that there are no trick questions. The correct answer is always among the list of choices.

2. Eliminate the obviously incorrect answer first to simplify your choices.

3. Answer all the questions. You aren't penalized for guessing.

4. Don't rush. Haste makes waste (or substitute the cliché of your choice).

However, the Networking Essentials exam now uses the *adaptive* format, where the next question you get depends upon whether you answer a question correctly or not. In this newer format, you can go back to review your questions, but you cannot change the answers. Now, you *must* answer questions. Choose the best possible answer, and guess if you have to.

After the Test

When you have completed an exam, the following happens:

- The testing tool gives you immediate, online notification of your pass or fail status, with the exception of beta exams. Because of the beta exam process, your exam results are mailed to you approximately six to eight weeks after the beta exam.

- The administrator gives you a printed Examination Score Report indicating your pass or fail status.

- Test scores are automatically forwarded to Microsoft within five working days after you take the test. If you pass the exam, you will receive written confirmation from Microsoft within two to four weeks.

If you don't pass a certification exam, do the following:

- Review your individual section scores, noting areas where your score must be improved. The section titles in your exam report generally correspond to specific groups of exam objectives.

- Review the exam information in this book, then get the latest Exam Preparation Guide, and focus on the topic areas that need strengthening. Visit Microsoft's Training & Certification Web site at http://www.microsoft.com/train_cert/ to ensure that you have the most recent Exam Preparation Guide.

- Intensify your effort to get your real-world, hands-on experience and practice with computer networking.

- Try taking one or more of the approved training courses.

- Review the suggested readings listed in Appendix F, "Suggested Reading," or in the Exam Preparation Guide.

- Take (or retake) the Networking Essentials Assessment Exam provided by Microsoft. You might also try using some of the exam preparation tools available, including sample tests. (For a list of vendors, look in Appendix G, "Internet Resources.")

- Call Sylvan Prometric to register, pay for, and reschedule the exam.

Contacting Microsoft

Microsoft encourages feedback from exam candidates, especially suggestions for improving any of the exams or preparation materials.

To provide program feedback, to find out more about Microsoft Education and Certification materials and programs, to register with Sylvan Prometric, or to receive additional information, check the following resources. If you live outside the United States or Canada, contact your local Microsoft office or Sylvan Prometric testing center.

Microsoft Certified Professional Program

(800) 636 7544 `http://www.microsoft.com/mcp/`

For information about the Microsoft Certified Professional program and exams. You can also contact the Microsoft Certified Professional Program by email at `mcp@msprograms.com`.

Sylvan Prometric Testing Centers

(800) 755-EXAM `http://www.prometric.com/`

To register to take a Microsoft Certified Professional exam at any of more than 2,000 Sylvan Prometric testing centers around the world. You can also now register through their Web site.

Virtual University Enterprises (VUE) Testing Centers

(800) TEST-REG   http://www.vue.com/

To register to take a Microsoft Certified Professional exam at any of more than 1,400 VUE testing centers around the world. You can also now register through their Web site.

Microsoft Sales Fax Service

(800) 727-3351

For Microsoft Certified Professional Exam Preparation Guides and Microsoft Official Curriculum course descriptions and schedules.

Education Program and Course Information

(800) SOLPROV   http://www.microsoft.com/train_cert

For information about Microsoft Official Curriculum courses, Microsoft education products, and the Microsoft Solution Provider Authorized Technical Education Center (ATEC) program, where you can attend a Microsoft Official Curriculum course.

Microsoft Certification Development Team

Fax: (425) 936-1311

To volunteer for participation in one or more exam development phases or to report a problem with an exam, address written correspondence to:

Certification Development Team
Microsoft Education and Certification
One Microsoft Way
Redmond, WA 98052

Microsoft TechNet Technical Information Network

(800) 344-2121   http://www.microsoft.com/technet/

For support professionals and system administrators. (Outside the U.S. and Canada, call your local Microsoft subsidiary for information.)

Microsoft Developer Network (MSDN)

(800) 759-5474 `http://msdn.microsoft.com/`

The official source for software development kits, device driver kits, operating systems, and information about developing applications for Microsoft Windows and Windows NT.

Microsoft Technical Support Options

(800) 936-3500 `http://www.microsoft.com/support/`

**APP
E**

For information about the technical support options available for Microsoft products, including technical support telephone numbers and Premier Support options. (Outside the U.S. and Canada, call your local Microsoft subsidiary for information.)

Suggested Reading

As you proceed in your career as a network professional, you will find a wealth of information available at your local bookstore. In fact, there are so many networking books that the task of determining which books are useful becomes overwhelming. To assist you in your further development, this appendix lists books from Que that will help you stay on top of the ever-changing world of computer networking.

Titles from Que

Que Corporation offers a wide variety of technical books for all levels of users. Following are some recommended titles that can provide you with additional information on many of the exam topics and objectives.

To order any books from Que Corporation or other imprints of Macmillan Computer Publishing (Sams, Ziff-Davis Press, and others), call 800-428-5331, visit Macmillan's Information SuperLibrary on the World Wide Web (http://www.mcp.com), or check your local bookseller.

Introduction to Networking, Fourth Edition

Author: Barry Nance

ISBN: 0-7897-1158-3

Upgrading and Repairing Networks, Second Edition

Author: Terry Ogletree

ISBN: 0-7897-2034-5

Special Edition Using ISDN, Second Edition

Author: James Y. Bryce

ISBN: 0-7897-0843-4

Special Edition Using NetWare 3.12

Authors: Bill Lawrence, et al.

ISBN: 1-56529-627-3

Special Edition Using NetWare 4.1, Second Edition

Authors: Bill Lawrence and Vangie Bazan

ISBN: 0-7897-0810-8

Windows 95 Communications Handbook

Authors: Jim Boyce, et al.

ISBN: 0-7897-0675-x

Windows 95 Connectivity

Author: Rob Cima

ISBN: 0-7897-0183-9

Special Edition Using TCP/IP

ISBN: 0-7897-1897-9

Author: John Ray

Special Edition Using NetWare 5

ISBN: 0-7897-2056-6

Authors: Peter Kuo, John Pence, Sally Specker

Windows NT Server 4 Security Handbook

ISBN: 0-7897-1213-X

Authors: Lee Hadfield, Dave Hatter, Dave Bixler, David Hatter

Practical Network Cabling

ISBN: 0-7897-2247-X

Authors: Frank Derfler, Les Freed

Practical Windows Peer Networking

ISBN: 0-7897-2233-X

Author: Jerry Ford

Platinum Edition Using Windows 95, Second Edition

Authors: Ron Person, et al.

ISBN: 0-7897-1383-7

Platinum Edition Using Windows 98

Authors: Ed Bott, Ron Person

ISBN: 0-7897-1489-2

APP
F

Internet Resources

It should come as no surprise that there are many networking resources available on the Internet. There are, in fact, enough resources that you could devote a thick book just to describing the different Web sites. However, this appendix brings you pointers to many of the best networking resources available online. The appendix is divided into two sections, covering each of the following Internet services:

- World Wide Web sites
- Newsgroups

Each section is further subdivided into categories.

World Wide Web

Computer networking resources can be found throughout the Web. In an effort to help organize your search for information, this section of the appendix is divided into the following categories:

- Books
- Certification Program
- Exam Preparation
- General Networking Information
- Hardware/Media
- Internet
- Periodicals
- Training

Each category contains pointers to sites that you might find useful as you continue your preparation for Microsoft certification exams.

Books

You can find information about books in print that will assist you in preparing to become an MCSE at the following two sites:

Que Corporation

URL address: `http://www.mcp.com/que/`

Find books to meet all your computer and training needs here.

Microsoft Press

URL address: `http://mspress.microsoft.com/`

Discover information about the latest books and products available from Microsoft Press.

Certification Program

As you proceed in your career as a Microsoft Certified Professional, you'll need to stay up-to-date on the latest levels of certification. The following two sites can help:

Microsoft Training & Certification Site

URL address: `http://www.microsoft.com/train_cert/`

This site includes anything and everything you need to know about the Microsoft Certified Professional program. You can find exam guides here as well as the latest developments in the certification process, such as new exams and certification areas of specialization.

MCP Magazine

URL address: `http://www.mcpmag.com/`

MCP Magazine focuses its site on helping Microsoft Certified Professionals stay on top of what is going on within the world of Microsoft Certification. The site provides certification updates, a searchable jobs database, a searchable training directory, and lists of online resources. There are also discussion forums covering all the certification exams with other Microsoft Certified Professionals who provide tips and tricks for taking the various exams.

Exam Preparation

As you prepare for upcoming Microsoft certification exams, you might want to take other sample exams. Microsoft provides some sample tests at its Training & Certification Web site, mentioned earlier, but some other exam preparation sites include the following:

Transcender Corporation

URL address: `http://www.transcender.com/`

BeachFrontQuizzer

URL address: `http://www.bfq.com/`

Self-Test Software

URL address: `http://stsware.com/microsts.htm`

General Networking Information

There are many sites on the Internet that cover general networking issues, but two you might find valuable are the following:

Network Professional Association

URL address: `http://www.npa.org/`

The Network Professional Association is a membership organization whose mission is to advance the network computing profession. Of particular interest are the lists of technical resources that include pointers to many online networking Web sites. One list has a rather lengthy but useful list on online computer publications.

Yahoo!

URL address: `http://www.yahoo.com/`

With new resources constantly appearing on the Internet, it is a constant struggle to stay up-to-date with new arrivals. You might find the following categories within the Yahoo! directory useful for following networking resources on the Internet:

`http://www.yahoo.com/Computers_and_Internet/mCommunications_and_Networking/`

`http://www.yahoo.com/Business_and_Economy/Companies/Computers/Networking/`

`http://www.yahoo.com/Science/Engineering/Electrical_Engineering/Telecommunications`

`http://www.yahoo.com/Computers_and_Internet/Software/Communications_and_Networking/`

Hardware/Media

For information about the physical media and network architectures, these vendor pages can be outstanding resources.

3Com Networking Support Center

URL address: `http://www.3com.com/nsc/`

As one of the largest manufacturers of network interface cards, 3Com's Web site has volumes of information about networking technologies. If you are interested in Fast Ethernet (100BaseT), it provides numerous tutorials and technical white papers.

Electronic Industries Association (EIA)

URL address: `http://www.eia.org/`

As a trade organization representing the manufacturers of a wide variety of electronic components, the EIA Web site has pointers to many manufacturers' pages.

Hewlett-Packard "Network City"

URL address: `http://www.hp.com/rnd/`

Hewlett-Packard's main site (`www.hp.com`) is worth checking out, but its Research & Development pages offer many insights into Ethernet and other technologies. As HP is the prime developer of 100VG-AnyLAN, you will find many pages devoted to that emerging technology.

IBM

URL address: `http://www.networking.ibm.com/`

IBM's site, of course, provides many resources for Token Ring networks, but IBM also manufactures a wide variety of products for other network architectures, such as Ethernet. Many technical white papers and product information pages are available.

Intel

URL address: `http://www.intel.com/network/`

Beyond manufacturing microprocessors, Intel is also a large vendor of networking hardware and makes available product information and technical resources.

IEEE

URL address: `http://www.ieee.org/`

The Web site for the Institute of Electrical and Electronics Engineers offers information about IEEE, its activities, and its standards.

Internet

If you would like to learn more about the Internet itself, the following sites might be of interest:

Internet Society

URL address: `http://www.isoc.org/`

The Internet Society is the nonprofit organization that oversees the overall administration and coordination of efforts relating to the Internet. Information can be found here about Internet standards, Internet governance, and new technologies.

Internet Engineering Task Force

URL address: `http://www.ietf.org/`

The IETF is the arm of the Internet Society that actually sets the standards used in Internet communication. Comprised of many committees and "working groups," its site provides information about all technical aspects of Internet operation.

InterNIC

URL address: `http://www.internic.net/`

The Internet Network Information Center (InterNIC) was the organization responsible for overall technical operations of the Internet. This site previously provided information about domain name registration, network operations, and a host of standards and historical information. However, at this time Network Solutions, Inc., the company that operated InterNIC under contract to the National Science Foundation, has changed the InterNIC Web site to point to its own information. Although the site is still useful, additional information can be found at the following two sites:

URL address: `http://www.arin.net`

The American Registry for Internet Numbers (ARIN) is a registration service for IPv6 address space. A nice tool that this site has is a who-is lookup service to locate information on networks, IP address allocations, and other related information.

URL address: http://www.icann.org/

The Internet Corporation for Assigned Names and Numbers is the new entity formed to take over some of the responsibilities that were handled by InterNIC and also by the Internet Assigned Numbers Authority (IANA), which is being phased out to be replaced by ICANN.

Internet Security

URL address: http://www.cert.org/

The Computer Emergency Response Term (CERT) has been monitoring Internet security issues since 1988 and serves as a source of security alerts and information related to ongoing and past incidents of attacks across the Internet. Any system administrator connected to the Internet really should be subscribing to CERT's alert mailing lists.

URL address: http://www.ciac.org/

The Computer Incident Advisory Cabability (CIAC) site is maintained by the U.S. Department of Energy. This site contains all the information that you would ever need about intrusion detection on your network and the vulnerabilities that exist with different operating systems.

The List

URL address: http://www.thelist.com/

If you are searching for an Internet Service Provider, you should check out this site. Perhaps one of the largest collections of pointers to ISPs, this site provides a searchable database of ISPs in your geographic area. For each ISP listed, information is available about services, costs, and contact information.

Periodicals

With the incredible pace of change in the world of computer networking, some of your best resources include the trade magazines that are produced on a weekly or monthly basis. Their Web sites provide not only searchable archives, but also pointers to other networking resources. A few periodicals are now including online chat or discussion areas as part of their Web sites. Although there are a large number of periodicals online, a few examples include the following:

Communications Week

URL address: `http://www.commweek.com/`

InfoWorld

URL address: `http://www.infoworld.com/`

LAN Magazine

URL address: `http://www.lanmag.com/`

LAN Times

URL address: `http://www.lantimes.com/`

Network Magazine Online

URL address: `http://www.networkmagazine.com/`

Windows NT Magazine

URL address: `http://www.winntmag.com/`

Training

As you continue along your path toward further Microsoft certifications, you might find that an instructor-led course at a Microsoft Authorized Technical Education Center will be just what you need to advance to the next level.

Productivity Point International

URL address: `http://www.propoint.com/`

PPI's Web site contains information about Productivity Point International and its training centers located throughout North America. You can find course descriptions, locations near you, and current schedules.

Other Training Resources

To find other training centers, visit Microsoft's Training and Certification site at `http://www.microsoft.com/train_cert/`.

Newsgroups

Although the Web alone provides volumes of information, newsgroups can also be a great source of information, particularly about breaking news items. Newsgroups are the discussion area of the Internet and provide much of interest to the network professional.

The following resources are divided into two categories:

- *Internet newsgroups* that you should be able to get from the news server of your Internet Service Provider.
- *Microsoft newsgroups* that you can access directly from Microsoft's news server.

In both cases, some of the newsgroups focusing on networking are in the following list. Because new newsgroups are constantly being added, there might be additional ones available by the time this book is published.

Within the following listings, an asterisk at the end of a newsgroup name is used to indicate that all the newsgroups within a specific category might be useful to you. For instance, the listing `microsoft.public.windowsnt.protocols.*` means that you might be interested in all the newsgroups inside that category, which include the following:

```
microsoft.public.windowsnt.protocols.ipx

microsoft.public.windowsnt.protocols.misc

microsoft.public.windowsnt.protocols.ras

microsoft.public.windowsnt.protocols.tcpip
```

This convention has been used to simplify the newsgroup listings.

Internet Newsgroups

To read Internet newsgroups, you should be able to simply open your newsreader and search through a list of available newsgroups. The large number of newsgroups available in the `comp.dcom.*` hierarchy are of special interest to networking professionals (dcom = data communications). Some examples include the following:

```
comp.dcom.*

comp.os.ms-windows.networking.*

comp.os.ms-windows.nt.admin.networking

comp.os.ms-windows.programmer.networks

comp.sys.ibm.pc.hardware.networks
```

Microsoft Newsgroups

Microsoft has made available its own news server for discussions of its products. The newsgroups on its server can provide a wealth of technical information. People reading and answering questions inside the newsgroups include Microsoft personnel as well as other highly skilled individuals. To connect to Microsoft's news server, you need to point your news server to `msnews.microsoft.com`.

If you are unsure of how to do this, look in the menus of your newsreader for an item about opening or connecting to a new server. Often, this function is found in the Options or Preferences window.

Some examples of Microsoft newsgroups include the following:

```
microsoft.public.windowsnt.protocols.*
microsoft.public.windowsnt.dns
microsoft.public.windowsnt.domain
microsoft.public.windowsnt.mail
microsoft.public.windows95.dialupnetworking
microsoft.public.windows95.networking
microsoft.public.exchange.*
microsoft.public.internet.*
microsoft.public.mail.*
microsoft.public.messaging.misc
microsoft.public.outlook97.*
microsoft.public.sqlserver.*
microsoft.public.snaserver.*
```

APP
G

Using the CD-ROM

The tests on this CD-ROM consist of performance-based questions. This means that rather than asking you what function an item would fulfill (knowledge-based question), you will be presented with a situation and asked for an answer that shows your capability of solving the problem.

Using the Self-Test Software

The program consists of three main test structures:

- *Non-Randomized Test.* This is useful when you first begin study and want to run through sections that you have read to make certain you understand them thoroughly before continuing on.

- *Adaptive Test.* This emulates an adaptive exam and randomly pulls questions from the database. You are asked 15 questions of varying difficulty. If you successfully answer a question, the next question you are asked is of higher difficulty because it tries to adapt to your skill level. If you miss a question, the next one asked is easier because it, again, tries to adapt to your skill level. This tool is useful for getting used to the adaptive format, but not for actual study because the number of questions presented is so low.

- *Random/Mastery Test.* This is the big one. This test is different from the two others in the sense that questions are pulled from all objective areas. You are asked 50 questions, and it simulates the exam situation. At the conclusion of the exam, you will get your overall score and the chance to view all wrong answers. You will also be able to print a report card featuring your test results.

All test questions are of the type currently in use by Microsoft on this exam. In some cases, that consists solely of the multiple-choice type questions offering four possible answers. In other cases, there will be exhibits, scenarios, and other question types.

Equipment Requirements

To run the self-test software, you must have at least the following equipment:

- IBM-compatible Pentium
- 16MB of RAM
- 256-color display adapter, configured as 800×600 display or larger
- Double-speed CD-ROM drive
- Approximately 5MB free disk space
- Microsoft Windows 95, 98, or NT 4.0 (Workstation or Server)

Running the Self-Test Software

Access the SETUP.EXE file, and the self-test software installs on your hard drive from the CD-ROM and runs directly from there. After you have followed the simple installation steps, you will find the software very intuitive and self-explanatory.

Lab Exercises

Although reading this book will help prepare you for the Networking Essentials exam, it is extremely important to also get some hands-on experience working with computer networks. Many of the ideas and concepts described in the chapters of this book will become even clearer when you actually experience them in action.

To assist you in gaining hands-on experience, the labs on the following pages have been designed to demonstrate many of the procedures in the book. Obviously, the material does pose some restrictions. In preparing for the exam, you are probably not going to rush out and install a WAN link using a T1 line between your office and house or set up a satellite link between sites. Likewise, it is probably beyond most budgets to install a 10-computer network using 10BASE-5 cables first, and reinstall the network cables several times using 10BASE-2, 10BASE-T, 100BASE-T, and finally, fiber-optic cables (although such an experiment would be a fantastic learning experience!).

Although the labs are designed to be independent of each other and can be done in any order, most of them do require network connectivity between two computers. Notes at the beginning of each lab indicate what is required for that specific lab. If you do not have an established network, Labs 1 through 3 describe the process of installing a network interface card (NIC) and a network protocol (TCP/IP), and joining a workgroup.

Equipment Requirements

Most of the lab exercises require two computers running Windows 95/98 or Windows NT 4.0 (Workstation or Server). There is no specific type of computer required, beyond what would be necessary to run the operating system. Note that although the Windows for Workgroups operating system can perform some of the functions in the lab exercises (such as sharing folders and printers), its networking functionality is limited compared to Windows 95 or Windows NT. Note that Windows NT 3.51 could also be used for many of the NT labs, although the exact steps will be different. Similarly, Windows 2000 could also be used for these labs.

Most importantly, you need a network to connect your two computers and to get the most from these lab exercises. If you are performing these lab exercises at work, any type of Ethernet network connection can work. If you want to set up a practice network at home, the materials are readily available to create an inexpensive network between two computers.

You will definitely need two network interface cards, many of which are now priced around $20–50. If you were equipping a production environment, you might want to examine the NIC characteristics and might spend significantly more for high-performance NICs. However, for a small home network linking two computers, any generic Ethernet NIC should work fine. To allow you to experiment with different media types, you might consider purchasing a NIC with multiple media connectors. For instance, Ethernet NICs can be purchased with connections for both 10BASE-T (an RJ-45 jack resembling a phone jack) and 10BASE-2 (thinnet BNC connector).

Note that if you are using a Windows NT PC, make sure that any NIC you intend to use is listed on the Windows NT Hardware Compatibility List (HCL). You can visit Microsoft's Web site at `http://www.microsoft.com/` to find the latest version of the HCL.

As far as cable media, here are two suggestions:

- You can purchase a small four-port 10BASE-T hub for well under $100 (often in the $50–70 range). Two 10BASE-T cables can be purchased for under $10.
- Alternatively, if you select network interface cards that have connections for both 10BASE-T and 10BASE-2 (thinnet), you can purchase a single thinnet cable for around $10. Additionally, you will need to spend a few dollars for terminators and possibly T-connectors (which are often provided with your NIC when it has a thinnet BNC connector). Your entire network investment, beyond your NICs, will be under $20.

Finally, if you will be performing these lab exercises on computers in your work environment, please record any network configuration settings prior to performing the exercises. Additionally, please check with your system administrators to be sure that they are okay about you modifying system settings.

Lab 1: Installing and Configuring a Network Interface Card

In this lab, you learn

- How to determine what interrupt requests (IRQs) are available
- How to install software drivers for a NIC

This lab requires a network interface card and a computer with Windows 95/98 or Windows NT.

Determining Available IRQs

If your computer uses Windows 95/98, open an MS-DOS prompt and type msd. (Note that if this file isn't in your system path, you might need to use the Find option from the Start menu to find msd.exe. When the computer has found it, double-click it in the window to execute it.) This opens the Microsoft System Diagnostics window and allows you to find out what IRQs are available.

If your computer uses Windows NT 4.0, choose Start, Programs, Administrative Tools, and Windows NT Diagnostics. Select the Resources tab. Click the appropriate button (IRQ) to see the IRQ resources currently being used.

APP
I

Installing the Card

If you do not have an adapter card, or if the card is already installed in your computer, you will need to skip to the next section on installing the adapter software.

Although the exact procedure for installing a NIC varies according to the type of computer you have, the general procedure can be listed as follows:

1. Shut down and unplug your computer.

2. Open up your computer case. This might involve removing screws.

3. At this point, you should be wearing a wrist strap to protect against electrostatic discharge before proceeding to touch components of your computer. If you do not have a wrist strap, you risk damaging your NIC. Although many companies take a relaxed attitude toward wrist straps, it would be in your best interest to proceed no further without first obtaining a wrist strap.

4. Locate an available expansion slot in your computer.

5. Remove the protective metal cover from the slot opening in the rear of your computer. This usually involves removing the retaining screw at the top of the slot opening inside your computer.

6. Examine your network interface card to determine if it has jumpers or a DIP switch to set the IRQ and Base I/O Port. If it does, make sure that you choose settings that are currently available. Common settings are IRQ3 and Base I/O Port 300h.

7. Gently insert the network interface card into the expansion slot. Make sure it is fully inserted as far as it will go into the slot. When properly seated, it should fit exactly into the hole on the back of your computer case.

8. Screw back in the retaining screw at the top of the slot opening to ensure that the NIC is securely fastened.

9. Close your computer case.

10. Plug the computer back in and power it on. If your operating system is Windows 95/98, it should detect the NIC as it starts up and should prompt you to install a driver and configure the new hardware. With other operating systems, you will need to manually initiate the driver installation process.

At this point, you should connect the network media to the NIC so that your computer can communicate on the network.

Installing the Adapter Software

This lab does not require the installation of a new NIC. It is possible to install the drivers for a nonexistent NIC. Before beginning this lab, you need to have access to the CD used to install your operating system. By default on some Windows 95/98 computers, the computer manufacturers put the CDROM files in the C:\WINDOWS\OPTIONS\ CABS subdirectory.

1. From the Control Panel, choose Network.

2. Open the Add Adapter window. If your computer uses Windows NT 4.0, select the Adapters tab, and click Add. If your computer uses Windows 95/98, click Add and then choose Adapter.

3. Choose an adapter type that matches your NIC. If your adapter type is not found and you are using Windows 95/98, select the Have Disk button, which allows you to supply a disk from the manufacturer. If this is the case and you are running Windows NT 4.0, scroll all the way down to the bottom of the list and choose an option allowing you to supply a disk from the manufacturer. If you do not have an actual NIC to install, you can choose any type to be your nonexistent NIC. Click OK. Note that in Windows 95, the manufacturers' names will appear in the left window pane. When you select a manufacturer, the specific drivers will appear in the right window pane.

4. Enter the appropriate IRQ level and Base I/O Port address.

5. If prompted for the bus type, choose the type of bus your NIC uses (most use ISA).

6. When prompted for the location of your files, enter the appropriate pathname.

7. If this is the first NIC installed in your computer, you might be prompted for additional protocol information. (As you install network protocols later, simply click OK and proceed through any prompts as best you can.) If not, you should see some protocol information flash by on your screen.

8. Restart your computer.

Your NIC should now be fully functional.

Determining What Protocols Are Bound to Your NIC

This procedure enables you to see what network protocols will use your NIC.

1. From the Control Panel, choose Network.

2. In Windows NT 4.0, select the Bindings tab. From the drop-down box, choose to view bindings by Protocol. In the resulting list of protocols, a "+" by each protocol will expand to show which NIC is bound to that protocol.

APP
I

3. In Windows 95/98, select the appropriate NIC and click the Properties button. Select the Bindings tab in the resulting dialog box.

4. You should now see the protocols bound to your NIC.

5. Cancel out of all dialog boxes.

Removing a Network Interface Card

This procedure demonstrates the steps to remove a network interface card. Note that if you proceed with the entire procedure, you will then need to reinstall the NIC before you can proceed with other lab exercises.

1. From the Control Panel, choose Network.

2. In Windows 95/98, select the appropriate adapter from the list of network components. In Windows NT 4.0, select the Adapters tab, and select the network component.

3. If you really want to remove the NIC, click the Remove button and confirm the prompts that follow. If you do not, press the Cancel button to exit the dialog box.

4. If you removed the NIC, restart your computer.

Lab 2: Installing TCP/IP

This lab requires one computer using Windows 95/98 or Windows NT to practice installation and configuration. The final exercise in this lab requires two computers.

You will need your original operating system installation media (CD or disks) to install the TCP/IP protocol.

Note that if you want to perform later labs that use two computers, both computers must use the same network protocol. If you want that protocol to be TCP/IP, you will need to repeat this lab on the second computer. Additional TCP/IP configuration information is provided for your second computer within the first exercise.

For your information, the IP addresses being used in this lab are part of the 192.168.0.0 block that is unassigned and available for private TCP/IP networks per RFC 1918. When establishing a private TCP/IP network not connected to the Internet, you can choose any IP addresses you want. However, should your network later be connected to the Internet, your addresses can cause conflicts with other sites on the Internet. To avoid this potential conflict, you can use addresses in the 192.168.0.0 range. Should you later connect your network to the Internet, there will be no conflicts.

In this lab, you learn how to install and configure the TCP/IP network protocol.

If your computer is using Windows 95/98, perform the following procedure:

1. From the Start menu, choose Settings, Control Panel.
2. Double-click the Network icon.
3. Click the Add button.
4. Double-click the Protocol option in the dialog box.
5. From the list of manufacturers, select Microsoft.
6. In the right-hand window pane, choose TCP/IP. Click OK and have your installation media ready to load the software needed.
7. Select TCP/IP and press the Properties button. The TCP/IP Properties window should appear.
8. For the IP Address, enter 192.168.24.1. (When repeating this procedure for the second computer, use 192.168.24.2.)
9. For the Subnet Mask, enter 255.255.255.0.
10. Select the Gateway tab and enter 192.168.24.100. (Note that this IP address does not exist and is used in this example for illustration. You will not be accessing the outside network and there will be no harm done in using this nonexistent address. We are pretending a router is at 192.168.24.100.)
11. Click the OK button to close the TCP/IP properties.
12. Click the OK button to close the Network Control Panel. Restart your computer.

If your computer uses Windows NT, perform the following procedure.

1. Open the Control Panel.
2. Double-click the Network icon.
3. In Windows NT 4.0, select the Protocol tab, and the Add button.
4. From the scroll list, choose TCP/IP Protocol and related components. Click Continue.
5. You do not need to select any additional services. Simply click Continue.
6. Enter the location of the installation media and click OK. After the appropriate software is loaded, you will next be prompted to enter configuration information.
7. For the IP Address, enter 192.168.24.1. (When repeating this exercise for the second computer, use 192.168.24.2.)

APP
I

8. For the Subnet Mask, enter 255.255.255.0.

9. For the Default Gateway, enter 192.168.24.100.

10. Click Continue until you exit the configuration dialog boxes.

11. Restart your computer.

Testing Your TCP/IP Configuration

There are several methods of testing your TCP/IP configuration, including the following:

- If you are using Windows 95/98, choose Run from the Start menu and type winipcfg. The resulting window will show you your TCP/IP configuration information.

- If you are using Windows NT, open a command prompt and type ipconfig to see TCP/IP information. Typing ipconfig -all will display additional information.

Additionally, the following commands can be used within a command prompt (Windows NT) or an MS-DOS prompt (Windows 95/98):

- netstat -rn displays your TCP/IP routing table. The command route print also provides similar information.

- netstat -e displays Ethernet information.

- netstat -s provides statistics about all protocols installed in your computer.

- ping 127.0.0.1 tests whether TCP/IP packets can be delivered to your NIC locally.

- ping your_ip_address tests whether your NIC responds to your IP address. In this lab, you would type ping 192.168.24.1 or ping 192.168.24.2 depending on which computer (1 or 2) you are using.

Viewing NetBIOS Names

Now that your computer is using TCP/IP, it has also been configured to allow the transport of NetBIOS names over TCP/IP. To view the list of NetBIOS names used by your computer, complete the following procedure:

1. Open a command prompt (Windows NT) or an MS-DOS prompt (Windows 95/98).

2. Type nbtstat -n to view the list of NetBIOS names used by your computer.

You will see names for both your computer and for your workgroup followed by a hexadecimal number that identifies a service running on your computer.

Testing the TCP/IP Connection Between Computers

This exercise requires two computers that are both configured with TCP/IP. This exercise uses the addresses provided earlier in the lab.

This exercise tests the TCP/IP configuration between your two computers.

1. On Computer1, open a command prompt (Windows NT) or an MS-DOS prompt (Windows 95/98).

2. Type ping 192.168.24.2. You should see a response back from the NIC on Computer2.

3. On Computer2, open a command prompt (Windows NT) or an MS-DOS prompt (Windows 95/98).

4. Type ping 192.168.24.1. You should see a response back from the NIC on Computer1.

Lab 3: Joining a Workgroup

This lab requires a computer using either Windows 95/98 or Windows NT.

If you are using Windows NT, make sure that your computer is not part of an existing domain or is not a domain controller. It would be best to use Windows NT Workstation rather than Windows NT Server.

In this lab, you learn how to join a workgroup to communicate with other computers.

Before computers can communicate and share resources within a Microsoft network, they need to be part of the same workgroup or domain. A workgroup, such as the one you will join here, is used primarily for a small peer-to-peer network. In a server-based network using Windows NT Server, computers join a domain instead of a workgroup. Joining a domain is covered in Lab 9, "Joining a Windows NT Domain."

If you want to use two computers for the other labs, you will need to perform these steps on both computers.

If your computer uses Windows 95/98 or Windows NT 4.0, perform the following steps:

1. From the Start menu, choose Settings, Control Panel, and the Network icon.

2. Select the Identification tab.

3. For a Workgroup name, enter WORKGROUP (it can be typed in either upper- or lowercase). Click OK.

4. Restart your computer.

APP

I

Lab 4: Using Shared Folders

This lab requires two computers networked together in the same workgroup or domain that uses either Windows 95/98, Windows NT, or Windows for Workgroups (WFW). These computers will be referred to as Computer1 and Computer2 in the following exercise. Ideally, Computer2 should use either Windows 95/98 or Windows NT 4.0. Note that although it *is* possible to perform this exercise using only one computer, much of the effect will be lost.

You will also need to have file sharing enabled. In Windows NT, the service is already available, but you need administrative privileges to share a network resource. In Windows 95/98, you will need to open the Network Control Panel and verify that "File and Printer Sharing for Microsoft Networks" is installed. If not, you will need to install that service before proceeding. Note that the word *folder* and the word *directory* are interchangeable in the later text.

In this lab, you learn

- How to share folders
- How to connect to shared folders

Sharing a Folder

The following exercise to share a folder will be performed on Computer1:

1. Create a new folder called C:\TEST. If you want, you can copy a few small files from some other folder into C:\TEST.
2. Display the contents of the C:\ drive. If you are using Windows 95/98 or Windows NT 4.0, open the My Computer window or Windows Explorer and navigate to where you see the C:.
3. Select the folder C:\TEST.
4. Open the Sharing dialog box. In Windows 95/98 or Windows NT 4.0, right-click the TEST folder and choose Sharing.
5. In Windows 95/98 or Windows NT 4.0, you will need to click Share As.
6. Enter the name of the share (15 characters, no spaces), and a comment. In Windows NT, enter the number of users that can access this share at any time.

If you use more than eight characters in a share name, the share is inaccessible to computers using MS-DOS or Windows for Workgroups. Additionally, when you do use more than eight characters (which works fine for Windows 95/98 and Windows NT), you need to click OK in the confirmation box that appears, which warns about the eight character limit for MS-DOS.

7. Establish who has permission to use the share. In Windows NT, click the Permissions button to add the appropriate users. For this example, set Everyone to Full Control (the default). In Windows 95/98 using share-level control, set the access type and, if desired, a password. In Windows 95/98 using user-level control, click Add, select The World under the User list, and press the arrow to move The World into the Full access box.

8. Click the OK button to activate the share. (You might need to click the OK button in the Permissions dialog box first.)

9. You should now see a hand along the bottom of the folder indicating that the folder is now shared.

Connecting to a Shared Folder

Within Microsoft operating systems, there are two mechanisms for accessing network resources. Windows 95/98 and Windows NT 4.0 provide a utility called the Network Neighborhood, which is used in a later exercise. However, all Microsoft operating systems can use the process of *mapping* a drive letter to a network resource.

The following procedure to access the folder you shared in the last exercise should be performed on Computer2 if it uses Windows 95/98 or Windows NT 4.0:

1. Open Windows Explorer.

2. From the Tools menu, choose Map Network Drive.

3. Select an appropriate drive letter. For our example, use G: unless you already have a G: drive.

4. In the Path entry box, type \\Computer1\test (where *Computer1* is the name of your first computer).

5. If you want to have this connection available to you in the future, check the box next to Reconnect at Logon.

6. Click OK.

7. You should now see drive G: added to your list of drives.

Disconnecting from a Shared Folder

When you are finished using a shared folder, you can disconnect from that shared folder using the following procedure (on Computer2):

1. Open your Windows Explorer.

2. From the Tools menu (Windows 95/98 or Windows NT 4.0), choose Disconnect Network Drive.

APP
I

3. Select G:*COMPUTER1*\TEST from the list and click OK (where *Computer1* is the name of your second computer).

4. You should see that drive G: is no longer available.

Using Network Neighborhood

This exercise can only be performed on a computer using Windows 95/98 or Windows NT 4.0. If you are following these exercises in order, this exercise should ideally be performed on Computer2.

Windows 95/98 or Windows NT 4.0 provides an additional utility called Network Neighborhood for accessing network resources. Network Neighborhood allows you to access files on a shared folder without going through the process of mapping a drive. You can use Network Neighborhood with the following procedure:

1. Double-click the Network Neighborhood icon on your desktop. You should see a list of all computers on your network.

2. Double-click the name of a computer that has shared folders. (*Computer1* in our earlier exercises.) You should see a list of all shared resources on that printer.

3. Double-click the shared folder TEST. You now can open files in this folder as if it were local to your machine.

Although the Network Neighborhood provides an easy means to access shared resources, some applications, particularly older Windows 3.x programs, require a mapped drive to function correctly. Such programs will not work with the Network Neighborhood.

Note that you can also access Network Neighborhood through the Windows Explorer. Additionally, when you have found a folder you want to access, you can easily map a drive to the folder by right-clicking the folder and choosing Map Network Drive.

For your information, the Network Neighborhood icon itself also provides a shortcut to the process of mapping a network drive, as described in the previous exercises. Simply right-click the Network Neighborhood icon on your desktop and choose Map Network Drive.

Stopping File Sharing

To stop sharing a folder, follow this procedure on Computer1:

1. Open a view of your file system and navigate to where you see the folder C:\TEST. In Windows 95/98 or Windows NT 4.0, you can use either My Computer Window or Windows Explorer.

2. In Windows 95/98 or Windows NT 4.0, right-click the folder and choose Sharing. In the resulting dialog box, choose Not Shared.

Lab 5: Using Shared Printers

This lab requires two networked computers that use either Windows 95/98 or Windows NT. These computers will be referred to as Computer1 and Computer2 in the following exercise.

Furthermore, this exercise assumes that you have a printer installed on Computer1. If you do not have a printer actually attached to the computer, you must at least create a fictitious printer on your system.

You will also need to have printer sharing enabled. In Windows NT, the service is already available, but you need administrative privileges to share a network resource. In Windows 95/98, you will need to open the Network Control Panel and verify that Printer Sharing is enabled. If not, you will need to install that service before proceeding.

Finally, you might need the original CD or disks for the operating system installed on Computer2 to connect to the printer on Computer1.

In this lab, you learn

- How to share a printer
- How to connect to a shared printer

Sharing a Printer

If Computer1 uses Windows 95/98 or Windows NT 4.0, the process of sharing the printer is as follows:

1. From the Start menu, choose Settings, Printers.
2. Right-click a local printer and choose Sharing.
3. Click the Shared As option button.
4. Enter a share name of PRINTER1 and click OK.

In Windows NT 4.0, the Sharing dialog box will also allow you to load printer drivers for additional operating systems. For the sake of simplicity, do not choose to install any additional drivers.

APP
I

Connecting to a Shared Printer

If Computer2 uses Windows 95/98 or Windows NT 4.0, perform the following procedure:

1. From the Start menu, choose Settings, Printers.
2. Double-click the Add Printer icon.
3. In the Add Printer Wizard, click Next.
4. In Windows 95/98, choose Network Printer. In Windows NT 4.0, select Network Printer Server. Click Next.
5. In Windows 95/98, for a pathname, type *Computer1*\PRINTER1 or click the Browse button to locate and select the printer on the network. In Windows NT 4.0, you will see a network browsing window. You will need to select the printer using that window. Click Next.
6. Select the type of printer used for PRINTER1. Click Next.
7. After you have supplied the original media and installed the printer driver, you will be asked if you want to make the printer your default printer. Select No and click Next.
8. You will be asked if you want to print a test page. If you have an actual printer, choose Yes. If not, choose No. Click Finish.

After you finish this process, the printer will install on your PC and can be used as if it is a local printer.

Disconnecting from a Network Printer

If Computer2 uses Windows 95/98 or Windows NT 4.0, the process of disconnecting from a network printer involves the following steps:

1. From the Start menu, choose Settings, Printers.
2. Right-click PRINTER1 and choose Delete.
3. After a confirmation prompt, the printer is deleted.

Stop Sharing a Printer

If Computer1 uses Windows 95/98 or Windows NT 4.0, complete the following procedure:

1. From the Start menu, choose Settings, Printers.
2. Right-click the shared printer and choose Sharing.
3. Choose Not Shared and click OK.

Lab 6: Microsoft Networking from the Command Line

This lab requires the use of two networked computers, running either Windows 95/98 or Windows NT. The computers are referenced in the lab as Computer1 and Computer2. When instructed to enter commands, you should use your actual computer names in place of Computer1 and Computer2.

In this lab, you learn how to use the command line to perform networking commands within Microsoft operating systems.

All commands are executed within a Windows 95 MS-DOS prompt or a Windows NT command prompt.

Viewing Other Computers

This exercise should be performed on Computer1:

1. From Computer1, type net view. You should see a list of other computers on your network.

2. Type net view \\Computer2 to see a list of shared resources for that particular computer.

Type net /? to view a list of command options available to you. Windows 95/98 and Windows NT differ in the options available.

Sharing and Accessing Network Resources

This exercise gives you practice in sharing and accessing various network resources.

If you already have a drive E: on your computer, you will need to substitute another drive letter in the following exercise.

1. On Computer2, create a folder at the top level of the C: drive called TEST1.

2. If Computer2 uses Windows 95/98, you need to open Windows Explorer, right click the new folder, select Sharing, and establish a shared folder.

3. If Computer2 uses Windows NT, type net share test1=C:\TEST1 to share the folder. Type net share again without any arguments to verify that TEST1 is now in your list of shares.

4. On Computer1, type net view \\Computer2. You should now see a share called TEST1.

APP

I

5. Type `net use e: \\Computer2\test1` to map drive E: to the new share on Computer2.

6. Type `net use` to verify that your share is active.

7. Change to drive E: to verify that you can access the drive.

8. Change back to drive C: in order to perform the next step of deleting the mapped drive connection.

9. Type `net use e: /delete` to remove the connection to Computer2.

10. Type `net use` to verify that the share connection is no longer active.

11. Return to Computer2 to stop sharing the TEST1 folder. If you are using Windows 95/98, you need to use Windows Explorer. Right-click the C:\TEST1 folder and choose Stop Sharing.

12. If Computer2 uses Windows NT, issue the command `net share test1 /delete` at the command prompt. Type `net share` to verify that TEST1 is no longer shared.

Synchronizing the Time

Microsoft networking includes the capability to synchronize the time between systems.

1. On Computer1, type `time` and note the current system time.

2. Type `net time \\Computer2` to find out the time on Computer2.

3. If Computer1 uses Windows 95/98, type `net time \\Computer2 /s /y` to set Computer1's time equal to that of Computer2.

4. If Computer1 uses Windows NT, type `net time \\Computer2 /set` to set Computer1's time equal to that of Computer2. Note that in Windows NT you must have administrative privileges to modify the system time.

5. On Computer1, type `time` and verify that the time now matches that of Computer2.

Lab 7: Administering User Accounts

This lab requires the use of a Windows NT computer. Additionally, you must have administrative privileges.

In this lab, you learn

- How to create user accounts
- How to modify user accounts
- How to delete user accounts

Creating User Accounts

To create user accounts, perform the following procedure:

1. In Windows NT 4.0, choose Start, Programs, Administrative Tools, and User Manager. (Note that if you are performing this command from a domain controller, you need to use User Manager for Domains.)

2. From the User menu, choose New User.

3. Enter a username. The username must be unique in the user account database and can be no longer than 20 characters. (The username is often a short name users use to log on to the system. Using the user's first name and last initial is a common naming scheme.)

4. Enter a full name and description.

5. Enter a password in both the Password and Confirm Password entry boxes.

6. If you want, click the Groups button and assign the user to a group.

7. Repeat this procedure to create three or four new users.

Modifying a User Account

There are times when user account information needs to be changed. For instance, people may change names or switch departments. Because Windows NT uses an underlying SID (security identification number) to identify users, the actual text data can be changed. To change information, perform the following procedure:

1. In Windows NT 4.0, choose Start, Programs, Administrative Tools, and User Manager.

2. Double-click the name of an existing user.

3. Edit the user information.

4. If you want to establish a new password, enter the new password in both the Password and Confirm Password dialog boxes.

5. If you want, click the Groups button and assign the user to groups.

6. Click OK when finished.

Deleting a User Account

User accounts can be easily deleted using the following process:

1. In Windows NT 4.0, choose Start, Programs, Administrative Tools, and User Manager.

2. Select the name of an existing user.

APP
I

3. From the User menu, select Delete. (Alternatively, press the Delete key on your keyboard.)

4. After multiple confirmation dialog boxes, the user account will be deleted.

Lab 8: Administering Group Accounts

This lab requires the use of a Windows NT computer. Additionally, you must have administrative privileges.

In this lab, you learn

- How to create group accounts
- How to modify group accounts
- How to delete group accounts

Group accounts are used within Windows NT when you want to assign permission to a group of users. For instance, the entire Human Resources department might need access to a particular folder on the server, but no one else should have access to that folder. Rather than assigning permission individually to each member of the HR department, all HR users would be placed into a group account. Access permissions would then be assigned to the group account. Users can be added and deleted from group accounts by network administrators. A user account can be a member of multiple group accounts.

Creating Group Accounts

To create group accounts, perform the following procedure:

1. In Windows NT 4.0, choose Start, Programs, Administrative Tools, and User Manager. (Note that if you are performing this command from a domain controller, you need to use User Manager for Domains.)

2. From the User menu, choose New Local Group.

3. Enter a group name. It must be unique within the user accounts database.

4. Enter a description.

5. Click the Add button and select users to be members of this group.

6. Click OK to return to the New Local Group window. You should now see your users listed in the window.

7. Click OK to add this group to the accounts database.

8. Repeat this procedure to create three new local groups.

Modifying a Group Account

There are times when group account information needs to be changed. For instance, departments can change. Like users, groups are identified within Windows NT through an underlying SID (security identification number). For this reason, the actual text data, such as the group name, can be changed.

Additionally, users might move around within an organization, and it might no longer be appropriate for a user to be part of a group account. Users can be added or deleted from the group account by administrators.

To change information, perform the following procedure:

1. In Windows NT 4.0, choose Start, Programs, Administrative Tools, and User Manager.
2. Double-click the name of an existing group.
3. Edit the group name and description, if desired.
4. If you want to add users to the group, click the Add button. Double-click user-names (or select the names and click the Add button). Click OK when finished.
5. If you want to remove a user from a group, select the user's name and click the Remove button.
6. Click OK when finished.

Deleting a Group Account

User accounts can be easily deleted using the following process:

1. In Windows NT 4.0, choose Start, Programs, Administrative Tools, and User Manager.
2. Select the name of an existing group.
3. From the User menu, select Delete. (Alternatively, press the Delete key on your keyboard.)
4. After multiple confirmation dialog boxes, the group account will be deleted.

Lab 9: Joining a Windows NT Domain

This lab requires the use of a Windows NT domain. The domain could be established using one computer running Windows NT Server, or it could be an already established domain on your network. Your client computer must be running Windows 95/98 or Windows NT. Note that if you are using Windows NT on your client, you must have administrative privileges on your computer and administrative privileges within the Windows NT domain.

APP
I

In order to log on to your computer when you finish this lab, you need to either have a valid account within the Windows NT domain or have the Guest account enabled in the domain.

In this lab, you learn how to add a computer to a Windows NT domain.

Within Microsoft networks, *workgroups* are peer-to-peer networks where security is maintained on each individual computer. However, *domains* are Windows NT Server–based networks where all access to network resources must be authenticated by a domain controller (either the Primary Domain Controller or a Backup Domain Controller). The later procedures indicate how you can add your computer to an existing Windows NT domain.

Joining a Domain from a Windows 95/98 Computer

If your client computer is using Windows 95/98, follow this procedure:

1. From the Control Panel, double-click the Network icon. (Alternatively, right-click the Network Neighborhood icon on your desktop and choose Properties.)
2. Select the Configuration tab if it is not already in view.
3. Double-click the Client for Microsoft Networks option in the Installed Components box.
4. Select the Logon to Windows NT Domain check box.
5. Enter the name of your Windows NT domain and click OK.
6. Make sure that Client for Microsoft Networks appears in the Primary Network Logon box in the lower half of the Configuration tab window.
7. Click OK.
8. Restart the computer.
9. At the logon prompt, you will now see not only the standard boxes for username and password, but also an additional box for the domain name. Assuming you have a valid user account in the domain, you will be able to log on now.

Joining a Domain from a Windows NT Computer

If your client computer is using Windows NT, follow this procedure:

1. From the Control Panel, double-click the Network icon. (Alternatively, in Windows NT 4.0, right-click the Network Neighborhood icon on your desktop and choose Properties.)

2. In Windows NT 4.0, you need to select the Identification tab before clicking the Change button.

3. Select the Domain option button and enter the name of your domain.

4. If your computer has previously connected to the domain, you do not need to do anything more in this window because an account for the computer has already been established within the domain.

5. If your computer has not previously connected to the domain, select the Create Computer Account in Domain check box and enter the username and password for a domain administrator.

6. Click OK to return to the Network Control Panel.

7. Click OK again to close the Network Control Panel.

8. Restart the computer.

9. In the logon dialog box, you will now see the domain name. Assuming you have a valid user account in the domain, you will be able to log on by entering that username and password.

Lab 10: Implementing User-Level Security

This lab requires a Windows 95/98 computer (referred to as *Computer1*) connected to a Windows NT computer (referred to as *NTComputer*). Both must be able to connect to share resources on the other computer.

Instead of using a single NT computer, you could also connect your Windows 95/98 computer into a network using a Windows NT domain.

In this lab, you learn how to switch a Windows 95/98 computer from using share-level security to using user-level security.

1. From the Control Panel, double-click the Network icon to open the Network properties windows. (As a shortcut, you can also right-click the Network Neighborhood icon and choose Properties.)

2. Select the Access Control tab and verify that Share-Level Access Control is selected. (This is the default setting for Windows 95/98.)

3. Close the Network Control Panel.

4. Open the Windows Explorer.

5. Create a new folder on your C: drive named TEST2.

APP
I

6. Right-click the folder TEST2 and choose Sharing.

7. Choose Share As. Notice the options you have for Read-Only, Full, and Depends On Password. Note that you can enter a password in the window if you want.

8. Click OK. You should see a hand on the bottom of the folder indicating that it is now shared.

9. From the Control Panel, double-click the Network icon.

10. Select the Access Control tab.

11. Select the User-Level Access Control check box and enter the name of your *NTComputer* in the entry box. (Alternatively, if your Windows 95/98 computer has joined a Windows NT domain, enter the domain name here.) Click OK.

12. You should see a warning dialog box indicating that you will lose all the shares you have currently established. Click Yes to continue.

13. Restart your computer.

14. Log back on to Windows 95/98 and open the Windows Explorer. Notice that your shared folders are gone.

15. Right-click TEST2 and choose Sharing.

16. Click the Share As button to notice your new options.

17. Click the Add button. You will see a list of users available from your Windows NT computer (or Windows NT domain). Move users into the appropriate categories and click OK.

18. Click OK to activate the share.

Note that switching back to share-level security would simply involve returning to the Access Control tab of the Network Control Panel. Once again, all established shares would be lost in the transition.

Lab 11: Establishing an Audit Policy

This lab requires a Windows NT computer. Additionally, you must have administrative privileges to perform this procedure.

In this lab, you learn

- How to establish an Audit Policy to monitor logon attempts
- How to use an Audit Policy to monitor application usage
- How to establish an Audit Policy to monitor file and folder access
- How to use an Audit Policy to monitor printer access

Monitoring Logon Attempts

An Audit Policy can be used to track logon attempts with the following procedure:

1. In Windows NT 4.0, choose Start, Programs, Administrative Tools, and User Manager. (Note that if you are performing this action on an NT domain controller, you will need to use User Manager for Domains.)
2. Under the Policies menu, choose Audit.
3. Click the Audit These Events option button to enable auditing.
4. Next to the Logon and Logoff option, select the check boxes in both the Success and Failure columns.
5. Click OK and then exit the User Manager.
6. Log off from Windows NT.
7. Begin the logon process, but enter an incorrect password.
8. Begin the logon process again, but again enter an incorrect password.
9. Log on using a correct password.
10. In Windows NT 4.0, choose Start, Programs, Administrative Tools, and Event Viewer.
11. From the Log menu, choose Security.
12. Notice the entries for the two unsuccessful and one successful logon attempts.
13. Exit the Event Viewer.

Monitoring Application Usage

The Windows NT Audit function allows you to monitor what applications are used by users of the Windows NT computer. All applications from user tools to games and system applications can be monitored using the following process:

1. In Windows NT 4.0, choose Start, Programs, Administrative Tools, and User Manager. (Note that if you perform this action on an NT domain controller, you need to use User Manager for Domains.)
2. Under the Policies menu, choose Audit.
3. Next to the Process Tracking option, select the check boxes in both the Success and Failure columns.
4. Click OK and then exit the User Manager.
5. From the Start menu or Program Manager, start Solitaire.

APP
I

6. In Windows NT 4.0, choose Start, Programs, Administrative Tools, and Event Viewer.

7. From the Log menu, choose Security.

8. Notice a new Detailed Tracking entry that records the start of SOL.EXE and a second Detailed Tracking entry that records the start of EVENTVWR.EXE.

9. Exit the Event Viewer.

Monitoring File and Folder Access

Because monitoring file and folder access can occur only on an NTFS partition, you must have an NTFS partition available for this exercise.

Windows NT provides the ability to monitor who uses a specific file or folder. Although the process is similar to that of the previous two exercises, it is a bit more involved:

1. Identify a folder with several files in it that you can open.

2. In Windows NT 4.0, choose Start, Programs, Administrative Tools, and User Manager. (Note that if you perform this action on Windows NT domain controller, you need to use User Manager for Domains.)

3. Under the Policies menu, choose Audit.

4. Next to the File and Object Access option, select the check boxes in both the Success and Failure columns.

5. Click OK and then exit the User Manager.

6. Open the Windows Explorer and navigate to the folder where you want to monitor files.

7. Right-click a file and choose Properties. Click the Security tab and choose Auditing. (Note that you can select several files by using the Ctrl or Shift keys before right-clicking.)

8. Click the Add button and add Everyone to the monitored users. Click OK.

9. Next to both Read and Write, check the boxes in both the Success and Failure columns.

10. Click OK to return to the Windows Explorer or File Manager.

11. Repeat steps 6–10 for as many files as you want to monitor.

12. Double-click or otherwise open the files that you monitored.

13. Close the files. Make changes to one file and close it after saving changes.

14. In Windows NT 4.0, choose Start, Programs, Administrative Tools, and Event Viewer.

15. From the Log menu, choose Security.

16. You should now see multiple ObjectAccess entries for the files that were modified.

17. Exit the Event Viewer.

18. Go back into the file properties and turn off auditing for the file (unless you want to continue to see events in your Event Viewer).

Monitoring Printer Access

For this exercise, you must have installed a printer (or at least a printer queue) onto your Windows NT computer.

Windows NT provides the ability to monitor who uses a printer. The process is similar to the previous exercise of monitoring file access:

1. If you have already enabled auditing of File and Object Access through the previous exercise, skip ahead to step 6.

2. In Windows NT 4.0, choose Start, Programs, Administrative Tools, and User Manager. (Note that if you perform this action on an NT domain controller, you need to use User Manager for Domains.)

3. Under the Policies menu, choose Audit.

4. Next to File and Object Access, check the boxes in both the Success and Failure columns.

5. Click OK and then exit the User Manager.

6. Open the Printers Control Panel.

7. Right-click a printer and choose Properties. Click the Security tab and choose Auditing.

8. Click the Add button and add Everyone to the monitored users. Click OK.

9. Next to Print, check the boxes in both the Success and Failure columns.

10. Click OK to return to the Print Control Panel or Print Manager.

11. Repeat steps 6–10 for as many printers as you want to monitor.

12. Print files to the printer(s).

13. Choose Start, Programs, Administrative Tools, and Event Viewer.

14. From the Log menu, choose Security.

15. You should now see multiple ObjectAccess entries indicating that the files were successfully printed.

16. Exit the Event Viewer.

APP

I

17. Go back into the printer(s) and turn off auditing if you no longer want to register events for the printer(s).

Lab 12: Monitoring Network Connections with Net Watcher

This lab requires two computers, one with Windows 95/98 (Computer1) and a second with either Windows 95/98 or Windows NT (Computer2).

In this lab, you learn how to use Net Watcher to monitor network connections in Windows 95/98.

Net Watcher is a utility provided with Windows 95/98 that allows you to monitor connections made to your computer. The procedure to use the program is as follows:

1. On Computer1, open the Windows Explorer.
2. Create a new folder called TEST2.
3. Share the folder with the share name TEST2.
4. From the Start menu, choose Programs, Accessories, System Tools, Net Watcher.

Net Watcher is not installed with Windows 95/98 by default. If you do not find Net Watcher in your System Tools menu, you need to open the Control Panel, and double-click the Add/Remove Programs icon. Next, select the Windows Setup tab, and look for the System Tools box. If it is gray, click the Change Option button and select the Net Watcher check box. You will then need to provide your Windows 95/98 installation CD to load the software into your computer.

5. From the View menu, choose Shared Folders. You should now see a list of shared resources.
6. In the Net Watcher window, select TEST2. The thin right-hand pane should be empty, indicating no current connections to TEST2.
7. On Computer2, connect to *Computer1*\TEST2 either using Network Neighborhood or through mapping a network drive in either the File Manager or Windows Explorer.
8. Back on Computer1, in the Net Watcher window you should now see a connection in the right-hand pane indicating that Computer2 has connected to TEST2.
9. From the View menu, choose By Connection. You should now see the connection to your computer from Computer2.

Lab 13: Using Performance Monitor

This lab requires two networked computers, one of which must have a version of Windows NT, the other of which can have Windows NT or Windows 95/98. This exercise will refer to the Windows NT computer as Computer1 and the other computer as Computer2.

In this lab, you learn how to use Performance Monitor to examine the flow of information between two computers.

To monitor the transfer of data between two computers, use the following procedure:

1. Before monitoring the transfer of data, you should identify some large folders that you can copy from one system to the other. Share the parent folders. Choose large folders for greater effect on the chart—for example, transferring the entire Microsoft Office folder from one computer to the other!

2. On Computer1 (your Windows NT computer), select the Performance Monitor from the Administrative Tools menu. You should see a blank chart.

3. Click the plus sign on the toolbar (or from the Edit menu, choose Add to Chart).

4. From the Object drop-down box, choose Redirector.

5. From the Counter window, choose Bytes Total/sec and click the Add button.

6. From the Object drop-down box, choose Server.

7. From the Counter window, choose Bytes Total/sec and click the Add button.

8. Click the Done button. You will now see the Performance Monitor window with little activity.

9. From the Options menu, choose Chart.

10. In the Vertical Maximum entry box, enter a low value such as 20 so that you will see a better line on your chart.

11. On Computer2, transfer the large folder from Computer1 to Computer2's disk drive.

12. On Computer1, you should now see a large increase in the Server line on the chart in Performance Monitor. (If it exceeds the Chart window, return to the Options menu, choose Chart, and enter a higher Vertical Maximum value.)

13. On Computer1, switch to File Manager and transfer a large folder from Computer2 to Computer1's hard drive.

14. Switching back to Performance Monitor, you should now see a spike in the Redirector line on the chart.

APP
I

15. Continue transferring folders and noticing the effect on Performance Monitor.

16. Experiment with adding other counters from the Server and Redirector to the chart and repeating the experiment.

17. As a variation, go back to the menu and open a second Performance Monitor window. Add the %Processor Time counter (from the Processor object) and repeat the exercise. Examine the changes in the Redirector and Server lines in one window and the Processor line in the other window.

18. Delete the folders you have copied and close Performance Monitor windows.

Lab 14: Backing Up Data

This lab requires a computer with Windows 95/98 or Windows NT.

In this lab, you learn how to use backup utilities to protect data

One of the frequent tasks of an effective network administrator is to protect the data resources available on the network.

Using Backup in Windows NT

If you are using Windows NT 4.0, unless you have a tape drive connected to your computer, you will not be able to go through the full Backup process. However, using the following steps you can see how the process will begin:

1. In Windows NT 4.0, choose Start, Programs, Administrative Tools, and Backup.

2. Assuming you do not have a tape device connected to your computer, you will receive an error message. Click OK to continue.

3. You will see a list of available hard drives to back up. If you have mapped any drives to shared folders on other computers, you will be able to back them up also. (If you would like to see this, exit Backup, map a drive to a shared folder, and then restart Backup.)

4. If you wanted to back up an entire drive, you can just check the box next to the drive name. However, if you want to select which files or folders you want to back up, double-click the drive icon.

5. Now, you will see a directory tree listing of the files and folders on your system. Check the boxes next to the files or folders you want to back up.

6. If you had a tape drive, you could at this point simply click the Backup button to save all the data. Without a tape drive, click Cancel to exit the window.

Using Backup in Windows 95/98

With Windows 95/98, you actually can perform a backup to a floppy disk. The procedure is as follows:

1. First, to have something to work with, create a folder called TEST on your C: drive and copy some small, trivial files to the folder.

2. From the Start menu, choose Programs, Accessories, System Tools, Backup.

3. Click OK after reading the welcome screen.

4. If you do not have a tape drive, you will see an error screen indicating that Backup cannot find a tape drive. Click OK to continue.

5. The Backup window will appear, and after a pause, a screen will appear stating that Microsoft Backup has created a Full System Backup file set for you. Click OK to continue. (This happens only the first time you run Backup.)

6. In the left pane of the Backup window, click the C: drive. You should see a list of the files and folders in the right pane. Notice that, as in Windows Explorer, you can expand the list of folders in the left pane. Note also that you see a list of all drives on your system, including those mapped to network resources.

7. Check the box next to the TEST folder.

8. Click the Next Step button at the top of the window.

9. Insert a floppy disk into your disk drive.

10. In the left pane, click your floppy drive as the destination of your backup.

11. Click the Start Backup button.

12. When prompted for a backup label, enter TEST.

13. You should now see your files being backed up. When Backup is finished, click OK, exit Backup, and remove your floppy disk.

Restoring a Backup in Windows 95/98

To do this exercise, you must have completed the previous exercise on creating a backup in Windows 95/98.

To restore a backup, complete the following steps.

1. Using your Windows Explorer or My Computer window, delete the folder C:\TEST.

2. Insert the floppy disk you created in the previous exercise into the floppy disk drive.

3. From the Start menu, choose Programs, Accessories, System Tools, Backup.

APP
I

4. Select the Restore tab.

5. In the left pane, click the icon for your floppy drive. After a pause, you should see a list of backup sets stored on the floppy disk.

6. In the right pane, select TEST and click the Next Step button.

7. You will now see a display of the contents of the TEST backup set. In the left pane, check the box next to the TEST folder. Notice as you do so, the files inside of TEST appear in the right pane. If you wanted, you could choose to only restore an individual file.

8. Click the Start Restore button.

9. The Backup program will now begin restoring your files. When it is completed, click OK to exit the dialog boxes.

10. Switch to your Windows Explorer or My Computer window and verify that the files have returned.

11. Switch back to Backup, exit the program, and remove your floppy disk from the disk drive.

Objectives Index

...continues

...continues

APP
J

Exam Topic	Exam Objective	Chapter	Chapter Topic Heading	Page
	conflicts for multiple network adapters in a token-ring or Ethernet network.			
		App. I	Lab 1: Installing and Configuring a Network Interface Card	509
	Implement a NetBIOS naming scheme for all computers on a given network.	9	NetBIOS Name Resolution	221
	Select the appropriate hardware and software tools to monitor trends in the network.	17	Network Performance Monitoring	394
		App. I	Lab 12: Monitoring Network Connections with Net Watcher	532
		App. I	Lab 13: Using Performance Monitor	533
Troubleshooting	Identify common errors associated with components required for communications.	18	Common Problems	427
	Diagnose and resolve common connectivity problems with cards, cables, and related hardware.	18	Entire chapter	415
	Resolve broadcast storms.	18	Protocol Analyzer	421
		18	Common Problems	427

...continues

APP
J

...continued

E

Q

R

Exam Guides

**MCSE Windows NT
Server 4.0
Enterprise in the
Exam Guide**
Emmett Dulaney
0-7897-2263-1
12/99

The One Source for Comprehensive Solutions™

The one stop shop for serious users, *Exam Guides* offer readers a thorough understanding of software and technologies. Intermediate to advanced users get detailed coverage that is clearly presented and to the point.

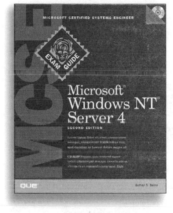

**MCSE Windows NT
Server 4.0 Exam
Guide**
Emmett Dulaney
0-7897-2264-x
12/99

Other Exam Guide Titles

**LPIC Linux Level 1
Test 1 Exam Guide**
Theresa Hadden
0-7897-2292-5
1/00

**MCSE Core+1
Certification Exam
Guide**
Emmett Dulaney
0-7897-2259-3
12/99

**Network+ Exam
Guide**
Jonathan Feldman
0-7897-2157-0
11/99

Coming Soon:

CCNA Exam Guide

**A+ Certification
Exam Guide**

**MCSE Windows
2000 Server
Exam Guide**

**MCSE Windows
2000 Professional
Exam Guide**

**MCSE TCP/IP Exam
Guide**

**MCSE Windows NT
Workstation 4.0
Exam Guide**
Emmett Dulaney
0-7897-2262-3
12/99

www.quecorp.com

All prices are subject to change.

What's on the CD-ROM

The companion CD-ROM contains Que's new TestPro test engine as well as *MCSE Networking Essentials, Second Edition* in Adobe PDF format.

Windows 95 Installation Instructions

1. Insert the CD-ROM disc into your CD-ROM drive.
2. From the Windows 95 desktop, double-click on the My Computer icon.
3. Double-click on the icon representing your CD-ROM drive.
4. Double-click on the icon titled START.EXE to run the installation program.

NOTE

If Windows 95 is installed on your computer, and you have the AutoPlay feature enabled, the START.EXE program starts automatically whenever you insert the disc into your CD-ROM drive.

Windows NT Installation Instructions

1. Insert the CD-ROM disc into your CD-ROM drive.
2. From File Manager or Program Manager, choose Run from the File menu.
3. Type `<drive>\START.EXE` and press Enter, where `<drive>` corresponds to the drive letter of your CD-ROM. For example, if your CD-ROM is drive D:, type `D:\START.EXE` and press Enter.

Technical Support from Macmillan

We can't help you with Windows or Macintosh problems or software from 3rd parties, but we can assist you if a problem arises with the CD-ROM itself.

Email Support: Send Email to http://www.mcp.com/support

Telephone: (317) 581-3833

Fax: (317) 581-4773

Mail: Macmillan USA

Attention: Support Department
201 West 103rd Street
Indianapolis, IN 46290-1093

Here's how to reach us on the Internet:

World-Wide Web